THREE WOMEN IN DARK TIMES

Three Women in Dark Times

EDITH STEIN, HANNAH ARENDT, SIMONE WEIL

or Amor fati, amor mundi

SYLVIE COURTINE-DENAMY

*translated from the French by
G. M. Goshgarian*

CORNELL UNIVERSITY PRESS
Ithaca and London

Originally published by Éditions Albin Michel S.A., 1997, under the title *Trois femmes dans de sombres temps: Edith Stein, Hannah Arendt, Simone Weil; or, Amor fati, amor mundi.*

The publisher gratefully acknowledges the assistance of the French Ministry of Culture-Centre national du livre.

First published 2000 by Cornell University Press
First printing, Cornell Paperbacks, 2001

Printed in the United States of America

Library of Congress Cataloging-in-Publication Data

Courtine-Denamy, Sylvie.
  [Trois femmes dans de sombres temps. English]
  Three women in dark times : Edith Stein, Hannah Arendt, Simone Weil / Sylvie Courtine-Denamy ; translated from the French by G.M. Goshgarian.
     p.   cm.
  Includes bibliographical references and index.
  ISBN 0-8014-3572-2 (cloth : alk. paper)
  ISBN 0-8014-8758-7 (pbk. : alk. paper)
  1. Stein, Edith, Saint, 1891–1942. 2. Arendt, Hannah. 3. Weil, Simone, 1909–1943.
4. Women philosophers—Europe—Biography. 5. Jewish philosophers—Europe—Biography. I. Title.
  B3332.S674 C6813 2000
  181'.06—dc21

                                                                        00-010475

Cornell University Press strives to use environmentally responsible suppliers and materials to the fullest extent possible in the publishing of its books. Such materials include vegetable-based, low-VOC inks, and acid-free papers that are recycled, totally chlorine-free, or partly composed of nonwood fibers. Books that bear the logo of the FSC (Forest Stewardship Council) use paper taken from forests that have been inspected and certified as meeting the highest standards for environmental and social responsibility. For further information, visit our website at www.cornellpress.cornell.edu.

Cloth printing   10   9   8   7   6   5   4   3   2   1
Paperback printing   10   9   8   7   6   5   4   3   2   1

FSC   FSC Trademark © 1996 Forest Stewardship Council A.C.
      SW-COC-098

To the Valiant: J. F., Gaspard, and Alban.

La Meriseraie, August 1995

The Greek philosophers whom one calls Stoics say that one must love fate; that one must love everything that fate brings, even when it brings misfortune.

Simone Weil, Letter to Antonio

Contents

x *Contents*

Acknowledgments

The author thanks the Committee for Philosophy at the French Centre national des Lettres for a grant that made it a great deal easier to complete this work. She also expresses her gratitude to Pierre Trotignon for his painstaking and balanced reading of the manuscript and to Jerome Kohn and Ursula Ludz for making unpublished texts by Hannah Arendt available to her.

S.C.-D.

THREE WOMEN IN DARK TIMES

Prologue

I always believed that "one is one's life."
—Hannah Arendt *Between Friends*

1933: In Germany, Hitler is granted the power to legislate by decree. Books are burned.

1943: The Warsaw Ghetto rebellion is crushed. People are burned.

1933–1943: Europe plunges into the "dark times" evoked by Bertolt Brecht in a poem in which he implores "those born later" to show indulgence in judging his generation, which was unable to "prepare the ground for friendliness."[1]

Dark times: against a backdrop of economic recession, Europe is being torn apart by the rise of anti-Semitism, the Nuremberg laws, and the persecutions of the Jews. Socialists and Communists join forces against the far Right. The Spanish Civil War breaks out. A slogan sums up the extreme political confusion sweeping over France: "Better Hitler than the Popular Front!"

Céline, Rebatet, Drieu la Rochelle, Brasillach, Bernanos, Giraudoux raise voices dripping with hate. The Italian fascists rally to the ideology of race. It is a time in which promises are broken and treaties are trampled underfoot. It is a time of dishonor: after signing the Munich Pact and then standing by while Germany annexed Czechoslovakia, are the French ready to die for Danzig? The Catholic Church lifts its ban on Action française. Yet had Pius XI not declared, only a year earlier, "spiritually we are Semites?"

The Trojan War will indeed take place. At first, it is "the phony war"; then come the French debacle and the exodus. Pétain, castigating "the spirit of hedonism," the source, he says, of all France's woes, preaches moral regeneration. Will Europe rid itself of the Jews by sending them to Madagascar?

1

The Vichy regime passes one law after another. It is the period of the mass roundups of Jews. Hitler makes the last preparations for the Final Solution, and the gas chambers go into operation. It is a time of indifference, a time of incredulity. The clergy—finally—protests. The Résistance begins to take shape. The Allies land in North Africa. The Unoccupied Zone in southern France is, in its turn, occupied by the Germans. French Jews too are deported; their national identity cards are stamped with the word "Jew." Léon Blum is interned at Buchenwald. Mussolini is overthrown: the Allies land in Sicily, then on the Italian peninsula.

To give these "dates their physiognomy,"[2] I have chosen to examine the lives of three women—Jews, philosophers, and contemporaries or near-contemporaries: Edith Stein (1891–1942), Hannah Arendt (1906–1975), and Simone Weil (1909–1943). All three were of Jewish descent, at a time when being born a Jew was enough to transform a life into a destiny. Edith Stein came from a family of practicing Jews, Simone Weil from an agnostic Jewish family, Hannah Arendt from a highly assimilated Jewish family. All three were drawn to religion in their youth. Two would feel a desire to embrace Catholicism; only one would pursue the conversion process to its conclusion. In 1933, Edith Stein entered the Carmelite order, without, however, repudiating her Jewish roots: Is the New Testament not a branch grafted onto the Old? Can one, then, speak of a "conversion"? Simone Weil, in contrast, called this filiation into question: the Old Testament and Jehovah, that omnipotent God "of hosts" without goodness, kept her from fully adhering to the Roman Church, which she considered catholic—universal—in name only. She would long hesitate on the threshold, without ever, it seems, making up her mind as to whether or not to be baptized. For Hannah Arendt, accepting her Jewishness was a matter of course, like the fact that she was a woman.

All three women were philosophers in a period in which not many women were. These three *Wunderkinder* made their choices early on: they opted for the philosophy that was then being forged. All three caught the eye of their teachers, illustrious rebels named Husserl, Heidegger, and Alain; yet all three dared to criticize them, and tried to go beyond them.

The teaching careers of all three suffered as a result of Hitler's accession to power, although only one, Edith Stein, failed to gain tenure as a professor because she was a woman. Is this why she was the only one to enlist actively in the feminist cause, however conservative her positions may seem to us today? Only one, Simone Weil, hated being a woman, refusing to acknowledge this basic fact of her existence just as she refused to acknowledge her Jewishness.

What reading of reality do these three women propose?

Two of them, Simone Weil and Hannah Arendt, considered themselves witnesses to dark times, "committed observers" who not only chronicled the war in newspapers and journals, but also participated actively in it and even engaged in combat. How did they conceive the relationship between politics and religion?

As early as 1933, Edith Stein petitioned the pope to promulgate an encyclical in favor of her people; she believed that a new curse was descending upon their heads. She never received a response. Arendt unhesitatingly chose to respond to Hitler in the terms of his attack: she made a personal commitment to the Zionist cause. Anti-Semitism had opened her eyes to history and politics. Weil, for her part, steadfastly refused to recognize the unprecedented character of anti-Semitism or racism. She regarded it as nothing more than the most recent avatar of an anti-Judaism that she herself espoused; it was, she thought, Hitler's way of standing the idea of a chosen race on its head. Thus, of the two pillars of the totalitarian Hell to which Arendt drew notice, anti-Semitism and imperialism, Weil perceived only the second: the colonial question, together with the oppression of the working class, wholly absorbed her attention. Yet she would discern, earlier than Arendt, the bankruptcy of the Communist Party and the fact that Communists and fascists defended theses that were politically and socially identical. Until Hitler marched into Prague, she opposed the idea of going to war with Germany; she compared Hitler's policies to those of the Roman Empire and dreaded the thought that France might become a colony of the Reich.

Weil and Arendt both invoked the example of the Trojan War to warn against the dangers of a conflict whose ultimate objective could only be the destruction of one whole region of the world. But whereas Weil blamed the emergence of totalitarianism on the decline of religion, Arendt, refusing to conflate authority with violence, strove to define the specificity of totalitarian ideologies, which she saw neither as susbstitutes for God nor as latter-day tyrannies.

The work of these women is inseparable from the tragic events that punctuated the period between the two World Wars. Revolutions, fascism, imperialism, democracy, totalitarianism, anti-Semitism—such was the breeding ground for the passionate thought of Simone Weil and Hannah Arendt. As for Edith Stein, she pursued her meditations on Saint John of the Cross even as, from the depths of her Carmelite convent, she heard echoes of the agony that men and women were suffering outside its walls.

All three women would experience exile. Arendt's exile took her first to France, from 1933 to 1941, and then to the United States, where she acquired citizenship in 1951. Weil's led her first to Marseilles, in the Unoccupied Zone, then to America, and, in the months immediately preceding her death, to London. Stein found asylum in Holland before being deported to Auschwitz and gassed, together with her sister Rose, on 9 August 1942.

The destinies of these women cross, even if we do not always find all three at the same moment. We shall be following them from 1933 to 1943. None of them can leave us indifferent; all three are compelling figures who move us with their fierce desire to understand a world out of joint, reconcile it with itself, and, despite everything, love it—*amor fati, amor mundi.*

PART I
THE FORMATIVE YEARS

Three Childhoods

Edith Stein was born in 1891 in Breslau, in the province of Silesia. She was the youngest of twelve children; four of her brothers and sisters died in childhood. Simone Weil, born in Paris in 1909, had a brother named André who was two years her senior. Hannah Arendt, born in Hanover in 1906, was an only child. Her mother's second husband, Martin Berwald, was a widower who already had two children by his previous marriage, Clara and Eva, both somewhat older than Hannah.

All three of the girls were sickly in their early years. Edith's autobiography[1] gives a large place to her own ailments and those of her brothers and sisters. Selma Weil often feared that she was about to lose Simone. Hannah's mother kept a day-to-day record she called *Unser Kind* in which she recorded her daughter's least little aches and pains, along with her triumphs.

Edith's was a family of practicing Jews: her great-grandfather, Joseph Burchard, who came from Posen, had been a cantor, and his grandchildren were sent to see him to learn how to pray properly. Edith's mother, Auguste Courant, who ran a lumber business, came from Lublinitz, a Hasidic stronghold. She observed Orthodox rites and celebrated religious holidays; Edith devotes a whole chapter of her autobiography to these celebrations. In addition to Passover and Rosh Hashanah, the Jewish New Year, Stein liked to recall how much Yom Kippur meant to her as a child, for the great Day of Atonement was also her birthday: "I believe this contributed more than anything else," she writes of her mother, "to her youngest's being especially dear to her."[2] Edith did not, however, go to the synagogue with her mother; she was happy to lie in bed reading and thinking about her dead father while waiting for her mother to come back from services. When she turned thirteen, she was allowed to fast until nightfall, a practice she kept up even after she had lost her faith and left the family home.

Simone came from a very cultivated, artistic family of "agnostics," even atheists. She knew nothing about her family background before the third grade; earlier, when reading Balzac, she had assumed that "Jew" was a synonym for usurer! Her mother had been slow to reveal Simone's background to her, since she herself, the child of a Galician father and Viennese mother, had been a victim of antisemitism in her youth. Yet Simone's paternal grandmother, whom Simone had known, was deeply attached to the Jewish faith and its dietary rules and would not have been able to bear seeing her granddaughter marry a *goy*. Simone's father, André Weil, was an Alsatian who had opted for French citizenship; her parents spoke German whenever they wanted to keep the children from understanding what was being said. Her maternal grandfather, a merchant, was a highly educated man with so thorough a command of Hebrew that he wrote poetry in it. Yet the first time Simone saw devout Jews praying in their phylacteries and *taleths* was in Casablanca in 1942, as she was about to set sail for the United States. The scene came as a real surprise to her. Comparing the fit of laughter that Hannah Arendt confessed came over her at Eichmann's trial—whose absurdity, in all its horror, had suddenly impressed itself upon her—to Simone Weil's laughter at Casablanca, Wladimir Rabi says: "She laughed, the fool, just as Simone Weil, every bit as foolish, had laughed in the camp at Casablanca in May 1942 while waiting for the boat that would take her to New York—she laughed at the sight of old Jews praying in their *taleths* as they waited alongside her."[3] Simone would not set foot in a synagogue until she went into exile in the United States; and, at that, the synagogue in question was one for Ethiopian Jews! She also faithfully attended Baptist church services during her stay in the United States.

Hannah's was also a family of assimilated, cultivated Jews. Her parents—Paul Arendt was an engineer, Martha had studied French and the piano—did not observe any of the religious practices but did allow Hannah to go to the synagogue with her grandparents for the Shabbat services. It was, perhaps, at their request that she was given a religious education, supervised by a Reformed rabbi from Königsberg named Hermann Vögelstein. However, Hannah would first come to feel her Jewishness not at home, but on the street, thanks to other children's antisemitic gibes. She became aware that she was a Jew "in the physical sense": "for example, as a child—a somewhat older child then—I knew that I looked Jewish. I looked different from other children."[4] Yet she feigned astonishment when Uwe Johnson boomed, "but, Hannah, you look like seven synagogues!"[5] In the interval, to be sure, the monstrous caricatures of Jews disseminated by the Nazis had done their damage: after her conversion, Edith Stein would condemn those "horrendous caricature [s that] looked out at us" "as if from a concave mirror" and deny that "having 'Jewish blood' cause[d] an inevitable consequence in the Jewish people." Still, young Hannah's newfound awareness of her Jewishness had by no means come as a shock. "That was just how it was": *amor fati*?

Edith's father died suddenly of sunstroke while on a business trip. Edith was still a baby. "I remember how [my mother] held me in her arms as he bade us farewell when he set out on the journey from which he was not to return alive. . . . So, for her, I was the final legacy from my father."[6]

Simone, for her part, was fortunate enough to have both her parents as long as she lived. They were very protective and followed her everywhere, sometimes even without her knowledge; whenever she managed to elude them, they would eventually catch up with her. It is true that she died very young, wasting away from tuberculosis and hunger in an English hospital; she was in England because she had begged Maurice Schumann, a former classmate at the Paris lycée Henri IV, to take her to London from the United States, where her family had dragged her into exile with them. Her parents would learn nothing of her death agony. To the last day of her life, she wrote them moving letters in which she bantered pleasantly and assured them that all was well.

Hannah lost her father when she was seven. That same year, 1913, her paternal grandfather, Max Arendt, also died. Hannah had doted on him; he had been a father-surrogate for her during the cruel illness of her own father, who was stricken with syphilis.

Edith's mother, who had had to take the family lumberyard in hand when her husband died, hardly had the time to look after her two youngest daughters. Erna, eighteen months older than Edith, remained very attached to her little sister to the end of her life, and wrote a volume of reminiscences about her.[7] The two girls were raised very much like twins by their older brothers: Paul, the eldest, lectured Edith on Goethe and Schiller while she was still a baby. Edith said that their mother "dispelled all of [her] pains and aches,"[8] catered to her every wish, and approved of all her daughter's decisions until the day Edith resolved to enter Carmel, a choice that caused her mother intense grief.

Selma Weil, whom her daughter called "darling," simply worshipped Simone. She kept a close eye on her as Simone moved from one teaching assignment to another in the French provinces, taking infinite pains to ease the spartan living conditions her daughter deliberately subjected herself to. It would seem that, unlike Edith's mother, Selma Weil had little interest in her daughter's religious development; she neither followed her in her mysticism nor disapproved of it.⁹ Yet the fact remains that she was worried her daughter might convert to Catholicism when, at a very early age, before becoming a student of the philosopher Alain, Simone was exposed to a Jewish teacher who had converted. "At that time, [our parents] would have disapproved completely [had she converted]," André Weil confided to Malcolm Muggeridge. "Being baptized was the most unpleasant thing that could happen to a person in a family with a Jewish background—they (the family) would certainly have expressed their opposition to it."[10]

Martha Arendt too was a "Jewish mother" who mollycoddled her child. She was, however, very liberally inclined, and, having discerned her strong-willed daughter's gifts and independence of mind very early on, took Hannah's part in her conflicts with teachers, protected her when she felt she needed it, shared her enthusiasm for Rosa Luxemburg, and joined her in her French and, later, American exiles. Of her mother, Hannah said, simply, "I owe her a lot, most of all an upbringing without prejudices and with all possibilities open to me."[11] She added that, however irreligious her mother might have been, she was without question "a Jew . . . I think she would have boxed my ears right and left if she had ever found out that I had denied being a Jew."[12] But, unlike Stein and Weil, Hannah was never tempted to disavow her Jewishness.

Schooling and Teachers

Arendt, Weil, and Stein were all brilliant students, wunderkinder. Edith, who was highly gifted, also had an excellent memory: she could reel off *Marie Stuart* by heart and corrected her family when, trying to fool her, they suggested the play was by Goethe. She was nicknamed "A Book with Seven Seals" while still quite young. She eagerly looked forward to growing up and going to school with her sister Erna and felt more at home (*heimischer*) there than in her own house. Her talent and intelligence set her apart from the other schoolchildren. German and history were her favorite subjects. She enjoyed writing compositions, as did Simone Weil, who handed in paper after paper to Alain, obeying his injunction to spend "two hours a day at the writing-table!" She would later teach her own students the same method. Edith's mother and brothers encouraged and rewarded the successes of "the smart one," as she was also called—to her profound dismay, for she disliked being made so much of, and liked it even less when people told her parents and acquaintances about her achievements at school. Yet, as a child, she "was convinced that [she] was destined for something great and that [she] did not belong at all in the narrow, bourgeois circumstances into which [she] had been born."[1] (Hannah's family, in contrast, never mentioned her successes or talked about her grades: these were things of no importance, and Hannah was simply oblivious to the matter.)[2] But, to everyone's surprise, Edith decided, in a show of her independence of mind, to leave school at the age of thirteen. Her mother sent her to Hamburg to stay with a married older sister who had children of her own: Edith lived with her for ten months before going back to school and completing *Gymnasium*. She took her *Abitur* with high honors.

Simone was no less gifted, despite the fact that her schooling was often interrupted, punctuated as much by childhood illnesses as by the frequent moves that her father, an army doctor, had to make during the first World War. She too learned long texts by heart, and would recite them in chorus with her brother André, much to the delight of the whole family: *Cyrano*, Corneille, Racine. When she invited friends over to her house, it was to put on plays. But she felt overshadowed by her brother, whose genius she compared to Pascal's.[3] He sat his first university entrance examination at the age of fourteen, whereas Simone was fifteen when she sat the same exam. He was admitted to the science department of the Ecole normale supérieure at sixteen; she would be admitted to the philosophy department only after her second try at the entrance exam—although she was, to be sure, the only girl in her class. At nineteen, her brother placed first in the highly competitive nationwide examination for teaching posts in mathematics; Simone took only seventh place in the 1931 exam for aspiring philosophy teachers, at a time when young women were awarded their credentials only if there was room left for them and on condition that they had scored at least as high as the boy with the lowest mark! Simone wanted to understand everything, to find out about everything, just like André; she had to work harder and progressed more slowly, something that, when she was in her teens, made her want to die with shame. André would later be awarded the Field Medallion, the highest distinction in mathematics. Simone's and André's maternal grandmother, whose native language was German, summed up Simone's attitude to her brother by saying that Simone was a *Kopiermaschine* (copying machine). Her outward appearance, dress, strong-mindedness, and opinions worried the old woman. The vice-principal at Henri IV had christened her "monstrum horrendum,"[4] while for Célestin Bouglé, director of the Ecole normale, she was "the Red Virgin."[5]

Hannah had merely to reach for the Greek and Latin classics on the shelves of the family library to satisfy her thirst for knowledge. Because her Greek class started too early in the morning to suit her, she convinced her mother to have her excused from it and hire a teacher to give her private lessons instead. She was even suspended from the *Luisenschule* for sassing back one of her teachers and had to take her exams for the *Abitur* as an independent candidate. Of course, she passed with flying colors.

Their secondary school diplomas in hand, the three girls had to settle on a major field of study. The parents of all three let them make up their own minds. In 1908, for the first time, female students in Prussia could enroll at university under the same conditions as their male classmates. Once again,

Edith surprised everyone: she chose philosophy. In April 1911, she enrolled in history and German language and literature; philosophy was included in the psychology classes taught by the professors William Stern and Hönigswald. As she would one day have to earn a living, she began preparing for a career as a teacher in the upper grades. Her mother gave her blessing to the plan.

Edith spent four semesters at the University of Breslau, studying, notably, with Stern, who led a "pedagogical group" he had organized; Edith was brought into it by her friend Rosa Guttmann. She would later say that she had spent her most rewarding hours at university with Stern, even if she ultimately pronounced a harsh judgment on her psychology courses, which had merely served to "persuade [her] that this science was still in its infancy; it still lacked clear basic concepts."[6] Yet Stern—whom Edith once likened, at a masked ball, to Nathan the Wise—considered himself a philosopher body and soul, and spoke out against creating separate chairs of philosophy and psychology. He avowed that his philosophical work *Person und Sache* meant more to him than anything else he had written—despite the fact that his publications in experimental psychology, based on observations of his three children (one, Günther, was to become Hannah Arendt's first husband), were to earn him an international reputation. After spending four terms at Breslau, Edith was attracted by the idea of going to study with Husserl, whose name she had repeatedly heard mentioned in 1912–1913 in Stern's seminar (Stern was then working on the psychology of thought in collaboration with the Würzburg school); indeed, she herself used Husserl as a major reference in the two presentations she made in this seminar. After once again convincing her family of the wisdom of her plans, she set out for Göttingen. In theory, she was to spend only one semester there, in view of the material sacrifices she was imposing on her mother, who also had to pay Rosa Guttmann's expenses so that this friend of Edith's could go with her. Dr. Moskiewicz, or "Mos," as he was called, brought her the second volume of Husserl's *Logische Untersuchungsh* (*Logical Investigations*), which had appeared in 1901, and painted an idyllic picture of Göttingen for her: "In Göttingen that's all you do: philosophize, day and night, at meals, in the street, everywhere. All you talk about is 'phenomena.' " At the same time, Edith saw, in a newspaper, a picture of Husserl's brilliant student Hedwig Martius, who had married a former student of his, Hans Theodor Conrad; Martius had just won a philosophy award. In addition, a cousin of Edith's who had recently been appointed *Privatdozent* for mathematics at the University of Göttingen sent her the schedule of lectures in philosophy there. Over the Christmas holiday, she studied the second volume of the *Logical Investigations* and became "convinced . . . that Husserl was *the* philosopher of our age." Edith herself, according to her friend Hedwig, was a "born phenomenologist."[7] Phenomenology "fascinated [her] . . . because it was precisely . . . a labor of clarification and because, through it, one forged one's own mental tools for the task at hand."[8] Edith would later say that phenomenological terminology constituted her "philosophical mother tongue."[9]

She was twenty-one when she arrived in Göttingen. On Moskiewicz's advice, the first thing she did after arriving was to introduce herself to Adolf Reinach, a Jewish convert to Christianity* who had a post as *Privatdozent* for philosophy. Reinach, Husserl's right-hand man, introduced Edith to him. Edmund Husserl, an Austrian born in Moravia, had converted to Protestantism when he was twenty-seven, along with his wife Malwine; they raised their children in the Protestant faith. It was at the University of Leipzig that Husserl, in the company of Gustav Albrecht and Thomas Masaryk, discovered the Bible and asked a minister to baptize him, even if another ten years were to pass before he would convert definitively, in a Lutheran church in Vienna. Vienna was also where he had met Franz Brentano, a priest who had broken with the Church. Brentano addressed this exhortation to a young Jewish friend of his, Samuel-Hugo Bergman: "Not only Jesus, but also the greatest and most progressive of the prophets before him, resolutely went beyond the idea of a chosen people and, high-minded, looked upon it as a narrow one. Therefore away with it, and with all the other old rubbish."[10]

Husserl was fifty-five years old. His first disciples—Adolf Reinach, Theodor Conrad, Abraham Geiger, Hans Lipps—had formed a circle around him, the "Göttinger Schule." It was not yet riven by the dissension caused by accusations that the man who claimed to have taken *zur Sache selbst* as his motto—go straight to the thing itself!—had "reverted to idealism." Husserl praised the "heroic achievement"[11] of Edith, who had read the whole of the second volume of *Logical Investigations*. He was, for her, simply "the Master." As the semester was getting underway, he published *Ideas Pertaining to a Pure Phenomenology and to a Phenomenological Philosophy*, which he dis-

---

*In 1917, Reinach and his wife, Anna, were baptized in the Protestant faith, at Anna's request, which her husband happily acceded to. The baptisms took place shortly before his death in the first World War, while he was on a leave of duty. It seems that, from the moment he was baptized, Reinach found an answer to his questions about the meaning of the horrors of the war: "they serve to bring men closer to God," he wrote on 23 May 1916 (*Gesammelte Schriften*, p. xxxvii). Nevertheless, before going to church to receive baptism, he appears to have been ill at ease: "I am very much afraid I am doing the wrong thing in accepting baptism thus. I am afraid that I have hurried to be baptized by a Protestant minister simply because I am not ready to enter the Catholic church." A year later, Reinach was killed in Flanders. His wife, followed by his sister, his brother and sister-in-law and their children, and many of their friends and students, later converted to Catholicism; his own sister and a nephew even chose to enter orders. Once she had become a Catholic, Mrs. Reinach was granted asylum in Spain during the persecutions of the Jews.

cussed during his seminar. In addition, he set aside one afternoon a week for his students, whom he received at home, listening attentively to their questions and thoughts. That summer, Husserl spoke on "Nature and Spirit," examining the foundations of the natural sciences and psychology; this was a theme he would take up again in the as yet unpublished second part of *Ideas*. It was during this summer as well that Edith read Max Scheler's *Formalism in Ethics and the Non-Formal Ethics of Values*; Scheler claimed to have fathered phenomenology without ever having studied under Husserl. Edith began to take an interest in the problem of *Einfühlung*, which explains her interest in Scheler's *The Nature and Forms of Sympathy*. But, over and above the philosophical influence Scheler had on her, the Catholic ideas of this converted Jew, as Edith would later acknowledge, constituted her "first encounter with this hitherto totally unknown world." Even if it did not yet lead her to the faith, it did open up for her "a region of 'phenomena' which [she] could then no longer bypass blindly. . . . The world of faith unfolded before [her]."[12] She adds: "In Göttingen I had learned to respect questions of faith and persons who had faith. With some of my women friends, I even went to one of the Protestant churches at times . . . [but] I had not yet found a way back to God."[13] The series of lectures on religious questions that Scheler delivered in Göttingen inspired many to convert: Dietrich von Hildebrand entered the Third Fransiscan Order, while Alexandre Koyré and his wife drew closer to the Catholic church. Adolf Reinach, for his part, converted to Catholicism during the first World War.

In addition to her interest in Husserl, the phenomenological circle, and Scheler, Stein also developed an interest—somewhat later, to be sure—in Saint Thomas, to whom she devoted a lengthy study, *Potenz und Akt* [Potentiality and act]. She was not, however, generally recognized by Thomists as one of them because of her "rather unorthodox Thomism."[14] Abandoning her plans to write a thesis under Stern's direction, she enrolled as one of Husserl's doctoral students. The subject she chose to work on was the concept of *Einfühlung* ("I wished to examine what empathy [*Einfühlung*] might be").[15] Husserl had taken the term from the work of Theodor Lipps, using it to designate intersubjective experience. But the war broke out. After taking the *Staatsexamen* in 1915 in order to acquire a teaching credential in German, history, and introductory philosophy, Edith temporarily set aside her work on her doctorate, *against* her mother's wishes this time, and applied for a job in a Red Cross military hospital in Mährisch-Weißkirchen. The hospital would eventually decorate her with a medal of valor for her devotion. She took *Ideas* and the *Odyssey* with her to read in her spare time.

During World War I, little Simone Weil secretly learned to read under the direction of her brother André: the boy wanted to spring a surprise on their father, who had been mobilized and sent to the front, when he came home on leave. Having become "godmother" to a soldier who had no family, Simone scrupulously fulfilled her obligations to her grown-up charge, renouncing sugar and chocolate so that she could give him her share. He came to stay with the Weils during a leave of absence in May 1917, shortly before being killed in action. A few months before her own death, in London, Simone would recall this period of her life in an exchange with Maurice Schumann: "since 1914, [war] has never left my thoughts."

Hannah and her mother, for their part, fled Königsberg at the end of August 1914, heading for Berlin amid cries of *Die Kosacken kommen*! This was just before the German troops and the second Russian army clashed near Tannenberg. The Arendts returned home ten weeks later, and life resumed its normal course, in spite of the war that was beginning to unfold on the Eastern and Western fronts.

EDITH SPENT ONLY A YEAR at the Red Cross hospital before going back to work on her dissertation, "The Problem of Intuition in Its Historical Development and as Reflected in Phenomenology." Husserl encouraged her, and was satisfied with the chapters she gave him to read. But she had not yet finished the thesis when he was named Heinrich Rickert's successor at the University of Freiburg. She followed him there. Husserl's new duties put such heavy demands on him that he could not find the time to read the bulky thesis. While she waited, Edith attended his classes four times a week, along with Mrs. Husserl and Roman Ingarden. Once the date of the oral defense (*rigorosum*) had been set, Husserl had no choice but to plunge into the dissertation, which so excited him that he suggested publishing it in the *Jahrbuch* together with his own *Ideas*. Had the student surpassed her master? "I have an impression that in your work you anticipate material in the second part of *Ideas*";[16] or, again, "you really are a very gifted young lady."[17] On 3 August 1916, Stein was awarded her doctoral degree with the highest possible honors, *summa cum laude*; she was the only doctoral student in Germany to be so honored that year. Her dissertation appeared in volume 5 of the *Jahrbuch*, under the title "Beiträge zur philosophischen Begründung der Psychologie und der Geisteswissenschaften" [partially translated into English as "Motivation as a Fundamental Law of the Life of the Mind"]. Heartened by this success, Edith applied to Husserl, who was overwhelmed by work, for a post as his graduate assistant. He was only too glad to give her the job, offering her a monthly salary of one hundred marks.[18] But putting his fifty-seven manuscripts in order and learning shorthand to decipher his scrawl, only to hear him subsequently order her to burn everything, was not Edith's idea of "assisting" him; she preferred to resign. Nevertheless, when he fell ill, as he did on October 1918, she rushed to his bedside to read aloud to him from Isaiah, Jeremiah, or the New Testament at his request, despite the fact that he had not yet converted.

On New Year's Eve, 1934, while on a visit to Sister Adelgundis Jaegerschmid, a Benedictine nun, former student, and family friend, Husserl recalled this episode; Sister Adelgundis offered to read to him as Edith had. After the doors of the University of Freiburg had been closed to him by Nazi Germany, Husserl often sought refuge in the priory of St. Lioba, Sister Adelgundis's convent. One morning in 1936, after reading the Gospels as he sat out in the sun, he said, "today two suns have shone on me." Hedwig Conrad-Martius reports that Husserl once said to his students: "Look at my New Testament. I always have it on my desk, but I never open it. If I were to begin reading it, I know that I would have to abandon philosophy." Was he drawn to the Catholic church in the closing years of his life? Did he fear, as John M. Oesterreicher suggests, that he no longer had enough time left for a conscientious study of all the Catholic dogmas? Mrs. Husserl, persecuted by the Nazis after her husband's death, received assistance from the Franciscan monk Leo Van Breda, who found her refuge in a Belgian convent, where she converted to Catholicism.

IN HER LAST YEAR of secondary school, Simone opted to study philosophy at the lycée Victor Duruy: she wanted to take a class with the philosopher René Le Senne. The class turned into a dialogue between the two of them. Le Senne later judged Weil to have been one of the five or six best students he had had in the course of his career. Yet he does not seem to have had any influence on her thinking, unlike her other mentor, Alain, who was to be her teacher in *khagne* at Henri IV. Alain's private nickname for her was "the Martian": "she had nothing of us and sovereignly judged us all."[19] She attended his two-hour class three times a week. Alain was an unusual thinker: he had no use for received ideas and insisted that his students cultivate their writing style, the translation of their thought. A philosopher without a system, he developed his ideas in short essays called *Propos*, which aimed to rethink everything. Simone would never forget the lesson she learned from him, for she writes: "not to understand new things, but to succeed by the strength of patience, effort, and a method to understand obvious truths with all of one's being."

Two great authors were on the syllabus every year, a philosopher and a poet or novelist. In 1925, Simone studied Plato and Balzac, and, in the year after, Kant's *Critiques* and the *Iliad*, a work that was to fascinate her for many years. She also studied Marcus Aurelius's *Meditations;* the Stoics' *amor fati* constitutes one of the leitmotifs of her work. The appraisals she received from Alain each trimester spoke of her in glowing terms: "excellent student," "a powerful and rare mind," "of the utmost originality," "shows an inventive mind," "one can predict brilliant results that may well prove astonishing." Yet Bouglé saw in her, as she was finishing her *khagne* course, "a combination of anarchist and sky pilot." Her compositions of the period do indeed testify to her sympathy for Catholicism: she was fond of citing the Old and New Testaments, Pascal—whom she criticized for maintaining that there could be no faith without miracles—and Saint Augustine. Although she liked Plato, Kant, and Spinoza, she preferred Descartes, and, in 1929–1930, wrote her DES thesis[20] on him, choosing as her topic "Science and Perception in Descartes." The thesis was directed by Léon Brunschvicg, who gave her the barely passing mark of ten out of twenty for it, the minimum she needed to pursue her studies at the Ecole normale. Alain profited from the occasion to address the following remark to his colleague: "Do you know why you only gave her ten out of twenty? Because she's Jewish":[21] Brunschvicg was apparently afraid of being accused of favoritism toward his co-religionists!

Philosophy aside, the only subject Simone studied seriously was Latin; she failed the entrance examination to the Ecole normale after her first year of *khagne* because she had so sovereignly neglected history. Even after she had been accepted at the Ecole normale, she still wished to attend Alain's classes, to the dismay of the principal of Henri IV. To prepare for the *agrégation*,[22] she drew up a colossal work program, studying for the exam under the direction of professors Puech, Alain, Laubier, a disciple of Alain's, and Brunschvicg. She passed, despite Bouglé's prophecy: "as for the Red Virgin, we shall leave her in peace to make bombs for the coming grand social upheaval."[23] She then came up for her first teaching assignment, and was named to a post in Le Puy. She showed up at the lycée accompanied by her mother, and was taken for a student! At Le Puy, she had fifteen students in philosophy and also taught freshman Greek. Teaching stints in Auxerre, Roanne, Bourges, and Saint-Quentin followed; they were interrupted by periods of sick leave, as well as an incursion into the "real world"—the factory.

PHILOSOPHY WAS THE ONLY conceivable choice for Hannah Arendt from the age of fourteen on—"I can either study philosophy or I can drown myself," she confided to a German television audience during a rare 1963 interview. By the age of fourteen, she had already read Kant, and, when it came out in 1920, *The Psychology of Worldviews* by her future dissertation director Karl Jaspers. She passionately loved poetry and Greek. Although she had "misgivings" as to whether "one could deal with [theology] if one was Jewish,"[24] she was given ample opportunity to do so while attending Rudolf Bultmann's seminar with her friend Hans Jonas and then writing her doctoral thesis on

"Love and Saint Augustine" under Jaspers's direction (she defended the thesis in Heidelberg in 1929). Jaspers did not award her the highest possible honors, as Husserl had in Edith's case, but only II-1, that is, *cum laude;* although he acknowledged that Arendt's work was "impressive, remarkable," it seems to have contained too many awkward passages, which Arendt had not succeeded in putting right despite the advice offered her. Since 1925, Jaspers had been bringing out his students' dissertations in the series *Philosophische Forschungen*, published by Springer in Berlin. The ninth and last to appear in this series was Hannah Arendt's. The work was not well received in academic circles: it was faulted for separating the thinker and the theologian in Augustine, to the benefit of the former, and also for its misunderstanding of contemporary theologians working in the Augustinian tradition. In 1930, the 1500th anniversary of Augustine's death, Arendt published an essay entitled "Augustine and Protestantism," in which she expressed surprise that only Catholics laid claim to his memory.

It was Martin Heidegger who had recommended his student Arendt to Jaspers (then still a close associate of Heidegger's), suggesting that he direct her doctoral thesis. Heidegger himself wished to avoid working with her, for fear of compromising himself even further than he already had. He and Arendt were having an affair—he was eighteen years her senior and the father of two boys—and their relationship had excited his wife Elfriede's jealousy. Let us read Hans Jonas's description of his friend as she was when she joined Heidegger's seminar at the age of eighteen:

> How I remember this singular newcomer! Shy and withdrawn, with striking, beautiful features and lonely eyes, she stood immediately out as "exceptional," as "unique" in an as yet undefinable [sic] way. Brightness of intellect was no rare article there. But here was an intensity, an inner direction, an instinct for quality, a groping for essence, a probing for depth, which cast a magic about her. One felt an absolute determination to be herself, with the toughness to carry it through in the face of great vulnerability. Her teachers felt it too: first Heidegger, later Karl Jaspers became from teachers lifelong friends.[25]

In an essay written to honor Heidegger on his eightieth birthday,[26] Arendt describes what it was about him that fascinated young German intellectuals of the day and brought them flocking to Marburg. Involved here was something "completely different from a 'circle' ":[27] there was "neither a secret nor membership," even if, as Arendt concedes, cliques later sprang up. Even more strangely, Heidegger's reputation, unlike Husserl's, did not rest on any written work—*Being and Time* was not to appear until 1927, whereas Hannah took Heidegger's seminar in 1924. Yet the philosopher's "name traveled all over Germany like the rumor of the hidden king." What was the gist of the rumor? That "there was someone who was actually attaining 'the things' that Husserl had proclaimed, someone who knew that these things were not academic, but the concerns of thinking men . . . and who, precisely because he knew that the thread of tradition was broken, was discovering the past anew."[28] In sum, the glad tidings that Arendt had heard, and which instantly convinced her to move to Marburg, given the "ocean of boredom" surrounding "the old academic discipline" as it was taught elsewhere, were that "there exists a teacher; one can perhaps learn to think."[29] What attracted her, like that which attracted Stein to Husserl or Weil to Alain, was the fact that "Heidegger never thinks 'about' something; he thinks something." His "thinking," like Husserl's or Alain's, " 'ha[d] the character of a regression' " [*Rückgang*]; like them, he offered "a fresh rethinking of what was already thought."[30] What captivated all three women was the fact that these "teachers" were, in a word, "rebels" who proposed to turn their backs on sterile academic erudition for the sake of "the matter of thought" [*die Sache des Denkens*].[31]

Heidegger and Jaspers were to remain Arendt's "friends for life," Jonas says. Yet Heidegger's Nazi "episode" is no secret ("ten short hectic months," as Arendt put it):[32] he conscientiously paid his Party dues down to 1945. Without going back over the details of this involvement yet again, let us nevertheless note that Arendt was a Jew; that she would face Nazi persecution; that, attacked "as a Jew," she would react by counter-attacking and assuming an active role in a Zionist organization; that she would be forced to become a stateless person, go into exile, and switch languages; and that her "career," which had, doubtless, been assured in advance in Germany, would be jeopardized until she had managed to win recognition in her adopted land, the United States (she became an American citizen in 1951). As for Heideggar, the "philosopher-king," he was to succumb to the temptation to "get involved in the world of human affairs."[33] On 22 April 1933—the year Hannah and her mother set out on the road to exile in France—he was all but unanimously elected to the post of Rector of the University of Freiburg, at a time when the autonomy of German universities had been suppressed in favor of the *Führerprinzip* and all civil servants "of non-Aryan races" packed off into retirement in conformity with a recently promulgated ordinance. How are we to explain the fact that Arendt, juggling euphemisms, was content to label this behavior an "escape from reality," an "error,"[34] invoking the "*déformation professionnelle*" philosophers are susceptible to?[35] True, there exist other texts, written when she was younger, in which she is much harsher. For example, in her first post-war philosophical article, "What Is Existential Philosophy?"[36] she displays great severity in her criticism of what she called Heidegger's solipsistic ontology, even if she subsequently retracted her hasty judgment. In her *Denktagebuch* or diary of 1953, she compares Heidegger to an old fox caught in his own trap.[37] At the end of the war, she resumed her correspondence with Jaspers. She had been given a mission by the Commission on European Jewish Cultural Reconstruction and returned to Europe in 1949 to carry it out. On her very first trip back to Germany, she chose to look up Heidegger again and talk things out with him. What did they say to each other? How did he plead his case? Bits and pieces of their conversation have filtered down to us by way of the correspondence between Arendt and Jaspers: she calls him a "little boy in short pants" who had no idea "what devil drove him into what he did," and she accuses him of a "lack of character."[38] Doubtless he failed to convince her. Yet a reading of *Men in Dark Times* would seem to indicate that she forgave him a great deal. As early as 1966, in the wake of an article on Heidegger that had appeared in *Der Spiegel* of 7 February, she could declare that, unlike Jaspers, she felt that "people ought to leave him in peace."[39]

Can enduring fascination, well into old age—and, let us not shy away from the word, enduring love as well—explain this "pardon," as Elzbieta Ettinger suggests in a recent book?[40]* The concept of "pardon" plays a key role in Arendt: "without being forgiven, released from the consequences of what we have done, our capacity to act would, as it were, be confined to one single deed from which we could never recover; we would remain the victims of its consequences forever, not unlike the sorcerer's apprentice who lacked the magic formula to break the spell."[41] Pardon emerges as the redemptive possibility of overcoming the irreversibility of action, "though we did not, and could not, have known what we were doing."[42] Arendt refers to Jesus of Nazareth here, for Jesus knew that the power to pardon "does not derive from God . . . but on the contrary must be mobilized by men toward each other before they can hope to be forgiven by God also."[43] If one must pardon, the reason is that " 'they know not what they do,' " since "crime and willed evil are rare." It is precisely because pardon "releases," quite as much as a promise "binds," that men can start out afresh and make things new. In other words, pardon is liberating. Indeed, only love can pardon, "precisely because it is unconcerned to the point of total unworldliness with *what* the loved person may be, with his qualities and shortcomings no less than with his achievements, failings, and transgressions."[44] And that is why love, being "unworldly," is "not only apolitical but antipolitical."[45] The conclusion would

*Regrettably, the author could only "consult," as she herself says, Heidegger's letters to Arendt, without providing references and precise, dated quotations.

appear to be that if Hannah Arendt forgave Heidegger much, the reason is that she loved him very much. The publication of the unabridged correspondence between the two should shed more light on the matter.

Arendt did not need to forgive Karl Jaspers for anything. Jaspers was the other teacher of her youth and a lifelong friend. She paid him homage on several occasions,[46] praising, in particular, his capacity for "inner emigration." Perhaps he more fully incarnated, in her eyes, the "respect," the *philia politike*—that "friendship without intimacy and without closeness"[47]—which she found in Aristotle and esteemed so highly. She waited until 1960 to send Heidegger one of her books, *The Human Condition*; he did not so much as acknowledge receipt. Jaspers, in contrast, hailed each new turn in her thought, dispensing advice, praise, and criticism. In a letter to him, Arendt comments on Heidegger's silence:

> I know that he finds it intolerable that my name appears in public, that I write books, etc. All my life I've pulled the wool over his eyes, so to speak, always acted as if none of that existed and as if I couldn't count to three, unless it was in the interpretation of his own works. Then he was always very pleased when it turned out that I could count to three and sometimes even to four. Then I suddenly felt this deception was becoming just too boring, and so I got a rap on the nose. I was very angry for a moment, but I'm not any longer. I feel instead that I somehow deserved what I got—that is, both for having deceived him and for suddenly having put an end to it.[48]

Arendt attended Husserl's seminar in Freiburg for only one semester. Yet his call to phenomenology—"the magic formula: back to the things themselves!"—doubtless left a lasting impression on her. When she tried to describe herself to an interviewer, however, she declared, "I am a sort of phenomenologist, but, *ach*, not in Hegel's way—or Husserl's."[49] A phenomenology owing nothing to Heidegger or Husserl would be one that refused to trace phenomena back to the consciousness of a subject in the way characteristic of modern thought since Descartes, a way which condemns us to solipsism, withdrawal into ourselves, and a loss of our sense of reality and of our human capacities. Arendt suggests that "there is nothing in the ordinary life of man that cannot become food for thought, that is, be subjected to the twofold transformation that readies a sense-object to become a suitable thought-object."[50]

"Amicus Plato, magis amica veritas"

(Aristotle): Criticizing Their Teachers

Because they had good heads on their shoulders and had put them to good use, Edith Stein, Hannah Arendt, and Simone Weil knew—indeed, it was a lesson which exposure to their teachers had taught them—that they had to rebel against those very teachers so as to think afresh things that had already been thought. They would, then, blaze their own paths. To begin with, they would criticize their teachers.

From Husserl to Saint Thomas

Although her Husserlian training was of great importance to her, Edith Stein repeatedly attempted, in the wake of her conversion, to bridge the gap between Husserl and St. Thomas. As soon as she began working as a German teacher at the Dominicans' convent school in Speyer, she set out to learn about the theoretical foundations of the Catholic world she now moved in; thus she undertook to translate Thomas's *Quaestiones disputatae de veritate* [Disputed questions on truth], a work that represented, in her eyes, "the only possible way into the world of Saint Thomas's thought." She did not, to be sure, wish to disavow either her Husserlian training, which made up her "philosophical fatherland," or the language of phenomenology, her "philosophical mother tongue"; but she did want to bring the worlds of Thomism and Husserlian phenomenology into confrontation, "and try to find the path leading to the immense cathedral of scholastic thought."[1] In addition to "Husserls Phänomenologie und die Philosophie des heiligen

Thomas von Aquino: Versuch einer Gegenüberstellung" [Husserl's phenomenology and the philosophy of St. Thomas of Aquinas: Attempt at a confrontation], an essay that dates from the same period as her translation of *Quaestiones*, Stein undertook preliminary work on a vast project entitled *Potent und Akt* [Potentiality and act] in 1931. This project would be postponed: she did not take it up again until 1935, on her superiors' urging. It now struck out in a new direction. Focused on the question of being, *Endliches und ewiges Sein* [Finite and eternal being, the title of the work that grew out of *Potentiality and Act*] provided Stein a fresh occasion to compare Husserl with St. Thomas, in whom she found "clear, precise" answers to questions that the medieval philosopher could not, of course, have posed in his day, but which could be posed in hers by "men who had nothing left to hold on to and were in search of something to sustain them . . . [men who] wanted a 'philosophy of life.' "[2] Stein lived in Speyer until March 1931. Dom Raphael Walzer, abbot at Beuron abbey and Stein's spiritual director, recommended that she give up teaching at the sisters' school of Saint Mary Magdalene and concentrate on her own work. She went back to Breslau for six months; several Jewish intellectuals there were in the process of converting to Catholicism, as was her sister Rosa, who was following her example.

Stein pays grateful homage to Husserl for discovering the realm of "pure consciousness" and trying to make it a field to which rigorous, fruitful methods of research could be applied. He had succeeded in calling attention to an area that had been poorly explored or even unknown until then: that of the "essential and necessary"—as opposed to the contingent and unrepeatable—nature of everyday experience and experimental science. Although this was no novelty from the vantage point of ancient and medieval philosophy, Stein remarks, it *is* new in the context of nineteenth-century materialism and empiricism.[3] Stein also commends Husserl's "way of directing attention to things themselves," a cognitive attitude she calls humble, because it is subordinated to the object; it freed people of their prejudices and, according to Stein, left many of Husserl's disciples "ready to accept the catholic truth," so that they were able to find "the way to the Church that he himself did not."[4] However, in the same text, Stein takes Husserl to task for failing to follow through on his commitments. His approach could have opened the way to the loftiest questions of ethics and the philosophy of religion: "it must be said that, in consequence of the absolutization of the monads, there is no place left for God—for our conception of God, which attributes absolute Being to Him alone, or even posits that He is absolute Being itself."[5] As a criterion for evaluating Husserl's modern conception of the world, Stein proposes "the faith and . . . heritage of our . . . catholic thinkers," who alone can eliminate all danger.[6]

Similarly, in her account of *The Crisis of the European Sciences and Transcendental Phenomenology*, in which she continues to situate herself as a "Christian thinker," Stein objects that Husserl has neglected "whole centuries of the Christian quest for the truth," because he treats Galileo, Descartes, the English empiricists and Kant as the sole links between the philosophy of his time and certain philosophical themes inherited from Antiquity. She suggests that the labor of self-criticism undertaken by modern philosophy be rounded out by an interrogation of the divagations of modern philosophy, given that modern philosophy proceeds from a break with the spiritual attitude of the Middle Ages. She also suggests, as a task for further research, that transcendental philosophy be compared with the classic doctrine of being of the *philosophia perennis*.

In September 1932, Stein participated in a colloquium at Juvisy within the framework of the *Journées d'études de la société thomiste*. There she asked whether it was necessary to bracket out existence, as Husserl does, in order to find an absolutely certain point of departure for philosophical activity. She suggested that it might be possible to forego the phenomenologists' transcendental reduction and "go back to an attitude of acceptance of the world based on belief."[7] In a review of the *Cartesian Meditations* she had published a year earlier, positing the cogito as *ens primum et absolutum* had appeared to her to be incompatible with Thomism; she had wondered if, "taking the *philosophia perennis* as a starting point," there might be a way of appropriating "the problematic of phenomenological constitution without simultaneously adopting what is called the transcendental idealism of phenomenology."[8]

Stein's comparison of Husserlian phenomenology with the philosophy of St. Thomas of Aquinas gave her an opportunity to point out, to begin with, that Husserl owed the rigor she so esteemed in him to his old teacher Franz Brentano, who had, precisely, "been brought up in the strict school of traditional Catholic philosophy."[9] But she went further, postulating a hidden relationship between Husserl—who acknowledged only Descartes and Hume as his teachers and masters—and Saint Thomas: "others have had an influence on him by way of invisible channels, an influence that did not really come to his conscious attention; St. Thomas is one of them"![10]

In support of her thesis, Stein cites the fact that Thomas and Husserl both practice philosophy as a rigorous science; that is, they share the conviction that everything which exists is rational, even if the two philosophers disagree as to where the limits of the understanding lie. In Husserl, reason as such does not admit of Thomas's distinction between natural and supernatural reason. On the other hand, a preoccupation with transcendental critique would have been foreign to Thomas, who interrogated reality "naively." If reason's path is endless for Thomas, as it is for Heidegger as well, it is also true that, for Thomas, the philosopher can never reach his goal because there exists another road to knowledge, one accessible to God alone, Who can, however, communicate something of it to us. This other road to knowledge is faith, "foreign to all modern philosophies." Even if Husserl acknowledges its existence, it lies, for him, beyond the scope of philosophy and rational cognition. But, Stein objects, insofar as it is precisely philosophy which claims to attain the broadest and most certain truth, philosophy depends on faith; the truths of faith constitute the criterion against which all other truths must be measured. To the objection of modern philosophy, which would here ask what guarantees the certainties of faith in their turn, the only possible response is the one Thomas gives: "faith is its own guarantee."[11] Stein concludes that a metaphysics, "which is what all philosophy secretly or openly tends toward, can only be secured by the joint efforts of natural and supernatural reason."[12]

Yet irreconcilable differences remain. To delimit the sphere of pure transcendental consciousness as Husserl does, and then proceed to mark off, within this consciousness, "a domain of authentic immanence, that is, a cognition [noesis] which is absolutely one with its object [noema], and therefore beyond all doubt," is incompatible with Thomism, for which Being and Knowledge coincide only in God. Furthermore, whereas Thomist philosophy endeavors to define the essence of this world, regarded as the most perfect of all possible worlds, Husserl, for his part, speculates about the constitution of a plurality of possible worlds by bracketing out empirical observation. Finally, Catholic philosophy cannot accept an ontology which posits human consciousness, rather than God, as the grounds for philosophical investigation.

Christian Philosophy and French Existentialism

Hannah Arendt takes a different view of the matter. Her approach is not, to be sure, that of a "Christian philosopher." For her, the great merit of Husserl's phenomenology resides in the fact that it liberates man from historicism, humanizing the world by putting man at the center of things and treating him as a philosophical theme. In Husserl, the reconstruction of the world sets out from consciousness. Husserl has, then, forged a new humanism in which man is at home in the world; that is, he has resolved the problem of man's feeling of alienation from the world. A conception of this sort replaces a "theocentric" with an "egocentric" perspective; it is thus radically counterposed to Stein's analyses.

But Arendt's interest in Husserl is not merely methodological; it also has to do with the fact that Husserl reestablishes the relation between Being and Thought via the detour of the intentional structure of consciousness. In so doing, he attains a certainty: the real object of my consciousness is independent of reality, which can therefore be bracketed. The tree which I *see*, though independent of the *real* tree, is no less real for that. (We have already seen Stein's Thomist objection: Being and Thought are only one for God.) However, Arendt considers it unfortunate that Husserl was unable to specify, in concrete terms, the contents of the philosophy of existence: man is not the creator of himself and the world. Stein was warning against precisely this kind of "danger" when she suggested that we should only consider the results of modern philosophy armed with "the worldview of our dogmatics and of classical philosophy."[13]

Another philosopher also felt "let down" by Husserl, if for different reasons: Hans Jonas. Jonas acknowledged that the self-exploration of a consciousness "pure" of all individual and empirical contingency had been, for him, a "marvelous school in which he learned his trade." But he said, wistfully, that it had only been a "dream," for it had not succeeded in making philosophy a "rigorous science" or accounting for "the existence of our own bodies."[14] It is surely no accident that not only Stein but also Arendt and Jonas turned from Husserlian phenomenology to the philosophy of Martin Heidegger.

In Arendt's view, modern philosophy, by radicalizing Husserl's method, goes further than Husserl: it seeks to make man the "Master of Being." Does it succeed? How does it go about matters? In a lecture delivered to the American Political Science Association in 1954, Arendt observes, as the title of her lecture says, that there has been a "Concern with Politics in Recent European Political Thought."[15] The two world wars, the phenomenon of totalitarianism, and "the dreaded prospect of atomic war" have brought to light "a deep-rooted crisis of Western civilization" and revealed the nihilism of the totalitarian movements: they have cast modern philosophical categories in tangible form. Observing that their categories and reality coincide, philosophers have descended from their ivory towers, Arendt claims, with the result that they are now more interested in politics than philosophy. Nihilism, she notes, has been interpreted as a consequence of the fact that philosophy has strayed from the path of Classical and Christian tradition. Certain Catholic philosophers, such as Jacques Maritain and Etienne Gilson in France or Romano Guardini and Josef Pieper in Germany, have accordingly called for a "science of order" that would reestablish the old hierarchy by subordinating the temporal and political realm to the spiritual. However remarkable Arendt finds the work of these men, she nevertheless points out its weakness, which consists in reaffirming old truths that have become inadequate. This defect is compounded by a failure to perceive that "the thread of tradition" has been broken once and for all. Hence these Catholic thinkers insist that it is possible to restore a world of the past; but they do not even say *which* world they think should be restored. Thus, in *Les métamorphoses de la Cité de Dieu*,[16] to mention only one of the examples Arendt cites, Etienne Gilson takes the unprecedented fact that contemporary events occur on a world-wide scale as proof that we must create a "universal society," something which would be possible only if all the world's nations were to adhere to a single principle transcending them all. Does this not come down to condemning ourselves, Arendt asks, to choosing between "totalitarianism, with its claim to global rule," or the "universal society" advocated by Christianity? Both alternatives jeopardize political freedom, which is possible only if an active "plurality" of "different principles of life and thought" is preserved.[17] Should this plurality disappear, we might well find ourselves facing the hypothetical situation that Arendt conjures up in *Was ist Politik?* [What is politics?] in order to suggest the irremediable "loss of a world" which total war would lead to:

> If as the result of some monstrous catastrophe, only one nation were left in the world, and all the members of this nation perceived and understood the world from the same standpoint, so that they lived in total harmony, then the world, in the historical and political sense of the term, would have come to an end. The people left on earth, deprived of a world, would have little more in common with us than did the tribes European civilization stumbled upon when it discovered new continents. These tribes had been dragging out their existence in isolation from the world, without relations to others; the Europeans either brought them back into the world of men, or else exterminated them before it ever dawned on European civilization that they too had been human.[18]

Arendt next examines another current of modern thought, French existentialism. As avowed atheists who refuse to refer to any philosophy antedating the French Revolution, the French existentialists represent "the opposite pole from the modern revival of Thomism" in France. During her eight-year exile in Paris, Arendt met Sartre, Camus, and Merleau-Ponty; after her arrival in New York, she published a short, enthusiastic essay called "French Existentialism."[19] In that essay as well, she praises the existentialists' tendency to look to politics for the solution of philosophical problems; she also commends them for giving priority to action, which they all, whatever their political disagreements, conceive as the necessary starting point for anything new and revolutionary. However, even if these philosophers have turned from contemplation to action and regard man as the supreme being, his own god, it would be inconsistent to expect them to produce a philosophy of political principles, that is, the new science of politics of which they make up only one premise among others. It is this science of politics that Arendt wants very much to see come into existence.

Simone Weil said of the existentialists, in a letter to Jean Wahl: "I will not hide from you that the 'existentialist' line of thought appears to me, so far as I know it, to be on the wrong side; on the side which is alien in thought to the revelation received and transmitted by Noah (to use that name for him)—on the side of force."[20] Yet, in her *Notebooks*, she wrote: "[*Dasein*—a truth in 'Existentialism,' but they have mixed with it a temptation]."[21]

The Philosophy of Existence in Germany

Arendt's hopes were materialized in the German philosophy of existence—more precisely, in that of Jaspers, who, as a convinced Kantian, had understood that the new global situation called for "limitless communication," and that thinking, far from being a solitary activity, must be "a practice carried out between men." Unlike, say, Gilson, who affirms that " 'reason is what divides us, faith is what unites us,' " a proposition that can be defended only as long as reason is conceived of as a solitary activity, Jaspers had seen that reason can become a universal bond on condition that it is neither entirely within the individual nor above him but rather constitutes, precisely, a bond *between* individuals. For Jaspers, however, this communication has its source in the encounter of an I and a Thou, that is, an experience close to that of the two-in-one, of the dialogue of solitary thought; it is not rooted in the public political sphere (for Arendt, it takes at least three to make a plurality). Hence it comes up, in its turn, against the difficulty that traditionally vexes political philosophy: "it lies in the nature of philosophy to deal with man in the singular, whereas politics could not even be conceived if men did not exist in the plural."[22]

Thus it is perhaps necessary to turn to the other German representative of modern philosophy, the man who, in Hans Jonas's opinion, represents a veritable "earthquake in philosophy," because he "made the entire, more or less visual, model of a consciousness which is essentially cognitive collapse, putting in its place the desiring, suffering, needy and mortal I."[23] And Arendt did indeed turn to Heidegger. The concept of the "world," central to Heidegger's philosophy, offers us, says Arendt, a way out of our predicament. By defining human existence as "being-in-the-world," Heidegger founds an ontology of daily life which can only be understood in terms of the relationships this "being" establishes with others. That, according to Arendt, is why Heidegger had avoided using the word "man" in his early writings, preferring *Dasein* or "being-there," whereas he speaks, in his last texts, of "mortals" in the plural, as the Greeks did.

Arendt had not always been so kindly disposed toward Heideggerian ontology. Had she not declared, in an earlier text, "What Is Existential Philosophy?" that, for lack of the second, long-awaited volume of *Being and Time*, Heidegger's ontology constituted merely a "provisional and inherently unintelligible answer" "to the question of the meaning of Being"?[24] This answer consists in the affirmation that being and temporality are identical and in the determination of man's being as a being toward death; as such, it reveals the identity of being and nothingness. Arendt also notes that the specification of *Dasein* as *Care*, as an existence constantly threatened by death, means that man is never at home in the world and can have the certainty of being a *Self* only in death; thus death, which takes him away from "the They," becomes "the absolute principium individuationis." Jonas was similarly disappointed, even if Heideggerian care, insofar as it is mortal, seemed to him to come closer to the natural rootedness of our being than Husserl's pure consciousness. By itself, care cannot account for physical need, the "I am hungry"; Heideggerian mortality is too abstract; and there is no ethics of decision in Heidegger.[25] Ultimately, Arendt criticizes Heidegger, in her 1946 essay—the criticism was retracted in 1954—for the "egoism" of the Self. In sum, she criticizes him for not being enough of a Kantian and thus missing what Kant had already clearly perceived, namely, that every individual represents all humanity. She does concede that he is to be credited for addressing questions Kant leaves in abeyance; for Kant, in his turn, fails to draw the consequences from his refutation of the ontological proof of the existence of God.

Edith Stein also underscores the "fascination" that Heidegger (whom she met for the first time at Husserl's house, when she was one of Husserl's doctoral students) exerted over academics; she confesses that she herself was deeply influenced by *Sein und Zeit* [Being and Time], which she read shortly after it appeared. Initially, she seemed uncertain about how to evaluate Heidegger's influence:

> It *may* make one more serious about life, because it focuses interest on the most decisive existential questions. But, when I consider the way it has done so heretofore, putting exclusive emphasis on the precariousness of *Dasein*, the darkness that precedes and follows it, and care, I can also imagine it promoting a pessimistic, or, indeed, nihilistic conception of things

and undercutting the orientation toward absolute being with which our Catholic faith stands and falls.[26]

But, while acknowledging the richness and power of Heidegger's analyses, Stein clearly sees that to affirm the identity of essence and existence in man is to compare man, if not to God—about whom, she notes, *Being and Time* has very little to say—then at least to a "little God," superior to all other beings.

Is the deliberate choice of the word *Dasein* not calculated to obviate the old body and soul duality? What, moreover, is to be said about Heidegger's treatment of the body, even if the existence of the body is not denied? And what of the imprecise treatment of the soul, even if Heidegger acknowledges the preeminence of mind? If *Dasein* is defined as "thrownness," who threw those who have been thrown, and where have they been thrown from? The distinction between the *Self* and the *They* does not provide the necessary explanation of authentic being. The *They* cannot constitute a decadent form of being-oneself from the moment one recognizes, as Heidegger does, that the individual is *thrown* into a community, into the *being-with* that sustains and guides him until he can accede to his being-himself, that is, to his responsibility. How can he "be-fallen"[27] if there is no Fall? The idea of fallenness makes sense only in relation to authentic being. For Stein, the matter is past doubt: "The Church's doctrine of the Fall is the solution to the enigma that results from Heidegger's description of fallen being."[28] *Dasein* is being for death, since death is the end of *Dasein* . . . Is there, then, a possibility of life after death? Death cannot be experienced through the *death* or *dying* of others, says Heidegger. But, if so, how are we to understand *Angst*, or to experience fear of anything, without the constant experience of the death of other people? Does *resoluteness*—man's capacity to project himself, comprehend an unprecedented situation, and grasp what it calls for in the *present moment*—not imply that he understands possibilities as a function of "an order and a plan that have not been drawn up by man himself?" What does *moment* mean in a doctrine of temporality in which the *image of eternity* figures only negatively? Stein pronounces her verdict on the ontological analysis of Heideggerian *Dasein*: not only does "the whole theory of time put forward in *Being and Time* have to be modified," but "the being of man as such is misrepresented" and described in "lacunary, incomplete" fashion; this is because Heidegger seeks to grasp being without taking essence into account, and because he focuses exclusively on a particular mode of being."[29]

Stein is no more favorably inclined toward the way Heidegger poses the question of the *meaning of being*, because once he has "restored the *I* to its full rights," that *I* can no longer emerge from itself to found the being of the world or the divine being, who is the ground for each of his creatures. Withdrawn into itself, the *I* does not constitute a point of departure from which it would be possible to accede to other modes of being; and, inasmuch as *essence* is not distinguished from *existence*, there can be no *eternal verities* either, for they would threaten to annul the temporality of being. Stein adds that Heidegger adopts an "infuriated, disdainful tone" in speaking of these eternal verities—for example, when he declares that they are among the "vestiges of Christian theology that have yet to be completely eliminated from the problematic of philosophy"; he does not, for all that, hesitate to appeal to the Scriptures, Paul, Jean, Saint Augustine, or Saint Thomas to clarify the concept of *world* in *The Essence of Reasons*, even if he persists in denying the existence of God. Stein further criticizes him for slighting medieval philosophy, for his ignorance of the tradition of the *analogia entis*, and for reducing *truth* to *judgment* where St. Thomas, for his part, finds a fourfold meaning at work in truth.

It should be clear by now that Stein criticizes Heidegger's philosophy for "retreating before the infinite, without which it is not possible to grasp anything finite, or the finite as such."[30] But does the fact that modern philosophy has taken its distance from faith necessarily mean relinquishing the idea of a collaboration between philosophers and theologians? Stein herself, situated as she was at the crossroads of phenomenology and Scholasticism, would later be concerned to show, in the wake of St. Thomas, that a Christian philosophy is by no means the "iron made of wood" Heidegger mockingly said it was. By this, she means that philosophy has to avail itself of the contributions of theology in order to make progress, inasmuch as human reason, unaided, is incapable of arriving at an understanding of the *logos* that governs the world. The task of Christian philosophy is to clear the way for truth; "only by so doing can it go part way down the path with unbelievers. . . . Later, perhaps, they will let themselves be conducted a bit further," even if they accept the truths of faith not as "theses," but as mere "hypotheses."[31]

Alain's *Propos*

It would seem that Simone Weil did not know Husserl or Heidegger well, unlike her former classmates Raymond Aron and Jean-Paul Sartre, both of whom traveled to Germany to study their thought. She was content merely to mention Husserl in her overview of philosophy: "In Europe in modern times one must cite Descartes and Kant; among the most recent thinkers,

Lagneau and Alain in France and Husserl in Germany."[32] She learned of Heidegger's existence from Simone Pétrement. Did Weil too, like Arendt and Stein, criticize her teacher? She seems to have remained quite faithful to him, philosophically speaking, to judge by her book *Oppression and Liberty* or by the notes one of her former students, Mme Anne Reynaud, took on the courses she gave at the Roanne lycée in 1933–1934 (Reynaud's notes were later published as *Leçons de philosophie*).[33] She even sent a copy of *Oppression and Liberty* to Alain, who wrote back: "Your work is of the first magnitude; we would like to see a sequel. All concepts must be re-examined, and the entire social analysis must be redone. Your example will give courage to the generations disappointed by ontology or ideology. Criticism awaits its workers."[34] Weil's affection for her old teacher never slackened, and she was deeply shaken when he was stricken by paralysis. He came to her defense when, to his amusement, she was accused of having "led" the miners' strikes in Le Puy, where she taught in the lycée. Alain pleaded her cause with the rector, Villard: "I am also very happy with the child Simone Weil. These are the things one does when young, and they are beautiful more than useful."[35] In her own teaching, Weil adopted the methods Alain had employed at the lycée Henri IV, which he never left for a university post: no textbooks, the great books, "the writing-table," memorization of passages from the great philosophers, courses focused, for the most part, on Descartes, Spinoza, Kant, and Marcus Aurelius, and syllabi that included not only philosphers but also great literary authors such as Balzac, Tolstoy, and Valéry.

Weil never lost the mistrust of organizations and parties that Alain had inculcated in her. Yet Alain himself was associated with the Radical movement. For Raymond Aron, he was "neither a Communist nor a socialist, but he belonged to the eternal left-wing, that group which does not exercise power since it defines itself by its rejection of power which is essentially predisposed to abuse and which corrupts those who exercise it." Alain was a citizen who opposed the authorities; he was a "sophist," according to Marcel Mauss. He nevertheless joined Rivet and Langevin, in the 1930s, at the head of the Vigilance Committee of Anti-Fascist Intellectuals, an organization that brought together communists, communist sympathizers, and socialists. To be sure, he usually arranged for Michel Alexandre, a colleague at Henri IV, to represent him at meetings. A convinced pacifist, Alain had nevertheless volunteered for service during World War I, at the age of forty-six, and fought in the artillery corps; he did so, he said, because he had "always needed to endure his share of misfortune with others in order to be happy."[36] Why did Weil complain, then, that "Alain's shortcoming is to have rejected pain"?[37] From this bloody catastrophe, which reduced men to slavery and annihilated the individual, Alain emerged a greater pacifist than ever. In 1927, Simone joined a pacifist group called the Will for Peace, even if, like Alain, she was to express a desire to take part in war once she had concluded it was inevitable. She did not, however, always endorse Alain's political views: "Is Alain going to continue to disgrace himself by supporting the Popular Front?" she once asked the Alexandres in a letter.[38]

Weil was also permanently influenced by Alain's mistrust of the scholarly community and the confiscation of thought by specialists; and, like him, she distrusted society. Anticlerical and, by his own definition, an unbeliever, Alain once wrote that the catechism one of his old friends taught was nothing more "than an occasion to give lessons in everyday morality."[39] Yet he was profoundly Christian, as his correspondence with Jacques Rivière attests: he says there that "only those who believe think," that "attention is religious, or it is not attention," and that it is unfortunate that omniscience, which he calls an idol dating "to before the Christian revolution,"[40] was, for Christians, one of the divine attributes. Weil did not forget this lesson, as we shall see later. Although she was hardly steeped in Husserl, she too would test her thought against the real world, which she would try to decipher, like a book; even before the invention of nuclear weapons, she diagnosed the risks of war engendered by the break between the ideal of Greek science, which had enlisted in the service of truth, and the efficiency of the science of her day, which had put itself in the service of technique. She deplored the fact that the modern age, which confused means and ends, neglected thought; she denounced the excessive increase in human power, the enslaving force that reduces men to things and destroys the world rather than assuming responsibility for it.

Three Ways of Being a Woman

$\textbf{W}$e have before us three rebels, or, rather, since virtually no obstacles were put in their path, three independent-minded women. All three could have said, as Arendt did, "I have always done what I liked to do."[1] They were women and philosophers at a time when philosophy counted very few women indeed among its ranks. Did none of them find herself confronting the issue of "women's liberation?"

"I Am Quite Used to Being a Woman"

Arendt, at any rate, did not. It has to be said that she took a rather conservative position on this question, as is shown by remarks she made in her interview with Günter Gaus.* "A beautiful magnetic woman with unerring discrimination between male and female friendship,"[2] Arendt apparently enjoyed being paid compliments by men, appreciated gallantry, and had no desire to forgo the privileges of being a woman, as her old friend Hans Jonas tells us. Her femininity was as obvious a fact for her as her Jewishness: "I am not disturbed at all about being a woman professor because I am quite used

---

*"I have always thought that there are certain occupations that are improper for women, that do not become them, if I may put it that way. It just doesn't look good when a woman gives orders. She should try not to get into such a situation if she wants to remain feminine. Whether I am right about this or not I do not know. I myself have always lived in accordance with this more or less unconsciously—or let us rather say, more or less consciously. The problem itself played no role for me personally" (Arendt, "Was bleibt?" pp. 10–11; "What Remains?" in *Essays in Understanding*, pp. 2–3).

to being a woman."³ Thus it irritated her to be introduced as the first woman to work in a field "generally thought to be a masculine occupation," namely, philosophy; "it does not have to remain a masculine occupation!" was her rejoinder to Gaus, "it is entirely possible that a woman will one day be a philosopher."⁴ She felt much the same irritation when it was pointed out to her that she was the first woman to lecture in the framework of the Christian Gauss seminars at Princeton. In a letter of 16 November 1953 to Kurt Blumenfeld, she objected to having to play the role of "exception woman" that people expected her to; it probably awakened painful memories of the role of "exceptional Jew."⁵ On the other hand, she was deeply touched when an enthusiastic student exclaimed, as he left one of her classes, "Rosa Luxemburg is back among us!" She had, indeed, written an essay on Luxemburg,⁶ actually a review of J. P. Nettl's biography, which she criticized for failing to give sufficient play to the fact that Rosa "was so 'self-consciously a woman.' " The proof, in Arendt's eyes, was Luxemburg's aversion for the women's liberation movement of her day: Rosa was a revolutionary who, like Hannah, set great store by "*la petite différence.*" Weil too wrote a review of Rosa Luxemburg's *Letters from Prison;* Luxemburg's stoic conception of life (*amor fati*) plainly had her unbounded sympathy and admiration.

"Intensely feminine and therefore no feminist," said Jonas as well.⁷ In 1933, Arendt had written, for *Die Gesellschaft*, a review of *Das Frauenproblem der Gegenwart: Eine psychologische Bilanz* [The woman problem today: a psychological balance sheet] by the Adlerian psychologist Alice Ruhle Gerstell. In this review, she criticizes the feminists of her day for only pressing claims of a strictly social nature rather than boldly and deliberately making new advances in the political arena; they thus doom themselves, she argues, to abstraction and ineffectiveness. Arendt accepted and even occasionally asserted her femininity. It is therefore quite surprising that she did not take exception to Jaspers's way of putting things when, in a letter of recommendation he wrote to help her obtain the compensation the German state offered refugees from Nazi Germany, he deemed it appropriate to say he was quite convinced that Arendt, who had studied under his direction as well as Heidegger's, "would have succeeded in an academic career in spite of being a woman" under the conditions prevailing before 1933.⁸ The fact remains that Arendt's "career" as an academic and writer was considerably retarded by her involuntary exile. Arriving in the United States in 1941, she made a name for herself only ten years later, with the publication of her first major book, *The Origins of Totalitarianism;* previously, she had to her account only her thesis on St. Augustine, published in 1929, the nearly completed manuscript of *Rahel Varnhagen: The Life of a Jewess,*⁹ and, it is true, countless articles. After 1951, she taught at prestigious universities, notably, from 1968 until her death, the New School for Social Research in New York. Not until 1972, after a lengthy procedural battle, did she obtain her reinstatement in higher education from the Federal German Republic. She had been excluded from German academia by the Nazis.

Edith Stein, Female Firebrand?

Did Stein accept the destiny of female philosopher with equal serenity? After defending her doctoral thesis, she would have liked to begin a career as a university teacher; the profession was, however, barred to women. Stein applied for the right to do a *Habilitation* nonetheless. Her application was rejected late in 1919. Husserl thereupon sent her a letter of recommendation intended for his colleagues at the University of Göttingen: "Should it one day become possible for women to pursue academic careers, I could recommend her very warmly as a first-rate candidate for the *Habilitation*."[10] A circular on the *Habilitation* of women in the universities was drawn up and sent out but to no effect. Edith, though not "shattered," was bitter. In 1928, after Husserl had retired, she thought of trying her luck again, at Freiburg this time. But she did not wish to apply to Heidegger, whom she had met at the Husserls' shortly before defending her dissertation and who had told her that, if she wanted a *katholische Berufung* (appointment to a Catholic school of higher learning)—she had converted in 1922—she would do better to turn to Martin Honecker. Thus she had to content herself with a job teaching literature to students in their last year at the Dominican convent school in Speyer. She was to remain in Speyer until 1931, when she was offered a post as associate professor at the Catholic Educational Institute in Münster, Westphalia. But, on 9 April 1933, she was forced to give it up in the wake of Hitler's accession to power. In her bedroom, pictures of Christian saints hung side by side with pictures of the heroines of her people, especially Judith and Esther.

In her last years at elementary school and again as a university student, Edith had been radically feminist, joining an activist feminist organization, the Prussian Association for Women's Suffrage. The end of the first World War saw the emergence of a number of problems involving woman's professional life, the family, education, politics, and the role of women in the Church. Stein gave her first public address on April 1928 in Ludwigshafen, at a congress of the Association of Bavarian Catholic Women Teachers; it bore the title "The Significance of Woman's Intrinsic Value in National Life." At the Conference of the Salzburg Academy that ran from 30 August to 3 September 1931—Edith was the only woman in attendance—she delivered a lecture called "The Ethos of Women's Professions." The least that can be said is that the lecture was hardly revolutionary. Opposed to requiring men and women to mix at the workplace, Stein maintained that women's mission consisted in marrying and raising families, that is, in behaving in conformity with their special nature; the Eucharist and liturgy offered them sufficient spiritual nourishment. In Zurich, she lectured on the "Mission of the Catholic Academic Woman" and the "Spirituality of the Christian Woman," and drew up a report on "Fundamental Principles of Women's Education" at the request of the German Catholic Women's Union; she also participated in a large number of radio programs on the subject. Her reflections were later brought together in a book, *Woman and Her Destiny*,[11] a collection of six essays in which Stein asks whether women have a specific nature, a "femininity," an "inner form which determines structure."[12] She finds little of use on the subject in experimental psychology. After evoking the work of Sister Thoma Angelica Walter—Walter, in her *Seinsrhytmik*, had drawn a distinction between *Dasein* (being-present, or woman) and *Sosein* (being-thus, or man), and argued that every individual is endowed with these two constituent elements to a greater or lesser degree—she goes on to reject Walter's classification in favor of the more classical distinction between essence and existence. The difference between the masculine and the feminine is, she says, one "of substantial form."[13] The capacity to observe the world, she adds, is an attribute of feminine nature; man is naturally predisposed to acquire knowledge of the world and act on it. This does not rule out the possibility of God's assigning men or women particular missions based on their individual talents. The "models" of womanhood are, for Stein, Elizabeth of Hungary and Mary, whom she celebrates for their "silent obedience" and what she calls the "ways of silence."[14]

Your Son, Simon

Simone Weil, for her part, detested being a woman. "The Martian," "monstrum horrendum," "the Red Virgin"—such were the hardly affectionate nicknames she had to put up with as an adolescent, as we have seen: her boyish ways and nonconformism seem to have shocked people. In 1957, Georges Bataille, who met her in the 1930s when both he and Simone were writing for *La critique sociale*, a review founded by Boris Souvarine, left a terrifying portrait of her in the person of Lazare, a character in *The Blue of Noon*;[15] he had already done a sketch for the portrait in an essay he published in *Critique* on *The Need for Roots*. In Weil's view, being born a woman was a misfortune; her biographer, Simone Pétrement, tells us that she was determined to "live like a man as much as possible."[16] She sometimes signed her letters to her parents "your respectful son"; her parents, in turn, humored her by calling her "Simon," "our second son," or even "*our khâgne boy.*" She was not very feminine, nor was she a feminist. In the context of the Group for Social Action that she formed in late 1927 together with a few other disciples of Alain's, she was once asked to discuss feminism, among other subjects; she peremptorily declared, in no uncertain terms, "I am not a feminist!" and arranged to be replaced by Mme Alexandre.[17] When Maurice Schumann told her as delicately as possible to be more attentive to her appearance so as to startle people less, she tearfully retorted that she had no time to lose on such frivolousness, and continued to waltz about in her threadbare cape and inevitable beret—except for the day when she had Simone Pétrement make her up because she hoped to land a job at the Renault plant! She felt she was unworthy of love; she once wrote to a former student of hers that

> when . . . I was tempted to try to get to know love, I decided not to— telling myself that it was better not to commit my life in a direction impossible to foresee until I was sufficiently mature to know what, in a general way, I wish from life and what I expect from it. . . . My conclusion . . . is not that one should avoid love, but that one should not seek it. . . . What matters is not to bungle one's life.[18]

For Simone too, Nazism would prove to be an obstacle, something that hindered her "being"—that, at least, was her diagnosis. In 1938 and in 1939, she took sick leave from her teaching because she was suffering from violent headaches that were becoming increasingly unbearable. In August 1940, having received no response to her request to be reinstated in her post, she wrote to the Minister of Public Education, the Latinist Jérôme Carcopino:

> I have conjectured that the text called "the Statutory Regulation on Jews," which I read some time ago in the press, perhaps has some bearing on the fact that I did not receive a reply. . . . I do not know the definition of the word Jew; this subject has never been part of my program of studies. . . . Does this word designate a religion? I have never entered a synagogue and I have never witnessed a Jewish religious ceremony . . . I recall that my paternal grandmother went to synagogue; I know that my mother's parents were both freethinkers. . . . Does this word designate a race? I have no reason to suppose that I have any sort of tie, either through my father or my mother, with the people who lived in Palestine two thousand years ago. . . . As far back as memory can go my father's family has lived in Alsace. . . . My

mother's family lived before this in a country with a Slavic population. . . . For the rest, one can conceive of the inheritance of a race, but it is difficult to conceive of the inheritance of a religion. As for myself, who do not practice any religion and never have done so, I have not inherited anything of the Jewish religion. . . . if there is a religious tradition that I regard as my patrimony, it is the Catholic tradition. The Christian, French, Hellenic tradition is mine; the Hebrew tradition is foreign to me.[19]

Weil would never be given another teaching job. She defied the 2 June 1940 decree that provided for a census of all Jews in the Unoccupied Zone: "I would much more prefer to go to jail," she said, "than to a ghetto."[20]

Is this superbly insolent text to be chalked up to the "self-hatred" often ascribed to Weil? [21] Pétrement reports that Weil went so far as to confess to Dr. Bercher in 1934: "Personally, I am an anti-Semite."[22] Be that as it may, the charge of self-hatred does not do justice to that Stoic *amor fati* which consists in a sense of being at home in the world, a "rootedness" that Weil always claimed was hers. Yet the fact remains that, in these texts dating from 1940 and 1941, she situates herself in the Christian and Catholic tradition and plays the Greeks off against the Hebrews. Even if she had been raised in an agnostic environment, as she claims she was, and even if she refused baptism to the very end, Weil, like Stein, made an abrupt volte-face that led the two of them to apprehend the world and their commitments to it very differently than Hannah Arendt.

Amor Fati *and the Fate of the Jews*

Sister Benedicta: Secretum meum mihi

Of her conversion to Catholicism, which took place in Speyer on 1 January 1922, Edith Stein would say to her friend Hedwig Conrad-Martius: "*Secretum meum mihi.*" Yet Edith must surely have been exposed to certain influences in order to embrace the Catholic faith and aspire to only one thing, to enter Carmel, for she had been brought up an Orthodox Jew (even if she completely rejected religion at the age of fifteen and defined herself as an atheist from then on). Meeting Max Scheler, as we have seen, had a certain importance for her; her friendship with the Reinachs was more important still. As Edith was sorting out Adolf Reinach's papers after his death at the front, she chanced upon a few notes on the power of prayer and the divinity of Jesus. The calm, Stoic attitude of Reinach's young widow also impressed her deeply: "It was the moment in which my unbelief was shattered; Judaism paled, and Christ streamed out upon me: Christ on the Cross."[1] A women who had stepped into the cathedral at Frankfurt to pray after going to market moved her tremendously; so did a farmer from the Black Forest saying his morning prayers with his farmhands before getting down to work.[2] Edith learned the Lord's Prayer in Gothic immediately thereafter. But the decisive moment came when, as a guest in the Conrad-Martiuses' home during the summer of 1921, she sat up all night reading the *Life* of Sister Teresa of Avila: like "this master of the inward life, seized in the depths of her being by a greater force," she felt that she too had encountered "the truth."[3] The day after she finished the book, she bought a catechism and missal and began regularly attending mass in Bergzabern: everything seemed familiar to her, and she understood the ceremonies down to the last

41

little detail. She requested baptism from the priest, receiving it on New Year's Day, 1922, and taking the baptismal name Teresia Hedwig. Hedwig Conrad-Martius stood godmother to her after obtaining an episcopal dispensation, for Conrad-Martius was a Protestant. On 2 February, Edith received the sacrament of confirmation; the ceremony of the laying on of hands was performed by Bishop Sebastian of Speyer. Is this conversion an instance of the much-discussed Jewish "self-hatred" of which Léon Poliakov has recently provided a number of illustrious portraits?[4]

Raised in the Jewish faith, Edith was perfectly aware that she was a Jew. She even identified with this heritage on the intellectual level, unlike Weil. This is attested by a remark she made to her classmate from Göttingen, Alexandre Koyré, after a 1931 conference at Juvisy at which the two of them agreed that the philosophers of the day—Husserl, Bergson, Meyerson—were "three of ours." When they spoke about Jews, they said, simply, "we."

The Little Personal Pronoun "We"

Saying "we" was precisely what Weil abhorred. The reasons had to do with her rejection of society as such, the "Great Beast" of book 6 of the *Republic*, and with her affirmation of the absolute supremacy of the individual. Let the reader judge: "the flesh impels us to say *me* and the devil impels us to say *us*"[5] or, again, more significantly for our purposes, "A Roman always thought in terms of *We*. A Hebrew also."[6] The Romans and the Hebrews were the devil in Weil's opinion, two peoples infatuated with themselves, convinced that they had been chosen above all others, idolaters of their respective nations. Weil wanted nothing to do with them; in her work, she never tires of excoriating their cruelty, fanaticism, colonialism, uprootedness, and rejection of "the true religion." As proof that the Hebrew people was accursed in the eyes of Antiquity, she points to Herodotus's total silence on the subject of the Hebrews—and yet Herodotus was curious about everything and had ventured as far as Tyr.[7] In a list of Weil's whipping boys and bêtes noires, Father Perrin includes "the Jews [, who] come first, of course! Then the Romans; the medieval Church; the people of Northern France; the Corsicans; Aristotle, St. Thomas, Maritain, etc.!"[8] As for Gustave Thibon, he does not hesitate to use the word "totalitarian" to describe an attitude that consisted in placing, on the side of grace, "the Egyptians, the Greeks, the Gauls, the Albigensians, who are wholly on the side of light, with the Romans and the Jews on the side of gravity."[9]

Yet, unlike Edith Stein, Weil did not change her religion. Indeed, did she not say that a "change of religion is for the soul like a change of language for a writer," since such a change can only lead, exceptions aside, to decline, impoverishment, and inevitable mediocrity? "As a rule it is better for a man to name God in his native tongue rather than in one that is foreign to him."[10] On this point, her views are similar to Simone Pétrement's. Pétrement confided to G. Aubourg: "I happened across some citations from Luther; they seemed to me to say more powerfully, and with greater freshness, what the Jansenists also said. I was tempted to convert to Lutheranism, but was held back by a kind of feeling that it is never a good idea to change one's religion; if I wasn't in agreement with the church I was born into, I doubtless never would be with any other Church."[11] But, as we know, Weil never ceased to repeat that she had neither a mother tongue nor a native religion—most certainly not the Jewish religion, which was the least suitable for reciting the name of God, of its blasphemous god Jehovah, a false god because he was an omnipotent god of hosts, not goodness, at least down to the exile. Whence the question that was to haunt Weil to her dying day—she demanded a "categorical" answer to it from Father Perrin: were the thirty-five obstacles to her joining the Church (she went on to name them one by one!) incompatible with baptism? Weil was to remain a "Christian outside the Church,"[12] confessing that she was "afraid of the Church patriotism which exists in Catholic circles."[13]

This refusal to belong, to maintain ties with a particular group, was paradoxical for someone who would repeatedly point out, in 1942, that participation in the life of a community, or rootedness, was the foremost "need of the human soul," because it enabled individuals to take up a position in the breach between the "treasures of the past . . . and expectations for the future."[14] Did Weil consider herself one of the uprooted? Taking Rome to task yet again, she affirmed that "our patriotism comes straight from the Romans," adding that the word was nothing but a screen for "idolatry with regard to [oneself]."[15] One can almost hear Alain here: "the divinity of our times," he writes, "is known as one's country."[16] Yet, a few pages further on, we find Weil inveighing against "those who don't want to defend their country"; she warns them that they risk losing, not "life or liberty, but purely and simply their country."[17] To be sure, even if a fatherland is, for Weil, only one of several "life-sustaining environments," whenever it is threatened with destruction, one is duty-bound to go to its aid. In 1942, in London, Weil took the full measure of the dangers France was facing and set out to re-invent the concept of fatherland: "From the social point of view . . . it will be impossible to avoid considering the notion of patriotism. Not considering it afresh, but considering it for the first time; for, unless I am mistaken, it has never been considered."[18] But, at a deeper level, God's children should love no fatherland short of the universe as a whole; that is why "one must . . . uproot oneself from the social and vegetative angles [and] have no native land on this earth that one may call one's own."[19] "[One can only] be rooted in the absence of a definite place."[20]

We are not dealing with a revelation in the strict sense in Simone Weil's case, for, in her own estimation, she had been "born . . . within the Christian inspiration"[21] and content to obey God and accept her fate: *amor fati*. Moreover, Weil's new awareness of Christianity, unlike Stein's, did not come by way of a reading of the mystics.* Nevertheless, her act of consent also had its decisive moments.

The first occurred in 1935, during a trip to Portugal: as Weil stood watching a procession of fishermen's wives, "the conviction was suddenly borne in upon [her] that Christianity is pre-eminently the religion of slaves, that slaves cannot help belonging to it, and [she] among others." That Simone felt she was a slave was due to the fact that she had only just put an exhausting year of factory work behind her—for ten years, it had been her "dream" to work in a factory. She had worked first for the Alsthom Company, then in the factory of J. J. Carnaud and Forges, and, finally, at the Renault plant. She had been, in turn, a lathe operator, a packer, and a milling machine operator and knew from personal experience what it meant to suffer to the point of physical and mental exhaustion. That was what she had been seeking, for she had been determined to kill herself if she proved unable to withstand the ordeal. Did this experience, this contact with real life, help her understand how the organization of industrial society could be brought into harmony with the working and living conditions of a free proletariat? Did she make the kind of progress she had hoped to on her book *Oppression and Liberty*, her "Great Work," her "Testament," as she called it, a book she had resolved to finish before starting work in the factory? In support of her application to the French Education Ministry for leave from her teaching, she said that she wanted "to prepare a philosophy thesis concerning the relationship of modern technique to the essential aspects of our civilization and . . . culture."[22] At the very least, her factory experience "changed [her] whole view of things, even [her] very feeling about life":[23] her relationship to time changed,** all the more so in that time in the factory was marked by an unbearable lack of thought*** and utter humiliation.**** This experience of humiliation, her

---

*"I had never read any mystical works" (Weil, *Attente de Dieu*, p. 43; *Waiting on God*, p. 22).

***"The days seem an eternity to me" (Weil, "Journal d'usine," *Œuvres complètes*, 2.2.250; "Factory Journal," p. 223).

****"It's only on Saturday afternoon and Sunday that a few memories and shreds of ideas return to me, and I remember that I am *also* a thinking being" (Weil, "Journal d'usine," p. 192; "Factory Journal," p. 171).

*****"Slavery has made me entirely lose the feeling of having any rights" (Weil, "Journal d'usine," p. 234; "Factory Journal," p. 211).

perceptions of the harshness of the situation, and the lack of the fraternity she had naively imagined to exist there, all inclined her to be rather pessimistic: "the class of those who do not count . . . and who will not count, ever, no matter what happens (notwithstanding the last line of the first verse of the *Internationale*)."[24] In the factory, she "received forever the mark of a slave, like the branding of the red-hot iron which the Romans put on the foreheads of their most despised slaves."[25] Just as she had wanted to see what working-class life was like from the inside, so she would later try to become familiar with the world of the peasantry: in *The Need for Roots: Prelude to a Declaration of Duties toward Mankind*, discussing the sickness that afflicted the modern world and the remedies for it, she would describe the uprootedness of workers and peasants and then endeavor to determine the spiritual "place that physical labor—[that] daily death—should occupy in a well-ordered social life."[26]

Her next exposure to Christianity came during her first journey to Italy, which she made alone, in 1937, traveling to Assisi, the very place where Christ had spoken to St. Francis. "There . . . something stronger than I compelled me for the first time in my life to go down on my knees."[27] Finally, there was the experience she had in 1938 during Holy Week, which she spent with her mother in Solesmes, going to all the church services. It was in Solesmes, she later said, that "the thought of the Passion of Christ entered my being once and for all."[28]

It is impossible to write about Simone Weil without mentioning Bernard Lazare, that other tormented Jew whom Charles Péguy describes, in his portrait of Lazare, as a "prophet of Israel."[29] Born in 1865 in Nîmes to an assimilated Sephardic family, Lazare too, like Weil, had not been given even the rudiments of a Jewish education: "I was raised as a Christian, taught not to be a Jew, to avoid, haughtily, those Jews who had not known the benefits [irony] of emancipation and were insulted and ridiculed as if they were slaves, not free citizens. . . ."[30] Lazare seems to have taken a certain pride in the fact that he was an assimilated Jew; indeed, he went so far as to distinguish "Israelites" (workers, merchants, soldiers, doctors, artists) from "Jews" (bankers and financiers), the very people who had, by compromising themselves in the Panama Canal scandal in 1884, provoked a recrudescence of anti-Semitism.* The anti-Semites, Lazare suggests, are beating the wrong horse. They would do better to be anti-Jewish; this would rally to their cause a good many of the Israelites who themselves looked askance at the influx of

---

*"Alongside this contemptible mass of Jews, there are other, very different people, Israelites . . . For years, they have been leading a peaceful existence; they feel attached to the land that has given them birth, on which untold generations have come and gone . . ." (Lazare, *Juifs et antisémites* [Paris: Allia, 1992], p. 6).

Eastern Jews seeking a safe haven after the 1892 pogroms, "those predatory, crude, filthy Tartars who, without good reason, come to batten off a country that does not belong to them."[31] But, the very same year, Lazare was to publish *Juifs et antisémites* [Jews and anti-Semites], a book in which he defied Drumont to come up with a solution to the Jewish question. Two years later, in 1894, he decided to take a stand against the anti-Semitism of the day, publishing *Antisemitism, its History and Causes*.[32] Drumont had not made anything up, Lazare said here: hostility toward Jews found its explanation in the fact that they had wished to survive as "a nation among the nations." Consequently, resolving the Jewish question seemed to Lazare to presuppose giving up the concept of nationality for that of cosmopolitanism. In the interval between the appearance of his two books, Lazare had apparently decided to "turn over a new leaf" and become what he was, a Jew: "I am a Jew, because I was born one. I do not care to change my name or join a Catholic church, Protestant church, or mosque. I have the right to remain a Jew and I will defend that right."[33] It was *this* "conversion" that Weil, who refused any kind of affiliation, was never able to make. "I belong to a group, and I wish to return to it and serve it in serving humanity," Lazare wrote.[34] The Dreyfus Affair gave him the chance he was looking for. He became the Dreyfus family's legal counselor, and succeeded in persuading Clemenceau, Zola, and Jaurès of the young captain's innocence with the publication of his lampoon, *Une erreur judiciaire: La vérité sur l'affaire Dreyfus* [A judicial error: the truth about the Dreyfus Affair]. Lazare had understood that the resolution of the Jewish question would not come about through assimilation or conversion but only as the result of a liberation struggle and a revolution in the ranks of his own people. The Jew was a pariah in everyone's eyes; he had, therefore, to become a conscious pariah. That presupposed rejecting the parvenus and getting rid of "this Jewish bourgeoisie, rich, not Jewish . . . our refuse, our dregs."[35]

Although Weil rejected any and all affiliation with Judaism, either on the grounds that she did not know how to define the word "Jew," or because the Jews were, in her judgment, "the poison of uprooting personified,"[36] she was not really prepared to join the Christian church. Her rejection of the word "us," her refusal, that is, to become part of a community, applied to Catholicism too. Moreover, she had not yet acquired the habit of praying—"I had never prayed; I was afraid of the power of suggestion that is in prayer—the very power for which Pascal recommends it."[37] She was content to recite George Herbert's poem "Love," to which a young Englishman she met at Solesmes had introduced her. It was during one of these recitations that, she said, "Christ himself came down and took possession of me."[38] Reciting this poem and also the Lord's Prayer transported her outside space, ushering her into the world of silence beyond the words. How are we to square these affirmations with the notion of "implicit faith" that Weil claims had been hers since early childhood? "Greece, Egypt, ancient India and ancient China, the beauty of the world . . . all these things have done as much as the visibly Christian ones to deliver me into Christ's hands as his captive. I think I might say even more."[39] To justify her refusal to join the Church, her stubborn insistence on remaining on the threshold, at the "intersection,"[40] she invoked her "genuine vocation,"[41] that is, the intellectual work she was planning to pursue.* Would the Church, like the factory, prevent her from engaging in the labor of thinking, because one had to devote oneself to it body and soul?

Edith seems to have shared the view that it would. After she had embraced the Catholic faith, it seemed, for a while, as if she had turned her back on all intellectual work, in the belief that "to lead a religious life meant one had to give up all that was secular and to live totally immersed in thoughts of the Divine." But she soon changed her mind: "Even in the contemplative life, one may not sever the connection with the world. I even believe that the deeper one is drawn into God, the more one must 'go out of oneself'; that is, one must go to the world in order to carry the divine life into it."[42] Edith made her return to philosophy by translating St. Thomas's *De ente et essentia* into German. (She had discovered Thomas—a philosopher Weil detested—in Speyer, and was later to write a long book about him, *Potentiality and Act.*) She then translated *De veritate*; the two translations were published in 1931 and 1932, respectively. Her return to philosophy was also marked by the publication, in a special supplementary volume to the 1929 *Jahrbuch*, of "Husserl's Phenomenology and the Philosophy of St. Thomas of Aquinas." The volume was a Festschrift for Husserl on his seventieth birthday.

But Weil named another obstacle to her joining the Church: the fact that it had not changed since the Inquisition. "After the fall of the Roman Empire, which had been totalitarian, it was the Church which was the first to establish a rough sort of totalitarianism in Europe in the XIIIth century, after the war with the Albigenses. . . . And the motive power of this totalitarianism was the use of those two little words: *anathema sit*."[43] Weil wanted nothing to do with this holy Church, "modeled on the holiness of Israel," this Church which declared, in the person of one of its Fathers, St. Augustine, that an infidel cannot do good simply by virtue of the fact that he is outside the Church, that is, "on the wrong road."[44] Father Perrin asked her to read a

---

*"My vocation imposes upon me the necessity of remaining outside the Church . . . for as long as I am not quite incapable of intellectual work" (Weil, *Attente de Dieu*, p. 65; *Waiting on God*, p. 35). Or again: "the love of those things which are outside visible Christianity keeps me outside the Church" (ibid., p. 65 / p. 42).

book by Father Sertillanges, *Le Catéchisme des incroyants* [The unbelievers' catechism], one whole chapter of which was devoted to the question of salvation outside the Church; but the book failed to convince her. Witness the fact that, late in March 1942, she questioned Canon Vidal in Carcassonne and Dom Clément Jacob of the Benedictine abbey in En-Calcat on the same subject. She takes it up yet again in her *Letter to a Priest*, posted from New York; and she would also confide to Maurice Schumann: "I am prevented from joining the Church . . . by its use of the words *anathema sit*." In Perrin's opinion, Weil's stubborn opposition to this formula can hardly be understood today, after the Second Vatican Council. Perrin also says that John XXIII, then papal nuncio in Paris, read Weil's *Waiting on God* and wrote Selma Weil to tell her how deeply it had moved him. After he became pope, the story goes, he called this to mind. In his opening address at Vatican II, he declared: "Today the spouse of Christ prefers to use the medicine of mercy rather than severity. She considers that she can best serve the needs of the present age by showing the validity of her teaching rather than by condemnations."[45]

Another of the arguments Weil cited had to do with her feelings about Israel. As Perrin observes, her attitude toward the Old Testament testifies to a backsliding and hardening of her positions. Weil's letter to Hélène Honnorat, written in Casablanca, is evidence of this:

> As to the human surroundings (rabbis, Polish for the most part), I would be curious to know how well the feelings Father Perrin expressed in his first letter to me, the one in which he set up our first appointment [Perrin had assured her of his support for, and sympathy with, the Jews], would hold up if he were to spend a few days here. . . . Father Perrin, if he could have seen us, would have been pained.[46]

Despite all this, Perrin prefers to speak of Weil's anti-Judaism rather than her anti-Semitism. The opposite holds for Gustave Thibon, who does not hesitate to say:

> No doubt she owed this hardness of green fruit . . . to her racial origin; she was indeed the daughter of that people marked with the sign of contradiction—that "stiff-necked" people whom the prophets sought to unbend—and her passionate anti-semitism is the most striking evidence of her descent. Is there anything more Jewish than the perpetual tension and uneasiness, the urge to examine and test the great realities—and the feverish search for eternity in the time order wherein we can recognize in the

noblest representatives of this chosen and rebellious race the ancient impatience for the Promised Land and a temporal kingdom?"[47]

Finally, in complaining that the Church "is not Catholic in fact as it is in name,"[48] Weil silently evokes Alain's definition: "Catholic means universal. It was, then, a great moment in human history when the catechism set out to teach the same doctrine to everyone, everywhere."[49] "We have to be catholic," Weil declares, "that is to say not bound by so much as a thread to any created thing, unless it be to creation in its totality."[50] To live in times like ours, "which have no precedent," we need to attain "universality": "in our present situation universality, which could formerly be implicit, has to be fully explicit."[51] One has to break free not only of the I, but also of the "we," that is, of "the social," which "is irremediably the domain of the devil . . . [who] impels us to say *us*; or else to say like the dictators *I* with a collective signification."[52]

Weil is extremely wary of collective sentiments, of the power that emanates from the group; she does not wish to belong to any "*milieu*" or circle, or to be part of any "us." Yet the fact is that she desires just that, ardently, as one desires anything one fears: "I should like it very much; I should find it all delightful. But I feel that it is not permissible for me." Thus she chooses to "be alone, a stranger and an exile in relation to every human circle without exception."[53]

Becoming What One Is

One finds not the slightest trace of religious or mystical torment in Hannah Arendt's life, even if Arendt too deliberately chose the pariahs' camp. She was Jewish and knew it, as we have seen, but attached no importance to the fact until Hitler's persecutions endangered German Jewry. At that point, she became truly Jewish, adopting a motto of Pindar's that Nietzsche cites: "become what you are." If she identified herself as Jewish, and, emphatically, as more and more Jewish, it was, to begin with, in reaction to Jaspers, who sought to win her over to a Weberian conception of a "German essence," a Germanness from which she wished to distance herself, if not intellectually and culturally, then at least historically; and, again, because the moment in which she attained this new consciousness of her Jewishness coincided with the one in which she abandoned her indifference to history and politics and resolved to become politically active, the moment in which she began to feel that she could no longer content herself with a spectator's role. Arendt's generation could no longer identify with the indignation of a Max Arendt, who, when Blumenfeld suggested that he join the Zionist movement, retorted, "when anyone calls my Germanness into question, I go for my gun!" Even if Arendt, like Weil, never joined a party—though people long believed that Weil had been a member the Communist Party, because she read *Humanité* and took an interest in the oppression of the working class—she would support Zionism. Does this mean that she was a "Sartrean" Jew, as is sometimes said—that is, a Jew only for the gaze of the other—or even that she made a virtue of necessity?

It is common knowledge that, for Sartre, "anti-Semitism makes the Jew," so much so that one must ask whether the Jew exists as such and if one is first a Jew or first a human being. Arendt's response is unambiguous. True, to the order Saladin gives Nathan the Wise—"Draw near, Jew!"—Nathan replies, "I am a human being"; but when one is attacked as a Jew, one must respond as a Jew, not in the name of universalism. Arendt was immediately able to take the true measure of events in Germany, making no mistake about just what was under way there, even if the Jewish establishment was by no means grateful to her for her insightfulness.

In any case, Arendt repeatedly asserted that, for her, the Jewish problem was posed in exclusively political terms. We must not, then, go looking for her on the terrain of faith. Nevertheless, it seems that she was thrown for a loss by the question Jaspers, after receiving *The Origins of Totalitarianism*, put to her in connection with the problem of evil: "Hasn't Jahwe faded too far out of sight?"[54] Arendt answered:

> Your question . . . has been on my mind for weeks now without my being able to come up with an answer to it. . . . On the personal level, I make my way through life with a kind of (childish? because unquestioned) trust [*Vertrauen*] in God (as distinguished from faith [*Glauben*], which always thinks it knows and therefore has to cope with doubts and paradoxes.) There's nothing much you can make of that, of course, except be happy. All traditional religion as such, whether Jewish or Christian, holds nothing whatsoever for me anymore. I don't think, either, that it can anywhere or in any way provide a basis for something so clearly political as laws. Evil has proved to be more radical than expected. In objective terms, modern crimes are not provided for in the Ten Commandments.[55]

Although Arendt must have known by this time that Hebrew has only one word, *emounah*, for both "confidence" and "faith," she remained convinced that religion could not provide an adequate basis for understanding the unprecedented atrocities associated with totalitarianism. Because faith and practical religion were no longer in season and religion was nowhere the source of political authority, she was to adopt the definition of Jewishness that Stein once gave a theologian: "we who grew up in Judaism have an obligation to give our testimony."[56] While Arendt was not a Jewish philosopher, that is, a philosopher who thought within the Jewish tradition, since she too, like Weil, identified with the Hellenic tradition, the fact remains that she never ceased to "give her testimony." She endorsed the imperative to remember precisely as expressed in the Jewish tradition, in the form of the injunction *zakhor*! She was untiring in her appeals for vigilance and unceasingly condemned those inclined to forget the Jewish tragedy, a tendency she was witness to from the moment the war ended. Nevertheless, she consistently declined to "play flattering homage" to the Jewish people, since, for her, belonging to it was not equivalent to loving it, even if she went to its defense.

Arendt always preferred Bernard Lazare, whom we mentioned a moment ago, to Theodor Herzl, witness an essay she wrote about both men, "Herzl and Lazare."[57] She took from Lazare the concepts of the parvenu and the pariah, along with the subdivision of the latter concept into two others, the conscious and the unconscious pariah. Like Lazare, she never tired of urging the Jewish people to combat its enemies by force of arms, as we shall see; she traced the origins of anti-Semitism, drew the lessons of the Dreyfus Affair, and attended Eichmann's trial in Jerusalem. The Jewish establishment raised a hue and cry against her book on the trial, pronouncing a veritable excommunication of its author; she became a pariah as a result. Arendt complained bitterly of this to Jaspers, despite the fact that she too loved to situate herself on the social periphery: "I'm more than ever of the opinion that a decent human existence is possible today only on the fringes of society, where one then runs the risk of starving or being stoned to death."[58] Besides Bernard Lazare, one might here evoke the figure of Rahel Varnhagen, that German Jew of the Romantic period Arendt wrote a biography of. Born a Jew and a woman, like Arendt, Varnhagen considered herself a loser, a schlemiel. She spent much of her life trying to make good what she called the "infamy of her birth" before finally coming to accept herself as she was: "the thing which all my life seemed to me the greatest shame, which was the misery and misfortune of my life—having been born a Jewess—this I should on no account now wish to have missed." Arendt, who did not need to make this long journey toward self-acceptance, comments: "it had taken her sixty-three years to come to terms with a problem which had its beginnings seventeen hundred years before her birth, which underwent a crucial upheaval during her life, and which one hundred years after her death—she died on March 7, 1833—was slated to come to an end."[59]

Philosophers, women, and Jews: that was the hand they were dealt. What would they make of it? What would they commit themselves to in the "spiritual situation" of the 1930s, characterized, in France, by the Catholic revival, the emergence of personalism, and, in politics, the rise of fascist movements?

PART II
COMMITMENT TO
THE THINGS OF THIS WORLD
(1933–1939)

1933

30 January: Hitler becomes Chancellor.

31 January: Edouard Daladier forms a government with a Radical majority.

27 February: the Reichstag fire. A decree entitled "For the Protection of People and State" provides Hitler the means to rid himself of his adversaries.

1 March: Léon Blum resigns after warning against the dangers of Daladier's project for thoroughgoing financial reform.

23 March: Hitler obtains the right to legislate by decree.

1 April: in Germany, the persecution of the Jews begins with a day-long boycott of Jewish shops. It does not call forth a single protest. A battery of anti-Semitic laws is put in place: Jews are excluded from the state administration and liberal professions.

7 April: a new law defines as Aryan "every German whose two parents and four grandparents are Christians and members of the white race." Civil service jobs are now reserved for Aryans.

10 May: Goebbels inaugurates a book-burning, declaring: "ich übergebe dem Feuer" [I consign to the flames] "the works of Freud, of Heinrich Mann, of Musil . . ." Raymond Aron comments: "Books burned *Unter den Linden* as the library of Alexandria had burned long before. The flames symbolized barbarity in power."[1] George Steiner recalls Heine's prophecy: "Where books are burned, human beings will also burn."[2]

July: the first concentration camp is set up in Dachau.

24 December: the beginnings of the Stavisky affair, which eventually implicates Serge Alexandre Stavisky, a Radical deputy to the National Assem-

bly and the mayor of Bayonne, in a swindle involving fraudulent municipal bonds. The right-wing press explodes in anger.

François Coty creates the far-right group Solidarité française.

Robert Brasillach, Lucien Rebatet, Pierre Drieu la Rochelle, and Bertrand de Jouvenel all contribute to *Je suis partout* [I am everywhere], an anti-Semitic weekly launched in 1930 by the publishing house Arthème Fayard.

Must One Turn One's Back On the World?

An Encyclical for the Jews

When Hitler took power, Edith Stein had a foreboding of the threat hanging over the heads of her people and over her own as well since, though baptized, she too was likely to suffer in the coming persecutions. Fearing for the lives of her people and, especially, of the German Jews—"suddenly it was luminously clear to me that once again God's hand lay heavily on His people, and that the destiny of this people was my own"[3]—she sought in vain to obtain a private audience with the pope. She had intended to urge him to issue an encyclical on the Jewish question. When she learned that, because of the large numbers of people flocking to Rome, she could not obtain a private audience, but only a "special audience"—in other words, that she could see the pope only as part of a small group—she gave up the idea of making the journey to the Vatican. Instead, she contented herself with sending Pius XI a written description of the situation of the Jews in Germany and also informed him of her fears for the Church's future. She never received an answer.

> I know that my letter was handed, sealed, to the Holy Father; and some time afterwards I received his blessing for myself and my family. There was no further result. But I have often wondered since whether my letter may sometimes have come into his mind. For what I predicted about the future of Catholics in Germany was fulfilled step by step in the following years.[4]

The tragedy unfolding in Germany threatened her personally: "I was almost relieved to find myself now involved in the common fate of my people; but I had of course to consider what I was to do."[5]

Did Pius XI recall Stein's letter when, on 22 June 1938, he assigned an American Jesuit named Paul LaFarge the task of drafting, in his name, an encyclical on the oneness of the human race, which was menaced by racist and anti-Semitic theories? The encyclical never saw the light. Is Pius's sudden death on 10 February 1939 sufficient explanation for this? Did the pope disapprove of the conclusions reached by the authors of the draft? Is it likely that Cardinal Pacelli, who succeeded Pius on St. Peter's throne on 2 March 1939, was unaware of the existence of this draft? Or was he, rather, reluctant to reveal its contents? All these questions are raised in a recently published book, *The Hidden Encyclical of Pius XI: The Vatican's Lost Opportunity to Oppose Nazi Racial Policies.*[6] We shall examine it in greater detail in our chapter about the year 1938.

A Carmelite

By April 1933, Edith Stein was certain that she would not be allowed to give a single lecture in the second term of academic year 1933–1934. After declining an offer to teach in Latin America, she made the decision—which she had been carefully weighing for twelve years—to enter Carmel: "since the summer of 1921 when the life of our holy mother St. Teresa had fallen into my hands . . . I had become a stranger in the world."[7]

Her mother was despondent over Edith's decision and would never recover from the shock, even if her daughter still occasionally accompanied her to synagogue to sing the Psalms: "Faith in the Messiah has nearly disappeared among today's Jews, even the believing ones. And, almost as much, the belief in eternal life. For that reason I was never able to make Mother comprehend either my conversion, or my entrance into the Order."[8] Edith felt no guilt about taking this step, convinced as she was that her mother would prefer to see her living in a German convent rather than teaching in South America.[9] All indications are that, once she was stripped of her German citizenship and forced to give up her post as an associate professor at the Catholic Pedagogical Institute in Münster, she set about creating a new identity for herself: "it is good to think about our having our citizenship in Heaven and the saints of Heaven as our fellow citizens and housemates. Then it is easier to bear the things . . . which are on earth."[10] She sought and found solace in a verse from the Letter to the Romans: "the '*Scimus, quoniam diligentibus Deum* . . . ' ['We know that, for those who love him, God turns everything to the good' (8: 28)] . . . offered me the greatest comfort and joy during the summer of 1933, in Münster, when my future was still shrouded in total darkness."[11] After crossing the threshold of the Discalced Carmelites on 14 October 1933, at the age of forty-two, Stein was clothed on 15 April 1934, taking the name Teresa Benedicta of the Cross. Husserl sent her a congratulatory telegram. Peter Wust comments: "she turned her back on the world and we returned to the world."[12] But did she really turn her back on the world, cutting herself off from it and wholly abandoning herself to her *amor fati*?

There exists a state of repose in God, of complete suspension of all intellectual activity, in which we are no longer capable either of making plans or of taking decisions, or, indeed, of doing anything at all, because we have entrusted the whole of our future to the Divine will and wholly abandoned ourselves to our destiny. I now feel that I am in this state, to a certain extent, after having had an experience that exceeds my own powers, totally consumes my energies, and robs me of all possibility of action. . . . [13]

Was Stein fleeing by entering Carmel at this critical juncture in the history of Germany Jewry? To a friend who expressed her joy at the thought that Edith was now safe from harm, she quickly replied: "No. I don't think so. I am sure that they will come and search me out here. In any case I should not count upon being left here in peace."[14] Edith was not mistaken. When the time came, she showed great courage: she proved ready to do her part in carrying the cross for the salvation of the Jewish people. Thus, when the Nazis staged a plebiscite as a show of popular support for the Führer, she did not go to cast her ballot, because the Jews had been stripped of citizenship. When two party members who intended to force her to vote came looking for her, she told them: "if the gentlemen attach such great importance to my 'no,' I am prepared to oblige them."

Responsible for the World

Discovering Zionism

We have emphasized that Hannah Arendt chose to confront the world and that she responded to attacks in the same terms she was attacked in. As she tells it, she had been preparing to go into exile for several years. Much more pessimistic and farsighted than her friend Anne Mendelssohn, for example, she had been convinced, since 1929 at the latest, not only that the Nazis were the enemies of the Jewish people but also that a great many Germans had fallen into step behind them. Although Arendt had no intention of living and working as a "second-class citizen," she nevertheless wanted to do something about the situation in Germany before leaving.

Kurt Blumenfeld entrusted her with the task of making as complete a collection as possible of the anti-Semitic propaganda in circulation in this period—what was then known as *Greuelpropaganda*. It was while on this mission that she was arrested and interrogated for a week by the Gestapo, then released for lack of proof. Her Berlin apartment was a haven for Communists persecuted by Hitler's regime.

Arendt fled Germany in 1933, without papers. Her exile led her first to Paris, where she stayed for eight years, and then, after a few weeks' internment in a camp at Gurs, to the United States. In Paris, she moved in step with the French intelligentsia. She made the acquaintance of Raymond Aron, Jean-Paul Sartre, and Albert Camus, attended Kojève's seminars, was reunited with other exiles, like Walter Benjamin, and met the man who was to become her second husband, Heinrich Blücher. To get by, she took jobs with Zionist organizations like *Agriculture et Artisanat* and *Youth Aliyah*, working with Baroness Germaine de Rothschild, the only member of the Rothschild family she could stand. This social and educational work, as she describes it, consisted essentially in helping Jews in their early teens who wanted to emigrate to Palestine by providing them food, clothing, and the necessary education. The work pleased her immensely and helped her forget the disappointment she had felt at seeing how many of her friends among the German intellectuals had made an accommodation with Hitler's regime. "Never again! I shall never again get involved in any kind of intellectual business. I want nothing to do with that lot," she later declared.[15]

A Frenchwoman in Berlin

But what was Simone Weil doing in 1932? She had made up her mind to go to Germany to try to understand where fascism found its base of support. Before leaving, she wrote a review of Trotsky's essay "What Next?"[16] She even arranged for Trotsky to stay briefly at her parents' apartment, together with his son, Leon Sedov, whom she nicknamed "The Crown Prince." There Weil and Trotsky engaged in heated discussions of the revolution. Simone berated him for his "superstitious" attachment to the German Communist Party; in his opinion, only the revitalization of the German Party and a call for armed struggle would ensure the victory of the revolution. But, for Simone, a party had to stay one step ahead of the masses, on the one hand, and maintain a united front, on the other. In a letter she wrote from Germany on 20 August, she drew up a balance sheet of the opposing forces in the country: "The Nazis do not only have petit-bourgeois elements on their side, but a great many unemployed people and a few workers. . . . Ninety percent of the Communists are on the dole. . . . The Communists and Social-Democrats have not formed a united front, a few exceptions aside."[17]

In Berlin, where she stayed for two months, she observed the street scene, immersing herself in the spectacle it offered. Her descriptions recall sequences from the films of Fritz Lang: "in Germany you see former engineers who manage to eat one cold meal a day by renting chairs in the public gardens; you see elderly men in stiff collars and bowler hats begging at subway exits or singing in cracked voices in the streets."[18] She wrote her parents reassuring letters: "I'm in the process of falling in love with the German people. . . . As for Berlin, it is at the moment the calmest city in the world. Everyone is in a state of expectancy and no one foresees any serious events before the autumn (October–November). Absolutely no feeling against foreigners. . . . Very few Nazis are seen in uniform, and those one sees keep quite calm."[19] Indeed, she concluded her letter by wondering whether she had not "come at an inopportune moment," given the absolute calm and her feeling of total security. Not long afterwards, however, she was to examine the question of the *Arbeitsdienst* [work service], which paid workers 10 Pfennige a week and was, in this period, intended for volunteers and the unemployed. She also commented on the incitations to murder communists that could be seen in the newspapers and drew attention to the monstrous capacity of Nazi ideology to win ever more converts even inside the Communist Party. However, she was at pains to make clear that, "once again, anti-Semitic and nationalist feelings don't appear at all in personal relations."[20]

Although Weil was by no means blind to the immense distress of the German people—of the more than eight million unemployed, only five and a half million received state aid, while the others either had to turn to their families for help or were reduced to stealing and begging—she focused on the paradox that the people as well as the existing organizations remained passive in a revolutionary situation, as if, "in the final analysis, fascism [were] a less frightening prospect for them than revolution."[21] Even the Berlin transport workers' strike of 3 November 1932, she noted, had failed to break up Hitler's party, though the Nazis did lose a million votes. On 23 March 1933, Hitler, who had been named Chancellor on 30 January, was vested with full legislative and executive powers. For the first time, in her essay "Sur la situation en Allemagne: Quelques remarques sur la réponse de la MOR" [On the situation in Germany: remarks on the reply of the M. O. R.],"[22] Weil pronounces the word "anti-Semitism": "antisemitism, with all that it involves, especially the looting of stores, is a powerful weapon . . . in the struggle to harness the socialist aspirations of the masses to different ends."[23] She concludes her essay with the bitter remark that "the best organized, most powerful, and most advanced proletariat in the world, the proletariat of Germany, has capitulated without a fight. . . . The tragedy that has taken place in Germany is a tragedy of international importance."[24] In November 1933, she still sees in German fascism nothing more than "the main enemy of the international proletariat." She compares the mode of industrial production, which subordinates workers to the instruments of production, with modern warfare, which subordinates combatants to the means of combat—with the difference that war demands still more: the sacrifice, not merely of labor-power, but of life itself. The point should be clear enough by now: for Weil, war is not a chapter in foreign policy, but a matter of domestic politics. She cites Karl Liebknecht: "the main enemy is to be found in our own country." If, then, "we don't want to renounce action, we must understand that we can fight against a state apparatus only from the inside."[25] In the same period, she raises questions about the nature of the USSR.*

Another Frenchman attracted to Germany by its culture and philosophy was in Cologne and Berlin from 1930 to 1933, at the newly created Institut français: Raymond Aron. He too observes, in his *Memoirs*, that even the students who were more or less in the National-Socialist ambit in 1930–1931 were by no means "monsters" and were amenable to dialogue; he adds that the changes which occurred after January 1933 did not become immediately apparent.** But he says at the same time that, from the spring of 1930 on, he sensed the irresistible upsurge of nationalism in Cologne and was, in this respect, "more aware than most Frenchmen that a storm was about to break over the world." Aron adds that, in this spring of 1930, he felt "the shock, which found its translation in Toynbee's dictum, 'history is again on the move.' " As early as July 1932, in an essay Aron published in the journal *Europe*, he declared that an authoritarian regime was inevitable, although he hesitated as to whether to predict the triumph of nationalism (Papen) or of National-Socialism (Hitler). Aron's stay in Germany in this period had a decisive impact on the development of his political thought: initially a pacifist flirting with socialism—influenced as he was by Alain, like his whole generation (and more than he cares to admit)—[26] he evolved toward a condemnation of Alain's "ahistoricism," which he was calling a source of blindness by February 1933, the date of his last essay in *Libres propos*. From 1933 on, Aron sought "to think rigorously even those realities the mind recoils from in horror."

Aron's *petit camarade* from the Ecole normale supérieure, Jean-Paul Sartre, took over Aron's post at the Institut français in 1933–1934. Sartre, unlike Aron, failed to perceive which way the winds of history were blowing:*** the year at the Institut français was for him an occasion to work on *La nausée*. It

---

*"It has never been of greater urgency for us to determine whether this workers' state is a reality or an illusion. If it is a reality, we must subordinate everything else to its defense. . . . If, on the other hand, no state in the world can lay claim to being the historical representative of the world proletariat, we shall have to count on nobody but ourselves, however weak we may be" (Simone Weil, "Le rôle de l'URSS dans la politique mondiale" [The role of the USSR in international politics], *Oeuvres complètes*, vol. 2, book 2: *L'expérience ouvrière et l'adieu à la révolution, juillet 1934–juin 1937*, ed. Géraldi Leroy and Anne Roche [Paris: Gallimard, 1991], p. 253).

**"What struck me most forcefully in the first weeks under the new regime was the fact that the great events of history are invisible" (Aron, *Mémoires* [Paris: Julliard, 1983], p. 55).

***"I had a year's holiday in Berlin, where I rediscovered the irresponsibility of youth (Jean-Paul Sartre, *Carnets de la drôle de guerre* [Paris: Gallimard, 1991], p. 100).

was not until 1938, at the time of the Czechoslovakian crisis and the Munich Pact, that he developed an interest in politics. In his preface to Paul Nizan's *Aden, Arabie*, he makes this remark about his indifference to politics: "I hated him to be involved in politics because I didn't feel the need for it myself."[27]

For Aron as for Arendt, the discovery of politics and the decision to act by wielding the pen—the wish, that is, to become a "committed spectator"— were contemporaneous with, and inseparable from, the rise of Nazism in Germany. However, those who, like Arendt, felt threatened in their own country assessed the German situation very differently. Thus it was that, in her interview with Günter Gaus, Arendt identified the twenty-seventh of February, date of the Reichstag fire, as the moment when she made her commitment to political activism: "this was an immediate shock for me, and from that moment on I felt responsible."[28]

But is Simone Weil to be believed when she unhesitatingly affirms, in the postscript to a letter she wrote to Father Perrin in 1942, that her "natural disposition is to be very easily influenced—and above all by anything collective"? "I know," she goes on to say, "that if at this moment I had before me a group of twenty young Germans singing Nazi songs in chorus, a part of my soul would instantly become Nazi. That is a very great weakness, but that is how I am."[29]

After returning from Germany, Simone participated in the grape harvest in Auxerre, harvested potatoes, was taught to weld by workers who were making repairs in the court of the lycée she taught at, and drew the lessons of what she had observed in Germany.* She helped the German refugees as best she could. Her articles on Germany came in for scathing criticism from orthodox marxists; she herself was happy to acknowledge that her ideas were "heretical" from every orthodox point of view. She does not seem to have become aware of the "Jewish question" at this time. Yet the May 1933 *Esprit* was given over to it; Wladimir Rabinovitch described "the tragedy of the Jewish people" in that issue of the review, while Emmanuel Mounier called for an international solution which, in his view, should have nothing to do with Zionism: "Palestine is an Arab country . . . there can be no question of mutilating a future Arab state for the benefit of a state created artificially, through a process of importation. . . . The essence of the solution lies in the creation of an international legal status for the Jews."[30]

---

*"In Germany I lost all the respect that in spite of myself I still felt for the Communist Party. . . . Actually it seems to me as culpable as the Social Democracy. . . . Trotsky himself seems to me to still retain a kind of timidity toward it that gives him some share of the responsibility for the Third International's crimes in Germany" (Simone Weil, letter to Urbain and Albertine Thévenon, cited in Simone Pétrement, *La vie de Simone Weil* [Paris: Fayard, 1983], 1:289–90; Pétrement, *Simone Weil*, p. 137).

1935

[J]anuary 1934: right-wing groups such as Action française and the Camelots du Roi [The royal newspapermen, the shock troops
of Action française], the Fédération nationale des contribuables [National
taxpayers' federation], and the Jeunesses patriotes [League of young patriots]
have mushroomed; they promote antiparlementarianism, xenophobia, and
anti-Semitism.

8 January: the body of Serge Alexandre Stavisky is discovered in a chalet
in Chamonix. The death is branded a "suicide," like Baron Reinach's in the
Panama Canal scandal and Colonel Henry's in the Dreyfus Affair.

6 February: taking as its pretext the Daladier government's decision to
transfer Jean Chiappe, the prefect of police, to Marocco—Chiappe supports
the far right—right-wing groups stage a riot in front of the lower house of
the National Assembly: twenty people are killed and some one hundred
wounded. Daladier resigns. Gaston Doumergue forms a new government.
The 21 February 1934 issue of the Socialist party daily *Le Populaire* lays responsibility for the riots at the door of Colonel de La Rocque, the "Führer
of the Croix de Feu," a veterans' organization which de La Rocque had transformed into a paramilitary group in 1930.[1]

9 February: a counter-demonstration called by the Communist Party and
the Confédération générale du travail unitaire, a Communist-dominated
trade-union federation, leads to nine deaths. In its 10 February edition, the
newspaper *Le Figaro* complains that the police lacked the necessary means to
arrest "the foreign scum: Levantines, Arabs, and wogs of all sorts."[2]

12 February: Communists and Socialists march side by side. The Popular
Front comes into being in response to the fascist threat in France.

63

March: the Vigilance Committee of Antifascist Intellectuals is formed; among the founding members are Paul Langevin and Paul Rivet, friends of the Socialist leader Léon Blum.

7 May: The National Front is founded, with Charles Trochu at its head. The Croix de Feu does not join it.

10 May: one year after the Nazi book-burning, the Free German Library is founded under the aegis of Lion Feuchtwanger, Heinrich Mann, and Romain Rolland.]

January 1935: the Saar Valley is returned to Germany after a plebiscite.

18 January: a giant unity meeting of the French Communist and Socialist parties.

9 March: Hitler officially announces that Germany will rebuild its Air Force.

16 March: Hitler reestablishes universal conscription.

11–14 April: presided over by Mussolini, the Conference of Stresa brings together the French and British governments, which reaffirm their commitment to protecting Austria's independence.

May: municipal elections in France.

2 May: the French government, with Piere-Etienne Flandin at its head, signs a five-year Mutual Assistance Pact with the Soviets.

Discussions between Stalin and French foreign minister Laval in Moscow.

16 May: Czechoslovakia signs an agreement with the USSR.

17 June: the Committee for Popular Unity is formed under the leadership of Victor Basch.

18 June: the London Agreement authorizes Germany to construct a battle fleet.

21 June: An International Conference on Culture, presided over by André Gide and André Malraux, vows to take up the struggle against fascist barbarity.

15 July: Léon Blum writes in *Le Populaire*: "We swear to remain united, disarm and dissolve all subversive groups, defend and develop democratic freedoms, and preserve peace for all mankind."

September: the anti-Semitic Nuremberg laws are enacted in Germany. Mixed marriages and extraconjugal relations between Jews and citizens of German blood are outlawed. Jews lose their German citizenship and can no longer vote or serve in the armed forces. All Jewish civil servants are forced to go into immediate retirement.

2 October: Italian troops enter Ethiopia. Italy declares that Ethiopia, with Eritrea and Somalia, now constitutes Italian East Africa. The emperor of Ethiopia calls for armed resistance. The dispute is formally submitted to the League of Nations for arbitration. Socialists, Communists, and Radicals form a united front to stop the advance of Fascism: the Popular Front is taking shape.

November: Jean Giraudoux stages *Tiger at the Gates*.

December: a decree on the sterilization of abnormal persons, incurable alcoholics, and those suffering from heriditary diseases goes into effect in Germany.

"At Home in the World of Thought"

A Tenured Philosophy Teacher Takes a Factory Job

Late in 1934, Simone Weil decided to take work in a factory to see what the "real world" was like. Always eager to measure herself against events where they actually took place and faithful to her principle that abolishing an evil requires first knowing what it consists of, she found a job as a power-press operator with the Alsthom Company in 1934, thanks in part to Boris Souvarine, who knew the managing directory of the firm, Auguste Detœuf. She thus came to experience first-hand the harsh conditions of working-class life. Of all her contacts with the real world, this was to be the most intense. It was one experience whose value she would never question.

What was a tenured philosophy teacher looking for in a factory? Before taking a factory job, Weil had wanted very much to finish what she called her "Great Work," her "Testament": *Oppression and Liberty*. By her own admission, writing it was an arduous process. Weil already knew that working-class life was marked by suffering and oppression. At the head of her manuscript was an epigraph drawn from Spinoza's *Political Treatise*: "with regard to human affairs, not to cry, not to become indignant, but to understand." Incidentally, Spinoza was, for Simone, the only great Jew, along with Charlie Chaplin! Let us note in passing that Hannah Arendt too has high praise for the character of the "suspect" created by Chaplin, one of the artists who belong to what she calls *Die verborgene Tradition* [The hidden tradition, the title of a collection of essays Arendt published in Germany]; she too would, late in life, come to recognize the importance of Spinoza after reading him at Jaspers's urging.

Weil wanted, then, to understand things, to get a firm grip on what she had only fleetingly glimpsed, and, perhaps, to correct certain misconceptions. In her DES[3] thesis, "Science and Perception in Descartes," she had begun to discuss "real action"—"to give it its true name, work." Now she wanted to see what "real action" consisted of. One of the major preconditions for arriving at an understanding of the world of work was a "critique of Marxism," the title of the opening section of *Oppression and Liberty*.[4] Did Weil, like Emmanuel Mounier, set the "hard-working revolution of the poor" over against the "revolution of parades" (the various forms of fascism), or had she already ceased to believe in the revolution? She did not travel to Russia, although she would have liked to, whereas she did go see things first-hand in Germany and Spain. Yet it seems that she was able (thanks especially to her friendship with Boris Souvarine, one of the founders of the French Communist Party, from which he was excluded in 1924 on the pretext that he was a "Trotskyist") to detect, very early, the defects and failures of communism and the hypocrisy of the Soviet regime, which was erecting a dictatorship and calling it freedom.

Comprehension, action, work: these are all concepts we find in Hannah Arendt as well. They hold a central place in her *The Human Condition*, a book its author defined as follows in a letter to Karl Jaspers: "I'm going to call the whole thing *Vita Activa* and will be focusing mainly on labor-work-action in their political implications."[5]

The Critique of Marx

Arendt and Weil proceed in much the same fashion: the two philosophers confront their thought with the real world, examine the role of labor in the range of human activities, and then attempt to draw political conclusions. We thus have good warrant for analyzing the two works together, notwithstanding the chronological distance between them. Comparison of the two is all the more justified in that Arendt had obviously read Weil, perhaps even more closely than she says—she cites her only once, in a note, as we shall see—and because Arendt too opens a chapter of her book about labor with a critique of Marx.[6] She is less caustic than Weil, who sarcastically rebukes the theoreticians of the Revolution for never having experienced factory life. Arendt quotes Benjamin Constant, who, compelled to attack Rousseau, declared: "certainly I shall avoid the company of detractors of great men."

That Arendt displays greater serenity in her critique of Marx is, perhaps, partly due to the fact that Weil has nothing to pit against the concept of Marxist revolution—that hollow word which, in her view, was to blame for so many deaths—except her own fiercely rebellious spirit and an ideal of "perfect liberty," which, she knows, is quite as utopian as Marx's doctrine. Beginning in 1934, she seems to have lost all hope in any kind of revolution whatsoever.* But, even if Marx sins by excessive optimism, Weil credits him

---

*"We are living through a period bereft of a future. . . . However, ever since 1789, there has been one magic word . . . revolution. . . . For more than a century, each new generation of revolutionaries has, in turn, placed its hopes in an impending revolution; today, these hopes have lost everything which was able to serve them as buttresses . . . for a long time now the working class has shown no sign of that spontaneity on which Rosa Luxembourg counted" (Weil, "Réflexions sur les causes," *Œuvres complètes.* 2.2.30; Weil, *Oppression and Liberty*, pp. 38–39).

for undertaking to study power relations in society just as a physicist would study matter.

In contrast, Arendt proffers, as her opening gambit, a *nemo ante me*: no one before her had distinguished Labor and Work (even if Locke had spoken of "the *Labor* of [our] Body, and the *Work* of [our] *Hands*").[7] Yet all European languages possess two distinct words to designate these two activities. Arendt has an explanation for this: no one before her had grasped the distinction because of the contempt which had, until the modern period, attached to work, perceived as "deforming the body" (Aristotle). To work was to be the slave of necessity; to free oneself of this necessity, one had to subject others to it by force—whence the existence of slavery. The modern period, on the other hand, glorifies work, which it regards as the source of all value: for moderns elevate the *animal laborans* to the rank formerly occupied by the *animal rationale*.

The contempt in which Antiquity held work is the one "gap" for which Weil faults "the miracle of Greece" and the ideal of human existence forged by the Greeks. In her opinion, it was Bacon who introduced the idea that man " 'cannot command nature except by obeying her.' " This, she says, is "the Bible of our times," the definition of work in the true sense; she adds that such work liberates men, because it constitutes "an act of constant submission to necessity."[8] In Arendt's view, work was given precedence over all else because of its productivity when Locke discovered that it was the source of all possessions, Smith, that it was the source of all wealth, and Marx, that it was the source not only of all productivity, but of our very humanity—in short, when Marx boldly advanced the blasphemous idea that "labor, not God, created man," that "labor, not reason distinguished man from the other animals."[9]

Arendt here seizes on the first contradiction at work in Marx: work, being the most natural of activities, is, for that very reason, "the least worldly" activity. We shall come back to this point. In Marx's view, the distinction between productive and unproductive labor, inherited from the Physiocrats, is more fundamental than that between skilled and unskilled labor, or even manual and intellectual labor—distinctions Marx treats as secondary. The distinction between productive and unproductive labor becomes more fundamental, because Marx scorned unproductive, "parasitic" labor, that of menial servants or domestics, for example. In fact, this distinction masks that of labor and work; if Marx failed to perceive it, it is because he was essentially concerned with the "productive forces of society"—in "labor power" conceived as a specifically human form of vital force, one as fully capable of producing a surplus, of creating surplus value, as nature is. This is a naturalist's point of view: Marx took little interest in "the question of a separate existence of worldly things, whose durability will survive and withstand the devouring processes of life."[10]

Weil appears to suggest the same thing when she says that "the human collectivity . . . has . . . taken in some sort nature's place to the point of crushing the individual in a similar manner."* Moreover, whenever the yoke imposed by natural necessity is lightened, social oppression increases in the same measure, so that "it would seem that man is born a slave, and that servitude is his natural condition."[11]

Furthermore, because Marx—the "greatest of modern labor theorists," according to Arendt—defines labor as " 'man's metabolism with nature,' " reification, the production of things, in no way delivers us from necessity: the effort of labor has always to be made all over again, remaining, as Marx himself put it, an " 'eternal necessity imposed by nature.' " Weil had apparently come to the same conclusion;** it is not because oppression is noxious that it can come to an end. What is the source of this oppression which, says Weil, Marx merely describes, without attempting to analyze it in depth? It stems from the existence of "privileges" instituted by the very nature of things— since confiscatory monopolies of power, work, and science are natural—and also from the struggle for power.*** But, above all, it has its source in the perversion, observable since the *Iliad*, which makes power, by definition only a means, function as an end from the moment men pursue it. And while it is true that power relations can occasionally be overturned, they cannot be abolished: from this period on, let us repeat, Weil no longer puts any faith in the revolutionary spontaneity that Luxemburg hoped for and believed in.

Weil and Arendt both expose the most basic contradiction in Marx's conception of what the revolution was to accomplish: not emancipation of the laboring classes, but rather man's emancipation from labor, even if Marx treats labor as the defining feature of the human being. While Weil pays tribute to Marx's idealism, acknowledging his heartfelt concern to lift "the ancient curse of work," she nevertheless criticizes this conception—which, she says, he has taken straight from Hegel—as "absolutely devoid of any scientific basis." In her view, Marx merely replaced the hidden mind which Hegel believed to be at work in a universe tending endlessly toward perfection with a new motor of history, namely, matter. Thus he attributed to matter "an unceasing aspiration towards the best."[12] In describing Marxism as "religious life of inferior quality," insofar as it assigns matter the power of "automatically creat[ing] the good,"[13] Weil was reiterating a criticism that

---

*"Thus, in spite of progress, man has not emerged from [his] servile condition." (Weil, "Réflexions sur les causes," p. 68; Weil *Oppression and Liberty*, p. 80).

**"Oppression is a necessity of social life" (Weil, "Réflexions sur les causes," p. 59; Weil, *Oppression and Liberty*, p. 70).

***"Thus the race for power enslaves everybody, strong and weak alike" (Weil, "Réflexions sur les causes," *Œuvres complètes*, 2.2. 57; Weil, *Oppression and Liberty*, p. 68).

Alain had already leveled at Marx's disciples.* This by no means prevented her from paying homage, in passing, to the "great idea" that in human society as well as in nature nothing takes place otherwise than through material transformations. Weil immediately adds, however, that Marx unfortunately failed to study the mode of production with a view toward improving the organization of society.[14] Yet the essential question is whether there are "any reasons for supposing that modern technique, at its present level, is capable . . . of guaranteeing to everyone sufficient welfare and leisure [to assure] the development of the individual."[15] This is "utopian," in her estimation—all the more so in that "Marx never explains why productive forces should tend to increase" until they attain a stage of development at which productivity calls for only minimal effort, with the result that the burden of necessity, and, concomitantly, social contraints, are reduced "until humanity reaches at last a truly paradisal state."[16]

Arendt had read Weil, and cites her:

> It is perhaps no exaggeration to say that Simone Weil's *La condition ouvrière* (1951) is the only book in the vast literature on the labor question which deals with the problem without prejudice and sentimentality. She chose as the motto for her diary, relating from day to day her experiences in a factory, the line from Homer: *poll' aekadzomene kratere d'epikeiset' anagke* ["much against your own will, since necessity lies more mightily upon you"],[17] and concludes that the hope for an eventual liberation from labor and necessity is the only utopian element of Marxism and at the same time the actual motor of all Marx-inspired revolutionary labor movements. It is the "opium of the people" which Marx had believed religion to be.[18]

For Arendt as well, emancipation from labor, and thus from necessity, and thus from consumption—from, that is, the natural metabolism which forms the very condition for human existence—is the only strictly utopian element in Marx's teachings. Yet Arendt wonders if yesterday's utopia will not be tomorrow's reality, in which case men will be confronted with a "serious social problem of leisure."[19] In Arendt's view, the hope of emancipating man from labor "rests on the illusion of a mechanistic philosophy which assumes that labor power, like any energy, can never be lost, so that if it is not spent and exhausted in the drudgery of life it will automatically nourish other, 'higher' activities." Weil, for her part, thinks that the Marxian utopia of the higher

*". . . who thought that the evolution of human affairs proceeded in accordance with a perfect mechanism that causes us to act, desire, fear, or hope, and in every case quite in vain, in step with the age and the particular moment. A theology without God" (Alain, *Propos sur la religion* [Paris: Presses Universitaires, de France, 1938], p. 10).

stage of communism is comparable to the utopian dream of "perpetual motion."*

Both women agree that the rationalization of labor and the myth of the "American robot" is nothing but a fiction, one they trace back to Aristotle. "Aristotle," Weil reminds us, "admitted that there would no longer be anything to stand in the way of the abolition of slavery if it were possible to have the indispensable jobs done by 'mechanical slaves.' "[20] Arendt points that "one hundred home appliances and half a dozen robots in the cellar will never replace the services of a maid. . . ." Aristotle once imagined, she says,

> something that has since become a reality, that "every tool could perform its own work when ordered . . . like the statues of Daedalus or the tripods of Hephaestus, which, says the poet, 'of their own accord entered the assembly of the gods.' " Then, the "shuttle would weave and the plectrum touch the lyre without a hand to guide them." This, he goes on to say, would indeed mean that the craftsman would no longer need human assistants, but it would not mean that household slaves could be dispensed with. For slaves are not instruments of making things or of production, but of living, which constantly consumes their services. (Aristotle, *Politics*, 1253b30–1254a18).[21]

In other words, "tools and instruments" can "ease pain and effort," but "they do not change the necessity itself." Weil had come to the same conclusion.**

Again, Weil and Arendt concur in their condemnation of the economy of "waste" and the creation of artificial needs, phenomena engendered by the race for progress and automation. "Besides," says Weil,

> automatic machines are only a paying proposition as long as they are used for mass production in enormous quantities; their functioning is therefore bound up with the chaos and waste involved in an excessive economic centralization; furthermore, they create the temptation to produce far more than is required to satisfy real needs, which leads to the squandering of precious stores of human energy and of raw materials . . . [to] the need for adapting other branches of production to this progress, [and to] the scrapping of old plant which is often discarded when it could still have served for a long time.[22]

---

*"It is solely the frenzy produced by the speed of technical progress that has brought about the mad idea that work might one day become unnecessary" (Weil, "Réflexions sur les causes," p. 45; Weil, *Oppression and Liberty*, p. 54).

**"No technique will ever relieve men of the necessity of continually adapting, by the sweat of their brow, the mechanical equipment they use" (Weil, "Réflexions sur les causes," p. 43; Weil, *Oppression and Liberty*, p. 52).

As if echoing Weil, Arendt observes that "we must consume, devour, as it were, our houses, furniture, and cars as though they were the 'good things' of nature which spoil uselessly if they are not drawn swiftly into the never-ending cycle of man's metabolism with nature."[23] However, for Arendt, once again, what is involved here is the perversion that consists in replacing *homo faber*'s ideals of permanence, duration, and stability with the *animal laborans*' ideal, the substitution of Work for Labor. Weil, in contrast, does not set much hope on art and literature: their sudden enthusiasms are not of much importance in her eyes.

We find the same critique of leisure society in our two authors. "The 'happiness of the greatest number' . . . the age-old dream of the poor and destitute . . . turns into a fool's paradise as soon as it is realized."[24] Precisely because the *animal laborans*' leisure time is devoted to consumption, Arendt fears "the grave danger that eventually no object of the world will be safe from consumption," that is, from "annihilation through consumption."

"Painless and effortless consumption would not change but would only increase the devouring character of biological life until a mankind altogether 'liberated' from the shackles of pain and effort would be free to 'consume' the whole world and to reproduce daily all things it wished to consume."[25] Does Weil not also declare, in her discussion of a possible reduction of the work-day in "Factory Work," that "the conversion of a people into a swarm of idlers, who for two hours a day would be slaves, is neither desirable nor morally possible, if materially so?" "No one," she continues, "would accept two daily hours of slavery. To be accepted, slavery must be of such a daily duration as to break something in a man."[26] An altogether superfluous activity borders on the absurd, she adds, just as a necessity whose ultimate purpose one fails to perceive is servile.*

Mechanical labor, creative work, and leisure were all much-discussed issues in the 1930s. In addition to the left-wing Catholic review *Esprit*, many new groups had sprung up in this period, such as Réaction, descended of Ac-

---

*In the manuscript of her open letter to Jules Romains, which was begun in early 1936, finished in Marseilles in June–July 1942, and published in the review *Economie et humanisme*, Weil had written: "the speech Marshal Pétain gave at Saint-Etienne has led me to reread the chapter of *Hommes de bonne volonté* [Men of good will] in which we find a description of factory life." The phrase may have been struck, the editor of these texts suggests, by Selma Weil. *Economie et humanisme*, for its part, did not hesitate to use two long quotations from Marshal Pétain as epigraphs to the essay. Incidentally, in *L'enracinement*, discussing the notions of the fatherland and regionalism, Weil boldly declares that the fact that "the Vichy Government should have put forward a regionalist doctrine is neither here nor there. Its only mistake in this connection has been in not applying it. Far from always preaching the exact opposite of its various battle-cries, we ought to adopt many of the ideas launched by the propaganda services of the National Revolution, but turn them into realities" (Simone Weil, *L'enracinement* [Paris: Gallimard, 1949], p. 211; Weil, *The Need for Roots: Prelude to a Declaration of Duties toward Mankind*, trans. Arthur Wills [London: Routledge and Kegan Paul, 1952], p. 158).

tion française, Plans, which had its roots in technocratic circles, and Ordre nouveau, part of a spiritualist current. The last-mentioned group brought together intellectuals like Robert Aron, Arnaud Dandieu, Denis de Rougemont, and Daniel-Rops, as well as technocrats. Between 1930 and 1938, the group published a journal that also bore the name *Ordre nouveau*. Its solution to the labor problem was to "divide up among the entire population the total quantity of mechanical, inhuman labor that bourgeois rationalization had imposed on the proletarians alone"; physical labor would be carried out as a civic duty during an eighteen-month stint of compulsory labor in a "civilian work service." Weil finds this idea unacceptable: "a people subjected to a short period of compulsory unpaid labour will not really work except under pressure from a despotic central power and under the threat of severe punishments."[27] Rejecting both individualism and collectivism, the movement called for a "spiritual revolution." Weil was familiar with these positions, which she condemns as "chimerical" in the draft of a 1934 article that went unpublished, "Sur le groupement de 'l'Ordre nouveau.' " In this text, she makes fun of Aron and Dandieu for their unconditional admiration of Paul Lafargue's *The Right to Be Lazy* as well as for their conception of the revolution: "It will doubtless not be long before one recognizes true revolutionaries by the fact that they are the only ones not to talk about revolution, because they are the only ones to realize that there is nothing in the present or the near future that deserves the name."[28]

While opposed to "demoralizing idleness," Weil nevertheless advocates providing working people access to the highest culture, which alone is capable of arming them against the danger represented by the will to power.* The high cultural level of the German proletariat had come as quite a surprise to her; she also marveled at the "enlightened, advanced" vintners of Auxerre when she worked in the grape harvest there. During a summer vacation at Villanueva, in 1933, she had even discovered a fisherman's guild which possessed a library containing only classics. She made a present of Rousseau's *Confessions* to the fisherman who was reading the second part of Goethe's *Faust*—from which she cites, in her "Testament," the lines, "If I could stand before thee, Nature, simply as a man, then it would be worth while being a human creature."

It is impossible not to think, here, of the "oasis" Hannah Arendt describes in telling Jaspers about her trip to California. She tells him that she met a longshoreman in San Francisco, a devoted reader of her own and Jaspers's works and a writer in his spare time, who showed her San Francisco "the way

---

*"The one sport which really inflames men, the sport whose objective is the domination of others" (Weil, "Avenir de la science," p. 179; "Scientism: A Review," p. 67).

a king shows his kingdom to an honored guest." He worked only three or four days a week. One also cannot help but recall her evocation of a neighbor of hers, a doctoral student from a disadvantaged background who had left the world of her childhood far behind; the young woman's room was crammed full of philosophy books.[29] Arendt is, moreover, at pains to specify that the oases she speaks of are not to be confused with relaxation or "taking it easy." Rather, they represent the world of culture and thought, of a thought which is not the unique province of the philosopher or specialist, not the *bios xenikos*, the "life of the stranger"—Aristotle's term, in the *Politics*, for professional thinkers. Every human being feels a need for such "forays 'out of order,' "[30] says Arendt, "reflection for its own sake that produces no concrete result." That is why she can only condemn "what is euphemistically called mass culture." Weil too excoriates the "miserable caricature of modern scientific culture, a caricature which, far from forming [the masses'] judgment, accustoms them to be credulous."[31]

Again, both thinkers observe that "the universal demand for happiness and the widespread unhappiness in our society"[32] (Arendt's phrase finds its pendant in Weil's "we are living through a period bereft of a future"[33]) are the symptoms of an imbalance between work and consumption. Is work the road to happiness and freedom? "We have begun," Arendt answers, "to live in a labor society which lacks enough laboring to keep it contented. For only the *animal laborans* . . . has ever . . . thought that mortal men could be happy."[34] For Weil, "the most fully human civilization would be that which had manual labour as its pivot, that in which manual labour constituted the supreme value." But she is at pains to add that "it is not a question of anything comparable to the religion of production which reigned in America during the period of prosperity, and has reigned in Russia since the Five-year Plan; for the true object of that religion is the product of work and not the worker, material objects and not man."[35] In July 1931, Weil published an essay in *L'Effort* entitled "URSS et Amérique" [The USSR and America] in which she criticized Stalin for expressing his admiration for American "efficiency" in an interview. Nowhere else, Simone affirmed, was the "subordination of the worker to the conditions of work" as clearly in evidence. But Alain issued her a warning: "I regard it as very important that the attacks on the USSR should be put aside in a work of *pure* criticism. The analysis (for example) of the bureaucracy must not rest on an inquiry concerning Stalin's government."[36] Simone must have been displeased, for she wrote shortly thereafter that "Chartier [Alain's real surname] has a very primitive, superficial view of mechanized society."[37]

The rehabilitation of manual work—one cannot but cite, here again, Locke's distinction between "the labor of our body and the work of our hands." If there is to be joy in the factory, this work, "the human activity par excellence," must be invested with an ultimate purpose. The worker, if he is to escape from the prison of immediacy, must grasp the why and the wherefore of his task and see the finished product, must have a sense of what he will be doing some two weeks in advance. He must be initiated into the mysteries of the machine and the productive process, which are a closed book for him because of his lack of training in mathematics. As things stand, he fails to perceive the relation between cause and effect, the "knack" involved.[38] Simone jotted down all these observations in her "Factory Journal." The misery known as the working man's condition, she says there, is that workers are everywhere like immigrants or exiles in their own land; they have no place they can call their own, no "home." "Bernanos has said that our workmen are not, after all, immigrants like those of Mr. Ford. The major social difficulty of our age proceeds from the fact that in a certain sense they *are* like them. Although they have remained geographically stationary, they have been morally uprooted, banished and then reinstated, as it were on sufferance, in the form of industrial brawn."[39] The primary consequence of affliction is the absence of thought; the worker lacks even the courage required to think about his affliction. But, for Weil as for Alain, only thought is action. If the factory is to become a place in which the worker finds satisfaction, then incentives more powerful than money must be found to motivate him. The worker must no longer be subjected to the tyranny of the present moment, must take a certain distance from his work and acquire a sense of how it will develop ten days to two weeks in advance if he is to take an interest and a measure of pride in it. In other words, a new "work stimulus" must be found. If it can be, work will once again take its place at the center of culture, which will no longer be a mere course of introduction to "real life." Here Weil remains sensitive to the influence of Alain, who, like her, took an active part in the People's Universities, less, he confesses, "to educate the people, than to establish clear ties of friendship with them, against the Castles, Academies, and V.I.P.s [he] does not like."[40] Like her brother André, Weil had participated in Lucien Cancouët's Social Education Group, which offered biweekly Sunday courses. She taught under its auspices from 1927 to 1931 while still a student of Alain's. During her stints in industry, one of her most cherished projects had involved publishing essays in which she expressed the hope that the workers "would feel at home in the world of thought." So that they might, it would be necessary, she thought, to close the gap between high culture and the masses, a legacy of the Renaissance. What was called for was not, however, "vulgarization,"* but rather "translation," that is, a method for

---

*"The term is as atrocious as the thing itself" (Weil, *Enracinement*, p. 89; *The Need for Roots*, p. 63).

bringing culture close to the hearts of people "whose feelings have been shaped by working-class conditions."[41] Her commentators all agree that Weil was a master of the art of translation, especially of the great Greek authors, like Homer, Heraclitus, Aeschylus, Sophocles, and Plato—whom she learned by heart. She wanted to introduce all sorts of people to them: Boris Pasternak, whom she met in a sanitarium, a peasant woman from the Ardèche region, the children on the ship that she took to New York. It was in this spirit that she published an essay on *Antigone* in the review *Entre nous*, whose editor-in-chief, an engineer by the name of Bernard, had given her a job in the factory in Rosières.[42] She intended to produce more such essays, in particular on *Electra*; however, Bernard's interest in publishing her work slackened. Beginning in 1929, she assigned work a privileged role, as is shown by her essays "De la perception ou l'aventure de Protée" [On perception, or, the adventure of Proteus], "Le travail comme médiation" [Labor as mediation], "La division du travail et l'égalité des salaires" [The division of labor and equal pay], and even her master's thesis, "Science and Perception in Descartes." From this period on, she speculated as to whether science hastens the emancipation of the workers, or, rather, contributes to their enslavement; she affirms that "the only wisdom consists in knowing that there is a world, that is, matter that work alone can change, and that, with the exception of the mind, there is nothing else."[43] In short, manual and intellectual labor would be united in her projected society.

Moreover, to perform this labor, "men would group themselves in small working collectivities, where co-operation would be the sovereign law."[44] Weil's choice of words bears emphasizing: "co-operation," not "division of labor"—for, as Hannah Arendt would observe, citing Viktor von Weizsäcker, in the "division of labor," "two men can put their labor power together and 'behave toward each other as if they were one.' " Such "division" points to "the unity of the species with regard to which every single member is the same and exchangeable."[45]

What, ultimately, do Arendt and Weil propose? In Arendt's case, the rehabilitation of the man of action: "as long as the *animal laborans* remains in possession of [the public realm], there can be no true public realm, but only private activities displayed in the open."[46] Let us recall that, for Arendt, the appearance of society, i.e., the advent of the "household," when it emerges from the shadows of the family hearth to take its place in the broad daylight of the public realm, excludes the possibility of action, for it demands that its members adopt a uniform, interchangeable, conformist mode of behavior, ipso facto ruling out all spontaneity, feats of prowess, or heroism. "Mass society, where man as a social animal rules supreme . . . can at the same time threaten humanity with extinction. . . . in a relatively short time the new social realm transformed all modern communities into societies of laborers and jobholders."[47] But, to gain access to the public domain, one must first be released from the grip of necessity, the realm of need: since "man cannot be free if he does not know that he is subject to necessity," he can throw off this burden "only by the use of servants."[48] The *animal laborans* has no means of access to the world, for his labor excludes him from it—as it did the slaves of Antiquity, regarded as *aneu logou*: "he is imprisoned in the privacy of his own body, caught in the fulfillment [*sic*] of needs."[49] Arendt accordingly proposes to humanize existence, for, "without being at home in the midst of things whose durability makes them fit for use and for erecting a world whose very permanence stands in direct contrast to life, this life would never be human."[50] The world is made up, "not of things that are consumed but of things that are used." Does Weil, for her part, not evoke Rimbaud's plaint in *A Season in Hell*: "we are not in the world," "true life is absent"?[51] Does she not rebel violently against society, that "Great Beast" which has a pernicious influence on men? Does she not counterpose real thought to the mere opinions one can have on anything and everything?

Weil is also aware that perfect liberty cannot consist in the disappearance of necessity; yet she knows that "nothing on earth can stop man from feeling himself born for liberty . . . for he is a thinking creature."[52] For Weil too, humanizing existence means making it possible for people to engage in thought and action: "life will be proportionately less inhuman according as the individual ability to think and act is greater."[53] However, "workers alone form a republic: this is why it is labor, not religion or love, which will be the basis for, and is the basis for, peace."[54] Weil does not, in fact, distinguish between work and action.* Righting the imbalance due to the inverted relationship between means and ends, reestablishing the balance that has been upset by excesses of all kinds—the excesses of science, mechanized society, bureaucracy, statistics, extreme centralization—restoring meaning to the individual in a social order that threatens to engulf him, and making workers socially useful again in a productive process invested with a sense of purpose—such would seem to be, for Weil, the means of overcoming the failure to think that dominates our times: "never have men been less capable of thought." In addition, Weil warns her contemporaries against the temptation of yielding to the attraction of the totalitarian regimes of the day.** Similarly, Arendt was

---

*"I feel a sense of my own value to the extent that I act. Only work brings peace" (Simone Weil, "Réflexions concernant le service civil" [Reflections on the civilian work service], *Œuvres complètes* 2.2.47–48).

**"In reality it is the lack of free thought which makes it possible to impose official doctrine by force" (Weil "Réflexions sur les causes," *Œuvres complètes*, 2.2.104; *Oppression and Liberty*, p. 119, translation modified).

to discover Eichmann's stupefying failure to think when, in 1963, she reported on his trial in Jerusalem.

"To Come to Know My People . . ."

"Islands of Perfection" in Palestine

For Simone Weil, no less than for Hannah Arendt, philosophy must enable us to understand the world; it must confront reality. On this point, Weil's thought is inseperable from that of her teacher Alain.* Even if, as Heidegger says, "thought does not yield knowledge as do the sciences . . . does not issue in practical wisdom . . . does not solve the enigmas of the universe . . . does not directly endow us with the power to act,"[55] Arendt had for her part also come to adopt, with Jaspers, the credo that "philosophy must become concrete and practical, without forgetting its origins for a minute."[56]

Arendt, as we have noted, had been so bitterly disappointed by her intellectual friends who, beginning in 1933, "fell into line" with the Nazi regime, that she no longer wanted to have anything to do with any kind of "intellectual business"; she therefore seized all the more enthusiastically opportunities offered her by the Paris Zionist organization to do social and educational work. In 1935, in the course of her work for the organization Agriculture et artisanat, she went to Palestine with a group of adolescents in her charge. She had obviously made careful preparations for the trip: "in order to come to know [her] people," she had taken Hebrew lessons from Chanan Klenbort, for whom she had found a job teaching Yiddish and Hebrew for Agriculture et artisanat.

"Her people" bears emphasizing; the use of the term is a deliberate affirmation of belonging on Arendt's part. In an exchange of letters with Gershom Scholem, Arendt initially uses the word "group": "I belong to the group of German Jews who were driven out of Germany early." But "group" does not mean the same thing as "people," even if Arendt, in a televised interview with Günter Gaus, had declared that, "in the first place, belonging to a group is a natural condition. You belong to some sort of group when you are born, always."[57] Speaking of her Germanness with Gaus, she went on to define what she meant by people: "I myself, for example, don't believe that I have ever considered myself a German—in the sense of belonging to the

---

*"It will be said that separating thought from acts is artificial; I hasten to remark that such a separation has never existed in my case" (Alain, *Propos d'économique* [Paris: Gallimard, Pléiade, 1958], LXI). Or again: "Men think . . . in accordance with the way they act" (Alain, *Les arts et les dieux* [Paris: Gallimard, Pléiade, 1958], p. 3).

people as opposed to being a citizen, if I may make that distinction."[58] Finally, let us note that Arendt falls back on the same term, "people," in her reply to Scholem's charge—inspired by the publication of her book on Eichmann— that she feels no love for the "Jewish people" (*Ahabath Israel*), although he "regard[s] her wholly as a daughter of our people, and in no other way."[59] Here is her response:

> I found it puzzling that you should write 'I regard you wholly as a daugh-
> ter of our people, and in no other way.' The truth is I have never pretended
> to anything else or to be in any way other than I am, and I have never even
> felt tempted in that direction. It would have been like saying that I was a
> man and not a woman—that is to say, kind of insane.[60]

Yet, while she acknowledges that it is a simple fact that she belongs to the Jewish people, Arendt rejects Scholem's basic criticism: for her, belonging to a people does not mean being duty-bound to love it. To begin with, Arendt feels an obligation to be impartial, in the Homeric sense—Homer heaps equal praise on Achilles and Hector, while Herodotus celebrates the heroic deeds of Greeks and barbarians alike. "If someone is not capable of this im- partiality because he pretends to love his people so much that he pays flat- tering homage to them all the time—well, then there's nothing to be done. I do not believe that people like that are patriots."[61] In other words, even if "that wrong done by my own people [Arendt is here referring to the role played by the Jewish ghetto councils] naturally grieves me more than the wrong done by other peoples," her pain is not for public consumption. This explains her choice of an "offhand," as opposed to a tragic, tone: she makes a duty of discretion, which is precisely what Scholem upbraids her for. Sec- ondly, as a member of the Jewish people, she regards as suspect the "love of the Jews" that, on Scholem's accusation, she utterly lacks: "I cannot love my- self or anything which I know is part and parcel of my own person." Lastly, love is, for Arendt, a category that, like pity or compassion, has no place in politics (she is highly critical of the role pity and compassion play in the gen- esis of the personality-type of the revolutionary): "I have never in my life 'loved' any people or collective—neither the German people, nor the French, nor the American, nor the working class or anything of that sort. I indeed love 'only' my friends and the only kind of love I know of and believe in is the love of persons."[62] This could hardly be clearer: love is a category for the private sphere, a fusion between two beings that abolishes the world by reducing it to a microcosm. Love, unlike politics, does not care about the world: politics begins only where the collectivity does, that is, whenever at least three people are present ("three's a crowd"). For Arendt, as we know, the German language, that is, one's mother tongue, is the true fatherland. Does her wish to learn Hebrew and become acquainted with her people justify the assumption that she was considering adopting a new fatherland?

Arendt was plainly excited by the new lifestyle forged by the settlers in the kibbutzim: she regarded it as a new political experiment cast in the form of a "peaceful, pragmatic revolution." At the level of relations between parents and children and also as far as its treatment of factory and farm work were concerned, this Jewish experiment in Palestine seemed to her to hold out a solution to problems common to humanity as a whole and present everywhere in modern life.[63] Yet she never considered emigrating, and, from this period on, criticized the "Palestino-centrism" of the settlers, absorbed as they were in their new way of life; she expressed reservations similar to those Nathalie Sarraute voiced on her return from Israel several years later. In a letter to Arendt dated 23 September 1969, Mary McCarthy gives her an account of Sarraute's enthusiastic reaction: "She was impressed by the *voluntary* communism of the kibbutzes, while acknowledging, somewhat later in the conversation, that this amounts to rule by your neighbors, which can have quite unpleasant features, particularly when it's the neighbors who decide whether you merit a trip outside the country or should be allowed to devote yourself to painting or writing . . ."[64] In her response to McCarthy, Arendt noted that she had reacted in much the same way: "I still remember my first reaction to the kibbutzim very well. I thought: a new aristocracy. I knew even then, of course, as she probably does too, that one could not live there. 'Rule by your neighbors,' that is of course what it finally amounts to. Still, if one honestly believes in equality, Israel is very impressive."[65] Yet, however keen her subsequent criticisms of Zionism, Arendt—like, for that matter, Sarraute—took the problem of Israel's survival to heart: "any real catastrophe in Israel would affect me more deeply than almost anything else." This did not prevent her from claiming that she "d[id] not share" "the survival passion" of the Jewish people, a passion that seemed to her be "something grand" and, at the same time, "something ignoble."[66] As early as 1941, she excoriated this will to survive at any price, this valorization of existence as such: "The Jewish people was beginning to resemble an old man who, at the age of eighty, had wagered that he would live to be one hundred twenty, and then adopted a carefully calculated diet and avoided all movement so that he could devote all his efforts to survival."[67] Calling for the creation of a Jewish army capable, if not of holding Hitler at bay, then at least of safeguarding the honor and reputation of the Jewish people, Arendt effectively urged Jews to invest this passion for survival with a national content. She takes the argument up again in a letter to McCarthy, in which she discusses the survival passion which has possessed this people since antiquity and has actually made it survive. The whole legislation since Esra and Nehemia has no other goal, and God knows it succeeded. . . . The argument: you need Israel in case another catastrophe happens in the Diaspora and/or because antisemitism is eternal etc., is specious. The Jews actually are as afraid of complete assimilation as they are of extermination. Weil, unlike Hannah Arendt, did not support the Zionist cause. Her contribution to a debate on Jewish immigration to Palestine in the pages of the review *Nouveaux cahiers* has been summed up as follows by Guillaume de Tarde:

> Weil saw yet another danger in Jewish settlement in Palestine: why create a new nationality? We were already suffering because of the existence of young nations born in the nineteenth century and animated by an exacerbated form of nationalism . . . Hence one should not create a nation today that, in fifty years, could become a threat for the Near East and the whole world. The fact that there exists an old Jewish tradition in Palestine is, precisely, a reason for creating a Jewish national home elsewhere than in Jerusalem.[68]

1936

7 January: conclusion of the Stavisky trial, which opened on 4 November 1935. Nine of the defendants are found guilty, including two former Radical deputies to the National Assembly.

22 January: Laval's cabinet disintegrates.

13 February: Léon Blum is the victim of an assassination attempt.

14 February: Hitler informs Mussolini that he intends to send troops into the Rhineland.

16 February: the Frente Popular wins the parliamentary elections in Spain, taking 260 of the 473 seats up for election.

28 February: Hitler grants Bertrand de Jouvenel an interview for *Paris Midi*.

26 April and 13 May: the Popular Front is swept to power in the French elections; the second round of voting gives it 378 seats in the National Assembly, 147 of which go to the Socialists. On the day after the elections, Blum writes in the Socialist daily *Le Populaire*: "We are ready to assume the role that is rightfully ours, that is, to form and lead a Popular Front government." However, Albert Lebrun, president of France since 1932, tries to persuade Blum to announce that he will not accept the post of head of government. The French Jewish community, for its part, has no "intention of becoming involved in the socialist experiment conducted by one of its members, who, although a member of the community, has taken his distance from it in order to enter public life (*Samedi*).[1]

Is Europe about to swing into the Left camp?

9 May: the Duce wins a triumphant victory in Ethiopia and announces the creation of the New Roman Empire.

Céline publishes *Death on the Installment Plan*.

May-June: a wave of strikes paralyzes the French economy. The strike movement deepens after 26 May: 35,000 workers occupy the Renault factories.

4 June: Blum, maître de requêtes in the Council of State, forms a government comprising Socialists and Radicals. The Chamber of Deputies now has seventy-two Communist members. The Communists, however, refuse to assume any direct responsibilities in the Blum government. In the Chamber, Xavier Vallat, deputy for the Ardèche region, voices his regrets over the fact that his "old Gallo-Roman country . . . [is] governed by a Jew."[2] The anti-Semitic newspapers run headlines railing against the "Talmudic Cabinet," the "man with the golden dinner service," "the government meetings that are now held in Yiddish." The mass-circulation paper *Gringoire* wonders if France, with its three million "foreign workers," has not become the world's garbage dump . . . filth from Naples, rags from the Levant, depressing Slavic odors, horrible Andalusian poverty, the seed of Abraham and the black pitch of Judea." Throughout the Popular Front period, Blum is the target of anti-Semitic attacks by the likes of Maurras, Béraud, and Daudet.

The Croix-de-Feu, disbanded by the Popular Front, reorganizes under a new name, the Parti social français. Jacques Doriot, a renegade from the Communist Party, founds the Parti populaire français, a nationwide anti-communist movement. Both of these parties are opposed to the idea of going to war with Germany. "Peace, even at the price of foreign domination," comments Hannah Arendt.

Broad social reforms are undertaken in the wake of working-class occupations of factories, workshops, and construction sites. The Confédération générale du travail, a pro-Communist trade-union confederation, quadruples its membership, which now reaches five million. French conservatives unite against Bolshevism, Blum, and the Jews.

Jean-Paul Sartre chooses not to vote.

Paul Claudel signs a text circulated by the World Jewish Congress to protest anti-Semitism in Germany, but remarks in private to Daniel-Rops that "everywhere, one finds Jews in the first ranks of the parties which are promoting social or religious subversion. It may well be that in assuming this destructive role, they are answering a sort of providential calling. But it is not surprising that that should provoke reactions."[3]

The Interior Minister, Roger Salengro, is accused by the far-right papers of having deserted and given information to the enemy in 1915. He commits suicide on 17 November.

17–18 July: Under Franco's lead, the Spanish generals rebel against their government. The ensuing fratricidal war, which comes to an end with the surrender of Madrid on 28 March 1939, is responsible for one million deaths.

20 July: the first appeal for help arrives from Spain. Under pressure from England, Blum, deeply divided and under attack from the Communists, decides not to send the Republicans arms: "I did not want to risk war for Spain. I *could* not."[4]

29 July: opponents of the Nazi regime try to organize Counter-Olympic Games in Barcelona. These games are not held because of the outbreak of the war in Spain.

1 August: the eleventh Olympic Games open in Berlin.

1 October: Franco sets up headquarters in Burgos, where he forms his junta.

14 October: the first contingent of the International Volunteer Brigades arrives in Spain. The French recruitment offices are permanently closed on 19 February 1937.

In France, the strikes resume in late autumn.

EDITH STEIN WROTE "The Prayer of the Church" in 1936; it was included in a collection entitled *Ich lebe und Ihr lebt*[5] [I am alive and all of you are alive], published on the initiative of priests and lay-people who wished to make their opposition to Nazi ideas a matter of public record. Prayer, especially the Lord's Prayer, seemed to them to be the "supreme salvation" in the face of the exactions of the period; each human being, they said, would become a "living building-block in the city of God." Stein's reaffirmation of her own Jewish tradition is particularly conspicuous in "The Prayer of the Church": "Christ prayed as a believing Jew and faithful follower of the Law"; or again, "Judaism had, and still has, its richly developed liturgy for public as well as domestic worship, for the great feasts as well as every ordinary day."[6] This liturgy, Stein notes, served as a prototype for that of the Catholic church.

The Fashion of Going to Spain

From Pacifism to Combat

As more and more of Europe fell under Hitler's control, Weil resigned herself to the idea that France would inevitably have to intervene. She accepted this idea, however, only after long resisting it, animated as she was by a pacifism she had learned from Alain. For her teacher, "power [wa]s like alcohol," and any leader was capable of becoming a tyrant if others allowed him to. Alain cited Stendhal: "the nation is drunk on glory; freedom, fare thee well."[7]

Drawing the lessons of the last war—"in the Great War . . . the object was always carnage"[8]—despite the fact that he had volunteered for service, he saw war, or even the simple threat of war, as the return "of the peoples to servitude in the name of freedom."[9] That is why he warned against fanatical, futile sacrifice of any kind: he considered himself duty-bound "to reveal all the causes of this brutal policy, whose sole objective is, always, to amass power and wealth, without drawing a single step closer to justice."[10] For his part, Alain aspired to attain the "good" by other methods.

The review *Esprit*, which also took an anti-war stance, had multiplied warnings against, and even attacks on, an electoral alliance which was hostile to the various forms of fascism and was accused by the right of war-mongering. Its repugnance for Stalinism notwithstanding, the review enthusiastically hailed the victory of the Popular Front. When war broke out in Spain, *Esprit* combated the Manichean vision shared by the Catholics, who saw the conflict as, simply, an ideological clash between communists and Catholics. The review's positions provoked the ire of Cardinal Baudrillart.[11]

Although Weil denounced the criminal utilization of hollow phraseology, her antifascism is no more open to doubt than the fact that she took part, unlike Raymond Aron and Jean-Paul Sartre, in the meetings of the Vigilance Committee of Antifascist Intellectuals led by Langevin and Alain. Nevertheless, in the summer of 1934, she told the Thévenons about her fears of the French-Soviet alliance advocated by the Communist Party.* That autumn, she wrote them another letter on the same theme: "everything that has happened since we parted—including the present events in Spain—has made me more and more determined to retire once and for all into my ivory tower, and not come out except for two reasons: the struggle against colonial oppression and the struggle against the maneuvers connected with the idea of passive defense in case of war."[12] From this moment on, indeed, Weil ceaselessly attacked imperialist designs, using economic arguments less than ethical and cultural ones. At the time, this was the position of a rather small minority.

She felt very ambivalent about the Popular Front. Keeping her distance from the (pro–Communist) Association of Revolutionary Writers and Artists founded by Henri Barbusse, she preferred to take part, on 10 and 11 August 1935, in an anti-war meeting unconnected with the Popular Front.

---

*"As for the anti-Fascist struggle, it is impossible to prosecute it without joining those who are preparing a fine little war side by side with Russia; so I abstain. . . . In any event, there's no point in getting upset about it: the alliance with the USSR is preparing us for a war of no mean proportions, but in the meantime preserves us from Fascism" (Weil, Letter to Urbain and Albertine Thévenon, autumn 1934, cited in Pétrement, *La vie de Simone Weil*, 2:9; Pétrement, *Simone Weil*, p. 218 [translation modified]).

On 23 August of the same year, she wrote to Claude Jamet: "A Popular Front government in France would inevitably bring us war—they would of course call it an 'antifascist war'—and fascism to boot."[13] On 26 September, Janet noted in his diary that she was "against Stalin, the USSR, and the Communist Party. . . . (Supreme) test of my faith! For the woman who is attacking it in this instance is above all suspicion. . . . A Trotskyist? Not since she met Trotsky. No, at the moment her political hopes find their last refuge in terrorism! . . . 'Malraux?' she said to me the other day. 'He worships nothing but force.' "[14] In 1933, in the draft of an unpublished piece on *Man's Fate*, Weil had criticized Malraux, even if she found his book very beautiful, for treating the revolution as a kind of "diversion, in the sense in which Pascal used the term," "a means of escaping the awareness of the nothingness of one's own existence . . . all diversion, including revolutionary action of this kind, is a disguised form of suicide. And revolutionary action, conceived, as in Kyo's case, as the most radical means of fending off awareness of the nothingness of human existence, tends naturally toward defeat and death."[15] It is not, then, revolution which should give meaning to life; one must first love life in order then to become a revolutionary. This love of life is precisely what Weil celebrates in Rosa Luxemburg. Her review of Luxemburg's *Letters from Prison* sets out from the paradoxical fact that these letters, written in the various prisons in which Luxemburg spent the war years and addressed to the companion of Karl Liebknecht,* who was himself a prisoner, constantly evoke flowers, birds, and nature—testify, in short, to Rosa's *joie de vivre*, to an aspiration to life, not a fascination for death. That is why Rosa seems to Weil to have very little of the Christian about her: "She is profoundly pagan. Every sentence in this collection breathes forth a feeling for the Stoic conception of life."[16]

Although peace remained Weil's paramount concern, she took part in the great strikes of June 1936 and the Bastille Day parade. She hailed the dignity and new responsibilities conferred upon the workers by the Matignon agreements, while pointing out the risk of totalitarian deviation inherent in the June movement.** Similarly, she gave unreserved approval to the Blum government's position on Spain. Blum, although cruelly torn himself, resisted Communist demands to send arms to the Spanish Republicans, thus playing into the hands of the Radicals, who pleaded in favor of non-intervention be-

---

*Karl Liebknecht (1871–1919) embodied the revolutionary opposition to the war within the Social-Democratic movement. He was twice imprisoned. With Luxemberg, he founded the Spartacus League and, on 1 January 1919, the German Communist Party.
**"Even capitalism is better than a totalitarian state of the U.S.S.R. type, toward which certain socialists would like to lead us straightaway" (Simone Weil, cited in Pétrement, *La vie de Simone Weil*, 2:132; Pétrement, *Simone Weil*, p. 293).

cause they feared, rightly, not only a war with the Axis powers (Berlin and Rome were backing Franco), but also a civil war in France. Yet, her support for Blum notwithstanding, Weil decided in early August to go to the Spanish front as a "journalist." Although she detested war, she had already begun participating morally in this war, for she consciously desired the victory of one side and the defeat of the other; she therefore joined an international corps of irregulars, learned how to handle a rifle, and, on 18–19 August, took part in a military operation on the banks of the Ebro. On 20 August, she had an unfortunate accident—she stepped into a pot of boiling oil she hadn't noticed—and was evacuated. On 22 May 1938, she wrote Georges Bernanos, after reading his *A Diary of My Times*: "I recognize the smell of civil war, the smell of blood and terror, which exhales from your book; I have breathed it too. I must admit that I neither saw nor heard of anything which quite equaled the ignominy of certain facts you relate, such as the murders of elderly peasants or the *Ballillas* chasing old people and beating them with truncheons." But she had heard enough to lose her illusions, and was now aware that "one sets out as a volunteer, with the idea of sacrifice, and finds oneself in the midst of a war which resembles a war of mercenaries." She had been particularly shocked by Buenaventura Durruti's attitude, although Durruti was a man she admired: he had not hesitated to execute a very young member of the Phalange after giving him twenty-four hours to join the anarchists. The boy had refused the ultimatum.[17]

Shortly after her return to Paris on 25 September, the international combat group she had joined was decimated at Perdiguera. Weil maintained her staunch support of the Republicans, attending meetings organized by the International Antifascist Rescue Committee (though she refused to stand up for the singing of the *Internationale*). But she gave up the idea of going back to Spain, for she now understood that the civil war had been transformed into a playing field for the conflicting ambitions of great powers like Russia, Germany, and Italy, and was turning, with increasing obviousness, into a contest between communism and fascism. Indeed, Clara Zetkin (1857–1933), who had participated in the Spartacus movement along with Liebknecht and Luxemburg and then joined the Communist Party while continuing to criticize the actions of the Communist International, had prophesied in 1923: "Fascism is the punishment for a proletariat that has proved incapable of pursuing the revolution begun in Russia."[18]

Back in France, Weil drafted a number of different essays. In an untitled fragment on Spain, she does not hesitate to mock "the fashion to take a little trip down there [Spain]"[19] and come back with a few more or less coherent observations on the country. Is this an exercise in self-criticism by someone who had written, just after arriving in Barcelona, that "power is in the hands of the people; the men in blue are in charge"?[20] In "Reflections That No One Is Going to Like," Weil denounces the organized lie perpetrated in Spain since 19 July 1936, the day Franco organized his military uprising.[21] "Do We Have To Grease Our Combat Boots?" warns against the danger of escalating a civil conflict into an international war and invites those who condemn the cowardice of the French government to go fight in Spain.[22] Thus, although she herself had chosen to fight side by side with the Republican forces, she approves Blum's policy of nonintervention as long as it preserves peace, even if there should be "an attack on our territory or the territories protected by us"; treaties mean less to her than "ties of flesh and blood."[23] While she clearly recognizes that Germany is "fascist," she nevertheless hopes that the Popular Front will be able to find areas of agreement with the Germans so as to avoid settling the Franco-German problem by "force";[24] she rejects the false alternative between "prestige" or peace, since no war, in her view, can achieve the legitimate ideals of justice, freedom, and social well-being.

The review *Esprit* had published an essay by Emile Hambresin entitled "La résurrection de l'Espagne et l'écrasement de l'anarchisme" [The resurrection of Spain and the destruction of anarchism] which triggered sharp protests from Weil and Victor Serge.* Although Weil acknowledges, in her reply, that the Confederación Nacional del Trabajo, a labor confederation of anarchist inspiration, welcomed suspect individuals to its ranks, it is slandering Joaquin Ascaso, she argues, to call him "an anarchist corrupted by the government," as the author of the article she is responding to does. But, she goes on,

> to hold him out as an example of "the scoundrels who claim to be anar-
> chists . . . to the sole end of enriching themselves" is to demonstrate an ig-

*Victor Serge (the pseudonym of Victor Lvovich Kibalchish, 1890–1947), in his youth an anarchist accused of complicity with the Bonnot gang, went to Russia when news of the October Revolution reached Western Europe. He made no secret of his disenchantment after his return to Russia and was arrested in 1927 and again in 1933. In November 1933, *Esprit* took up the cudgels for him in an article entitled "Où va la révolution russe? L'affaire Victor Serge" [Where is the Russian revolution heading?: the Victor Serge affair]; the article was sharply critical of the USSR. Weil evokes Serge's case again in an essay entitled "Le problème de l'URSS" [The problem of the USSR], published in *L'effort* on 2 December 1933: "The question of the 'proletarian dictatorship' is a very cloudy one, and has already betrayed us into making disastrous mistakes. The example of the USSR tends to promote acceptance of the principle that the individual can be sacrificed. . . . Thus many people think it quite revolutionary to show no interest in the fate of Victor Serge—who has been deported without a trial, had his manuscripts taken away from him, and been deprived of all means of making a living—on the pretext that Serge is only an 'individual'. . . . The collective interest always and without exception signifies the interests of those in power." (Weil, "Le problème de l'URSS," *Œuvres complètes*, 2.1. 310; partially translated in Pétrement, *Simone Weil*, p. 184) Beginning in 1936, after Romain Rolland had intervened with Stalin to obtain his freedom, Serge became a regular contributor to *Esprit*.

norance so profound as to disarm indignation . . . the incomparable friend of Durruti (the most popular of the leading activists in the CNT), and a man killed in action on the second day of the civil war. . . . One is saddened to see an article in *Esprit* repeat such a disgraceful statement as if it were uncontested truth.[25]

In 1938, Weil would say about the Spanish Civil War: "it was the operetta *Miles gloriosus*: after their country had been liberated, the leaders of the P.O.U.M. were planning to liberate Rome, before marching on to Berlin!"[26]

The Battle of the "isms"

The Alternative: Communism or Fascism?

Weil sounded the alarm against the dangers that starting another Trojan War would involve, given the colossal power of the weapons of destruction mankind had invented. She added that the objective for which the Trojan War had been fought, Helen, had now been replaced by another: meaningless words, abstract, absolute entities, "isms." Fascism and communism seemed to her to be "two almost identical political and social conceptions," characterized by intrusive state control over private life, outrageous militarization, a one-party system, and "serfdom": "no two nations are more similar in structure than Germany and Russia."[27]

"Nazi Germany and Soviet Russia started from . . . circumstances in many respects almost diametrically opposed, yet still arrived at certain results which are structurally identical,"[28] Arendt too would say in 1954, emphasizing that the Soviet Union had "embarked upon the road to totalitarianism" around 1930, Germany around 1938, and adding that the USSR was much more "fully totalitarian" than Germany. Yet, in the introduction she wrote in June 1966 for the third American edition of *The Origins of Totalitarianism*, she set these dates back, tracing the creation of a truly totalitarian regime to 1929 in the Soviet Union and 1933 in Germany. In June 1945, taking stock of events, she maintains that "anti-semitism was indubitably the feature which gave the fascist movement its international appeal": hence, to eliminate fascism once and for all, it was necessary to start by rooting out anti-Semitism.[29] As is well known, organizations responsible for spreading anti-Semitic propaganda developed in France over the years 1936 and 1937: the National Propaganda Organization, the French Anti-Jewish League, the Center for Documentation and Propaganda, and the Colonial Anti-Jewish

Movement all relayed Action française. Mass-circulation papers and magazines like *Candide* or *Gringoire* moved closer to *Je suis partout*. Arendt worked enthusiastically for the International League Against Antisemitism and helped defend the Jewish medical student David Frankfurter, who had assassinated a Nazi leader, at a time when the Consistoire, holding high the slogan "No politics!", had refused to demonstrate the least solidarity. Arendt, who would marry a former Communist, Heinrich Blücher, in 1940, expected no help from the Communist Party: "the extreme Left had forgotten its traditional pacifism in favor of old nationalist slogans."[30]

This explains why Arendt joins Weil in her condemnation of "isms." "I call all ideologies in this context *isms* that pretend to have found the key explanation for all the mysteries of life and the world."[31] The great danger of ideology lies in the fact that it purports to be independent of reality, and, as it does not possess multiple perspectives and has no reliable criterion for distinguishing truth from falsehood, does not scruple to bend reality to meet the requirements of its own discourse: it arranges facts in accordance with a logical procedure that sets out from an axiom and deduces everything else from it. Thus the Nazis

> destroyed Germany to show that they were right when they said the German people were fighting for its very existence; which was, at the outset, a pure lie. They instituted chaos in order to show that they were right when they said that Europe had only the alternative between Nazi rule and chaos. They dragged out the war until the Russians actually stood at the Elbe and the Adriatic so as to give their lies about the danger of Bolshevism a *post facto* basis in reality.[32]

In its extreme form, that is, stripped of all content, ideology suppresses thought. Witness "the disconcerting ease with which so many people changed from a red shirt into a brown one. These changes seem to indicate that it is not even the ideologies, with their demonstrable content, which set people into action, but the logic of their reasoning all by itself and almost independent of content."[33]

By way of illustrating this war of "isms," which "makes the Trojan war look perfectly reasonable," Weil recounts how, in the summer of 1932 in Berlin, when a Communist and a Nazi fell to arguing in the street, it inevitably "became clear to both disputants that they were defending exactly the same programme." She observes that this merely "exacerbated in each of them his hatred for an opponent separated from him by such a gulf as to remain an enemy even when expressing the same ideas. That was four and a half years ago; the Nazis are still torturing German communists in the concentration camps today, and it is by no means certain that France is not threatened with a war of extermination between anti-fascists and anti-communists."[34]*

Is "the distinction between dictatorship and democracy" any more tenable, or is it also a "vacuous entity"? Does democracy constitute a stake important enough to justify going to war? Weil often recalls that political regimes are unstable and that Germany's attitude is explained by the humiliation inflicted upon the country by the Treaty of Versailles. She suggests that helping change Germany's situation to bring about "an alteration of these conditions, in such a way as to make possible some relaxation of the State authority in Germany, might be more effective than killing the young men of Berlin and Hamburg."[35] "The notion of national prestige must give way to a new principle of foreign policy."[36]

Alain had already pilloried, in 1922, the absurdity of the wars of our times: "They are caused by honor and boredom, those twin brothers."[37] His disciple adds a warning against the desire to "keep France strong" at the risk of undoing all the social gains achieved under the Popular Front, gearing production exclusively toward the manufacture of arms, and making overtime and speed-ups necessary.

---

*See also Weil, *Cahiers*, 3:138; Weil, *Notebooks, 1940–1942*, 2:497: "Opposites. Nowadays, people thirst after and are nauseated by totalitarianism; and almost everyone loves one kind of totalitarianism and hates another kind. Is there always, thus, an identity between what we love and what we hate?"

1938

[**E**arly 1937: Blum's government is floundering; it has come under fire for its purely defensive stance on both economic policy and the war in Spain.

22 February: the German Foreign Minister goes to Vienna. The Austrian Nazis greet him with cries of "Ein Volk! Ein Reich! Ein Führer!" Schuschnigg, who wants a Christian, independent Austria, says that he intends to restore the authority of the Hapsburgs.

Hitler and Mussolini oppose the legitimists.

Céline publishes *Bagatelles pour un massacre* [Bagatelle for a Massacre];[1] Malraux publishes *Man's Hope*.

March: Pius XI promulgates two encyclicals in the space of a few days: *Mit brennender Sorge*, in which he condemns racial hatred and Nazism, and *Divini Redemptoris*. Cardinal Verdier in Paris, Monsignor Saliège, archbishop of Toulouse, and Cardinal Maurin in Lyons (who once supported Action française) condemn anti-Semitism as unchristian.

16 March: thirty-six people are killed in Clichy, a Paris suburb, in a shootout between rank-and-file militants of the Parti social français and supporters of the Popular Front.

21 May: Hitler declares that "Germany neither wishes nor intends to interfere in Austria's internal affairs, annex Austria, or bring about *Anschluß*."

21 June: the Blum government, losing its majority, is toppled by the Radicals. Blum becomes vice-president of the Council in the Chautemps government, whose Socialist members resign on 14 January 1938.

June: Bernanos publishes *A Diary of My Times*.

Unrest breaks out among the minorities in the Sudetenland; they represent a quarter of its population and are, for the most part, concentrated in a ring of territory surrounding Bohemia. They demand a number of reforms: abolition of the national state, the right to uphold Nazi theories, termination of the alliance with France and Russia, and a federal state. In a treaty of friendship signed in January 1924 and confirmed in October 1925 with the Locarno Pact, France had pledged to protect Czechoslovakia.

19 July: in Munich, Hitler inaugurates an exhibition of "degenerate art" (*entartete Kunst*).]

5 February 1938: At the Théâtre des Ambassadeurs, Jacques Maritain delivers a lecture entitled "Les juifs parmi les nations" [The Jews among the nations].

5 March: Hitler declares that he needs more space in Europe and intends to settle the Austrian and Czechoslovakian questions.

8 March: the Chautemps government resigns. Albert Lebrun recalls Blum. The second Blum government is formed, but lasts only four weeks.

9 March: Schuschnigg announces a plebiscite for the 12th; voters will be asked to endorse a "free, independent, social and Christian Austria." The Austrian Nazis alert Hitler, who declares that he intends to invade Austria to defend the interests of the pro-German population.

Schuschnigg resigns: "May God protect Austria!"

12 March: *Anschluß*. The German army marches into Austria; Hitler is acclaimed by large crowds. Schuschnigg is thrown into prison, where he will remain until 1945. Eichmann, an SS-Hauptsturmführer, unleashes a terror campaign: the Nazis begin hunting down Jews. Every day, thousands of Jews unsuccessfully seek to obtain visas for the United States.

Darquier de Pellepoix's Anti-Jewish League puts out a new leaflet: "It is the Jews who want war because war is the only way to avoid defeat and pursue their dream of world domination."[2] Colonel de La Rocque explicitly refuses to throw in his lot with the anti-Semites, sowing division in the ranks of the Parti social français.

Lucien Rebatet gives Action française a new name: "Inaction française." Celine calls for racism: "If you really want to get rid of the Jews, then, not thirty-six thousand remedies, thirty-six thousand grimaces: racism! And not a little bit, with the fingertips, but all the way! Totally! Inexorably! Like complete Pasteur sterilization."[3] Robert Brasillach, in an editorial in the 15 April 1938 issue of *Je suis partout*, demands a Statute on Foreign Jews. A year later, Rebatet will propose a statute on the French Jews as well.

Cardinal Gerlier, who succeeds Cardinal Maurin in Lyons, presides over a meeting against racism and anti-Semitism.

14 March: Blum's government reaffirms its support for Czechoslovakia.
March-April: influx of Jewish-Austrian refugees in the wake of *Anschluß*.
8 April: resignation of the Blum government.

10 April: in a plebiscite, Greater Germany ratifies the annexation of Austria. Ninety-nine percent of those who go to the polls approve.
The Daladier government is formed.

Mitteleuropa takes shape. The noose tightens around Czechoslovakia, which counts three million Germans.

Italian Fascism, initially oblivious to the notion of race, rallies to anti-Semitism after the Ethiopian adventure; it believes that the Jews are at the bottom of the antifascist movements.

A set of measures unfavorable to foreigners is passed into law; their objective is to apply quotas to certain professions. A number of people are deported or imprisoned, provoking a spate of suicides among refugees.

July: Roosevelt convenes an international conference on refugees; none of the thirty-six participating countries wishes to raise its quotas for German Jews. France, which has let in approximately twenty-five thousand refugees from Germany since 1933, continues to accept more than any other country until 1938, when the United States and Great-Britain overtake it.

September: the 200,000 foreign Jews who have settled in Italy since 1919 are ordered to leave the country in six months; those who have been naturalized are stripped of their citizenship.

15–29 September: the Czechoslovakian crisis.

25 September: Berlin advises all German citizens in Czechoslovakia to return to Germany without delay.

28 September: Germany is on the point of ordering a general mobilization.

After the Duce intervenes, the mobilization order is postponed for twenty-four hours.

29 September: the Prime Ministers of England, France, and Italy meet at a conference in Munich.

30 September: Hitler is allowed to annex the regions of Czechoslovakia with majority German populations.

On their return to Paris, Daladier and Bonnet are given a hero's welcome: France believes that the threat of war is fading.

5 October: in the Chamber of Deputies, 535 deputies ratify France's abandonment of its Czech ally. There are seventy-five nay votes, seventy-three of them cast by Communists.

1–10 October: German troops march into Czechoslovakia and occupy the territories ceded to Germany. The Czechs put up no resistance.

7 November: Hermann Grynszpan, a young Polish Jew, assassinates a sec-

retary at the German Embassy in Paris, Ernst von Rath. A new set of decrees on undocumented foreigners goes into effect.

7–8 November: In retaliation for the assassination of Rath, Goebbels organizes *Kristallnacht*. Ninety-one people are killed, hundreds are injured, 191 synagogues are destroyed, and 7,500 Jewish businesses suffer damages. Jewish refugees flock to the borders.

The leaders of France's Jewish community do not protest even now, with the exception of the Jewish magazine *Samedi*, which understands that Nazi Germany has declared war on all Jews.

December: Walter Benjamin writes to Theodor Adorno, "it is very difficult to live here without a constant, oppressive sense of anxiety."

Raymond Aron enriches his courses at the Ecole normale in Saint-Cloud with a series of "reflections on the crisis."

"The time is out of joint" (Shakespeare, *Hamlet*)

In January 1938, in Germany, Jews were massacred and synagogues burned down. "Woe to this country," Sister Benedicta-Edith Stein exclaimed, "when God comes to avenge the outrages visited on the Jews!"[4] Echoes of the Jews' ordeal had penetrated the walls of her convent: she had learned from American newspapers of the atrocities perpetrated against them. "These were unconfirmed reports which I will not repeat. I had indeed already heard of severe measures being taken against the Jews. But now suddenly it was luminously clear to me that once again God's hand lay heavy on His people, and that the destiny of this people was my own." This time, however, Stein did not reveal her background to her interlocutor.[5] In the spring of 1938, Sister Benedicta took her simple vows and donned the veil. On 21 April, she pronounced her solemn, perpetual vows. "No words can express," she wrote to the philosopher Roman Ingarden, "what it means to be taken by God forever."[6]* Husserl had died on 17 April.

"When the whole world is out of joint, I simply try to understand the what and the why of what is happening, and, from the moment I do my duty, I recover my calm and my good spirits." This sentence, which is to be found in a letter Rosa Luxemburg wrote to Louise Kautsky on 26 January 1917 from her prison in the Wronke fortress, might also be applied to the period in question here.[7] On the eve of the second World War, anti-Semitism was an issue which dominated public discussion, deeply dividing Catholics and pro-

---

*Weil would use much the same expression: "Christ himself . . . took possession of me."

voking passionate reactions, broken friendships, professions of faith, and even conversions.

In a lecture delivered at the Théâtre des Ambassadeurs on 5 February 1938, Jacques Maritain affirmed that "the racists are indebted to the Old Testament, as the Communists are to the New. It is the Scriptures from which the former drew, only to corrupt it, the idea of a chosen people, a people of God; it is the Gospels from which the latter received, only to denature it, the idea of universal salvation and human brotherhood."[8] Weil— we will come back to this point—was to take up the first part of this comparison and what it implied about the notion of a chosen race. One also finds in Weil the notion that socialism consists in praise for the vanquished, whereas racism associates the good with the victors.

In June 1938, Maritain, responding to André Gide in *La Nouvelle revue française*,[9] declared that contemporary anti-Semitism was not a matter to be treated lightly. Two months earlier, Gide had published, in the same journal, an essay entitled "Les Juifs, Céline et Maritain," in which he expressed surprise that the critics had taken Céline's *Bagatelle for a Massacre* seriously; he himself considered it nothing but a "game" in which "the Jews were only a pretext," like the maggots that devour the hero's stock of potatoes in *Death on the Installment Plan*. A few years earlier, Gide had been swept up in the wave of Belle Epoque conversions which Henriette Psichari-Renan[10] portrays as a symptomatic reaction to the separation of Church and state realized in 1905; he had nearly "converted," and only the examples of Francis Jammes, Paul Claudel, and Charles Du Bos had made him think better of it. Although he had been a classmate of Léon Blum's at the lycée Henri IV, Gide gave free rein to his anti-Semitism, remarking, in a discussion of Blum's *Nouvelles Conversations avec Eckermann* [New conversations with Eckermann], that Blum had "a semitic, yet extremely sharp, mind."[11] Worse, in 1914 he had written in his *Journal* that Blum "doubtless sees a chance for the [Jewish] race to make it at last. Doubtless he sees, in this success of the race, the solution to a host of social and political problems. The Jews' day will come, he thinks, and it is already crucial to recognize and establish Jewish superiority in every category, every field, every branch of learning, industry, and the arts." In 1938, Gide charged Maritain with dodging the issue of race in general and of the Jewish race in particular in his lecture "A Christian Looks at the Jewish Question"; a discussion of race could, according to Gide, have shed light on the Jewish question. Gide added that Maritain misinterpreted a sentence of Léon Bloy's which he nevertheless often quoted: " 'the history of the Jews thwarts the history of the human race as a dike thwarts the flood, to raise its level.' "[12] Gide offered his own interpretation: "I should have liked to hear Maritain say more about this positive aspect of the contribution made by the Jewish race."[13] But Gide forgot the end of Bloy's sentence: "they are immovable forever and all one can do is to clear them by leaping over them, with more or less fuss, but with no hope of destroying them."

The title *Le Salut par les Juifs* (*Salus ex judaeis quia Salus a judaeis*) [Salvation is of the Jews] alludes to the fourth chapter of the Gospel according to St. John, a text at antipodes from Drumont's theses. Yet Bloy confesses that he is not inclined to make the slightest change to the "lovely page" he wrote six years earlier in the "angry book" *Le Désespéré* [The desperate one]. Let the reader judge:

> The Middle Ages had the common sense to confine [the Jews] to reserved pens and special clothing which allowed everyone to avoid them. When one had to have something to do with these rotters, one hid from them as from something vile and then purified oneself as fast as one could. The shame and danger that contact with them brought was the antidote to the pestilence they represented—for God has decreed that these vermin shall exist til the end of time. Now that Christianity seems to be groaning under the boots of the very people who believe in it, now that the Church has lost all credit, we foolishly wax indignant over the fact that the Jews have become the masters of the world; the rabid nay-sayers to the apostolic tradition are the first to be surprised. First we outlaw disinfectant, then we complain about lice. That is the characteristic imbecility of modern times.

Bloy concludes:

> For me, it is more obvious than ever that Christian society is infested with a most disgusting breed, and it is terrible to think that this pack is, by the will of God, to endure *forever*. From a twofold point of view, moral and physical, the modern Yid would seem to be the magnet for all the hideousness in the world.[14]

The Maritains nevertheless chose Bloy as their godfather.

HIGHLY SENSITIVIZED to the colonial question, Simone Weil had made plans to go to Indochina and then Albania, but later gave them up. She failed to convince Malraux that the Stalinist regime was as oppressive as fascism. Relieved of her teaching duties for health reasons in January, she read voraciously in 1938: Roman history, the *Iliad*, Sophocles, and Aeschylus, but also modern writers, the history of religion, the Old Testament in the official version published by the French rabbinate—she was outraged by what she found in it—and *The Seven Pillars of Wisdom* by T. E. Lawrence, whom she ranked as high as Homer.

THE POPULAR FRONT had collapsed; the government fell into the hands of the Radical party. France was riven by dissension. Within the ranks of the government itself, Paul Reynaud, who opposed the Popular Front and advocated a free-market economy, also opposed the Munich Agreement and Gaston Bonnet's foreign policy. A clear-cut choice was beginning to emerge: France had either to bar the road to the fascist advance at the risk of war or defend peace at any price at the risk of contributing to the construction of a National-Socialist Europe.

In March 1938, in the wake of *Anschluß*, Weil joined forty other antifascist intellectuals in calling for "immediate negotiations"; she endorsed Chamberlain's policy and warned of the dangers to which the arms race was exposing the economy.[15] Though well aware that the government could no longer advocate a policy of nonviolence, she declared, after attending a lecture by Henri Bouché on "The French Problem of National Defense," that she was in favor of "a particular form of resistance . . . that would more closely resemble guerrilla warfare than regular war."[16] In May 1938, she still believed that Hitler's sole objective was to rectify Germany's borders. She acknowledged Germany's "totalitarian" nature, but, in the same breath, pointed out the instability of its political regime. She understood "the distress of our time," yet did not think that what was at stake in Czechoslovakia mattered enough to warrant Europe's abandoning its security and going to war.[17] "The preservation of the Czechoslovakian state as it presently exists" did not seem to her a sufficiently important objective, whether "from the point of view . . . of rights as such, the balance of power . . . or France's treaty commitments": "can we allow a whole young generation to die for a treaty it did not ratify?" She was prepared to see Czechoslovakia become "a German satellite," venturing so far as to say that "the Czechs [could] ban the Communist Party and exclude Jews from all relatively important positions without losing anything of their national life. In short, injustice for injustice— since there must be some form of injustice in any case—let us choose the one that has the least risk of war."[18] She did not find the prospect of German hegemony in Europe any more alarming than an unyielding attitude on France's part, with the concomitant risks of war, defeat, and invasion. Despite her esteem for Gaston Bergery, founder of the Parti frontiste (initially called the Front commun, and, later, the Front social), she was shocked by an article he published on 1 April in his newspaper *La Flèche*: his antiwar positions notwithstanding, Bergerey was for barring the way to German control of central Europe. If France were to countenance German hegemony in the region, Weil wrote, the country would soon find itself "adopting certain laws of exclusion, chiefly against Communists and Jews—which is, in my eyes and probably in the eyes of the majority of Frenchmen, nearly an indifferent matter in itself."[19] What grounds does Simone Pétrement have for saying about this letter that Weil's "disinterestedness made her prefer, of the two evils, the one of which she personally would be the victim"?[20] The same year, Weil spent Holy Week in Solesmes, with its Benedictine monastery; she followed the mass with her mother and was entranced by the plain-chants. The recitation of George Herbert's poem "Love" "had the virtue of a prayer" for her.[21] It made Christ a living presence, "a presence more personal, more certain, and more real than that of a human being; it was inaccessible both to sense and to imagination, and it resembled . . . love."[22] This was, as we have seen, Weil's third exposure to Christianity, "the religion of slaves."

By the Munich Agreement, signed on 30 September 1938, Hitler, Mussolini, Chamberlain, and Daladier recognized Germany's right to annex the Sudetenland. While Weil approved of their decision, she did not believe that the threat of war had been definitively averted. Emmanuel Mounier, who emphatically disapproved of the Munich Agreement, voiced his indignation in an editorial in the October *Esprit*: "When men or regimes or countries, after championing the rights of small nations and the idea that one must keep one's word, deliberately go back on their engagements, and, in the space of twenty-four hours, with a kind of irritated haste smacking of the basest sort of crime, drive those they have taken under their 'protection' toward suicide, how can one not speak of dishonor?"[23] But not all the contributors to *Esprit* agreed. Maurice de Gandillac, Roger Labrousse, Marcel Moré, and Bernard Serampuy (François Goguel) disavowed the stance taken by the review. Georges Bernanos lashed out at them in *Nous autres français* [We French]:

> At the hour of the Munich diktat, four of *Esprit*'s contributors, whose names one had best not pronounce in front of a pregnant woman, lest she give birth to a coward—Messieurs de Gandillac, Labrousse, Moré, and Serampuy—not only categorically refused to endorse the courageous attitude taken by the review, but also felt compelled to write five pages designed to justify what they call, in their priceless language, "a retreat to modest positions." Five pages against honor is too much. A single line would have been enough.[24]

On 6 September, Pius XI declared, before a group of Belgians on a pilgrimage to Rome, "spiritually we are Semites." Jacques Maritain singled his words out for comment on 8 February of the following year, in another lecture delivered at the Théâtre des Ambassadeurs: "anti-Semitism . . . is a movement in which we Christians can have no part whatsoever. . . . *Spiritually we are Semites*: no stronger words have been spoken by a Christian against anti-Semitism, and this Christian is the successor of the apostle Peter."[25] The pope's witness strengthened the Maritains' new faith in the unity of the two Testaments: "we pass from one [Testament] to another by means of Christ."[26] Both Maritains were converts. Jacques had been baptized in the Protestant faith while still a child. Raïssa came from a Jewish family; her maternal grandfather was Hasidic. Léon Bloy and his wife acted as their godfather and godmother. To the Maritains, the Nazis' anti-Semitism seemed to be a kind of "Christophobia"; the persecution of the Jews took the form of the Cross. "Nazi anti-Semitism is in essence a rabid aversion to the Revelation of Sinai and the Law of the Decalogue; above all, it is . . . a kind of preternatural hatred and fear of Christianity and the Law of the Gospel which do not dare speak their name, as well as of the King of the Jews Who is the Word Incarnate . . . and Who became flesh in a Virgin of Israel."[27] The Maritains had sponsored a new edition of Bloy's *Salvation Is of the Jews* in 1906. It bears the following dedication: "I dedicate these pages, written for the catholic glory of the God of Abraham, Isaac, and Jacob, to Raïssa Maritain." The reason for what the Maritains saw as the "monstrosity" of Christian anti-Semitism could only reside, they thought, in the anti-Semites' need for an alibi "to clear themselves of their sense of guilt for the death of Christ—but if Christ did not die for their sins, then they flee from the mercy of Christ! In reality, they want not to be redeemed."[28] Maritain urged his listeners to purge their language of the cliché "deicidal race." "Who put Christ to death? The Jews? The Romans? I myself have put Him to death, I put Him to death every day by sinning. . . . Jews, Romans, executioners—all were mere instruments, wretched, freely consenting instruments of the will for redemption and sacrifice. That is what Christian teachers should teach their students."[29] The Maritains, especially Jacques, were often vilified for their pro-Jewish positions. One of the most vicious attacks—Maritain did not deign to respond to it, although it so unnerved his wife that she immediately began to consider exile—was unleashed by Lucien Rebatet in *Je suis partout*: "Mr. Maritain . . . that 'singular Catholic' . . . is married to a Jew. He has Judaized his life and doctrine. His theology and dialectic are bogus, like the passport of a Jewish spy. Mr. Maritain represents, body and soul, what the Germans so rightly call a '*Rassenschänder*,' a defiler of the race." Rebatet blamed the Maritains for the resurgence of paganism among the Germans, on the grounds that they were guilty of "confusing Roman Catholicism . . . with its worst enemy, the vagabond, anarchic messianism that still awaits its god, except where it has replaced him, in the form of marxism, with deadly subversion."[30]

Let us also note the attack that Marcel de Corte published in March 1939, in *La Revue catholique des idées et des faits*, under the title "Jacques Maritain et la 'question juive.' " Claiming that his concern was only with "ideas," de Corte criticized Maritain's *Questions de conscience* (i.e., *L'Impossible antisémitisme*) for conflating the temporal and the spiritual, nature and grace. Maritain, said de Corte, mistakenly believed that "Israel [was] still a chosen people," "a mystical body" with a "supernatural vocation"; he had misinterpreted Paul's phrase about the "mystery of the Jews" and invented "a labor 'of terrestrial activation' " that he assigned to the people of Israel. This was a dangerous fiction, as it "providentially legitimates the revolutionary work that Israel is today carrying out in society. . . ." We shall not examine Maritain's "replies" to each of these charges, but shall merely content ourselves with noting that while de Corte announces his position from the outset—he says he is neither "anti-Semitic" nor "pro-Semitic," and considers racist policies to be "philosophically inadmissible"—his solution to the Jewish question is "segregation." That is, he advocates the solution of the Middle Ages, notwithstanding his belief that the Jewish question of his day is posed in economic and political rather than religious terms. A return to the ghetto is inevitable because "the doctrine that the Jews can be assimilated has definitively proven its bankruptcy." Paradoxically, "the more fully Israel assimilates, the more it accentuates its characteristic features: rationalism, hyperintellectualism, attrition of the sense for the concrete, coupled with a concrete sense of egotistical interests, pushiness, activism, and a taste for scandal and intrigue." But isolation necessarily implies "special status, and rules out full equality before the law." In short, although de Corte claims he is not an anti-Semite, he feels that the Jews should stay in their place: they are merely "guests." To be sure, he recommends that Christians show them "charity at the individual level," but he simultaneously calls for Christian "severity at the collective level."[31]

In his response, entitled "The Mystery of Israel," Maritain seizes on this last phrase and the idea that the Jewish question can only be solved by segregating the Jews. This is, he says, simply a "process of barbarization" that creates "demeaning racial categories." He scoffs at the "singular theology [that] would please Mr. Julius Streicher and encourage him to continue on his present path." The conclusion of his essay shows how much information he had at his disposal by 1939 about the treatment reserved for the victims of Nazi persecution:

At a time when anti-Semitic persecutions have reached unprecedented levels, when thousands upon thousands of wretched souls are deprived of the protection of the law, subjected to unspeakable brutalities and humilia-

tions, lingering deaths, "spontaneous" acts of popular violence or the horrors of the concentration camps—at a time when one hears daily that the
epidemic of Jewish suicides continues to rage in Vienna and elsewhere, or
that, as happened last winter, cold and hunger are decimating whole train-
loads of Jews blocked at closed borders, or that, as is happening as I write
these lines, boats overcharged with Jews dying of distress are drifting from
one Mediterranean port to another, turned away wherever they go, then
the only realism befitting, not only a Christian, but, I say, any man still
possessed of natural feelings, of *caritas humani generis*, is to refrain from uttering or writing a single word that can serve degrading hatred as a pretext
and, one day, be stained with the blood or laden with the despair of beings
created by God.[32]

At this time, Arendt was in exile in Paris. Besides doing social work with
refugees for Zionist organizations there, she was attending Alexandre Kojève's seminars on Hegel at the Ecole des hautes études, thanks to Raymond
Aron, who had become Secretary of the Social Studies Center at the Ecole
normale supérieure. Alexandre Koyré, who also attended these seminars, introduced her to Jean Wahl, whom she would later describe to Jaspers as "a
nice person but a bit dumb."[33] While she never spoke out publicly in France,
as befitted her status as a foreigner and, soon, enemy alien, she must surely
have attended to all these polemics. The first major article she was to publish after her arrival in the United States, "From the Dreyfus Affair to France
Today,"[34] shows that she had kept a close eye on the activities of Action
française.* Clemenceau, in her view, had played the key role in the Dreyfus
Affair. Arendt approvingly cites, in a number of different passages of her
work, his famous dictum, "by infringing on the rights of one you infringe on
the rights of all." Thus, in her review of a book by Bruno Weil, she criticizes
Weil for having failed to appreciate "the consuming passion for justice" that
distinguished Clemenceau, "one of the few true friends modern Jewry has
known," a man who regarded even "the Rothschilds as the members of a
downtrodden people."[35] Walter Benjamin, a distant cousin of her first husband, Günther Stern—Arendt had met Stern in Paris—had, incidentally,
also taken out a subscription to the paper *Action française*. Besides attending
Kojève's seminars, Arendt frequented a group of Marxists of different back-
grounds who gravitated around Benjamin's apartment in the rue Dombasle.
In another, less well known essay, "Christianity and Revolution," she reviewed, notably, the American edition of a book by Raïssa Maritain, *Adven-*

---

*Arendt sent a copy of this text to Jacques Maritain, whom she held in high esteem. She had
met Maritain through Paul Tillich.

tures in Grace.[36] The essay shows just how well informed she was. She sets out from the observation that the old anticlerical passions had plainly ebbed in France, as they had not in Spain and Italy, and speculates as to the probability of a Catholic revival in French intellectual life comparable to the one that had been in full swing at the time of the Dreyfus Affair. She notes the role played in this revival by "Catholics without faith," the "degenerated disciples" of Joseph de Maistre and future founders of Action française. "Condemned by the Pope in 1926, [they] ended by bowing before their real master, Mr. Hitler." The contempt in which these "cerebral" Catholics held the Christian faith stemmed from their deep hatred of democracy and their "disgust for the teachings of charity and the equality of men." But, Arendt adds, alongside "these dilettantes of fascism" there emerged a very different Catholic revival movement, embodied by men like Charles Péguy or Georges Bernanos in France and Chesterton in England. These Catholics too were hostile to modernity[37] and "sometimes stumbled into unhappy alliances with the 'Catholics without faith,' alliances in which they naturally were destined to play the role of suckers. Witness Jacques Maritain's relations with Action française."

Maritain had indeed drawn closer to Charles Maurras after breaking with Bergson in 1907 or 1908. He did not join the political party Action française, but, under the influence of Father Humbert Clérissac,[38] took out a subscription to Maurras's daily in 1911. He also contributed to Jacques Bainville's *Revue universelle* from 1920 to 1927; this brought him into contact with Léon Daudet. His aim was to oppose a "party of intelligence" to socialism and communism. Although he was careful, in his essay "A propos de la question juive" [On the Jewish question], to avoid "all hatred or contempt for the Jewish race and the religion of Israel,"[39] Maritain did not hesitate to write:

> An essentially messianic people like the Jewish people, from the instant that it refuses the true Messiah, must play a fatal role of subversion in the world, I do not mean by reason of a preconceived plan, I mean by reason of a metaphysical necessity which makes of the Messianic hope and of the passion for absolute Justice, when they descend from the supernatural to the natural plane, and are falsely applied, the most active revolutionary ferment.

Maritain goes so far as to advocate "a struggle against the Judeo-Masonic societies and cosmopolitan finance with a view to assuring national security," and he acknowledges "the need to take a certain number of preventive measures that were, to be frank, easier to settle upon when culture was officially Christian."[40] However, Maritain ceased collaborating with the *Revue uni-*

verselle in 1927, setting out in a new direction with his book *Primauté du spirituel* [Primacy of the spiritual]. The shift in his thought was confirmed by his March 1928 essay, "Situation du sionisme" [The situation of Zionism].

But let us turn back to Arendt's essay. What men hated in the modern world, she says there, was the lack of democracy: "they were indeed struggling against something very ominous, which very few socialists—whose political party, according to Péguy, 'is completely composed of bourgeois intellectuals'—clearly realized, namely, the all-pervading influence of bourgeois mentality in the modern world." She notes the victory of "these Catholic converts or neo-Catholics," declaring that it was Péguy "who discovered and defined the essential difference between poverty—which was always a virtue, for Roman republicans as well as for medieval Christians—and destitution, which is the modern plague reserved for those who refuse the pursuit of money and the humiliations of success." Similarly, she credits Bernanos, "a knight without fear or reproach," with having written "the most passionate denunciation of fascism—*Les Grands Cimetières sous la lune*" [Vast graveyards under the moon].

Bernanos had, to be sure, launched his famous "A Dieu" on 21 May 1932 in *Le Figaro*; but it was in January 1937 that he broke categorically with Action française, having become aware of the terror, masked as a "crusade," exercised by the Spanish Civil War. Earlier, however, he had spoken of "the prerevolutionary period" in Spain, which he had seen and experienced firsthand "with a handful of young Phalangistas under the command of José Antonio Primo de Riveira"—his son among them. He had even declared that Primo de Riveira was animated by a "furious sense of social justice."[41] But his illusions about Franco lasted only a few weeks. Thereafter, he mercilessly criticized Franco's terror regime, in which the fate of Spain's citizens, deprived of the protection of the law, was determined by denunciations and the whims of the police; the key to the whole was the word "purge." Bernanos prophesied that "the Spanish tragedy, a charnel-house . . . [was] a foretaste of the tragedy of the universe" in which "men of good will" no longer had "any country" or a place in "any party." One finds another portrait of these "men of good will" in Arendt's interpretation of Kafka's *The Castle*, a novel which, as she reads it, illustrates the real tragedy of assimilation: Kafka's hero vainly seeks to obtain at the individual level something that is every man's natural right—the right "to establish himself, to become a fellow-citizen, build up a life and marry, find work, and be a useful member of society."[42] That the harshest indictment of fascism should have been the work of a man who was a royalist all his life and had harbored the wildest illusions about the Spanish Phalange is, in Arendt's view, a good illustration of the collapse of the European party system.[43] Yet Bernanos, despite his break with Maurras, his denunciation of "communion with the obscure forces of Race,"[44] and his condemnation of the "inhumanity" and "excesses" of the totalitarian countries, continued to deplore, in the 1938 text *We French*, Jacques Maritain's "womanish reveries about the Jews and democracy, which earn him the plaudits of the public that frequents the Théâtre des Ambassadeurs."[45] He even said that "there is a Jewish question; I believe in the peril to which the Jewish nation, the Jewish spirit, the Jewish genius, admirably defined by Bernard Lazare and Péguy, expose faltering Christendom."[46] Arendt suggested that it would be a mistake to dwell on Bernanos's "false, dangerous ideas—like the notion of race," or his "obscure, dangerous prejudices, like his antipathy for Italians and Jews," since they matter little when weighed against the insights for which, she says, we are indebted to him: the fact that fascism, in spite of all its fine rhetoric about the young generation, is responsible for killing childhood; the fact that humanity has reverted to worshipping idols, and that the world has been plunged into a fit of delirium tremens precisely by those who trust in nothing save the moderation and philistine wisdom of the petite-bourgeoisie. In 1942, Arendt would also sing the praises of Bernanos's *Lettre aux Anglais* [Letter to the English], which she calls a "valiant engagement, fought in the name of man."[47]

In any case, she goes on to say, the Catholic revival did not produce a single great philosopher or artist, any more than it produced a great theologian. In passing, she dismisses Bloy as "sometimes approach[ing] the borderline of bohemian *Kitsch*." Yet she expresses her gratitude to these men for venturing onto the terrain of politics and endeavoring to become "true revolutionaries" (like, perhaps, Bernard Lazare, whom she celebrates?); she commends them for being "more radical than the radicals" and taking their arms from the "oldest arsenal," Christianity's, not modernity's. "In Péguy's endless repetition, 'All evil comes from the bourgeoisie,' is more elementary hatred than in the collected speeches of Jaurès."

However, referring to Raïssa Maritain's book, *We Have Been Friends Together*, Arendt establishes a distinction between Péguy and Jacques Maritain. Unlike Péguy or even Chesterton, Maritain was led to convert less by political considerations than by a longing for spirituality: "the Maritains converted after having been exposed to the anti-intellectualism of Bergson." While Arendt plainly approves of Maritain's frightened reaction to Bergsonian attacks on reason, she criticizes him for having "so quickly and desperately sought shelter, despite being a philosopher," for, that is, seeking "one certainty which would lead him out of the complexities and confusions of a world that does not even know what a man is talking about if he takes the word truth into his mouth." The certainties of the Thomists seem to her far superior to all those invented at the end of philosophy; yet the fact remains

that "a system of certainties is the end of philosophy." That is why she concludes her essay by expressing strong doubts "that Thomism will ever be able
to bring about a revival of philosophy."

IN APRIL 1938, after reading the American Jesuit Paul LaFarge's *Interracial
Justice*, published in 1937, a book which demonstrates that there is no scientific or biological basis for the concept of race, the pope invited LaFarge to
Castelgandolfo. Did he, as he issued the invitation, recall the letter Edith
Stein sent him in 1933, just before entering Carmel? That, at any case, is the
hypothesis put forward by Jan H. Nota,[48] a Dutch Jesuit who has devoted his
life to studying and teaching the thought of Edith Stein. Nota first heard of
Humani Generis Unitas while he was attempting to locate, precisely, Stein's
letter to Pius XI. On 13 April, the pope had instructed the Sacred Congregation to send all Catholic universities a list of racialist propositions that had
been declared unacceptable. This list was published on 3 May.

Though bound to secrecy by the pope, Paul LaFarge left two versions, one
public and the other private, of his audience with the eighty-one-year-old
Pius XI, who was suffering from diabetes and a heart condition:

> *Confidential.* Father Maher may have written to you what really did happen
> at the audience. What happened was that the Pope put me under secrecy,
> and enjoined upon me to write the text of an Encyclical for the universal
> Church, on the topic which he considered is most burning at the present
> time . . . '*Say simply,*' he told me, '*what you would say if you yourself were
> pope*'. . . . Frankly, I am simply stunned, and all I can say is that the Rock of
> Peter has fallen on my head. Had I anticipated such a terrific development,
> nothing would have persuaded me to go to Rome, much less see the
> Pope.[49]

LaFarge teamed up with a French and a German Jesuit, Gustave Des-
buquois and Gustav Gundlach. For three months, the three men worked in
Paris on the commission they had received from Pius XI. After a fourth Jesuit had translated their work into Latin, it was submitted to the pope.

In the summer and fall of 1938, the Holy See repeatedly tried to block passage of an Italian law forbidding interracial marriages; Pius XI even wrote a
personal letter to the Duce and the King on the matter. This persistence
prompted Ciano, Mussolini's son-in-law, to note in his diary, "row with the
Church in sight." But the Vatican's efforts were fruitless: the law was promulgated on 7 November 1938.

Pius XI died on 10 February 1939. He had been planning to deliver a
speech on the eleventh denouncing the Italian race laws for violating the

Concordat, but he did not have time to finish drafting it. It was not until 6 February 1959 that John XXIII quoted fragments of the speech in a letter to the Italian bishops that was published in *L'Osservatore romano* three days later. As to the existence of the commission that had been charged with drawing up the encyclical on anti-Semitism, it was not revealed to the American public and the world press until 1972, when a story on it appeared in the *National Catholic Reporter* (Kansas City).

Paragraph 144 of this draft encyclical explicitly condemns anti-Semitism:

> That such persecutory methods are totally at variance with the true spirit of the Catholic Church is shown by the decree of the Sacred Congregation of the Holy Office for March 25, 1928: "The Catholic Church habitually prays for the Jewish people who were the bearers of the Divine revelation up to the time of Christ; this despite, indeed, on account of, their spiritual blindness. Actuated by this love, the Apostolic See has protected this people against unjust oppression and, just as every kind of envy and jealousy among the nations must be disapproved of, so in an especial manner must be that hatred which is generally termed anti-Semitism."

Paragraph 147 states that "anti-Semitism becomes an excuse for attacking the sacred Person of the Savior Himself, who assumed human flesh as the Son of a Jewish maiden; it becomes a war against Christianity, its teachings, practices, and institutions."[50] Paragraph 144 cites a Decree of the Sacred Congregation in which, with the approval of Pius XI, the Holy Office had decreed the suppression of the association of the Friends of Israel, created in 1925 and devoted to the conversion of the Jews. The grounds for this decision was that the association had "adopted a manner of acting and thinking that is contrary to the sense and spirit of the Church, to the thought of the Holy Fathers and the liturgy."[51] While the Friends of Israel had been right not "to make 'deicide' a sort of 'original sin' borne by every Jew," the promoters of the association could not remain silent, said the Holy Office, "about Israel's unfaithfulness to its mission [or] its participation in Christ's death." Even less could they ban the word "conversion" and replace it with the words "return" or "passage" of the Jews. Henceforth the tendency "to magnify the [Jewish] race would be condemned," for it could only issue in a separatism that would heighten Jewish national pride.

But the more basic question is how to construe what Emmanuel Mounier was already calling, in 1939, the "silences of Pius XII," silences Father Jean Tonneau exonerated him for as early as 1942, in *Le Pape, la guerre et la paix: Pie XII a-t-il parlé?* [The pope, the war, and the peace: Has Pius XII spoken out?][52] Must we accept Georges Passelecq's and Bernard Suchecky's judgment? "One must bluntly say," Passelecq and Suchecky declare, "that the Jews, on the eve of the World War, were not really anybody's problem. Could ten righteous men have been found to stop the crime?" Was the encyclical *Mit brennender Sorge* of 14 March 1937 not exclusively given over to denouncing the dangers threatening Catholicism in Germany? It declares:

> Anyone who wants to see Biblical history and the wisdom of the teachings of the Old Testament banished from the Church and the schools blasphemes against the Almighty's plan of salvation, raises up a narrow and limited human thought and judges Divine designs on the history of the world. He renounces faith in the true Christ, as he appeared in the flesh, in the Christ who received his human nature from a people who were to crucify him.

And was *Divini Redemptoris*, published three days later, not exclusively concerned with the struggle against atheistic communism?

ON 9 NOVEMBER 1938, *Kristallnacht*, Sister Renata de Spiritu Sancto wrote: "Sister Benedicta herself was almost paralysed with grief. 'It is the shadow of the Cross which is falling upon my people. If only they would see this! It is the fulfillment of the curse which my people called upon its own head. Cain must be persecuted, but woe to whoever lays hands upon Cain. Woe also to this city and this country when God's wrath descends upon them for what they are now doing to the Jews.' "[53] On 31 December, Edith Stein left Germany for Holland.

1939

3o January: Hitler declares that the Jewish race will be annihilated in Europe.

17 February: the weekly *Je suis partout* strikes up a campaign called "The Jews and France."

24 February: the Chamber of Deputies recognizes Franco's government by a vote of 323 to 261.

1 March: by way of reply to *Je suis partout*, *Le Voltigeur*—an offshoot of *Esprit*—runs the headline, "Anti-Semitism vs. France." On the first page is a cartoon showing a death's-head crowned with a German helmet and the caption "je suis partout." The paper also publishes texts taken from Péguy's *Notre Jeunesse* [Our youth], under the title: "Open Letter from Charles Péguy to M. Robert Brasillach and other junior Rebatets."[1]

15 March: Hitler enters Prague and annexes Czechoslovakia, violating his commitment, made in Munich, to guarantee its independence.

22 March: Germany puts pressure on Lithuania, which ultimately cedes its rights to Memel.

31 March: in the Chamber of Commons, Chamberlain declares that Great Britain will go to Poland's aid if it is threatened.

3 April: Hitler, unhappy about the rapprochement between Warsaw and London, speeds up preparations for war with Poland, while attempting to avoid a simultaneous conflict with the Western powers.

7 April: Italy, in its turn, upsets the status quo in the Mediterranean by invading Albania.

23 April: Germany forces Romania to sign a draconian trade agreement.

27 April: for the first time in its history, England institutes a draft; it applies to all twenty-one-year-old men. The British government has begun to pay attention to the Nazis' racist theories in the wake of Hitler's entry into Prague and the annexation of seven million Czechs of "foreign race." Great Britain accepts the idea that a war will be necessary to stop Hitler.

10 May: following the promulgation, on 21 April, of the law for the protection of racial minorities, Céline's *Bagatelle for a Massacre* and *The School of Corpses* are withdrawn by their publisher, Denoël. Both books are condemned for defamation in June.

22 May: Germany and Italy sign a military alliance, the Pact of Steel.

The United States proclaims its neutrality, although it would prefer to see a victory of the democracies in the event of war. On 15 April, Roosevelt sends Hitler and Mussolini a peace message with a list of twenty-nine countries which he asks them to promise not to attack for a period of twenty-five years. He never receives an official response.

The USSR, which has made a rapprochement with the Western powers after Hitler's entry into Prague, seems to be the only country capable of providing Rumania and Poland (already assured of Western protection) tangible support if they are attacked. Churchill attempts to encourage cooperation between Warsaw and Moscow, but the Poles show no interest whatsoever in concluding an agreement with the USSR. Negotiations come to a virtual standstill; each clan is suspicious of the other.

1 August: Paul Claudel writes: "All the sacred writers call Israel a witness; but the Greek word for witness is martyr."[2]

Pius XII lifts the ban on Action française. From now on, any good Catholic can read Charles Maurras with impunity.

Anti-Semitism makes inroads even in the government: Daladier appoints Jean Giraudoux to the post of Commissioner-General of Information. Giraudoux has just published *Pleins pouvoirs* [Full powers]: "Our land has become a land of invasion. The invasion is carried out just as it was in the Roman Empire, not by armies but by a continual infiltration of barbarians."[3] Because France had been overrun by "hundreds of thousands of Ashkhenazis escaped from Polish or Rumanian ghettos," Giraudoux hopes to see the creation of a Ministry of physiology and psychology: "what more beautiful mission could there be than to shape lovingly one's own race!" He feels that Hitler was entirely right "to proclaim that a policy reaches its highest form only if it is racial, for that was also what Colbert and Richelieu thought."[4]

20 August–14 September: the Danzig crisis. "When people talk, in France, about 'dying for Danzig,' they are uttering a solemn absurdity" (Emmanuel Mounier).

23 August: Germany and the USSR sign a non-aggression pact. Partial mobilization in France.

Blum condemns the Soviet attitude and the French Communists. After the Ribbentrop-Molotov pact is signed, many Communists leave the French Communist Party and rally to the Socialist camp.

30 August: Parisian schoolchildren are evacuated to the provinces.

1 September: Germany attacks Poland without declaring war. France orders a general mobilization.

3 September: France and Great Britain declare war on Germany.

17 September: Soviet troops enter Poland.

26 September: the Communist Party is dissolved and the Communist deputies to the National Assembly are placed under arrest.

Late September: the "phony war" settles over the French front; it lasts seven months.

October: the Reich annexes the western part of Poland.

8 November: an attempt on Hitler's life fails.

Late November: the Russians attack Finland.

December: Pierre Drieu la Rochelle publishes *Gilles*, a novel whose hero hates the Radical party, "which left France childless, which let her be invaded and overrun by millions of foreigners, Jews, half-breeds, Negroes, Indochinese."[5]

The Destruction of Carthage

In Anne Frank's Country

Because German Jews no longer had the right to emigrate to Palestine, the prioress of the Breslau Carmel appealed to the Carmel in Echt, near the Dutch town of Roermond, to help smuggle Sister Benedicta across the border on 31 December 1938. She learned Dutch and served humbly in the refectory in Echt. Her sister Erna, bound for the United States with her family, writes: "I was reassured at the thought that she was safe from Hitler in her convent, and that my sister Rosa, who, with Edith's help, had also found refuge in Echt, was out of danger as well."[6]

On 9 April 1939, Edith made out her last will and testament:

I joyfully accept in advance the death God has appointed for me, in perfect submission to his most holy will. . . . for the Jewish people, that the Lord may be received by his own and his kingdom come in glory, for the deliverance of Germany and peace throughout the world, and finally, for all my relatives living and dead and all whom God has given me: may none of them be lost.[7]

Hitler Equals Caesar

Hitler's entry into Prague brought about a sharp turn in Simone Weil's thinking: she gradually abandoned her anti-war positions, without, however, giving up all hope that war might be avoided through negotiation. After the Germans put down a student revolt in Prague, she devised a plan to parachute troops and weapons into Czechoslovakia, hoping to participate in the operation herself. She sought the assistance of a number of people in key positions, who, however, kept their distance from her because of her reputation for being a communist. Yet Weil had never had a Party card. Indeed, in 1943, in her essay "Note sur la suppression générale des partis politiques" [Note on the general suppression of political parties], she defines parties as "organizations that are publicly, officially constituted in such a way as to destroy the sense of truth and justice in people's souls": partisan attitudes seem to her to be a kind of "leprosy" that is gaining ground everywhere.[8]

Analyzing the prevailing situation in the spring and summer of 1939, Weil recognizes that "Europe finds itself at a tragic juncture," one she compares to the historical moment when Carthage was razed by Rome. In her opinion, Hitler and the Romans show striking similarities. She names two main points of resemblance. First, the Germans, like the Romans, think of themselves as a chosen race, born to command. Weil cites Virgil: "Your task, Roman, is to rule in sovereign fashion over the peoples." Second, both Rome and Germany are treacherous. Indeed, Weil describes the Hebrews in the same way, lumping them together with the Romans and condemning both peoples in the same breath. For Weil, unlike Arendt (who follows Mommsen on this point), the "twin peoples" who became cognizant of their historical existence in one and the same undertaking, the war against Troy, were not the Greeks and Romans, but rather the Hebrews and Romans, twins in infamy.

In order to take the full measure of Weil's iconoclasm, let us begin by examining Arendt's analyses of Rome. For Arendt, the Romans were "the most political people . . . ever known."[9] Indeed, Roman policy can even be said to have given rise to a "Western world," in that the Romans politicized the space between the peoples—they had, that is, a *foreign* policy. The Romans laid the foundations of the "Western world, conceived *as* a world"; it was Rome which transformed the desert into a world.

Many extraordinarily rich, great civilizations existed before the Romans, yet what lay between them was not a world, but a desert. When times were good, links were established across this desert; they resembled slender threads, or paths running through uncultivated regions. When times were bad, the desert spread, in the form of wars of annihilation that destroyed the world as it then was.[10]

Roman foreign policy was a policy of alliances or pacts that changed yesterday's enemies into tomorrow's allies: "pacts and alliances . . . were closely bound up with warfare between peoples; as the Romans conceived them, they represented, so to speak, the natural continuation of every war." This implies that even combat, "the most hostile of human encounters, brought something into being which the [parties] had in common thereafter"[11]— combat gave rise, once action and suffering had come to an end, to a new world, a new "in-between." Arendt regards "the inviolability of agreements and treaties (*pacta sunt servanda*)" as the origin of the promise: the concept of the promise is a means of countering the "unpredictability" of human affairs. She adds that "the great variety of contract theories since the Romans attests to the fact that the power of making promises has occupied the center of political thought over the centuries."[12] Similarly, the concept of pardon, which makes it possible to annul an act and make a new beginning, has its source in the Roman principle of sparing the vanquished (*parcere subiectis*), or even in the Roman practice of commuting death sentences.

One finds no such praise for the Romans in Weil, for whom Rome's "foreign policy was conducted in the same spirit as Hitler's, with the same ruthless arrogance, the same skill in inflicting humiliation, the same bad faith."[13] Weil would certainly not have agreed with Arendt that

what the Romans themselves aspired to was not so much the *imperium romanum*—that Roman domination over peoples and countries which, as we have known since Mommsen, developed more or less against their will, imposing itself on them—as it was the *societas romana*, a system of alliances that had been established by Rome and could be infinitely extended, in which peoples and countries were not simply bound to Rome by temporary, renewable treaties, but became eternal allies.[14]

Weil took the opposite view, emphasizing the similarity between Hitler and Caesar: "Hitler and his men do not love war; they love domination and dream of nothing but peace—a peace in which their will is supreme, of course. Ancient Rome did likewise."[15] Moreover, the Romans did not at all know "what tender feelings were." "Natural pride, whether it be in good times or in bad, is incapable of creating any real, ardent sense of fraternity. This didn't exist among the Romans."[16]

What is to be said of promises? Here too Weil charges the Romans, that "people of brigands," with treacherousness. In a letter to an anonymous correspondent written in 1938 or 1939, she says that the breaking of a promise has to be a "rather exceptional act, surrounded by such mysterious circumstances or directed against adversaries who are so reliable that one's reputation for keeping one's promises remains untarnished with those who do not look at matters closely—which is to say, the overwhelming majority of people." Unless, that is, breaking one's promise leads to "the almost total massacre of the victims, so that they are no longer able to complain." Last hypothesis: "the person who breaks his promise must be so powerful that nobody dares criticize him, or even notice."[17] By way of example, Weil mentions Caesar, who defeated the Germans in Gaul by resorting to the basest sort of treason to terrorize the Gauls. Caesar was, moreover, not unique: beginning with the Punic Wars and the victory over Hannibal, the history of Rome is a history of banditry. Weil's conclusion is that keeping promises is more or less superfluous from the moment that "fear and hope are powerful enough to create by themselves, unaided by judgement, belief in promises and threats in men's souls."[18] The worst act of banditry imputable to the Romans, and, indeed, one of the most atrocious events in history, is, in Weil's view, the destruction of Rome's rival Carthage.[19]

To justify the destruction of Carthage, historians have given posterity to understand that the Carthaginians were the treacherous party: they are supposed to have broken their engagements to the Romans, with whom they had concluded a treaty of alliance in which they pledged not to go to war without first obtaining Rome's approval. Could one ask for better proof that "history never heeds the defeated"? Arendt often cited Cato the Elder's phrase: "Victrix causa deis placuit, sed victa Catoni" [the victorious cause pleased the gods, but the defeated one pleases Cato]. But Carthage ultimately took up arms, exasperated by countless Numidian invasions. It was defeated and destroyed. Rome profited from this situation to declare war on the Carthaginians in order to punish them for failing to respect their agreement. Carthage sued for peace: the Romans responded by imposing conditions as harsh as those Hitler imposed on Emil Hacha, the President of the Republic of Czechoslovakia, when, on 15 March 1939 in Berlin, he forced him to agree to let Germany send troops to Bohemia. Violating the treaty in which they had agreed to spare Carthage, the Romans now threatened to raze it to the ground, besieging it for three years. This proves, according to Weil, that "extreme submission was no defense against . . . Roman cruelty."[20] Weil makes no distinction between Roman nationalism, whose fundamental political principle "was to maintain the maximum degree of prestige" by dint of propaganda, and Hitlerite racism.* In Berlin as in ancient Rome, one finds the same antiphilosophical, antireligious, antijuridical attitudes, the same cruelty, the same perfidy,[21] the same political objective, and the same methods: racism, nationalism,[22] and affirmation of the superiority of one's own race.[23] In both regimes, Weil detects the same contempt for labor, the same bellicosity,[24] the same seriousness and discipline.[25] Hitler equals Caesar. Nevertheless, unlike the Romans, Hitler is not yet master of the world; he has not yet annihilated Carthage, that is, England: "The principle difference between Hitler and the Romans is that he has established a totalitarian dictatorship before becoming master of the world, and this will probably prevent him from conquering the world; for it seems that a totalitarian dictatorship is better at oppressing its own subjects than at conquering many new ones."[26]

Arendt too draws a comparison with Carthage, but only in order to evoke the destruction of European Jewry in 1942; she says that the Jews "are the victims of a sacrifice of a kind that has not occurred since the age of Carthage and the destruction wrought by Moloch."[27] It is, however, only in a much later text, a 1958 fragment of a projected book she was planning to call *Introduction to Politics*, that she develops her analysis of the destruction of Carthage in detail. What was destroyed, she spells out in this fragmentary text, was by no means Roman "clemency"; nor was it the power of this military and commercial rival of Rome's in the Mediterranean basin. What was destroyed was " 'a government which never kept its promises and never forgave,' and which thus embodied the anti-Roman political principle per se . . . [Carthage] would have destroyed Rome if Rome had not destroyed it."[28] The value of this example lies, then, in the fact that Carthage constituted an exception to the politics of alliance and contract characteristic of the Roman *lex*, which, as we have seen, Arendt unreservedly admires. Out of fidelity to its own principles, Rome, she suggests, should have "allowed the city to continue to exist as a rival," not out of charity, but "for the sake of enlarging the city [of Rome], which could thereafter have included this completely foreign element within a new alliance."[29] Thus the Romans' failure consisted in their inability to accept coexistence with Carthage in the modern sense of the term.[30] In the final analysis, the Romans failed to see "that there could exist something radically different from, and yet as great as Rome, something which was equally worthy of being remembered by history."[31] In short, Arendt accuses Rome of having abandoned Homeric impartiality.

---

*"Any specifically Germanic frills that Hitler has added to the Roman tradition are purely literary and mythological patchwork" (Weil, "Quelques réflexions sur les origines de l'hitlerisme," in *Œuvres complètes*, 2.3. 198; "The Great Beast," in *Selected Essays*, p. 112).

Total War: The Trojan War As Paradigm

Weil finally admits that "German domination of the world would be a disaster," because "unlimited war," a term she says she prefers to the specialists' "absolute" or "total" war, is a new phenomenon in Europe, whose equal can only be found, once again, in Rome. Since Germany was bent on world domination, the goal of the democratic powers, should a war break out, had to be the annihilation of Germany. This excess, this imbalance disturbed her. Arms should be used to a purpose: "either . . . extermination of the enemy . . . or to obtain certain limited and definite advantages . . . in the negotiation . . . or to create among the enemy the desire for peace (defensive war)."[32] For Weil, a partisan of nonviolence, this new type of war is a disaster. It can end only with the exhaustion—Arendt says annihilation (*Vernichtung*)—of both victor and vanquished, since the sole aim a nation can pursue in such a war is self-preservation. Moreover, it "can only be followed by a peace which itself constitutes a new disaster."

On this point too, Weil's thought invites comparison with that of Arendt, who, like Weil's "specialists," speaks of total war in *Was ist Politik?* [What is politics?]. Arendt assigns a very precise meaning to this term, which came into general use after the first World War. Thus Ernst Jünger in *Krieg und Krieger* (1930) employs the expression "die totale Mobilmachung" (total mobilization) to designate the changes that had occurred in the art of warfare, having to do with the kinds of weapons used, the fact that resignation and fatalism had replaced the traditional virtue of courage, and the total mobilization of labor, with the subordination of the workforce to arms production implied by such mobilization. The conditions of war have been so thoroughly transformed, Arendt observes, that ancient warfare now seems to us to be a "lost paradise": whereas war was once simply "the pursuit of politics by other means, that is, could always be avoided if one of the conflicting parties chose to bow to the other's demands,"[33] the bombings of Coventry, Dresden, and Hiroshima have shown that war is not only capable of decimating entire peoples, but also of "turning the world they inhabit into a desert."[34]

Simone Weil died in 1943, and thus did not witness all these tragic episodes. If Arendt can speak of total war, it is, to be sure, because the discovery of atomic weapons depends on processes which are not natural, but derive from the universe, and have been mastered by man, whose behavior is no longer that of a natural living creature. But this kind of war is also total in the sense that its objective is unlimited: it targets the brute existence of a whole country and people. Such a phenomenon is not new. There have been excesses since Antiquity; we had simply forgotten them until the totalitarian regimes made us aware of them again:

For the first time, perhaps, in the modern era, though certainly not for the first time in recorded history, people exceeded an inherent limit that sought to contain the use of violence—the limit that said that the means of violence could only be used to bring about partial destruction, could only be brought to bear on small parts of the world and on a restricted number of human lives, but never on an entire country or people.[35]

The excess consists in the fact that, since what is destroyed is never something that was merely produced, it can, by the same token, never be restored. It is not so much the destruction of the city of Troy that matters, although the city was so thoroughly razed that many believed it had never existed. Nor is the crucial consideration the number of victims. Far more important is the destruction of the "world of human relations conjured up by words and action."[36] What is annihilated in this way is a constitutive part of the world, a unique worldview that enables a certain reality to exist and endure: "The more peoples there are in the world . . . the more world will be created in the space between them, and the greater and richer this world will be."[37] The reality of the world is attested solely by the infinite multitude of viewpoints of those who are part of it.

For both Arendt and Weil, the Trojan War stands as the archetype of total war or the war of annihilation, which Weil anticipates, dreads, and warns against, while Arendt lives through it to the bitter end. Arendt evokes this archetype to show that from the moment politics, which is concerned with the world *between* men, turns destructive, it negates itself. All moral considerations aside, wars of annihilation can have no place in politics.

But if the Romans are despicable because they razed Carthage, so that Weil continued to fear them even as an adult, why do the Greeks fare better at her hands? After all, she admits that Greek history too has its origins in an abominable crime, the Trojan War. How are we to explain the emotion she felt upon reading "The *Iliad*, Poem of Might,"[38] given her celebration of the fact that "the Cathars carried the horror of force to the point of practicing nonviolence. . . . That was going far, but no further than the Gospel"[39]? Indeed, Weil often compares Greek and Occitan civilization. The theme common to the *Iliad*, centered on Troy, and the (in Weil's view) epic poem *Song of the Crusade Against the Albigensians*, which takes Toulouse as its center, is the theme of the death-agony of an entire civilization, stricken "by force of arms" and "fated to disappear for ever." Moreover, the Trojan War is for Weil one of the most tragic instances of Japheth's and Shem's hatred for their brother Ham. In a text called "The Three Sons of Noah," she presents "Noah, drunk with wine . . . sleeping naked in his tent," as a "representation of Christ."[40] Ham, who steals a glance at his naked father, inherits supreme wisdom which he passes on to his heirs; in contrast, Noah's other two sons and all their descendants—including, of course, the Jews—reject this revelation once and for all. Ham comes under the curse Noah pronounces upon him, together

> with all those things and beings which are destined to suffer affliction on account of an excess of beauty or purity. . . . Each time that the invader has given himself up to the spirit of the place which is the spirit of Ham, and has drunk of its inspiration, there has been a civilisation. Each time that he has preferred to maintain his proud ignorance, there has been barbarism, and darkness worse than death has covered the land for centuries.[41]

On the Trojan side, needless to say, we find "only people descended from Ham"; none of Ham's descendants are to be found on the opposing side. If the Bible makes no mention of the Trojan war, Weil adds, and if the Hebrews' conquest of Palestine left not a trace in the traditions of the Greeks, the reason is that the Hebrews made their way into Palestine at a time when the country had been "emptied of its warriors by the Trojan War, the men of Troy having called . . . distant peoples to their assistance." Thus the Hebrews were able to massacre whole peoples with impunity, for these peoples had no one left to defend them. It is no accident that the Hebrew conquests came to an end precisely when the warriors returned home.

Yet even if Greek history traces its origins to this atrocious crime, it is the great merit of the Greeks that, far from having prided themselves on it, they were haunted by it and racked by remorse. "Homer always calls Troy 'Holy Ilion.' This [war] was the original sin of the Greeks, and filled them with remorse. By their remorse, they, the executioners, were found worthy to inherit something of the inspiration of their victims."[42] The genius of the Greeks resides in the fact that the world of force, "which makes a thing of anybody who comes under its sway . . . [which] makes him a corpse,"[43] simultaneously "evokes the far-off world, precarious and touching, of peace, the family, that world wherein each man is, for those who surround him, all that counts most [a hot bath when a man returns from battle]." "Nearly all the *Iliad* takes place far from hot baths."[44] In other words, it is the *Iliad*'s rare moments of grace which give us a sense of what force and violence destroy forever. Weil describes what she identifies as the supreme merit of the *Iliad* in an early version of the conclusion to her essay, "The *Iliad*, Poem of Might": "the same bitterness, as just as the sunlight, spreads over the Greeks and the Trojans, the eminent and the obscure, the powerful and the weak, victory and defeat."[45]

Arendt, whose views on this point are similar to Weil's, also celebrates

Homeric impartiality at great length. She argues that it provides the basis for Greek historiography:

> It is of the utmost importance that Homer's epic does not fail to mention the defeated, that it testifies in favor of Hector no less than Achilles, and that, although the Greek victory and Trojan defeat have been predetermined in a council of the gods, this victory does not exalt Achilles or debase Hector, does not make the Greek cause more just or the defense of Troy less so.[46]

Singing of the war of annihilation, Homer in some sense undoes that annihilation, according to Arendt. Arendt and Weil both raise a cry of alarm: "let us not start another Trojan War," a war which would no longer be fought, says Weil, for Helen, "a woman of perfect beauty," but would rather turn on abstractions or hollow words. Weil is speaking before Auschwitz, at a moment when she still had an anti-war position and did not want to commit herself to the defense of Czechoslovakia, although France had promised to protect it in a 1924 treaty confirmed in 1925 by the Locarno Pact. Arendt has gone through the bitter experience of Auschwitz and Hiroshima, and warns against the dangers of the desert, which would put us back in a pre-Roman situation; today's wars, she observes, are no more "storms of steel"[47] that clear the political skies of clouds than they are "a mere continuation of policy by other means."[48] Rather, foreign policy—or rather, the danger that permanently haunts international relations—will henceforth be at the heart of politics. The consequence is that Clausewitz's dictum has been stood on its head: politics has now become a continuation of war in which ruse is temporarily substituted for violence.[49] Even worse, the arms race shows that Kant's statement—"nothing should occur in wartime which makes peace impossible afterwards"—has also been stood on its head, with the result that we are now living in "a peace in which no effort is spared to keep the possibility of waging war open after all."[50] Both Arendt and Weil underscore the perversity of the fact that violence has become a necessity. But Arendt is writing in 1958, in the context of the Cold War; her warning has to do with the eventuality of a third world war, a total war, a war of annihilation, an atomic war this time, "in consequence of the monstrous development of the modern means of annihilation, over which states have the monopoly."[51]

Weil concludes her essay with a discussion of Hitler, whom she regards as neither a madman nor a monster, and still less as a mediocrity, but rather as a ruthless, extremely lucid and bold individual, whose will and imagination will not be checked by humanitarian considerations of any kind.[52] Weil had seen, before Arendt, what Hitler's "genius" consisted in: he subordinated industry and technology to the armed forces and the state, won the allegiance of the rootless, atomized masses of modern society by holding the illusory possibility of unity up before them with a view to establishing and increasing his own power, maintained various front organizations, and continued to use certain slogans while divesting them of all meaning, thus neutralizing resistance of any kind in advance. Turning back to her comparison between the Germans of Gaul and the Romans, Weil does not hesitate to say: "We should be strangely simple, even simpler than the Hitler youth, if we saw anything in the slightest degree serious in the cult of Wotan, the neo-Wagnerian romanticism, and the religion of blood and soil, or if we believed that racialism is anything at all except a rather more romantic name for nationalism."[53]

France—a Colony of the Reich?

Is Hitler a barbarian? Weil asks. "Would to heaven he were! There was always a limit to the harm done by the ravages of the barbarians."[54] The present danger, far graver in her eyes, is that of becoming one of the "independent countries threatened with colonization," since "Bohemia is no more oppressed by Hitler than the provinces were by Rome,"[55] or the Indochinese by France. "Is it not just as easy to be ignorant of the cruelties of the Germans towards the Jews or the Czechs as it is of those of the French towards the Annamites?"[56] Between 1937 and 1940, Weil's political thought is, indeed, indissociable from the colonial question. She goes so far as to say that "a number of Frenchmen, having found it perfectly natural to talk about collaboration to the oppressed natives of the French colonies, went on making use of this word without any trouble in talking with their German masters."[57]

On 26 November 1939, Jean Giraudoux, who had been appointed Commissioner-General of Information, gave a radio speech in which he spoke about the French colonies' attachment to the metropolitan center. Weil read about the speech in *Le Temps*, and wrote Giraudoux a letter in reaction: "I have always been proud of you as one of those whose names can be mentioned when one is looking for reasons to love present-day France. . . ." Undaunted by the fact that her letter could land her in prison under the terms of the decree of 24 May 1938, she proceeded to list the injustices the Indochinese had suffered at the hands of the French:

> How many men we are now compelling to die for our country after depriving them of their own! Did not France acquire Annam by conquest? . . . . We have killed their culture. . . . Although there is chronic famine in the north of their country, the plentiful rice of the south is ex-

ported abroad. There is an annual tax which is the same for the poor as for the rich. Parents are reduced to selling their children, as they used to in the Roman provinces. Families sell the shrines of their ancestors, their most valued possession, and not even so as to get food, but simply to pay the tax. . . . Has anyone dared to deny the atrocities after the Yen-Bay troubles?[58]

We do not know whether Weil posted this letter.

For Hannah Arendt, imperialism was one of the pillars of the totalitarian hell. But, unlike Weil, she did not limit herself to considering only its French variant. The nation-states' determination to expand and seek colonies, which emerged in 1884, and which she analyzed down to 1914, was marked by the race for Africa, Pan-Germanism, and other annexationist movements. In fewer than twenty years, Arendt reminds us, the British Empire acquired twelve million square kilometers and sixty-six million new subjects; Belgium conquered two million, three hundred thousand square kilometers and acquired eight million new subjects. Imperialism encountered virtually no opposition, she explains, because it appeared to provide an ideal market for capitalist production and forged common interests in nations that had previously been divided into antagonistic classes. Hence the alliance between capitalism and the "mob," with the attendant risk that such an alliance might "take the form of transformation of nations into races" for lack of any "other unifying bond available between individuals who in the very process of power accumulation and expansion are losing all natural connections with their fellow-men."[59]

For Arendt, however, anti-Semitism—which Weil does not so much as mention, so strong is her aversion to the Hebrews of Antiquity and so blind is she to the reality of the phenomenon—constitutes the first pillar of totalitarianism. She distinguishes two kinds of anti-Semitism in modern times. There is, to begin with,

the anti-Semitism of the nation-state (beginning with the Wars of Liberation in Germany, ending with the Dreyfus affair in France), which came about because the Jews emerged as a group particularly useful to the state and receiving special protection from it. As a consequence of that, every group in the population that came into conflict with the state became anti-Semitic. Then comes the anti-Semitism of the imperial age (which began in the 1880s).[60]

Arendt also underscores the similarities between English racialist thought, represented, notably, by Benjamin Disraeli, and the myth of the "Aryan race," which first makes its appearance in Germany. She contrasts them with the current of anti-Semitic thought dominant in France, a country where hatred for the Jews is contemporaneous with their emancipation in the Revolutionary period: thus the Count of Clermont-Tonnerre declared that he would accord them everything as individuals and refuse them everything as a nation. This anti-Semitism never waned; it took root in both the French Left and the Right over the course of the nineteenth century. Most French Jews came from the middle ranks of the bourgeoisie and did not practice their religion; they were indifferent to their tradition and ready to assimilate. The same did not, however, hold for a considerable number of Jews who had emigrated from Eastern Europe to France, especially in the 1880s and again after 1918. Their customs and the fact that they continued to speak Yiddish fueled the propaganda of Action française, which then found it easy to widen the gap between the assimilated Jews who, if Action française was to be believed, had taken control of France, and the non-assimilated Jews, who, for their part, were said to embody a foreign threat. It was above all these non-assimilated or, to use Sartre's term, "authentic" Jews whom the Vichy regime would later persecute. During her French exile, Arendt had an opportunity to observe first-hand the extremist Catholic milieux around Action française (let us recall that the excommunication of this movement for heresy in 1926 had been annulled by Pius XII in July 1939!) which lashed out at Free Masons, Protestants, and foreigners, this last being the category in which they put the Jews. It was in France that she worked up the raw material which would later enable her to write the first essay she published after arriving in the United States, "From the Dreyfus Affair to France Today."[61] In a little notebook she used for her lectures to the Women's International Zionist Organization on French anti-Semitism, she jotted down quotations, thoughts, and ideas in the air at the time. In her lectures, she defends the hypothesis that anti-Semitism had persisted uninterruptedly from the days of the Dreyfus Affair down to the Vichy period; she points out that, during Pétain's trial, the Lille newspaper *La Voix du Nord* compared the trial to Dreyfus's. She retraces the history of the notion of race, which was not, in her view, a German invention, but an idea whose roots reach back to the eighteenth century and appear simultaneously in all the Western countries, especially France, in the course of the nineteenth.[62] In 1845, a disciple of Fourier's, Alphonse de Toussenel, vilified the Jews in a book called *Les Juifs, rois de l'époque* [The Jews, kings of the age] which gave the medieval caricature of Jews as social parasites a new lease on life. Between 1853 and 1855, Arthur de Gobineau published *The Inequality of Human Races*: poorly received in France, it was welcomed with open arms in the Germany of the 1890s, and its theses were then "scientifically" recast in the work of the ethnological and anthropological societies active in France in the 1920s. 1882 saw the publication of Father E. A. Chabouty's *Les Juifs, nos maîtres* [The Jews, our masters]; in 1883, the review *L'Antisémitique* began "an investigation of the Jews"; in 1886, Gougenot de Mousseaux published, in his turn, *Le Juif, le judaïsme et la judaïsation des peuples chrétiens* [Jews, Judaism, and the Judaization of the Christian peoples]. Drumont's *La France juive* [France of the Jews], published the same year by Marpon and Flammarion at Léon Daudet's urging, went through fourteen editions and sold two million copies. Along with Renan's *Vie de Jésus* [Life of Jesus], it was the greatest publishing success of the century.[63] Is there any need to recall that Maurice Barrès, a disciple of Soury's and Gustave Le Bon's who claimed to be "purging Christianity of its vile 'Jewish leaven,' " had high praise for *La France juive*?[64] Georges Bernanos himself, before writing *A Diary of My Times*, had, in 1931, published *La Grande Peur des bien-pensants* [The panic of right-thinking folk]. Here he surveyed the history of the Third Republic and denounced the barbarity of so-called modern society, characterized by an absence of faith, the disappearance of patriotism, and social misery, which he proposed to combat "by limiting the number of births and eliminating the infirm and indolent."[65] At the same time, he painted an exalted portrait of Drumont, his "old teacher," whom he had discovered at the age of thirteen on his father's recommendation. He insisted heavily, in *La Grande Peur*, on the idea that Drumont had a "vocation," and underscored the "duty" which Drumont, "that French knight"—whom Daudet had once hailed "with the sublime name of Revealer of the Race"—felt called upon to fulfill at the sight of "the Jewish conquest":

> A handful of convulsively active foreigners, who had been kept on the fringes of national life for centuries, but were suddenly cast into the midst of a society whose leading elements had been crushed or impoverished by the war, seized control of the sources of money with seeming spontaneity, and then promptly set about organizing their conquest, patiently, silently, with a superb sense of what modern man is, of his prejudices, failings, and immense, foolish hopes. After making themselves the masters of the nation's gold, they were soon convinced that they could at the same time, in an egalitarian democracy, become the masters of public opinion, that is, of public morals. [They put] their vices [on display] . . . impudence, a frantic desire to show off, and a cruelty worthy of the satrap.[66]

Then, after recalling the Panama scandal and the Dreyfus affair, Bernanos prophesied: "We will see something quite different when, after the minuscule Jewish bug has devoured the brains of the American giant, the mindless monster attacks the Russian colossus, likewise emptied of his brains."[67]

Weil's whole critique of the notion of race is encapsulated in a "Negro story of 1890 about the differences of colour" which she simply retells. The story has it that God summoned three white men to the edge of a river, ordering them to dive in and fetch three bundles from the opposite bank. The first of the three, who was not at all afraid, swam over and brought back a bundle of books, papers, and pens. The second jumped anxiously into the already dirty water and came back out all yellow: his bundle contained farming tools. By the time the third man dove into the water, it was black; he became black in his turn. "He turned to God and said to him: 'Lord! Leave me, I pray thee, something white.' " His bundle contained a whip and chains. Seeing him weep, God took pity on him and "left him some white in the palms of his hands and on the soles of his feet."[68]

"The Disease of Agnosticism"*

Politics, a Secular Religion?

For both Simone Weil and Hannah Arendt, the defining feature of the modern masses resides in the fact that "they do not have common interests to bind them together or any kind of common 'consent' which, according to Cicero, constitutes *inter-est*."[69] This homelessness or lack of roots explains, says Arendt, why mass-man offers the ideal raw material for movements in which men are pressed "so tightly together that it is as though their plurality had disappeared into One Man."[70] Yet might Weil not have agreed with Eric Voegelin's criticism of Arendt? Voegelin argues that Arendt fails to see that the origins of totalitarianism lie in "the spiritual disease of agnosticism." In April 1938, a few weeks after *Anschluß* had been officially proclaimed, Voegelin published *Political Religions;* the book was confiscated by the Gestapo, which promptly put its author's name on the black list. To Voegelin, morality and humanitarian sentiments seemed altogether inadequate to combat the "satanic force" represented by National Socialism, the living incarnation of Evil in the world. In his opinion, the struggle against Nazism required that one take into account its "roots in religiosity."[71] Far from considering National Socialism, as others did, to be simply a form of "regression toward barbarity" and medieval obscurantism, Voegelin argued that it was engendered by, precisely, secularization. Human life in political communities is not, says Voegelin, exclusively secular; it does not only consist of a system of juridical and power relations, but is also pervaded by the

---

*We have borrowed the expression "the disease of agnosticism" from Eric Voegelin, the founder of the New Institute for Political Science at the University of Munich.

divine. Thus, after calling attention to the similarity between politics and the religion of the Egyptian Empire under Akhenaton, as well as the symbolic system of the chosen people of Abraham, Voegelin notes that the theoreticians of Italian fascism, like their National Socialist counterparts, spoke of their respective regimes as if they involved a religious idea and a religious politics which both had their source in the same sacred substance, the *Volksgeist*: "the worldly God speaks to the *Führer* as the otherworldly God spoke to Abraham, and the *Führer* transforms the divine words into orders for his followers and people."[72] For his part, Raymond Aron somewhat later proposed the term " 'secular religions' " for "those doctrines which have taken the place of waning faith in the souls of our contemporaries, and which locate the salvation of mankind in this world, in a distant future, in the form of a social order that must be constructed."[73]

Weil would surely have agreed, for she affirms that "if children are brought up not to think about God, they will become Fascist or Communist for want of something to which to give themselves."[74] *The Need for Roots*, a work commissioned by the Free French movement in London, deals explicitly with the links between politics and religion, setting out to show that, even when God's transcendence is no longer acknowledged, there subsists an active need for a transcendent reality that is *other*, whatever the object of that need might be—matter, science, or revolution. For Weil, the simultaneous emergence of totalitarianism and the secular religions leaves no room for doubt: as soon as man, not God, is taken as the measure of all things, what ensues is "the errors of our time . . . the result of Christianity minus the supernatural element. This is due to 'laïcisme' (secularization), and, in the first place, to humanism."[75] However, for Weil, modern totalitarianism represents the radicalization not only of Roman totalitarianism, but also of the Catholic totalitarianism of the thirteenth century. By thus denying what Arendt calls the "horrible originality" of totalitarianism,[76] she appears to confirm what the Ecclesiast tells us: that there can be nothing new under the sun. However, the originality Arendt has in mind does not involve some new "idea," but rather the fact that the actions totalitarianism inspires constitute "a break with all our traditions"; this break consists in transforming the Biblical commandment "thou shalt not kill!" into its exact opposite, "thou shalt kill!" When Weil uses the world "totalitarianism," it would appear that she makes no distinction between authority and violence. Arendt emphasizes that the use of this term is relatively new in political science, and that it has merely taken the place of the word "imperialism," used "to denote aggression in foreign politics." The term totalitarianism has served, since the downfall of imperialism, "to denote lust for power, the will to dominate, terror, and a so-called monolithic state structure."[77]

Arendt, in contrast, while evoking the "devil" and "evil spell[ ]tion with Hitler and referring to the camps as an "image of H[ ]any assimilation of political ideology to religion. In 1950, responding, along with other intellectuals, to a *Partisan Review* inquiry into "the new turn toward religion among intellectuals and the growing disfavor with which secular attitudes and perspectives are now regarded," she vigorously protests against using religion as a weapon or even as a simple buffer against totalitarianism. Recent history seems to her to have demonstrated religion's impotence, notwithstanding the good will or even the heroism of some of the clergy of all the various confessions.[79] She also remarks in this essay that while the overwhelming majority of people have ceased to believe that there will be a Last Judgment at the end of time, yet "the same masses, at any rate hardly bothering to think of the old mysteries, like the Incarnation or the Trinity, are quite willing to believe—well, just anything." Their attitude, as she sees it, is one of "plain superstitiousness."[80] But it is above all in the essay "Religion and Politics"—originally written for a Harvard conference on the subject "Is the Struggle between the Free World and Communism Essentially Religious?" and later published in the journal *Confluence*, edited by Henry Kissinger*—that Arendt stakes out a clear-cut position on the relationship between politics and religion. She takes issue, in particular, with the conception of "political religions" put forward by Voegelin and defended by Waldemar Gurian in *Bolshevism: An Introduction to Soviet Communism*.[81] From the fact that the crisis of the modern world is the indisputable result of a breakdown in authority and tradition, it by no means follows, says Arendt, that this crisis is religious or has a religious origin. Her second argument is that freedom, which is the central concern of politics, is by no means a religious category; this shows the profoundly non-religious nature of public affairs. She alerts us to the danger of "blasphemy" inherent in the use of the term "secular religion," which tends to identify Hitler and Jesus on the grounds that they fulfilled the same social function. Coming back to the demise of the belief in Hell, the only element in the religious tradition powerful enough to have served as an instrument of political authority, she concludes that it proves that there has been a "separation of the religious and political realms of life." Finally, she sounds a warning: "if we try to inspire public-political life once more with 'religious passion' or to use religion as a means of political distinctions, the result may very well be the transformation and perversion of religion into an ideology and the corruption of our

---

*Raymond Aron put out the call for papers for the conference (see "The Diffusion of Ideologies," *Confluence* 2, no. 3 [1953]: 3–12) and contributed a paper himself, "Totalitarianism and Freedom." Arendt's essay appeared in *Confluence* 2, no. 3 (1953): 105–12.

fight against totalitarianism by a fanaticism which is utterly alien to the very essence of freedom."[82]

In her response to Voegelin's review of *The Origins of Totalitarianism* in the *Review of Politics*,[83] Arendt once again affirms that totalitarian ideologies cannot take the place of the Divinity and that atheism is at most a "condition *sine qua non*, nothing which could positively explain whatever happened afterward. Thus those who conclude from the frightening events of our times that we have got to go back to religion for political reasons seem to me to show just as much lack of faith in God as their opponents."[84] In Arendt's view, such an interpretation, apart from its failure to recognize the specificity of the crimes committed, neglects modern society's tendency toward atheism.[85]

Scientists, Scholars, and Politics

Weil also blames others for Hitler's rise, including scholars and scientists: "savants and all those who write about science . . . are possibly guiltier of Hitler's crimes than Hitler himself."[86] This is what a passage she quotes from *Mein Kampf* would seem to indicate. Here Hitler shows he has understood that to take oneself for the lord and master of nature, where force alone holds sway, is simultaneously to authorize oneself to dominate men, who are not subject to different laws. Modern science is guilty, in Weil's eyes, of demanding for itself the same respect religion once commanded. However, scientists' motivations are not pure; furthermore, science is subject to the whims of fashion, and fails to live up to its definition, which is to be "the study of the beauty of the world."[87] Alain too was aware of the link between science and the domination of man by man.*

On this point, Weil appears to agree with Arendt, who also points out that Hitler showed great insight into the nature of modern propaganda when he suddenly realized the necessity of employing " 'scientific' arguments and refused to use the standard crackpot ones of traditional anti-Semitic propaganda." But Arendt observes further that the Nazis did not make use of the ideas offered them by the "respectable German professors" who volunteered their services to the Nazis: "The Nazis had their own ideas; what they needed were techniques and technicians with no ideas at all or educated from the beginning in only Nazi ideas. The scholars first put to one side by the Nazis as of relatively little use to them were old-fashioned nationalists like

---

*"Tyrannies will always be reasonable, in the sense that they will always seek out specialists, as the army does today, and with ever greater success. Conversely, reason will always be tyrannical, because the man who knows never tolerates the choice and freedom of the man who does not. Thus tyrants and scientists are by nature allies; the most odious things will find themselves bound up ever more closely with the things which command the greatest respect" (Alain, *Politique*, LXIX, p. 215).

Heidegger, whose enthusiasm for the Third Reich was matched only by his glaring ignorance of what he was talking about."[88] Arendt mentions Alfred Bäumler and Walter Frank in this connection.

Immortal Fame

In her discussion of the Nazis, which preceded Arendt's, Weil puts the accent on the disproportion between Nazi crimes and any conceivable punishment. Thus she remarks in 1942 that none of the punishments one might inflict on Hitler can involve more than "an historical death, an historical suffering—in fact, History." Declaring, in 1946, that genocide transcends questions of crime and innocence, Arendt, for her part, wished to show that "an organized attempt was made to eradicate the concept of the human being."[89]

Weil too pointed out that Hitler had only one objective: to go down in history, to enjoy the immortality that fame brings. And he succeeded. Hence the only exemplary punishment for Hitler, in Weil's opinion, would involve "such a total transformation of the meaning attached to greatness that he should thereby be excluded from it."[90] We are, in some sort, responsible for Hitler, as are all those who contribute to perpetuating this "conception of greatness." Indeed, we may be even guiltier than Hitler himself. If he had not read a "tenth-rate work on Sulla," he would perhaps have been able to perceive some form of greatness other than crime.[91] Reading Roman history is to blame, says Weil, who also deals Péguy and Maritain a blow in passing here. Against Péguy, she objects: "if one admires the Roman Empire, why be angry with Germany which is trying to reconstitute it on a vaster scale by the use of almost identical methods?"[92] As for Maritain, she criticizes him for speaking, in connection with God, of the *rights* He has over His creatures and of the fact that He has no moral obligation toward them. This comes down, she says, to turning God "into the infinite equivalent of a Roman slaveholder."[93]

But the fundamental problem consists in avoiding a situation in which, "in twenty, fifty, a hundred or two hundred years' time, some solitary little dreamer . . . [will] see in Hitler a superb figure."[94] This is, for Weil, a problem of education, a matter of properly understanding the way history should be taught and of choosing the right "motivations." To suppress the teaching of history would be absurd, for "without history there can be no sense of patriotism." It would be quite as wrong to eliminate stories of war, or to place wars "in the background":[95] tragedies, like epics, are a part of reality, which is why the *Iliad* still has the emotional power it does. History and descriptions of war must, however, be presented differently: Weil demands that facts be accurately stated and "shown in their true perspective relatively to good and evil."[96] She proposes meeting out severe punishments to all those—

journalists, writers, historians—responsible for diffusing untruths, so great is her aversion to all forms of lying propaganda and so uncompromising her advocacy of "the spirit of truth," which, she believes, is sorely lacking in our civilization.[97] Two years later, in a letter addressed to *Cahiers du Sud*, Weil would write: "I believe in the responsibility of the writers of recent years for the disaster of our time. By that I don't mean only the defeat of France; the disaster of our time extends much further. It extends to the whole world, that is to say, to Europe, to America, and to the other continents in so far as Western influence has penetrated them."[98] The dadaists and surrealists, by lending their voices to the "drunkenness of licence," like Gide's *Fruits of the Earth* and *Lafcadio's Adventures*, which offer no criteria for distinguishing good from evil, are, she thinks, more harmful than cocaine.[99]

Does Arendt, for her part, not adopt the Roman definition of what a cultivated person ought to be, namely, "one who knows how to choose his company among men, among things, among thoughts, in the present as well as in the past"?[100] She refers us to Plato, for whom poetry, like painting or inspiring examples, educates future generations by "glorifying the countless mighty deeds of ancient times."[101] In her correspondence with Mary McCarthy, Arendt, deeply shaken by the recent death of her friend W. H. Auden, recalls Homer's way of justifying the misfortunes of men:

> Homer said that the gods spin ruin to men that there might be song and remembrance. Helen said in the Iliad: Zeus brought evil on her and Paris "so that in days to come we shall be a song for men yet to be" and Hecuba (in Euripides) about to be carried off into slavery, says—consoles herself?—without this disaster "we would be unfamed, unsung, not something to be remembered by mortals in the future."[102]

Arendt is not unaware, then, of the problematic nature of fame; she too denounces this strange perversity of modern times, which testifies to the "loss of the public realm" and is characterized by a confusion between "the striving for immortality" and "the private vice of vanity."[103] Hans Jonas, in an essay on "Immortality" dedicated to his friend Hannah Arendt, likewise questions the perverse state of affairs in which the names of the innocent victims of the Hitlers and Stalins are not recorded in the "Book of Life," while those of their murderers are.[104] Yet the fact that the murderers have attained historical immortality, and that, in our times, only the frivolous are concerned to immortalize their names, does not, as Arendt sees it, call the status and content of history into question so much as it clearly shows the degree to which public opinion is fabricated or manipulated: today a good name and infamy are of equal value.

Part III
Exile (1940–1943)

1940

9 April: the Germans invade Norway and Denmark.

10 May: German offensive in the West. Hitler overcomes Dutch and Belgian resistance in a few days. The Battle of France begins in the Ardennes. The Pope breaks his neutrality a second time—the first occurred when Russia invaded Finland—to condemn Hitler's aggression.

Holland is occupied. Dutch Jews are excluded from the civil service, isolated from the rest of the population, put under house arrest, not allowed to enter most stores or use public transportation, and required to wear the yellow star. The Germans set up "Jewish Councils," the largest of which is in Amsterdam, and appoint notables in the Jewish communities to head them.

14 May: Rotterdam is bombed.

27 May: Belgium surrenders.

June: publication of the last issue of *Esprit* to appear before the Armistice and the collapse of the Third Republic.

4 June: Dunkirk falls. Italy enters the war alongside the Germans. A New German offensive begins in the regions of the Aisne and the Somme.

10 June: Mussolini announces that Italy has entered the war.

Paris is declared an open city. The Parisians begin to desert the capital.

12 June: General Weygand declares at Cangé castle that the French should lay down their arms. Paul Reynaud, the President of the Council of Ministers, and the twenty-four deputies who are present reject Weygand's proposal as "inadmissible." The vote is nearly unanimous; only Marshal Pétain supports Weygand.

13 June: Bouthillier, Baudouin, and Ybarnégaray rally to the idea of an

armistice; Pétain assumes the leadership of the movement. The government joins the exodus, traveling first to Tours and then to Bordeaux. Laval takes possession of Paris's City Hall. Pétain has convinced Admiral Darlan of the "need for a change in regime."

15 June: Camille Chautemps submits an armistice proposal; thirteen members of the Council vote in favor, six against.

16 June: Churchill proposes a Franco-British union; the idea is rejected by the French cabinet. Paul Reynaud tenders his resignation to Lebrun, designating Pétain as his successor.

De Gaulle leaves Bordeaux on an English airplane when Pétain forms his government, whose legitimacy is recognized by nearly forty states, including the U.S. and the USSR.

17 June: Pétain forms his cabinet, which asks to be informed of the Germans' conditions for an armistice.

18 June: from London, where Churchill has arranged for him to speak on the radio, General de Gaulle appeals to the French to keep fighting: "France has lost a battle, but it has not lost the war . . . because this war is a world war." Few Frenchmen listen to his appeal. De Gaulle creates a dissident movement, the Free French, and an embryonic French government, the National French Committee; a central bureau for intelligence and action is attached to the committee. The bureau's mission is to make contact with the clandestine French Resistance. It attracts a steady stream of volunteers and soon commands a small army that will later fight in Ethiopia, the Sahara, Libya, and on the Atlantic. However, the English do not recognize de Gaulle as representing France. Nor do many Frenchmen follow his lead, at least down to November 1942; Pétain enjoys the confidence of the large majority of the French population.

At this time, Jacques Maritain is on a mission for the French Foreign Ministry at the Institute for Medieval Studies in Toronto. Unlike Mauriac, Claudel, and Gide, who are, for the moment, under Pétain's spell, Maritain staunchly opposes him; so does Bernanos, who is in Brazil. But, while Maritain approves of de Gaulle's appeal, he does not join the Free French.

21 June: France and Germany sign an armistice. Hitler receives the French delegation at Rethondes in the same railway-car in which Foch dictated his conditions to the German plenipotentiaries in 1918.

21 June: Sartre is captured by the Germans.

23 June: Raymond Aron leaves for England.

20–25 June: the government establishes its seat in Vichy. Pétain explains the reasons for his actions in a series of messages to the French.

25 June: in one of these messages, Pétain proclaims: "Our defeat is due to the slackening of our moral standards. The spirit of hedonism is destroying

what the spirit of sacrifice had built up. I invite you to undertake a process of moral and intellectual recovery."¹ This program of *redressement*, or moral restoration, will be christened the National Revolution. The Church will soon follow Pétain's lead; the slogan of the National Revolution, "Work, Family, Fatherland," is directly inspired by its teachings. Thus Father Tellier de Poncheville condemns the return to paganism and materialism. As for the new archbishop of Paris, Cardinal Suhard, he hails the armistice, "thanks to which French blood is no longer being spilled on the battlefield," and proclaims his support for the Marshal: "Is Marshal Pétain not a Frenchman beyond reproach? A Frenchman whose one desire is to serve? . . . When, in a difficult, grave moment, a leader of his caliber speaks out, we should put our trust in him!"

6 July: Raïssa Maritain writes: "There is no longer any future for me in this world. Life for me draws to a close, ended by the catastrophe that has plunged France into mourning, and, with France, the world."²

10 July: the French parliament votes Pétain full powers. Xavier Vallat, who has successively been a member of Action française, Georges Valois's Faisceau, and Colonel de La Rocque's Croix de Feu, is appointed Secretary for Veterans' Affairs. Even after France is liberated, he will stubbornly maintain, before the High Court of Justice, that "the Jew is not only an unassimilable foreigner living in a community which tends to constitute a state within the state; he is also, by temperament, a foreigner bent on domination who tends to create, with others of his kind, a super-state within the state."

22 July: Raphaël Alibert, the French Justice Minister, decides to reexamine all the acts of naturalization carried out on the basis of the 1927 Citizenship Law.

25 July: *Le Petit Journal* (de La Rocque's paper) proposes to weed out "offensive" Anglicisms, such as "grill-room," "lavatory," and "five o'clock tea."³

30 July: inciting a French soldier or sailor to join an "enemy" army is made punishable by death.⁴

31 July: Bernanos writes: "I am an opponent of M. Philippe Pétain's governemnt because . . . he is betting on totalitarian victory, and I am betting on totalitarian defeat."⁵ On the BBC, Bernanos ridicules Vichy, which he calls an "agricultural dictatorship"; France has become "totalitarian Europe's peaceful vegetable garden . . . charged with providing the workers in Germany's gigantic factories with fresh vegetables."⁶

Hitler notifies Mussolini of the possibility of establishing a Jewish state in Madagascar under French supervision (the project has been in the air since 1931).

4 August: the newspaper *Paris Soir* reports a new decree "to promote French morality"; it outlaws shorts for women and requires that bathing-

suits go down to the knee. The Catholic paper *La Croix* declares that "victory does not always mean what the common man understands it to mean . . . Our victory probably began in June 1940."[7]

6 August: "Editorial in *Le Temps*: New Order will be based on Continental collaboration; *frontier rectifications are of no consequence;* there will be good understanding among the nations because all will live under a corporative, authoritarian, totalitarian régime."[8]

7 August: in the absence of German pressure, all male foreigners between the ages of eighteen and forty-five who can play no useful role in the French economy are interned in concentration camps.

The teaching methods best suited to French schools become a subject of public debate: "the French teacher must become a peasant again and teach little future peasants; French girls must learn cooking and sewing—not Latin or mathematics" (*Paris Soir*).[9] School inspectors are "no longer selected by competitive examination, but appointed by the Ministry."

13 August: Pétain alludes to the Jews neither in his speech of 13 August—drafted by René Gillouin, "the Marshal's friend"—nor in that of 10 October, written by Gaston Bergery and titled, "L'ordre nouveau est une nécessité française" [The New Order is a French imperative], nor, again, in the series of articles he publishes in *La Revue des deux mondes* in the fall.

Secret societies are outlawed.

The first Jewish shop windows are smashed in Marseilles and Lyons in the name of the National Revolution. The Paris Opera reopens and stages Berlioz's *Damnation de Faust* for the occupation authorities.[10]

16 August: the trade-union confederations are dissolved.

24 August: a court martial is commissioned to judge the Gaullists in summary proceedings.

27 August: abrogation of the 1938 Marchandeau Law, which had outlawed anti-Semitic propaganda.

Crimes of opinion are put back on the books; belonging to certain groups is now a criminal offense as well.

No one whose father is not French can enter French public service.

All French citizens who left metropolitain France for a foreign destination between 10 May and 30 June lose their citizenship.

28 August: an ordonnance requires that a number of Catholic movements cease and desist from all activity. This does not prevent Georges Lamirand, Minister for Youth and Sports, from attempting to convince the French bishops of the importance of his campaign to maintain National Youth teams or create new ones. Where necessary, he helps rebuild the most important Catholic movements by demobilizing their staff members.[11]

29 August: a new law creates the Veterans' Legion.

September: the authorities conduct a census of Jews in the Occupied Zone. Raymond Aron's books are put on the Germans' "Otto list" of banned writings. Jean-Paul Sartre later describes what he was in this period: "during the Occupation, I was a writer who participated in the Resistance, not a resistance fighter who wrote."

Emmanuel Mounier, offered a post in the United States, declares: "this is not the moment to desert."[12]

Late September: the Unoccupied Zone in southern France counts thirty-one concentration camps; there are forty-one more camps in northern France. A total of 50,000 Jews are interned in these camps. Some 15,000 more are detained in camps in North Africa.

15 September: the arrest of Léon Blum is greeted with jubilation by the right-wing press.

October or November: Philippe Viannay (alias André Philip) and Robert Salmon create Défense de la France.

3 October: in Vichy, the Council of Ministers enacts the Statute on the Jews. Public opinion is utterly unmoved. German law defines Jews in terms of religion; Vichy's Statute speaks of race. German law defines all those who have more than two Jewish grandparents as Jews; for Vichy, two grandparents are enough if one's wife is also Jewish.

7 October: repeal of the 1870 Crémieux Decree, which had granted Algerian Jews French citizenship.

8 October: Léon Blum is accused of having committed crimes in the exercise of his functions, of responsibility for France's entry into the war, and of endangering state security.

Claire Girard, executed on 27 August 1944 after taking part in the liberation of Paris, says in a letter to her family: "Anti-Semitism is on the rise here and is beginning to do serious damage; it is terrible. Certain shops, cafés, and restaurants are off-limits for Jews. Their homes are looted before their very eyes. Just yesterday, as I was walking with Anise [Annie Girard, who would become, after returning from Ravensbrück, Anise Postel-Vinay] near the Bois de Boulogne, in a quarter where there are many Jewish homes, I saw German 'potato bugs' stacking whole trucks high with furniture, objets d'art, and paintings before the horrified owners' very eyes." In the same breath, she says: "where you are, in the South of France, nobody seems to realize what is going on here."[13]

24 October: Pétain holds a meeting with Hitler at Montoire, dashing the hopes of many resistance fighters, who thought that he was secretly preparing to resist the Germans. Défense de la France is not alone in assuming that Pétain is resisting the German diktats and that the problem is not Pétain, but Laval.

30 October: Pétain declares, "today, honorably, and in order to maintain French unity, I begin collaborating . . . as part of the process of building a new order in Europe."[14] In November, Cardinal Baudrillart, Rector of the Institut catholique in Paris, endorses the agreement Pétain and Hitler announce they have reached. Cardinal Gerlier, of Lyons, exclaims, "Pétain is France, and France is Pétain!" The Protestant minister Boegner seconds him. Monsignor Suhard and the clergy as a whole are more mistrustful.[15]

November: Blum is transferred to the Château de Chazeron in Bourassol, near Riom, where he is to go on trial.

December: Hitler signs Directive 21, Operation Barbarossa; Himmler and Heydrich begin preparing the "Final Solution."

13 December: Pierre Laval is arrested. There is a new burst of hope and an upsurge of confidence in Pétain. Emmanuel Mounier, however, is not fooled: "Have confidence in the Marshal! people cry out on all sides. Well, we are not lacking in good will! But what fateful coincidence made him choose Darlan after Laval? And who will it be after Darlan? How can one help but think that his blue eyes and undoubtedly guileless heart are providing a kind of cover for all the dirty deeds being done in his name?"[16]

AFTER THE 1940 DEFEAT, Pierre Dunoyer de Segonzac had submitted to the Ministry for Youth and Sports a project for the creation of a training school for people entering the national administration. The result was the creation of the School for National Adminstration at Uriage, near Grenoble; more than four thousand people were trained there in the course of the next few years. The head of the school was a monarchist; the students pledged allegiance to the flag and sang "Maréchal, nous voilà"; in the *Cahiers d'Uriage*, the Marshal's youth policies were praised as fulsomely as in *Jeunesse de la France*. Among those at the School were military men whose education had been shaped by the ideas of Charles Maurras. There were also clergymen who drew their spiritual inspiration from Marc Sangnier's Sillon movement and were alarmed by the decline of Christianity in France: Father de Naurois, the school's chaplain; Monsignor Bruno de Solages; Father de Lubac; Father Fraisse; and Father Chenu. Intellectuals also played an active role in Uriage: P. H. Chombart de Lauwe, E. Mounier, J.-M. Domenach, Joffre Dumazedier, S. Nora, B. Cacérès, G. Gadoffre, P. Delouvrier. These men were united by their Catholicism, patriotism, and opposition to Nazi ideas. Their aim was to organize spiritual resistance, seeking, as they were, a third way, a new civilization, and the advent of a new man whose nature was to be defined by personalist doctrine. Gradually, however, their relations with the Vichy regime deteriorated. Henri Massis, after paying a visit to Uriage, became the chief adversary of the School in Vichy.[17]

En Route for Freedom

Simone Weil had no desire to leave Paris. Shortly before the Germans launched their offensive, she had drawn up a "project to send nurses to the front lines" to treat the wounded and dying in the heat of combat. She wanted, of course, to be one of those nurses, even if it meant risking her life. She submitted the project to several influential people, none of whom took it very seriously. Somewhat earlier, she had read the English White Paper on the concentration camps in Germany as well as newspaper reports on the massive arrests of students in Bohemia. She was "obsessed by these horrors." They led her, as we have just seen, to draw up a "semi-political, semi-military project" to parachute weapons and volunteers prepared to sacrifice their lives into various concentration camps; these volunteers were to arm and train the prisoners and massacre the SS guards.[18]

"Since 1940, I have closely followed all measures bearing on the deportations and ghettos," Hannah Arendt wrote on 3 September 1943;[19] she had begun to draw up, retrospectively, an inventory of the methods the Nazis used to foment anti-Semitism among the population of various countries. One proof that they had deliberately sought to do so was the fact that French supplies were sold to the German soldiers through Jewish intermediaries. This created the impression that the soldiers were under direct orders to buy in Jewish neighborhoods and led to a massive return of Polish-Jewish refugees from Toulouse.[20] A few months later, these Jews were arrested and sent to concentration camps. Massive destruction of Jewish life only took place, Arendt goes on to say, when manifestations of sympathy for the Jews attracted too much attention; the Nazis, she adds, preferred that the killing take place in uninhabited regions.[21]

La Gursienne

Hannah Arendt, who had married Heinrich Blücher in January, was arrested after the *Gouverneur général* of Paris issued a decree ordering that all "enemy aliens" be rounded up on 15 May 1940 and brought to the Vélodrome d'hiver, an indoor sports arena in the French capital. The men were either packed off to Buffalo stadium, if they were "enemy aliens," or Roland-Garros stadium, if they were considered "suspect." Arendt spent a week in the Vélodrome d'hiver before being transferred by bus, along with other women internees, to a Paris railway station, the Gare de Lyons. From there she was sent to Gurs, in Southwestern France, not far from the Spanish border, where there was an internment camp in which Spanish refugees and militants of the International Brigades had been living since April 1939. Eighteen thousand Jews and a hundred or so French resistance fighters would eventually pass through the camp. It seems that Arendt, like other internees, had her moments of despair, but that she rapidly got over them:

> At the camp of Gurs . . . where I had the opportunity to spend some time, I heard only once about suicide, and that was the suggestion of a collective action, apparently a kind of protest in order to vex the French. When some of us remarked that we had been shipped there '*pour crever*' in any case, the general mood turned suddenly into a violent courage of life.[22]

Lotte Eisner, a film critic who also ended up in this camp, later described the conditions the deportees were subjected to:

> People have been far too indulgent in describing the camp. [There were] barracks housing sixty women at a time, most of whom became hysterical. . . . We were in Block J. Every night, the officer responsible for this block came with his dog-whip to look for the prettiest girl to sleep with. He would give her something to eat in exchange. When, after the armistice was signed, the German officers arrived, he fraternized with them.[23]

A few weeks after Arendt's arrival in Gurs, France had gone down to defeat. Arendt managed to escape from the camp after laying hands on false identity papers. Of a total of seven thousand women interned with her, two hundred managed to flee. In *Scum of the Earth*, Arthur Koestler describes these *Gursiennes*, or "women of Gurs," wandering in a daze down the roads of Southwestern France two and a half miles from the camp at Vernet, where he himself was being held: "Peasants lend rooms to them or let them work in fields *au pair*. They look undernourished, exhausted, but tidy. All wear turbans *à la mode*, a coloured handkerchief round the head."[24] In 1962, Arendt herself described how she left the camp in a letter to the magazine *Midstream*:

> None of us could 'describe' what lay in store for those who remained behind. All that we could do was to tell them what we expected would happen—the camp would be handed over to the victorious Germans. . . . This happened, indeed, but since the camp lay in what later became Vichy-France, it happened years later than we expected. The delay did not help the inmates. After a few days of chaos, everything became very regular again and escape was almost impossible. We rightly predicted this return to normalcy. It was a unique chance, but it meant that one had

to leave with nothing but a toothbrush since there existed no means of transportation.[25]

Let us note in passing that Arendt's brief sojourn in the camp was later the occasion for a tiff between her and Mary McCarthy. In 1945, after mentioning the hostility of the French toward the German occupiers, McCarthy had declared, a bit flippantly, that she " 'felt sorry for Hitler, who was so absurd as to want the love of his victims.' Arendt, incensed, shot back, 'How can you say such a thing in front of me—a victim of Hitler, a person who has been in a concentration camp!' " It was three years before they were reconciled: McCarthy apologized for her remark, and Arendt admitted that Gurs had only been an internment camp.[26] After getting out of Gurs, Arendt found refuge in Montauban with her friends the Cohn-Bendits; Montauban's socialist mayor was an opponent of the Vichy government. Two simultaneously promulgated decrees testify to the confusion that reigned in this region of the country: the prefect gave orders to the effect that all foreigners formerly interned at Gurs had to leave the *département* within twenty-four hours, while the government forbade all travel by foreigners. Arendt's biographer reports that she read Proust, Clausewitz, and Simenon in Montauban.

The "Free" Zone

In Simone Weil's *Cahiers inédits* [Unpublished notebooks], which date from mid-September 1940 to January 1941, we find the phrase, "[ms. 28. Notes on the camp at Gurs.]"[27] Weil was in Marseilles at the time. As Paris had been declared an open city on 10 June 1940, she yielded to her parents' insistent demands and fled with them to Nevers. The Germans arrived in Nevers by night; by 14 June, they had reached Paris. The Weils' exodus then took them to Vichy, which they reached in the first days of July. The French Premier, Paul Reynaud, had resigned, the parliament had voted constituent powers to Pétain, and the armistice agreement had been signed.

Simone was indignant and deeply regretted her earlier anti-war positions: now she was resolved to go to England to join the combatants. As a faithful disciple of Alain's, she wrote to Georges Bernanos: "I do not love war; but what has always seemed to me most horrible in war is the position of those in the rear. When I realized that, try as I would, I could not prevent myself from participating morally in that war—in other words, from hoping all day and every day for the victory of one side and the defeat of the other—I decided that, for me, Paris was the rear." The Weils moved closer to Toulouse in hopes of using it as a springboard to leave France; in September 1940, they went on to Marseilles.

On 3 October 1940, Jews in the Unoccupied Zone were ordered to register with the police. Günther Stern, Arendt's first husband, helped Hannah and Blücher obtain visas. Only 238 of the 1,137 visa applications received by the Vichy governement between August and December 1940 were approved: the government was extremely reluctant to issue exit visas. At the same time, Spain and Portugal were issuing transit visas in highly arbitrary fashion. Walter Benjamin, for example, failed to obtain a French exit visa and joined a small group planning to sneak across the border near Port-Bou. Unfortunately for him, the Spanish government had decreed that Spanish transit visas were not valid on the day he tried to cross the border. Benjamin committed suicide by taking half a box of sleeping pills that he had half-heartedly agreed to split with Arthur Koestler (his neighbor at 10, rue Dombasle and a partner in their Saturday night poker games) the last time they had seen one another in Marseilles. In January 1941, the Vichy government briefly relaxed its stringent policy on exit visas; Arendt and her husband were able to board a train for Lisbon, where they had to put up with another three-month wait. They had taken a suitcase full of manuscripts that Benjamin had entrusted to them; Arendt and Blücher read Benjamin's "Theses on History" to their fellow refugees. Lisbon, the last open port in Europe from which it was possible to set sail for America, witnessed the "procession of despair" Koestler describes:

> And they marched past two by two, the Polish aristocrat and the Jewish pedlar, the French nationalist and the German pacifist, the Catholic father and the Communist comrade; and they queued up, two by two, in front of the Arks, the sons of Shem and the sons of Japheth. . . . And the flood was forty days upon the earth and the waters prevailed upon the earth; but there was still no rainbow set in the clouds.[28]

The Religion of *Blut und Boden*

Simone Weil lived in Marseilles from October 1940 to May 1942. She chose this period to write "Israël et les Gentils" [Israel and the Gentiles], which attacked Judaism and the Hebrew God. What were her grievances against the religion of Israel? Where did they originate?

"Wotan Is Now Trying to Supplant Jehovah"[29]

We have already mentioned Weil's critique of the Romans' imperialistic policies, anti-juridical spirit, and treacherousness. It culminates in Weil's critique of Roman religion, which "can scarcely be said to deserve the name of religion at all," and is less "suitable" than any other "for the recitation of the name of the Lord."[30] But since the Romans and the Hebrews were, for Weil, twin peoples in religion as in other respects, her condemnation of the Romans' religion encompasses that of the Jews as well, for Judaism too was based on an idolatrous conception of the chosen people, a conception that barred the way to universalism. "The idol was the State. People adored the Emperor. As all other forms of religious life had to be subordinated to that one, none could rise above idolatry."[31] As for Hebrew religion, the fact that it was monotheistic did not make it any less idolatrous. Its idolatry consisted, on the one hand, in affirming—at least down to Moses and excepting the Book of Job, the Song of Songs, and David's Psalms—that God was omnipotent rather than good and, on the other hand, in defending the idea of a chosen people. "The Hebrews took for their idol, not something made of metal or wood, but a race, a nation, something just as earthly. Their religion is essentially inseparable from such idolatry, because of the notion of the 'chosen people.' "[32] But, if Israel had indeed been chosen, in that Christ was born there, it was likewise Israel which put him to death: "Judas was chosen to nourish Christ—and Judas was chosen to betray Him."[33] This murder was provoked by the fact that Christ had done only good: "if He had shown that He could put tens of thousands of men to death with a single word, these same priests and Pharisees would have hailed Him as the Messiah." In the final analysis, the Jews simply took the logic of their tradition to its natural conclusion when they crucified Christ.[34] In adopting Christianity as the religion of the Roman Empire, Rome merely deepened the blemish that the Old Testament had already put on the face of Christianity.* The Hebrews imposed their Scripture everywhere.[35] They were Christianity's evil inspiration,[36] and transmitted their prejudices to the early Christians.[37] Far from owing a debt to Israel,[38] we must purge Christianity of its influence. The close relationship, which Weil so strongly disapproved of, between the New Testament and the Old constituted one of the major obstacles to her joining the Church, which was too Roman for her taste and thus too closely tied up with society, that Great Beast.** While it is true that the situation changed

---

*"Thus by a twofold historical accident the twofold Hebraic and Roman tradition has in great measure negated, for two thousand years, the divine inspiration of Christianity" (Simone Weil, "Quelques réflexions sur les origines de l'hitlerisme," *Œuvres complètes*, vol. 2: *Ecrits historiques et politiques*, book 3: *Vers la guerre, 1937–1940*, ed. Simone Fraisse [Paris: Gallimard, 1989], p. 213; Weil, "The Great Beast," *Selected Essays, 1931–1943*, ed. and trans. Richard Rees [London: Oxford University Press, 1962], p. 133).

**"Rome is the Great Beast of atheism and materialism, adoring nothing but itself. Israel is the Great Beast of religion. Neither the one nor the other is likeable. The Great Beast is always repulsive" (Simone Weil, *La pesanteur et la grâce* [Paris: Plon, 1988], p. 183; Weil, *Gravity and Grace*, trans. Arthur Wills [Lincoln: University of Nebraska Press, 1997], p. 219).

with Moses, with, that is, the appearance of commandments of an ethical nature, Moses did nothing more than apply the wisdom he had received from
the Egyptians when he defined God as Being—though not yet as Good.
Moreover, injunctions to be charitable are rare in the Mosaic tradition. In
particular, Jehovah seemed to Weil to be sorely lacking in pity. Greek
philosophers had held that, whenever a wretched creature implored pity, it
was Zeus himself who was begging for pity through her; they even went so
far as to say, not "Zeus, protector of suppliants," but "suppliant Zeus." In
contrast, an expression like "suppliant Jehovah" is unthinkable.[39] Apparently
Weil was ignorant of the Book of Isaiah (63:9), in which it is written that God
is afflicted in the afflictions of men, and of Psalms 91:15: "I will be with him
in trouble." In her eyes, Moses was above all the founder of a state, the mes-
senger of an all-powerful God who, like the Devil, made only worldly
promises. Further evidence that the Hebrew people did not carry God in its
heart can be seen in the fact that rather than enduing the Egyptian slavery
"that had been provoked by their previous exactions, [the Hebrews pre-
ferred] to win their freedom by massacring all the inhabitants of the lands
they were to occupy."[40]

Weil emphatically states that the rootlessness of our times can make
people want to "belong unconditionally to some brown, red or other totalitarian system" which gives them "a solid illusion of inward unity" and thus
constitutes a very "strong temptation for . . . many distraught minds."[41] Yet,
unlike Arendt, she sees nothing more in the concept of race than a "romantic" version of the idea of the "nation," in the Hebrew or Roman sense of the
word. Hitler, she argues, simply turned the notion of "chosen race"[42] back
against the Jews: "the Jews were persecuted because, once the Church had
annexed their privilege, their claim that they had still kept it made them too
embarrassing. . . . Hitler persecutes the Jews for the same reason. He would
like to imitate them by calling the German collective soul Wotan and saying
that Wotan created heaven and earth."[43] On this point, let us note in passing,
Weil simply reiterates a thesis that Alain,* and even Bernanos,** had defended before her. Does she misunderstand the notion of a chosen people,
which has much less to do with domination than responsibility, that is, the
idea of being entrusted with a mission? That is what Father Perrin suggests,
citing the following verses from Exodus: "Now therefore, if ye will obey my
voice indeed, and keep my covenant, then ye shall be a peculiar treasure unto

---

*"Here, then, the Germans fail to recognize their brothers, the other chosen people; they fail
to recognize their own fanaticism in the Bible, which they have read too much" (Alain, *Politique*
[Paris: Presses universitaires de France, 1962], XCVII, p. 292).

**"The totalitarian states must necessarily eliminate their Jews, since each citizen of those
states believes himself one of God's elect, and there is no room in the world for two Chosen
Peoples" (Georges Bernanos, *A Diary of My Times*, trans. Pamela Morris [London: Boriswood,
1938], pp. 255–256).

me above all people: for all the earth is mine: And ye shall be unto me a kingdom of priests, and an holy nation." (Exodus 19: 5–6). Similarly, Emmanuel Lévinas criticizes Weil's conception of the election of the Jews, which was in no sense a gift of grace and, far from being defined in terms of privilege, is entirely a matter of responsibility: "every person, as a person—that is to say, one conscious of his freedom—is chosen." The idea that there is a chosen people, Weil intimates, is at odds with the universality of the divine principle. But "if being chosen takes on a national appearance, it is because only in this form can a civilization be constituted, be maintained, be transformed."[44] Martin Buber, finally, believes that Weil turned her back on a Judaism that she did not really know, even if one takes "Judaism" to mean the conventional Christian conception of the religion of the Jews. For Buber, Weil was in error about what was at stake in Judaism and Christianity. He cannot, he says, however much he would like to, take her by the hand and bring her to see that "becoming a people of God means rather that the attributes of God revealed to it, justice and love, are to be made effective in its own life, in the lives of its members with one another. . . . Of the two, however, love is the higher, the transcending principle."[45]

A Gnostic Anti-Judaism?

One may choose to see nothing more than a little joke in the remark Weil is supposed to have made to Dr. Bercher around 1933: "personally, I am an anti-Semite,"[46] and consequently speak only of her anti-Judaism. But what is one to make of the "the hatred for the Bible," as Lévinas puts it,[47] of a woman who "lived like a saint and bore the suffering of the world"? Was she abysmally ignorant of Judaism, as Lévinas claims, because she never had the opportunity to meet "a real teacher of Judaism," unlike Lévinas himself, who had met Benjamin Chouchani and been powerfully impressed by him?[48] Perrin, Thibon, Buber, and Lévinas all underscore not only Weil's profound misunderstanding of the Jewish religion but also her unfair treatment of it.

Thus, speaking of a difference of opinion with Weil as to how to understand the expression "Yaveh Sabaoth," Perrin says, after honestly admitting that neither he nor she knew Hebrew: "relying on certain notes, I did not want to interpret the phrase as meaning anything save 'God of the Heavenly Hosts'—of stars and angels—whereas Simone wanted to see in it only the God of Israel's 'Armies.' "[49] Another point of disagreement involved Weil's interpretation of a Biblical passage in her essay "Les trois fils de Noé" [The three sons of Noah], written at about the same time as "Israel and the Gentiles." Not only is Noah presented "as a 'figure of Christ' " in this essay, as we have seen, but, contrary to the traditional interpretation, which takes *Ham* to be the accursed son because he saw the nakedness of his father, Weil affirms that what he saw made him heir to the highest wisdom, which he transmitted to his heirs, the Canaanites. In contrast, she says, Shem, Japheth, and their descendants remained eternally ignorant.[50] Turning next to Weil's essay on the *Iliad*, Perrin asks:

> Why does Simone forget that the revelation of God and of creation was vouchsafed to Israel? That it was given to Moses to formulate the Great Commandment? Why does she pass over in silence the fact that the Old Testament was unique in forbidding human sacrifices? Why does she not quote the admirable injunctions concerning pity for the stranger, the needy ... even to the goat which must not be cooked in its mother's milk?[51]

Lévinas is no more favorably disposed toward Weil's acceptance of evil. Evil, she says, derives from the superabundance of God's goodness and by no means prevents one from loving God; on the contrary, only to those who have never ceased to love Him will it one day be vouchsafed to "hear ... the very silence as something infinitely more full of significance than any response, like God himself speaking."[52] Ideas of this kind horrified Lévinas, however respectful he was of Christianity, because, for him, the continued existence of evil in the world was a call to action, not a reason for resignation and silent suffering.[53] Yet Lévinas argues not from a theological but from a logical point of view. Moreover, his intention is less to criticize Weil than to address Jews she might have "wounded or troubled." And he reassures us that the Gnostic anti-Judaism Weil represents has "nothing in common with Hitler's. How comforting!"[54] He is the more indulgent with her because her writings were all posthumous.

Did Weil know the Gnostic any better than the Hebrew tradition? She repeatedly calls attention to her sympathy for the Gnostics, Marcion and Valentinus in particular. Her high praise for the Cathares, Manicheans, and other Gnostic sects, her aversion to certain passages in the Old Testament, together with the contempt in which she held the Hebrews, her reflections on affliction and de-creation, her ascetic way of life, and, finally, her death— which has been compared to the *endura* practiced by the *perfecti*, the Cathar priests—are all, according to some commentators, points of resemblance between her philosophy and that of the Gnostics.* Moreover, her close friend-

---

*P. Danon, "A propos du catharisme," *Cahiers Simone Weil* 12, no. 2 (June 1989): 187. Maura A. Dalyin, "Simone Weil gnostique?" (*Cahiers Simone Weil* 11, no. 3 [September 1988]), and A. Biron, "Simone Weil et le catharisme" (*Cahiers Simone Weil* 6, no. 4 [December 1983]), attempt, on the other hand, to show that Weil was ignorant of Gnostic doctrine and to point out basic features of her philosophy distinguishing her from the Gnostics.

ship with her future biographer Simone Pétrement is well known, as is the fact that Pétrement made a close study of Gnostic philosophy, writing two monographs on the subject.[55]

In a draft of a letter to her brother, Weil wrote that "there is no trace of mysticism [that is, investigations of states of spiritual ecstasy] before the neo-Platonists and the Gnostics."[56] Pétrement does not know which Gnostic texts Weil might have read by this time and cannot recall ever having spoken to her about Gnosticism.[57] Yet she expresses surprise at some of the ideas found in *Gravity and Grace* and affirms that "it was probably at the beginning of 1939 that I brought her the collection of *Manichean Homilies* found in Fayum."[58] By the same token, she acknowledges, in many different passages in *A Separate God*, that certain of her ideas were suggested to her by Weil. This holds for the notion that the mysterious woman of chapter 12 of the Apocalypse represents the Holy Spirit;[59] it also applies to her reflections on the Docetic heresy, "the only heresy that Simone Weil was said to bear to see condemned."[60]

In Perrin's opinion, Weil was ignorant of all the Gnostics except Marcion:

> Her position was complicated and made more unyielding by her encounter with Marcion, a second-century Gnostic. . . . Motivated by his hatred for the Old Testament, this heretic imagined an absolute dualism, and eventually decided that an evil principle had inspired the whole of the Old Testament; he was successful enough to be able to found an anti-Church which found adherents in a number of different places. . . . Simone was deeply impressed by Marcion, as I learned only much later, when *Pensées sans ordre* was published.[61]

Marcion, who was born in Sinope, in Pontus, would appear to hold a place apart among the Gnostics. He alone took Paul and no one else as his authority (whereas Gnosticism generally proceeds from both Paul and John) and preferred the Gospel of Paul's disciple Luke, although he pruned it of a great many passages so as to rule out Judaicizing interpretations. Marcion was much more open and tolerant than Valentinus. In Weil too, one finds a distinction between a legalistic, vindictive God, the God of the Old Testament, and his anthithesis, the true God, Who is as "good" as He is "alien," "other," "unknown," and "hidden." This is the transcendent God of the Gospels, known to us only through Christ. However, there is in Weil no trace of the anti-cosmism found in Marcion, for whom the world appeared as *haec cellula creatoris*, this miniscule cell of the Creator's; for Weil, "the universe is beautiful, even including evil."[62] Nor does Weil share the Gnostics' hatred for the instability and inconstancy of time: even if "we are abandoned in time,"[63] even if "time carries us wither we do not wish to go,"[64] we must accept this alienation by obeying God.

In an essay entitled "Un nouveau 'front' religieux" [A new religious 'front'], published in *Israël et la foi chrétienne* [Israel and the Christian faith][65] an essay that, according to André Latreille, circulated in occupied France, Henri de Lubac denounces the "formidable pagan impulse" at work in the Hitlerites' persecutions of religion. Identifying their war of conquest as anti-Christian, de Lubac vented his wrath at the French tradition, distinct from the German. For these traditions, the whole tragedy of Christianity stemmed from the fact that the Christians had been unable to break with the Jewish Bible, as the Gnostics had long ago urged them to do:

> We reject, as at once silly and blasphemous, the contradiction some are trying to establish between a "Semitic Old Testament" and an "Aryan New Testament." We shall maintain the indissoluble bond between both our Testaments, always interpreting the Old, in the final analysis, in terms of the New, but also always basing the New on the Old. . . . In truth, our heritage includes all of that. All of that has become our flesh. We shall not suffer anyone to wrest it from us. And, should someone take anti-Semitism as his pretext for laying hands on it, we shall repeat the cry, so perfectly just, of the great Pius XI: "Spiritually we are Semites!"[66]

Arendt's Version of the Critique of the Notion of a Chosen People

Unlike Weil, Arendt seldom alludes to the Old Testament. In a passage in *The Human Condition*, she does, however, emphasize that in the Old Testament, as opposed to classical Antiquity, life was held sacred. Neither work nor death was considered evil, so that the patriarchs were not concerned with individual, earthly immortality or the immortality of the soul.[67] Somewhat further on, Arendt remarks that "the melancholy wisdom" of *Ecclesiastes*— " 'vanity of vanities; all is vanity . . . there is no new thing under the sun' " is strong evidence of a lack of faith in the world, "as a place fit for human appearance, for action and speech," the things capable of renewing the world.[68] Finally, Arendt notes that the concept of promising can be traced back through the Romans to its origins in "Abraham, the man from Ur, whose whole story, as the Bible tells it, shows such a passionate drive toward covenants that it is as though he departed from his country for no other reason than to try out the power of mutual promise in the wilderness of the world, until eventually God himself agreed to make a Covenant with him."[69] Yet Arendt too regards the "non-separation of religion and state in Israel"[70] as "disastrous," and is highly critical of the notion of a chosen people, even if her arguments, unlike Weil's, are not rooted in opposition to the Judaism of the Bible. Thus, on 13 May 1942, at a meeting of the Jewish Youth Group which she founded together with another member of *Aufbau*'s editorial committee, Joseph Meier, Arendt said that she detected, in the Jews' claim that they were the chosen people, a "secret aversion to normalcy . . . the privilege of being different." The baneful consequence of this was Jewish indifference to the fate of the world and the course of history—that is, worldlessness—an attitude which, in the nineteenth century, was enshrined in the theory of the "salt of the earth" and the figure of the "exception Jew." The same year, although she hailed the publication of Jacques Maritain's *Ransoming the Time*,[71] recommended it to the "pious and the unbelievers who have not yet sold their souls to the devil," and urged them to begin by reading the chapter on "My Neighbor," she warned "those among us who do not limit themselves to observing the 613 commandments and interdictions, and do not pray for the coming of the Messiah," against Maritain's ideas about the election of Israel, "which he identifies with the Jewish people as a whole." Far from putting the accent, as Weil does, on the death of Jesus, and reiterating the accusation that the Jews were a deicidal people, Arendt says that the fact that Jesus of Nazareth was a Jew could constitute "the symbol, both for us and for the Christian peoples, of our belonging to the world of Hellenic and Judeo-Christian culture." The only claim the Jews can—indeed, must—press is that of being "a people like all others," men among men, inasmuch as the sole law that should preside over human affairs is "the law of normalcy": "in the world we are living in, any exception is a monstrosity." Arendt reminds us that what is at stake for the Jewish people, the definition of "Jewishness" as a "political and national affiliation," is not a matter to be decided by rabbis alone, any more than it is a purely theological debate, as Paul Tillich and Jacques Maritain had understood it to be. Where Weil invokes a universal religion, Arendt speaks of the normalizing human condition; yet, for her, this does not signify assimilation or disavowal of one's community affiliation, but only a relinquishing of the idea of Jewish privilege.

In maintaining that Hitler simply turned the notion of "chosen race" back against the Jews, does Weil not deny, before the fact, the specificity of Auschwitz—that is, as Arendt remarks, the circumstance that for the first time in the history of the persecution of the Jews, they were not persecuted for their religion? Here is what Hans Jonas, an old friend of Arendt's, says on the subject, as if he were echoing her remarks:

> Here [at Auschwitz] there was neither faith nor infidelity, neither belief
> nor unbelief, neither ordeal nor witness, neither hope nor redemption,
> there was not even strength or weakness, heroism or cowardice, defiance

or submission. No; of all that, Auschwitz, which devoured even babies, knew nothing at all. . . . Those who died there did not die for love of their faith (as the Jehova's Witnesses still could), nor were they murdered for their faith or some freely chosen personal orientation. Their agony was preceded by the ultimate abjection or destitution.[72]

Similarly, in maintaining that Hitler did not fall from the sky, but had historical antecedents, does Weil—who unhesitatingly compares the German dictator to Caesar, or even Richelieu and Louis XIV[73]—not contest the unprecedented nature of totalitarianism, which Arendt, for her part, forcefully emphasizes? Arendt vigorously protests the assimilation of totalitarianism to any evil familiar from the past, although she does acknowledge that tyranny and despotism resemble it in certain ways: "but many other forms of government have denied freedom, albeit never so radically as the totalitarian regimes."[74] Or again: "despite the novelty of totalitarianism, they equate totalitarian domination with tyranny or one-party dictatorship."[75] The points of resemblance are the absence of hierarchy; the tendency to despoliation, terror, torture, and spying; and the tendency to consign opponents to oblivion, while concentrating power in the hands of a single individual, who exercises it in the name of a *Führerprinzip* and reduces everyone else to impotence. What, precisely, does Arendt mean by totalitarianism? She contents herself with remarking that the term "is not much more than about five years old"[76] and that it emerged "after the liquidation of the British Empire and the reception of India into the British Commonwealth." Earlier, people used the words "imperialism" or "racist imperialism" to designate aggressiveness in foreign policy.[77] Today the word totalitarianism serves "to denote lust for power, the will to dominate, terror, and a so-called monolithic state structure."[78] In other words, Arendt suggests that the term imposed itself after the downfall of imperialism.

However, while totalitarianism does not have "causes," its emergence was facilitated by certain "crystallizing" elements found in mass society, that is, by those strata of disorganized, neutral, and indifferent people without social ties who, whatever their position in society support totalitarian regimes. What, for Arendt, does the novelty or originality of totalitarianism consist of? To begin with, in the fact that it "constitute[s] a break with all our traditions" and "explode[s] our categories of political thought and standards for moral judgment";[79] secondly, in its reliance on violence and terror, directed not only against the regime's opponents, but, before long, against its partisans, so that it soon makes only innocent victims. But are these victims truly innocent for Weil and Stein? Did Stein, in particular, not exclaim, during

Kristallnacht, "this is the fulfillment of the curse that my people has called down upon itself"?

The reversal of values that comes about under totalitarianism culminates, for Arendt, in "loneliness," in which man is "abandoned to his own company," "mute," condemned to an absence of dialogue, to the "desert."[80] Above all, totalitarianism has revealed the existence of

> crimes which men can neither punish nor forgive. When the impossible was made possible it became the unpunishable, unforgivable absolute evil. . . . Just as the victims in the death factories or the holes of oblivion are no longer "human" in the eyes of their executioners, so this newest species of criminals is beyond the pale even of solidarity in human sinfulness.[81]

In her discussion of this "absolute" or "radical" crime, Arendt observes that it "has emerged in connection with a system in which all men have become equally superfluous."[82]

Weil sees nothing more in the concentration camps than an extension of Roman inhumanity—"the concentration camps are not a more murderous affront to human goodness than were the gladiatorial games and the sufferings inflicted on slaves."[83] As an example of the kind of torture practiced in the camps, she describes the act "consisting of moving a stone from B to A, then from A to B again, and so on during the whole day"—in other words, absurd, mindless labor.[84] Yet she is fully aware that people are tortured in the camps, for she also writes: "Let us suppose a man whose entire family has perished amidst tortures, and who himself was long exposed to torture in a concentration camp . . . if [he] ever believed in God's mercy, [he] either believe[s] in it no longer, or else conceive[s] it in an entirely different fashion from that in which [he] did before."[85] Arendt, for her part, distinguishes three types of concentration camps "corresponding to the three basic Western conceptions of life after death: Hades, Purgatory, and Hell." In "Hades," individuals—in the non-totalitarian countries, refugees, stateless persons, and the asocial—are simply put "out of the way"; "Purgatory is represented by the Soviet Union's labor camps"; "Hell" is embodied by the Nazi camps. . . ."[86] The one thing all three have in common is that "the human masses sealed off in them are treated as if they no longer existed."

Arendt was often criticized for making this "amalgam" between Auschwitz and the Gulag, notably by Raymond Aron in his 1954 review of *Le Système totalitaire* [a separately published French translation of roughly one-third of *The Origins of Totalitarianism*] for the journal *Critique*. Aron criticized her for her method, "which tends to fasten on the essential." But that was precisely her aim: in her view, understanding what an unprecedented regime *is* means grasping not its causes or origins, as the title of her book misled people into thinking, but its essence. Aron further criticized Arendt for contradicting herself by treating totalitarianism as a political regime, one whose originality he felt she exaggerated. Totalitarianism, she says, is not animated by a "principle," not even the principle of fear, from which one may at least try to escape. In this it differs from other regimes, monarchical, republican, or tyrannical—all of which are ruled by a clear-cut "principle," i.e., honor, virtue, and fear, respectively. But if this is so, Aron maintains, then totalitarianism is not a regime. In *Was ist Politik?* [What is politics?], Arendt discusses the meaning of the word "principle" at length; she carefully distinguishes it from "significance," "purpose," and "goal."

> In addition to these three elements, constitutive of every political act—the purpose it seeks to realize, the goal it pursues and orients itself toward, and the significance it reveals as it unfolds—there is a fourth. Although it never provides the immediate occasion for any political act, this fourth element is nonetheless what sets it in motion. I propose to call it the "principle" of action, following Montesquieu, who was the first to single out this principle in his discussion of the different types of states in *The Spirit of the Laws.*[87]

Arendt observes that, in our times, political activity is characterized by opportunism, that is, by the absence of all principle.* Aron asks whether a regime which has no principle is still a regime:

> *Qua* regime, it exists only in the author's imagination. In other words, Mrs. Arendt transforms certain aspects of the Hitlerite and Stalinist phenomena into a regime or political essence; she isolates and probably exaggerates the originality of Russian or German totalitarianism. Taking this real originality for the equivalent of a basic regime leads her to consider our time as a negation of traditional philosophies. She thus drifts insensibly into a contradiction which consists in defining a functioning regime by an essence which implies, as it were, the impossibility of its functioning.[88]

It should, however, be recalled that Arendt was not the first to compare the two one-party states represented by Nazi Germany and the USSR. In

---

*"Political action [today] clings opportunistically to the surface of daily events, with the result that they carry it off in every imaginable direction; thus what is praised today is always in contradiction with what occurred yesterday." (Arendt, *Was ist Politik?* p. 129).

1935, Waldemar Gurian,[89] a friend of Arendt's to whom she has devoted a moving essay, addressed the question of their similarities in *The Future of Bolshevism*.[90] On 28 November 1936, in a lecture entitled "The Era of Tyrannies,"[91] Elie Halévy also compared communism, fascism, and National Socialism. Admittedly, none of these writers uses the term "totalitarianism," as Arendt does. She was not, however, the first to do so:[92] the adjective "totalitarian" was gaining ever wider currency throughout 1920s Europe, particularly Italy, where it was promoted by the Fascists. Goebbels himself uses it, if Hitler does not; and, as we have seen, Ernst Jünger considered *total* and *Totalität* appropriate terms to describe the mobilizations for the first World War. François Furet nevertheless acknowledges the audacity of Arendt's conception; she was able to go beyond the "purely negative idea of anti-fascism" and define, through her use of the new word totalitarianism, a type of regime that was indeed unprecedented, one in which society was totally subjugated by a Party-State that ensured its domination by means of ideology and the terror exercised by a despotic leader.

Lastly, Raymond Aron upbraids Arendt for failing to ask how long totalitarianism would endure. This was, he felt, the more important question: "Is it a temporary, pathological phenomenon that accompanies certain transformations? Or is it, despite its intrinsic absurdity, capable of enduring as a kind of permanent dehumanization of human societies?"[93] Aron prudently refrained from trying to settle the question, although he argued that "we would be mistaken to treat the fact of human unreason as something definitively acquired." Furet is fairer to Arendt. The central idea behind the comparison developed in *Le Système totalitaire*—a book he calls "disjointed," "important, and yet sloppily written," like Gurian's—is, he emphasizes, that "the age of the concentration camps is not over."[94] Since the collapse of the Communist regimes and the consequent opening of their archives, we have, indeed, observed a new interest in comparison of the two systems. Ernst Nolte initiated this new trend with his provocative thesis to the effect that the Nazis' "racial genocide" was a reaction to the "class genocide" perpetrated earlier by the Bolsheviks.[95]

1941

January: Field Marshal Rommel goes to the aid of the Italians in Libya.

February: first major public reaction to the arrests of Jews in Amsterdam.

Following a set of decrees issued by Education Minister Jacques Chevalier, who intends to put God back into the public schools, *Esprit* launches a comprehensive inquiry into the question of "God in the Schools," sparking the ire of the French episcopate.

10 February: Darlan replaces Laval in Pétain's immediate entourage, becoming the Marshal's heir apparent.

29 March: Xavier Vallat becomes the new Commissioner-General for the Jewish Question.

30 March: Hitler declares, in a long speech: "The Communists have never been and never will be our friends. The fight which is about to begin is a war of extermination. If Germany does not embark upon it in this spirit, she may well defeat the enemy, but thirty years from now he will once again rise up and confront her."[1]

April: the Wehrmacht invades Yugoslavia and Greece.

14 May: Three thousand four hundred Jews, most of them Polish, are taken prisoner in a big round-up.

The Nazi propaganda film *The Jew Süß*, screened at the Scala movie theater in Lyons, touches off student protest and an article in *Temps nouveau* of 9 May. As a result, the paper is suspended for four months. A joke makes the rounds in Lyons: "*Temps nouveau* Süß-pended."[2] In June, *Esprit* too protests against projection of the film, which had been imposed by the Germans.

2 June: a revised Statute on the Jews promulgated by the Vichy regime stipulates that the only valid proof that one is not of the Jewish faith is a baptismal certificate dated prior to 25 June 1940. An exception is made for Jewish families which count three generations of war veterans (1870, 1914, 1939) and for Sephardic Jews. Jewish businesses come under temporary Aryan administration. A *numerus clausus* restricts admission of Jews to universities and the liberal professions not already closed to them. The Theological Faculty in Lyons stands alone in denouncing the Statute of 17 June.

22 June: Operation Barbarossa begins with the German assault on Russia.

July: *Esprit* publishes "Supplément aux *Mémoires d'un âne*" [Supplement to *Memoirs of an Ass*]. Written in the style of the Countess de Ségur, it rakes those collaborating with the Germans over the coals.

10 July: Pierre Boutang attacks *Esprit* in *Action française*.

Vichy orders Pierre Dunoyer de Segonzac to break with Mounier and Father de Naurois.

24 July: *La Gerbe* attacks the personalist ideology that dominates the School of National Administration at Uriage.

Drieu la Rochelle writes, in the August issue of *La Nouvelle Revue française*: "Four million foreigners in France, including a million Jews, gave me the occupation blues long before you [the Germans]."[3]

August: The authorities ban *Esprit*.

The first issue of *Défense de la France* appears. A majority of Frenchmen still do not know who Charles de Gaulle is. Left-wing Resistance fighters, with their antimiliatrist positions, do not trust him because he is a general; those on the right have misgivings about his individualism: "De Gaulle was regarded as ambitious and unstable. It was a mistake to mix politics with military matters."[4] Many feel that the Resistance should remain a strictly French affair: "neither Germans, nor Russians, nor Englishmen."[5] The French collapse, they believe, should be interpreted more in moral than in military or political terms—the Germans are barbarians, while Nazism is the absolute enemy, the enemy to be destroyed. These people appeal to Bergson and Péguy as their moral authorities.

9–12 August: the Atlantic conference.

12 August: at the Grand Casino in Vichy, Pétain announces new measures: the obligation to take an oath of allegiance is extended from the army to the judiciary and all civil servants. The insignia of the French battle axe [symbol of Vichy France] is created.

20 August: some 3,500 Jews are rounded up. The camp at Drancy opens. The revised Statute on the Jews goes into effect in North Africa. Xavier Vallat advocates stamping the letter "J" on Jews' national identity cards. The Secretary-General for the National Police in the Interior Ministry, René

Bousquet, is opposed to the idea but would like to see music by the composers Darius Milhaud and Jacques Ibert banned from the airwaves.

September: the Germans demand that a census of Jews be conducted in the Occupied Zone.

Monsignor Cholet comments: "We have no right to criticize the Leader himself or his orders. Subordinates are to obey without question or enquiry. . . . In the name of our religious conscience we will be the most united and the most disciplined of citizens."[6] Cardinal Gerlier is more hesitant. On the one hand, he makes no secret of his deep personal admiration for Pétain, who, he feels, embodies the moral "restoration" of France; he openly endorses the slogans of the National Revolution; and he shows sympathy for Franco's regime. On the other hand, he abhors Nazi ideology. Yet he limits himself to denouncing the inhuman conditions at the camp in Gurs—where internees are starving to death—and demanding that the Statute on the Jews be applied with "justice and charity." It is René Gillouin, a traditionalist Protestant and friend of Marshal Pétain's, who goes furthest in his denunciation of Vichy's treatment of the Jews: while admitting that he "professed a state antisemitism," he compares the persecutions of the day to the Repeal of the Edict of Nantes, which, he tells Pétain, looks like a "picnic beside your Jewish laws, *Monsieur le Maréchal.*" Although Archbishop Saliège of Toulouse, hostile to the anti-Jewish measures from the outset, is an exception to the rule, resistance within the Church comes mainly from the lower clergy and laypeople, as is attested by the first issue of *Témoignage chrétien*, which appears in November. Entitled "France, prends garde de perdre ton âme!" [France, beware of losing your soul!], it bears the signature of Gaston Fessard.

For the first time, gas is used to put someone to death at Auschwitz.

Leningrad comes under siege.

October: the first issue of *Combat* appears. Henri Frenay, initiator of the Mouvement de libération nationale, is its editor-in-chief; he had settled in Lyons in early 1941. *Combat* is followed by *Franc-Tireur*.

7 December: Pearl Harbor: Japan demolishes the American Pacific fleet. At Roosevelt's behest, the United States declares war on the Axis Powers. The Japanese move into Malaysia and Thailand.

December: the Germans stand at the gates of Moscow.

9 December: a Vichy communiqué authorizes the internment of all foreign Jews who have entered France after 1 January 1936.

12 December: creation of the Service d'ordre légionnaire, a prototype of the Milice.

24 December: Paul Claudel, who had supported Pétain in 1940, writes to the Grand Rabbi of France to tell him of "the disgust, horror, and indigna-

tion felt by all good Frenchmen, particularly Catholics, who are witness to the injustice, despoilment, and manifold forms of ill-treatment [their] Jewish compatriots are currently being subjected to."[7] The text of the letter is communicated to the inmates of the camp at Drancy in 1942. Xavier Vallat demands that the Secretary-General for the National Police bring his authority to bear to prevent further utilization of the "audacious opinions on the government's actions that personalities like M. Paul Claudel see fit to express." A police investigation and search are carried out at the château in Brangues before the case is finally closed.

The Carmelites are expelled from Luxemburg.

The Nazis put the last touches on the Final Solution of the Jewish question. The mass slaughter begins.

The German Reich includes, beyond the borders of Germany as defined by the Versailles Treaty, Austria, the Sudetenland, western Poland, Luxemburg, Alsace-Lorraine, Eupen and Malmedy, part of Slovenia, and Bialysok, all of which are Germanized and Nazified. The Reich has satellite states as well: Slovakia, Romania, and Croatia, ruled by fascist regimes.

Italy, in its turn, has annexed a few mountain valleys in the French Alps, part of Menton, part of Eipeiros and Thessaly, the Dalmatian islands and Dalmatian coast, Croatia, Montenegro, Albania, and Libya. It has imposed its language, laws, currency, and courts in all these areas.

Spain is an ideological ally of the Greater German Reich.

A campaign gets under way to hire "volunteers" to work in Germany. "Germany has shed its blood to protect you from Bolshevism; your duty is to lend your arms to help Germany build a new Europe." The campaign is accompanied by blackmail: one prisoner of war is released for every three Frenchmen who go to work for the Germans.[8]

Many-Colored Stars

Concentration camps were set up as soon as the Nazis came to power. They were originally intended for the "re-education" of Germans hostile to Nazism, for communists, Social Democrats, Christian Democrats, and conscientious objectors. Thus camps were successively opened at Dachau (in 1934, in Bavaria), Buchenwald (in 1937, near Weimar), Mauthausen (in 1938, in Austria). Later foreigners of all nationalities were also transferred to these camps. In 1941, Heydrich, head of the security police, classified the camps in four categories: Category I was for deportees, Category II for old people or those whose poor health made it unlikely that they would ever be fit for work, Category III for prisoners representing a danger for the Reich, and Category IV for those slated to receive the harshest treatment. In addition to the striped pajamas that all inmates had to wear, common criminals were to wear a green triangle, political prisoners a red one, homosexuals a pink one, asocial elements a black one, and conscientious objectors a purple one; resistance fighters had, in addition, the dubious privilege of displaying the letters "NN" (*Nacht und Nebel* [night and fog]) on their uniforms. The apex of all these triangles pointed downward. If a deportee was Jewish, a second, yellow triangle, pointing upward, was drawn under the first; the two triangles thus formed a star of David.

"Ave Crux, Spes Unica!"

The Stein sisters, whom the Prioress of the Carmel in Echt was trying to smuggle into Switzerland, were repeatedly summoned by the Gestapo for questioning. Whenever Edith walked into the Gestapo office, she would greet the dumbfounded officers with a *"Gelobt sei Jesus Christ!"* She and her sister were required to wear the yellow star. Who had informed on them? "I am satisfied with everything," Stein writes. "A *scientia crucis* [knowledge of the Cross] can be gained only when one comes to feel the cross radically. I have been convinced of that from the first moment and have said, *Ave Crux, spes unica* [Hail, Cross, our only hope]."[9] *Amor fati.*

Early in 1941, Sister Benedicta was dispensed from all her chores so that she might finish her last work—which, moreover, she was not to finish—in time to commemorate the quadracentennial of the birth of St. John of the Cross. This text, which she had outlined in 1931, was called *The Science of the Cross.*

To Xavier Vallat

Simone Weil met a number of Dominicans, among them Father Perrin, to whom she was introduced by Hélène Honnorat, a history professor who faithfully attended services at the university chapel. Her friendship with Honnorat was strengthened by the fact that the two women's brothers were also friends. Weil expressed a desire to become a servant on a farm. Perrin wrote her on 3 June 1941, "your friend has perhaps told you of my love for Israel, and its present misfortunes can only increase this desire to serve it."[10] Perrin believed he would be helping a potential victim of Nazism. Haunted by the problems of faith, baptism, and salvation outside the Church, Weil told him, at the very outset of their relationship, of her spiritual opposition to the Old Testament. "I don't think I had ever encountered such a lack of understanding. I don't believe her position on the matter ever changed,"

Perrin comments.[11] Be that as it may, he put her in contact with his friend Gustave Thibon, who owned a farm in Saint-Marcel d'Ardèche; Perrin was "certain that their political disagreements would not matter, given all they had in common."[12] Simone offered her services to Thibon out of a desire to experience the life of the peasants firsthand. She was working to the point of exhaustion, for she had observed that "people's intellectual acuity inevitably diminished" as they grew older. Yet this was an intensely productive period in her life. "Our first contacts were rather hard," Thibon confesses;

> we were far from having the same tastes in art or the same opinions in philosophy and politics. . . . Without mixing directly in political action, I recognized the legitimacy of the Vichy Government, whereas Simone Weil was already a whole-hearted "résistante." . . . Simone Weil . . . never showed the slightest intolerance towards me and did not hold my preferences against me. I have since learned that later on, in America, she defended the poor "Vichyists" against the final and unqualified anathema fulminated by certain emigrants.[13]

Perrin too, recalling her consternation when Paris was declared an open city, describes Simone as having been "among the earliest *résistants*."[14]

Shortly after arriving in Marseille, Weil met Jean Ballard, the editor-in-chief of *Cahiers du Sud*, as well as Lanza del Vasto, René Daumal, and an important figure in the "Combat" Résistance network, Gaston Berger. She published her first essay, "The *Iliad* or the Poem of Might," in the December 1940–January 1941 issue of *Cahiers du Sud*, signing it with the pseudonym Emile Novis, an anagram of her name. She also published two essays on the language of Oc: "L'agonie d'une civilisation à travers un poème épique" [The death agony of a civilisation as reflected in an epic poem] and "The Romanesque Renaissance." Jean Ballard put her in touch with Déodat Roché, the "Cathar bishop," to whom she would later write a long letter.[15] Like Joë Bousquet, she defended the thesis that the Romanesque civilization of the tenth and eleventh centuries had constituted the real renaissance of the Greek spirit; she contrasted it with "the other, false Renaissance" of the sixteenth century. In a letter to Jean Ballard, Bousquet says that her essay is an "arrow which soars higher than the clouds . . . we can never do enough to call people's attention to this text."[16] Through Jean Tortel, whom Simone met in the fall of 1940, she was put in touch with the Résistance network "Témoignage chrétien." Pierre Vidal-Naquet, then a lycée student in Marseilles old ladies would point to, saying "there's the fellow who doesn't like the Maréchal," was charged by his teacher Léon Augé with the task of taking Simone bundles of the *Cahiers du Témoignage chrétien.*

Weil distributed clandestine literature for four months, not only in Marseilles and the Bouches-du-Rhône region but also in the Var region and in the Upper and Lower Alps. She was helped by a young protégée of Perrin's, Marie-Louise Blum, née David; known as Malou in the Résistance, this young woman from a conservative, Catholic, Pétainist family was responsible for *Témoignage chrétien* in Marseilles and the surrounding areas from December 1941 to 1943. Weil distributed three hundred copies of the first three issues of the journal; she was frequently apprehended by the police. Credit for the first, November 1941 issue, entitled "France, beware of losing your soul," went to Father Gaston Fessard. As a pretext for denouncing Nazism, the paper seized on the fact that, during a lecture which Baldur von Schirach, the leader of the Hitler Youth, had given at the invitation of the Cercle de la Rive gauche, the *Horst Wessel Lied* was sung. The second issue of *Témoignage chrétien*, entitled "Notre Combat" [Our struggle], was put under the direction of Father Pierre Chaillet, the journal's founder. Chaillet insisted that his movement maintain total independence from both the Free French forces and all political parties: "we are not a Résistance movement," he declared. Finally, before sailing for New York, Weil found the time to help distribute the third issue, "Les racistes peints par eux-mêmes" [The racists as portrayed by themselves], which had been produced by Fathers Chaillet, Ganne and de Lubac. Looking back on this period, Blum-David writes:[17]

> Our mission was to ensure, to the best of our ability, that each issue would (given the high risk involved in producing the paper) reach at least five persons, and, if possible, ten. Copies had, then, to be put into absolutely reliable hands, which meant that we had to spend a great deal of time finding the right people for the job and motivating them to do it. . . . Without the least hesitation, [Weil] took part in the Résistance, distributed the nearly 300 copies of each issue of *Cahiers du Témoignage chrétien* that I left with her, and also had me forge the identity papers needed by one or another individual, and, of course, Jews. I affirm this categorically.[18]

Simone was aware of the fascination she exercised over Malou[19] ("I was fascinated by her cultivation, her intelligence, her compelling personality") and made a point of explaining her views on the notion of disobedience in the young woman's presence:

> Disobeying the law is a very serious business. . . . One has to think it over a long time before taking the step, after assuring oneself that one has no

other recourse, and that the cause which requires us to break the law is truly that of justice and truth. There can be no democracy if a country's citizens do not obey its laws. We are encouraging young people to break into city halls to steal stamps and seals, we are inciting young men to assume false identities or go into hiding to avoid the S[ervice du] T[ravail] O[bligatoire]. This is a necessary evil, but we should never forget that it is an evil.[20]

Much later, in 1970, Arendt too considered the problems of conscience with which the law sometimes confronts citizens. She cited Socrates and Thoreau as emblematic figures. Her concern was "to find a recognized niche for civil disobedience in our institutions of government" when we are confronted with an " 'illegal and immoral war,' " undue expansion of the executive branch of government, or "chronic deception."[21]

Malou further states that Weil was fully cognizant of the persecutions the Jews were suffering. Weil, she says, gave her two documents on Nazism to alert her to the risks they were taking. "One was a story about the friendship between a Jew and a Nazi; it ended in tragedy. The other described how Jewish intellectuals, particularly lawyers, were treated in the concentration camps in Germany, and how the Nazis tried to humiliate them."[22]

Gustave Thibon once told Weil that he could not understand why, given her publicly advertised positions, she deprived herself of food, scrupulously limiting herself to official rations. He took this as a sign of loyalty to a government she deemed illegitimate. Weil retorted: "We owe obedience to the powers that be in all things which do not compromise our conscience; if I were to carry out the ideological and political recommendations of Vichy, I should soil my soul, but in observing its rules concerning rationing, I only risk, at the very most, dying of hunger, and that is not a sin."[23] It was during this visit to Thibon that she learned a chanted Greek version of the Lord's Prayer. She had made up her mind to study the Lord's Prayer very closely; she was apparently unaware, Perrin comments, that "most of the demands in the Pater noster are taken, word for word, from the Jewish daily prayer . . . 'Father' is the translation of the Aramaic word 'Abba'—our Papa; an Eastern liturgy, the Syriac, seems to have preserved the Aramaic text exactly as it came from Christ's lips."[24] Jacques Maritain, for his part, read a poem called "Deus Excelsus Terribilis" (later published by Raïssa) as part of a radio message broadcast in New York on 12 January 1944: "If we cry abba! Father! / You do not accept our cry / It returns to us like an arrow / Which has struck the impenetrable target. . . ."[25]

On October 18, as the grape harvest was coming to an end, Weil wrote

Xavier Vallat,* Commissioner-General for Jewish Affairs, to say that she had yet to receive a response to her request for reinstatement in the French public school system. Like her letter to Carcopino, this one too is a veritable anthology piece. Weil notes that, although she does not always understand what the word Jew means, she supposes that the fact that the Ministry of Education has not responded to her demand for reinstatement has to do with "the presumption of Jewish origin that attaches to [her] name." "It is true," she adds, ironically, "that [it has] also abstained from paying me the indemnity provided for in such cases by the statute concerning Jews, which gives me a lively feeling of satisfaction at having no part in the country's financial difficulties." She continues in the same tone, once again recalling that she has no ties to Jewish tradition and does not feel drawn by it; nevertheless, since "the government has proclaimed its desire that Jews should go into production, and preferably go to work on the land," she has obeyed to the best of her ability, because she is

> at this moment working in a grape harvest; I have cut grapes eight hours a day every day for four weeks, in the employ of a grape-grower in the Gard region. My employer has honored me by saying that I hold up my end of the work. . . . He does not know, it is true, that simply because of my name I have an original defect that it would be inhuman for me to transmit to children. . . . I consider the statute concerning the Jews in a general way as being unjust and absurd, for how can one believe that a university graduate in mathematics could harm children who study geometry by the mere fact that three of his grandparents attended a synagogue?[26]

The letter closes with expressions of gratitude to the government, which has provided Weil an occasion to withdraw from the category of intellectual and go back to the land! Injustice, absurdity: is that all she damns the Vichy regime for? While it is true that she denounces the Statute on the Jews, she

---

*Michelle Vaudoyer, a niece of Daniel Halévy's and Jean-Louis Vaudoyer's—Vaudoyer was manager of the *Théâtre français* and a member of the French Academy—has written a short personal recollection, "Quand je déjeunais avec Simone Weil" [When I had lunch with Simone Weil], in which she says that she met Weil at least twice, at political luncheons organized at Xavier Vallat's home in 1934 and 1938: "She listened to what was said about politics and social questions with an almost comic avidity. . . . She proved very far-sighted when, in 1941, she wrote to Vallat: 'You would do better to busy yourself with your vines than with politics!' How marvellously sharp her eye was! She had a luminous mind: in her (unpublished) letters to Vallat, it seems she had accurately predicted the political events of the post-war period. Had she also had a premonition that Vallat would be condemned to ten years in prison for collaborating with the enemy? As might be expected, he manifested extraordinary reserve on this subject in later years . . ." ("Quand je déjeunais avec Simone Weil," *Cahiers Simone Weil* 4, no. 3 [September 1981], pp. 183–184).

does so less to express her solidarity with the Jews than to demonstrate, yet again, how much separates her from them.

When, after reaching the United States, Simone's brother André urged his family to join him, Simone wrote back: "[The Americans'] hospitality is a purely philanthropic matter, and it is repugnant to me to be the object of philanthropy. . . . It is more flattering, taking it all in all, to be the object of persecution." She would only consent to leave for America if she could be "certain that that would permit [her] to realize [her] project" to organize a group of front-line nurses.[27] In fact, as she confides in a dedication of the copy of her translation of *Antigone* that she presented to the Ballards' grand-daughter Françoise, she felt "at home in Marseilles, at a time when so many people thought they were in exile."[28]

"I can only say with Jefferson: as for the rest, *Ceterum censeo*"*

"It's your business!"

Hannah Arendt and her husband Heinrich Blücher arrived in the United States in May 1941, one year before Weil. Hannah had to learn to write in another language—"and that is *the* problem of emigration," she would say to Jaspers (English was her third language). She defined herself as "a kind of free-lance writer, something between a historian and a political journalist."[29] She was hired on as an editorialist by the newspaper *Aufbau*, which published for German-speaking refugees. Manfred George, *Aufbau*'s editor-in-chief, had particularly appreciated the polemical tone of her "Open Letter to Jules Romains," published in the columns of his paper on 24 October 1941.[30] Romains, who had been taken sharply to task in *Aufbau* on 7 February, had re-acted by rattling off a list of his illustrious antifascist deeds, recalling that he had helped Jewish refugees by getting them visas or securing their release from French concentration camps. His plea in his own defense culminated in the words, "I hope the French Jews have not forgotten." Arendt's letter provided new proof of her familiarity with the French political scene: thus she pointed out that it was thanks to the book *Full Powers*, by Daladier's clos-est friend Jean Giraudoux, later Commissioner-General for Information in the Vichy government, that anti-Semitic remarks had become acceptable in

---

* These are the opening words of a speech by Cato the Elder (Arendt, letter of 19 February 1965, in *Arendt–Jaspers: Briefwechsel*, p. 619; Arendt, *Correspondence*, p. 583). Arendt used them as the title of an essay she published in *Aufbau* ("Ceterum Censeo," *Aufbau*, 24 December 1941, p. 2).

French parlor-room conversation for the first time since the Dreyfus Affair. She also vented her indignation over the cynicism of the notorious anti-Semite Sarraut, who had, with the help of the magic formula "released on condition that he join the French Foreign Legion," discovered a means of dispatching thousands of young Jewish men to the Sahara. Arendt's critique of Romains ran along the same lines as her critique of Jewish philanthropists: "benevolent gestures on the part of a protector wound more deeply than the enmity of declared anti-Semites." That is why she ends her open letter with a reminder of Clemenceau's attitude. Clemenceau had understood that, in political struggles, there are neither benefactors nor protectors but only friends and enemies: "one of the problems of those who struggle for justice is that they have ranged against them, along with the hate of the oppressors, the weakness and, all too often, the faint hearts of the oppressed."

But the first real essay that Arendt was to publish in *Aufbau* bears the title, "Die jüdische Armee—Der Beginn einer jüdischen Politik?" [The Jewish army—the beginnings of a Jewish politics?].[31] Here she returns to the question, raised in a lecture by Kurt Blumenfeld, as to whether or not it would be opportune for Jews to create an army. If they are to assume the heritage left by their dead, Arendt says in 1941, "the Jews have to leave the realm of utopia behind": they must take up arms against Hitler.

Responsible for the rubric "This means you!" in *Aufbau*, Arendt untiringly called for the creation of a Jewish army in Palestine. Only through combat could the Jewish people gain access to the world of politics. The defense of Palestine seemed to her to be a struggle for Jewish freedom; freedom was neither a "gift" nor a "reward for one's sufferings."[32] Only combat could give real content to the will to *live*, not merely to "survive at any price." A Jewish army is by no means utopian if all the Jews want one and volunteer for service; its success depends only to a very limited extent on Jewish dignitaries and diplomats. The interest of an army resides in the fact that it can give Jews the possibility of meeting attacks with armed force: "someone who is attacked as a Jew cannot defend himself as an Englishman or Frenchman, for, if he does, the whole world can only conclude that, simply, he is not defending himself."[33] The traditional refusal to take the Palestinian Jews into consideration must become a thing of the past, so that they too can "hoist the Jewish flag." Participating in the war is a prerequisite for preparing the peace, so true is it, says Arendt, citing Nahum Goldmann, that "someone who is not at war is not at peace either."[34] Arendt fears that abstaining from combat will deprive the Jews of the right to take part in the peace negotiations; she is afraid that "the people of the Book will be transformed into a people of paper" and that the United Nations will not be prepared to sit down at the same table "with the pariah among the peoples" or welcome it into its ranks.[35]

But who is to blame for this state of affairs, which Arendt calls "rootlessness"? She accuses, first and foremost, the Jewish theoreticians themselves, because they have led the Jews to believe that they are simply what antiSemites say they are—except when other theoreticians have led them to believe that, because anti-Semitism was "the superstructure of a necessary economic process," it would disappear as soon as the Jews had lost their privileges. Finally, says Arendt, the Jews have succumbed to the illusion that anti-Semitism was merely the natural aversion of one people for another, so that the only possible solution lay in flight. She has Herzl in mind here, but also, more generally, the Zionists, to the extent that, Chaim Weizmann not excepted, they are guilty of what Arendt calls "worldlessness." She concludes that a political response to anti-Semitism has yet to be found. In May 1942, observing that the Jewish army had been officially buried, and that it had been dubbed the "so-called Jewish army" at the extraordinary Congress of the World Zionist Organization, Arendt points the finger at still other culprits. Chamberlain, "by sacrificing remote Czechoslovakia," and the French, who "scoffed at the idea of dying for Danzig or Prague," have demonstrated what Realpolitik is:[36] a game of poker. Why do the Colonial Office and the English General Staff so obstinately ignore their potential allies in the Near East? Because those allies were Jews, Arendt answers, and because accepting their support would have been tantamount to fueling Nazi propaganda and admitting that Hitler was right. For Hitler quite "simply" argued that only two peoples, the Jews and the Germans, really had a stake in this war, for better or for worse: all the others had been dragged into it by their governments.[37] Only the Germans and the Jews were legitimately represented by their governments—with the one difference that the Jewish government was "occult." As all the other peoples except the Germans were ruled by the Jews, the Jews, because they did not want to fight, but merely contented themselves with manipulating other governments to achieve "world domination," bore the blame for all the suffering. The Jews in Palestine were ignored, then, so as not to make it seem that Hitler had been right. The second reason they were ignored, according to Arendt, was that they had taken it into their heads to live like Jews, that is, "like other peoples, as God had created them, without covering their nakedness with the fig leaf of any other nationality whatsoever." Hence they would not be satisfied to don the trenchcoats of this or that other nation, or consent to die a "universal death" for the British Empire "rather than a particular death for their country, their women and children, and the honor of their own people."[38]

The English attitude is fraught with consequences, because it condemns the Jews to live a hand-to-mouth existence, hoping and despairing at the same time, and operating, in any case, "in a world of appearances in which nothing corresponds to reality." That brand of politics may appear realistic in London, but "everywhere else, and, first of all, in Palestine, it looks like a way of committing suicide or destroying one's own reality."[39] Indeed, if the Jewish "crazies" had their own army, they would try to take a few thousand German soldiers prisoner, like brave little Betty[40] or the resistance fighters in the Warsaw ghetto (Arendt would later undertake to chart the stages marking "the day-to-day transformation of these Jewish rebels").[41] In short, they would strive to "transform the law of extermination and the law of flight by means of the law of combat,"[42] for they know that there is no "miracle" save the law of action. Indeed, they might eventually gain the immortality they had been denied and write their names in the "Book of Life," for, "when life is hunted and harried . . . when death begins to assert its horrible domination, precisely when life has become the supreme good, we can no longer aspire to immortality."[43] These Jewish fighters might also succeed in refuting the notion that there is a "supernaturally good" and a "supernaturally evil" people and demonstrate that all those endowed with the human form are "originally and unconditionally equal."[44] Finally, they might give the lie to everyone who continued to affirm that the Jews have always been the victims and objects of history. If they failed to, they risked being excluded without appeal, like all persecuted peoples, from human history.

1942

"**G**oebbels has explained, in the Nazi weekly *Das Reich*, that the extermination of the Jews of Europe is about to begin, together, perhaps, 'with that of the non-European Jews.' The murder of some five thousand Jews in Berlin, Vienna, and Prague will signal the start of the massacre, the first 'response' to the extraordinary fact that all the peoples of Europe, as well as those beyond its borders, are resolved to put an end to Nazi domination, whatever the cost."[1]

14 January: Darlan writes to Moysset: "I have the impression that Monsieur Xavier Vallat is acting a bit overzealously and that he is not following the orders 'not to bother the long-established French Jews.' "[2] Vallat is caught between the hesitations of the government and increasingly insistent German demands.

15 January: Mounier, who has been arrested and imprisoned, goes on a hunger strike. He is acquitted on 30 October at the end of the "Combat" trial for lack of conclusive proof that he participated in the operation initiated by Henri Frenay. Frenay is accused of membership in a movement "of foreign inspiration, since its acknowledged leader is de Gaulle, and everybody knows that former general de Gaulle is today in the pay of England."[3]

20 January: the Wannsee Conference takes place; it had originally been scheduled for 9 December 1941 but was postponed because of Japan's entry into the war and Germany's declaration of war on the United States.

February: Stefan Zweig commits suicide.

27 March: 1,112 Jews leave Compiègne, bound for Auschwitz. Nineteen return at the end of the war. The Dutch Jews reach Auschwitz in July, the

Belgian and Yugoslavian Jews in August, the Czech Jews in October, the Norwegian and German Jews in December.[4]

18 April: Darlan resigns. Laval, a political foe of Léon Blum's who was driven out of politics in 1940, joins the government again. He wants a peace treaty in due form with the Germans and proposes a new census to distinguish French from foreign Jews.

6 May: Vallat is removed from office, to be replaced by Darquier de Pellepoix, who, in 1935, left the Croix de Feu because he did not consider it sufficiently hard-line. Darquier de Pellepoix has also clashed with Action française, calling Léon Daudet and Charles Maurras Jews! In addition to the Anti-Jewish League, he has founded the National Club Against Wogs and the Association for the Defense of the Race. René Bousquet is named Secretary-General for the National Police.

25 May: Jacques Maritain writes to General de Gaulle: "can one imagine Joan of Arc troubling her head over exercising political power and making preparations to form a government?"[5] André Philip replies: "It seems to me that that was precisely the essence of her mission. Her voices told her to go have the king crowned at Reims, so that he could recover his lost sovereignty. We expect de Gaulle to show us the way to elections so that the French people can recover its lost freedoms."[6]

28 May: after the attempted assassination of Heydrich, three hundred Jews are arrested and stood before a firing squad in Berlin; their families are sent to concentration camps.

6 June: After long postponing the measure, the Vichy authorities require all Jews over six to wear the yellow star.

10 June: one thousand Jews are deported from Prague to Maidenek and Sobibor.

The ancient myth of Jewish ritual murder resurfaces. The gas chambers go into operation. "Even if I were not Jewish, but belonged to some other European people, my hair would stand on end if a single hair on the head of a single Jew were harmed," Hannah Arendt writes on 19 June 1942.[7] It is now dangerous to help Jews. The Socialist Party keeps silent. The Communist Party, hostile to Pétain and Vichy, does not organize massive mobilizations against the race laws.

The first issue of the *Cahiers OCM* (clandestine organ of the Organisation civile et militaire, a Résistance movement) is distributed. It is a special issue devoted to the "national minorities."

22 June: Pierre Laval declares: "I am hoping for a German victory, because, without Germany, Bolshevism would establish itself everywhere."

4 July: Bousquet announces that, at the last cabinet meeting, Marshal Pétain and the President of the Council of Ministers, Pierre Laval, agreed to

the deportation, "as a first step, of all stateless Jews from the Occupied and Unoccupied zones."[8]

6 July: Laval proposes that children under sixteen be included in the convoys of deportees sent from the Unoccupied to the Occupied zone.

16–17 July: On Laval's orders, the operation "Spring Wind" is launched: its objective is to round up 28,000 Jews. The victims are held in the "Vélodrome d'hiver." Some one hundred people commit suicide. The internees are sent on to camps in Pithiviers, Beaune-la-Rolande, and Drancy. In all, 13,000 people are arrested.

August and September: those interned in the camp at Les Milles are sent en masse to the East.

23 August: as a sign of protest, the Cardinals and Archbishops meet in Paris. They do not issue a joint declaration, but Cardinal Suhard goes in person to see Pétain. Monsignor Saliège writes a pastoral letter that is read out in all the churches of the Toulouse diocese and published in *Témoignage chrétien*, *Le Franc-tireur*, and *Combat*; it is also broadcast by the BBC. On 30 August, Monsignor Théas, the bishop of Montauban, publishes a pastoral letter of his own.

4 September: the Germans impose the Service du travail obligatoire, a system of forced labor that only applies to Frenchmen. The Jewish Question fades into the background.

8 September: in New York, Jacques Maritain protests on the radio against Vichy's complicity in the persecutions of the Jews: "a new disgrace has been inflicted upon our country: heinous measures have been taken against the Jews not only of the Occupied zone, but of the so-called "free zone" as well. Two hundred thousand foreign Jews have been taken into custody by the Germans in the Occupied zone. In the Unoccupied zone, the police are hunting down thirteen thousand more . . . the Pope has stepped in to ask for mercy . . . the French bishops have protested, Monsignor Saliège in Toulouse [among them] . . . Marshal Pétain is providing cover for Laval. . . . People of France, humiliated and abandoned, you alone, confronted with this disgrace and all the others countenanced by abject governments, can save France's soul by showing pity for the oppressed and expressing your wrath against the oppressors."[9] Maritain goes so far as to propose that, on Yom Kippur, Christians pray for the Jews and demand pardon for the persecutions that are being visited on them.[10]

15 September: In his *Journal*, Lucien Vidal-Naquet denounces "a few of the most representative infamies amongst the many we have committed. We have handed the Nazis political refugees who trusted us; we have just thrown the foreign Jews who had found asylum with us to the lions; we have created . . . a French regiment that fights under French colors but in German

uniforms! . . . We have ordered our troops in Syria and Madagascar to resist the English forces; we have refused to fight the enemy, reserving our heroism for our conflicts with our allies! Disgusting!"

23 September: Léon Blum's younger brother René, after being interned first in Drancy and then in Beaune-la-Rolande and Pithiviers, sets out for Auschwitz in convoy 36 along with another thousand or so Jews. Eichmann is advised by wire that the brother of the former president of the French Council of Ministers is arriving with the convoy.

2 October: Jean Moulin unifies the internal French Résistance movement, first in Southern and then in Northern France, then sets about organizing France's political future. Emmanuel d'Astier de la Vigerie (active in the Résistance group Libération Sud) and Henri Frenay (active in Combat) arrive in London. An agreement is reached between France combattante and the two movements operating in Southern France. Franc-tireur joins forces with them.[11]

Various bodies are created to represent the Résistance as a whole: a study commitee, a clandestine press agency, a solidarity committee, and a bureau charged with infiltrating fighters into France by land and by parachute. Gaullism is born. Although the General's political authority has not yet been accepted, Pétain's popularity is on the wane.

Laval returns to office and curbs Résistance activity in the French Armistice Army.

10 October: here is yet another extract from Lucien Vidal-Naquet's *Journal*: "I say that France's crime lies not in accepting the war, but in abandoning the fight and crawling abjectly at Hitler's feet. Agnostic that I am and shall remain, I declare my fervent faith in the slogan '*Liberté, égalité, fraternité*,' in which this country's soul has found expression for more than a century and a half. . . ."

29 October: Cardinals Suhard and Gerlier meet with Laval and Pétain. All four men then attend a military parade together. To defuse the protests of the French bishops, Laval holds out the prospect of state subsidies for Catholic schools.

November: Stalingrad becomes a crucial stake in the war. Rommel is defeated at El Alamein.

8 November: Operation Torch: the British and Americans land in North Africa. The joint operation is under the command of General Eisenhower. The Americans have kept General de Gaulle and the "so-called Free French" in the dark; they have opted to treat General Giraud as the leader of the French Résistance and raise his hopes of assuming the supreme command of all Allied troops in North Africa.

When the Algiers putsch occurs, Giraud is in Gibraltar for discussions

with Eisenhower. When he arrives in Algiers, the military refuses to acknowledge his authority. Darlan secures Pétain's official endorsement of his
commanding position. De Gaulle protests from London. The Résistance
follows suit. Darlan and Giraud continue to enforce the measures adopted
by the National Revolution.

9 November: Vidal-Naquet again:

> Yesterday morning, someone called us to say . . . that American troops had
> landed in North Africa. We make a rush for the wireless; we listen to Roo-
> sevelt's emotional appeal to the French people as well as the message ad-
> dressed to the peoples of North Africa by the general commanding the op-
> eration. News comes pouring in. Algiers is occupied. Algiers surrenders.
> American troops came ashore in massive numbers. General Giraud enjoins
> the army to do its duty. On the radio, General de Gaulle makes an impas-
> sioned speech that leaves us delirious with joy. Every one of us has tears in
> his eyes; all of us, children or adults, feel the solemnity of the moment, and
> understand that this is a turning point in the war, that the tide has now
> turned against the enemy. . . . resistance is never impossible. By resisting
> when resistance is called for, in the face of all hope, one saves one's honor,
> and, consequently, everything else into the bargain.[12]

November 1942 is also a turning point for Défense de la France, im-
planted in the Unoccupied zone by Suzanne Guyotat. The organization now
establishes relations with Combat and Témoignage chrétien.

The School of Administration at Uriage makes contact with Giraud and
also with the Organisation de résistance de l'armée, Défense de la France,
Economie et humanisme, and the Résistance fighters in the Vercors maquis.

11 November: the Germans retaliate by invading the Unoccupied zone.
Pétain protests for the sake of appearances. Marseilles, which has been a
place of transit for hundreds of thousands of refugees, is gradually transformed into a "hoop net; the Nazis can scoop whatever they want out of it."[13]
The invasion of the Unoccupied zone quashes the myth that Pétain is part
of the Résistance.

15 November: Darlan seizes power in Algiers. Pétain relieves him of his
command, replacing him with Laval.

27 November: the French fleet is scuttled in Toulon.

10 December: Hitler issues orders to deport all Jews and other enemies of
Germany from France.

11 December: the word "Jew" is stamped on national identity cards and
food ration cards. In a speech before civil service trainees at the School of
Administration in Uriage, Xavier Vallat declares: "Jews can be put up with in

homeopathic doses . . . that is, as long as they are diluted sufficiently for the indisputable qualities of their race to be stimulating rather than dangerous." In the same talk, he refers to the Jews as "worms that love gangrenous wounds."[14]

13 December: "This is a religious war," Laval repeats. "The German victory will save our civilization from sinking into the quagmire of communism."

19 December: The Führer criticizes Laval, who retorts: "What do you want me to do? Wherever I turn, I hear nothing but cries of 'string up Laval!' "

27 December: Laval signs a decree closing the School in Uriage. It is reorganized in spring 1943 in La Thébaïde, in the Vercors maquis.

"I Feel Like a Deserter"

Ethiopian Jews in New York

Despite her unwillingness to leave France, Simone Weil reluctantly set sail for America on 14 May 1942, together with her parents, who were alarmed by the persecution of the Jews. "The thought of having left France continues to lacerate me,"[15] she wrote. She felt like a "deserter." Refusing to take a first-class berth, she slept in the hold and tried to teach the children on board about *Antigone*. On 6 July, the Weils arrived in New York, moving into an apartment at 549 Riverside Drive, where they would live from mid-July to November 1942. From the moment she read an account of a Bastille Day demonstration that left two dead and several injured in Marseilles, Weil's one wish was to leave New York.

In New York, Weil finished her *Letter to a Priest*. Jean Wahl, in Marseilles, informed her that certain French refugees in the United States took her for a Vichy sympathizer. She denied it:

> Ever since the day when I decided, after a very painful inner struggle, that in spite of my pacifist inclinations it had become an overriding obligation in my eyes to work for Hitler's destruction, with or without any chance of success, ever since that day I have never swerved from my resolve; and that day was the one on which Hitler entered Prague. . . . My decision was tardy, perhaps. Indeed, I think so, and I bitterly reproach myself for it. But anyhow, since I adopted this position, I haven't budged. . . . What may have given rise to such rumors is the fact that I don't much like to hear perfectly comfortable people using words like coward and traitor about

people in France getting by as best they can in a terrible situation. There is only a small number of Frenchmen who almost certainly deserve such epithets. . . . There was a collective act of cowardice and betrayal, namely the armistice; the whole nation bears the responsibility, including Paul Reynaud, who ought never to have resigned. I myself was immediately appalled by the armistice, but in spite of that, I think that all the French, including myself, are as much to blame for it as Pétain. From what I saw at the time, the nation as a whole welcomed the armistice with relief. . . . On the other hand, I think that since then, Pétain has done just about as much as the general situation and his own physical and mental state allowed to limit the damage. The word traitor should only be used for those for whom one feels certain that they desire Germany's victory and are doing what they can to that end. As for the others, some of those who are prepared to work with Vichy or even with the Germans may have honorable motives that are justified by particular situations. And others may be constrained by pressures that they could only resist if they were heroes. Most of the people here, however, who set themselves up as judges have never had an opportunity to find out if they themselves are heroes. . . .[16]

In a work we have often cited, Pierre Vidal-Naquet examines the positions Jacques Maritain adopted in America, remarking that it was "easier to make oneself heard loud and clear in New York than in Lyons or Marseilles. However, Vichy France had no lack of supporters in the United States, which had not yet recalled its ambassador from France."[17]

In New York, Weil prayed every day at Corpus Christi, a Catholic church on 121st Street. On Sundays, she went to a Baptist church in Harlem. It was also in New York that, as we have seen, she first set foot in a synagogue—one for Ethiopian Jews! Hardly had she arrived in the city than she began making persistent requests to be sent on a mission to London. From July 1942 on, she begged Maurice Schumann and Jacques Soustelle, who were working in various Free French organizations, to call her to London and entrust her with a sabotage mission or the task of transmitting general instructions to the internal French Résistance movement; she pointed to her familiarity with the clandestine movements, especially *Cahiers du Témoignage chrétien*. On 27 July, she wrote to Jacques Maritain, whom she had met at a Free French reception on Bastille Day; she laid out her project to send nurses to the front lines, enclosing letters of recommendation from Father Jacob and Father Perrin, both of whom urged Maritain to back her plan. She also attempted to explain her "spiritual position" to Maritain, naming some of the obstacles that prevented her from receiving baptism. In his response of 4 August, Maritain told her that if she wished to present her project to the Free

French military authorities, she should contact Alexandre Koyré, who was about to leave for London. He also recommended that she arrange to meet Father Couturier and advised her to read St. Paul. In the meantime, she had approached Admiral Leahy, the U.S. ambassador to Vichy France, who informed her that her project had been taken under study.[18]

Schumann had spoken of Weil to André Philip, Commissioner-General of Labor and Domestic Affairs in the Free French National Committee. While she failed to convince him to support her project to dispatch nurses to the front lines, she did manage to obtain his authorization to set sail for London on 10 November aboard the *Vaalaren*. The ship docked in Liverpool on 26 November.

Theresienstadt

"Greetings from Those on Their Way to Poland"

In early 1942, the Prioress of the Carmel in Echt attempted to bring the Stein sisters across the Swiss border to the Carmel in Le Pâquier, near Fribourg. But their departure was delayed. In June, Edith wrote: "For months, I have been carrying, over my heart, a little piece of paper with these words of Christ's: 'But when they persecute you in this city, flee ye into another.' "[19] On 28 July, her brother Paul, his wife, and his daughter were sent to Theresienstadt, in Bohemia, where they were later put to death. Eichmann was responsible for the Theresienstadt *Altersghetto* [old people's ghetto], set aside in 1942 as a place of internment for "privileged" families. When it became overcrowded, as it soon did, these families were evacuated and sent on to Auschwitz. Theresienstadt was subsequently transformed into a model ghetto to which the Nazis would bring representatives of the Red Cross.

On 11 July, the Dutch Catholic bishops protested against the mass deportation of Jews, refusing to enforce a number of Nazi decrees excluding young Jewish converts to Catholicism from parochial schools and denying Jews access to public buildings. On 4 June, the bishops had sent the Reichskommissar a telegram which pointed out that these mass deportations violated God's commandment to show justice and mercy. Rome did not back this protest. The sole concession made to the bishops was a decision not to deport Christian Jews. Not satisfied with this exception to the general rule, the bishops had a pastoral letter read out in the Catholic churches. It ran as follows:

> All of us are living through a period of great distress. . . . But there are two sets of people whose distress is deeper and more poignant than that of oth-

ers . . . the Jews and . . . those who are deported to work abroad. Such great distress should be of the utmost concern to us all; and it is the purpose of this pastoral letter to bring it to your attention. To that end, we are making public the telegram of protest we sent to the occupying powers two weeks ago. When we survey the frightful misery that has for nearly three years been threatening the whole world with destruction, we cannot help thinking of today's Gospel lesson, which shows us Jesus weeping over Jerusalem's blindness and prophesying that God would judge the city. His tears and dire prophecies apply equally well to us today.

The Nazi reprisals were not long in coming. On 2 August, the authorities arrested two hundred forty-five Catholic converts who had found asylum in Dutch convents and monasteries. "Catholic full-Jews we must consider our worst enemies and for this reason we must see to it that, as soon as possible, they are deported to the East," declared a circular signed by the Reichskommissar. Those detained were transferred to the camp at Amerfort, and taken from there to Westerbork; this was the camp where Etty Hillesum,* who had arrived on 30 July as a "social worker for populations in transit," not as a deportee, wrote her *Letters from Westerbork*.[20] The first refugees were interned in this camp, which had been set up in 1939, in October of the same year. Between July 1942 and September 1944, 100,000 Dutch Jews passed through it "in transit" before being dispatched to Auschwitz, Sobibor, Theresienstadt, and Bergen-Belsen in the convoys that set out for the East every Tuesday. When the Stein sisters arrived in Westerbork, twelve hundred Catholic Jews, including ten or twelve nuns and priests, had been herded together there.

Has Edith Stein not written that "the abandonment of our wills, something which God demands of all of us and of which we are all capable—this abandonment is the measure of our holiness"?[21] She was prepared to die a saintly death:

> I joyfully accept the death that God has appointed for me, in perfect submission to his most holy will. May the Lord accept my life and death for the honor and glory of his name, for the needs of his holy Church . . . that the Lord may be received by his own and his Kingdom come in glory, for the deliverance of Germany and peace throughout the world, and, finally, for all my relatives living and dead and all whom God has given me: may none of them be lost.[22]

*On 7 September 1943, Etty Hillesum was deported to Auschwitz, where she perished in the gas chamber.

On 2 August, the Stein sisters' names appeared along with thirty-one others on a list drawn up for the security police in Maastricht: Edith and her sister Rosa were numbers 23 and 24 on the list. On 7 August, they were deported to Poland in a convoy of 987 internees. En route, on the platform of the railway station in Schifferstadt, Germany, Sister Benedicta spotted a former student of hers: "give my love to the sisters of Saint Magdalene—I am on my way to the East!" she cried out to the woman through the train door. She had just time enough to scrawl on a piece of paper, "Greetings from those on their way to Poland. Sister Teresa Benedicta."[23] On 9 August, Edith and Rosa died in the gas chamber, together with those in their convoy and 766 Jews from Drancy.

J. M. Oesterreicher remarks that "Edith Stein's life was not lost at Auschwitz, but rather completely fulfilled."

"No One Will Sing the Kaddish for Them"

"No one will chant the mass, no one will recite the kaddish. These victims will leave no written testament behind; they will scarcely leave a name,"[24] Hannah Arendt wrote on 19 June 1942 about these anonymous dead. Her remarks apply to Stein, whom Hannah Arendt probably learned about from Rolf Hochhuth's play *The Deputy*. Jaspers had brought the play to her attention in 1963. "There exists the strangely moving story of the German-Jewish nun, Edith Stein . . . who, in 1938,* still unmolested in her German convent, wrote a letter to Pius XI, asking him to issue an encyclical about the Jews. That she did not succeed is not surprising, but is it also so natural that she never received an answer?" Arendt writes in "The Deputy: Guilt by Silence?"[25] an essay on Hochhuth's play.

A Christian on St. Peter's Chair?

The Deputy, which questioned Pope Pius XII and the role played by the Catholic Church during the World War II persecutions of the Jews, created a stir when it was staged in Basel; Jaspers compared the reactions it touched off to the intrigues set in motion by the publication of Arendt's book *Eichmann in Jerusalem*. The play reveals incontrovertible facts, says Arendt in her review of it, even if the Vatican refuses to "open its archives for contemporary history." Like her own book about Eichmann, it is a "report" which

---

*Arendt is plainly in error here, for reasons that can be chalked up to Hochhuth's account. As we have seen, it was in 1933 that Stein sent a sealed letter to Pius XI after failing to gain an audience with him. The Pope's sole response was to send her and her family his blessings.

shows that the Pope was fully apprised of the Nazis' deportations and "re-settlement" of the Jews. Yet he preferred to dispatch nuncios throughout Nazi-occupied Europe to inform the heads of government in Catholic countries rather than instructing the bishops to tell their flocks what was happening.

Why did the Pope not raise his voice in protest when, after the Nazis occupied Rome, Jews, including Catholic Jews—that is, Jews converted to Catholicism—were rounded up? Why did he not mobilize four hundred million faithful Catholics? Would "an attitude of protest and condemnation . . . have been not only futile but harmful,"[26] as Cardinal Montini, the future Pope Paul VI, claimed? Arendt points out that "more than 40 per cent of the Reich's population was Catholic at the outbreak of the war," while "almost all Nazi-occupied countries as well as most of Germany's allies had Catholic majorities." As for the argument that it was necessary "for the Church to remain neutral in case of war," this "was the price the Church had to pay," says Arendt, "for the separation of Church and State," now that the old distinction between a "just and unjust war had become . . . inapplicable." But since, as we have seen, "the Pope had broken his neutrality twice . . . at the occasion of Russia's attack on Finland, and . . . when Germany violated the neutrality of Holland, Belgium and Luxemburg," why did the Vatican not also "protest against the massacres in the East, when, after all, not only Jews and gypsies but Poles and Polish priests were involved?" The guilt of " 'official Christianity in Germany' " has been established, she reminds us, by reputable Catholic historians like Gordon Zahn, Friedrich Heer, and Waldemar Gurian. Their studies show that the Vatican's guilt was even greater than had been assumed. In 1930, "the German episcopate had condemned racism, neo-Paganism, and the rest of Nazi ideology," but the Vatican newspaper *L'Osservatore Romano* considered it appropriate to "point out," as Waldemar Gurian notes, "that the condemnation of its religious and cultural program did not necesssarily imply refusal to co-operate politically." For the Holy See, the sworn enemy was not Nazism, but Bolshevism, as Pius XI reminded his readers in a 1937 encyclical which stated that "socialism [was] irreconcilable with the teachings of the Church."

"In July 1949, the Holy Office excommunicated all persons who were members of the Communist Party, including those who read Communist books or magazines"; it "renewed this decree in April 1959"! In the summer of 1933, the Vatican signed a Concordat with Hitler that was never abrogated, even if, as we have already seen, Pius XI had been planning to make an address on 11 February 1939 on the occasion of the tenth anniversary of the Lateran treaty and the Concordat between the Holy See and Italy. But the same Pius XI, who had entrusted Paul LaFarge with the project of writ-

ing an encyclical, also favored Hitler with a handshake. When asked to help
determine whether people were of Jewish origin, the Church extended
prompt and full co-operation. "The German shepherds followed their
flocks, they did not lead them," Arendt comments bitterly.[27] In 1935, the
Nuremberg race laws outlawed mixed marriages, in violation of certain
clauses of the Concordat, and the German clergy had to to deny the sacrament to certain Catholics. Moreover, these laws implictly contested the validity of Jewish conversions to Catholicism.

Arendt concludes her essay with these words:

> I can't help thinking that if there was any group of people during the years
> of the Final Solution who were more forsaken by all mankind than the
> Jews traveling to their death, it must have been these Catholic "non-
> Aryans" who had left Judaism and who now were singled out, as a group
> apart, by the highest dignitaries of the Church. We don't know what they
> thought on their way to the gas chambers—are there no survivors among
> them?—but it is difficult to gainsay Hochhuth's remark that they were
> "abandoned by everyone, abandoned even by the Deputy of Christ." So it
> was in Europe from 1941 to 1944.[28]

Hochhuth raises a further question: "had there been a better pope," would
the Vatican have kept silent? In *Men in Dark Times*, Arendt paints a portrait
of John XXIII,[29] whose sole ambition, she says, was "to be similar to the good
Jesus," although he knew "perfectly well" that this meant "being treated as a
madman." Mary McCarthy seems not to have liked this portrait; she criticized Arendt for not being "close enough to the churchman—stone and mar-
ble vs. wood." Arendt replied:

> I think it was precisely the churchman in him whom he discarded as
> Pope—and the consequences, as we now know, have been pretty serious.
> You cannot be a Christian and preserve the hierarchy, even if, as in Ron-
> calli's case, you have no heretical thoughts whatsoever. Without *nulla salus
> extra ecclesiam* [no salvation outside the Church], which he repudiated on
> excellent theological authority, the hierarchy can't be maintained.[30]

Appointed the Vatican's representative in Bulgaria in 1925, Monseigneur
Roncalli (the future Pope John XXIII) was subsequently transferred to Is-
tanbul before being named papal nuncio in Paris in 1944. He profited from
his stay in Turkey to forge contacts with Jewish organizations and prevented
the Turkish government from shipping some hundred Jewish children back

to Germany: "Could I not, should I not," he asked later, "have done more, have made a more decided effort and gone against the inclinations of my nature? Did the search for calm and peace, which I considered to be more in harmony with the Lord's spirit, not perhaps mask a certain unwillingness to take up the sword?"[31] It so happens that John XXIII read Hochhuth's play a few months before his death. When he was asked what could be done against it, he responded: "Do against it? What can you do against the truth?" John XXIII might have been Hochhuth's "better pope."

On 25 September 1942, Arendt published an essay in *Aufbau* which hailed "the sudden outburst of indignation on the part of the French people, so effectively seconded by the Catholic clergy, over Vichy's plans to carry out mass deportations of Jews."[32] In the people's anger, she saw the awakening of the conscience of the French nation, which, precisely "because it was born of the Revolution, had become the European nation par excellence." She believed that this new solidarity afforded the Jewish people, the people which had faced the fiercest persecution at Hitler's hands, a far better chance of achieving national emancipation than the grand liberal projects drawn up by various Jewish institutions in anticipation of a peace conference.

But the Vichy regime in France had its advocates in the upper echelons of the Church—so much so that, when the country was liberated, de Gaulle initiated a "purge of the episcopate" that he intended to pursue with the Vatican's approval. Jacques Maritain, a professor at the Institut Catholique in Paris on a guest lectureship at Princeton University when the war caught him by surprise, was to serve as the intermediary between de Gaulle and the Church. After France had once again taken its place in the international community, Maritain was charged with representing it at the Vatican; thus it was that his wife Raïssa, who had persuaded first one and then the other of her parents to receive baptism, found herself the wife of the French ambassador to the Vatican in 1945. On 12 July 1946, Jacques Maritain directed a personal note to the attention of Monsignor J.-B. Montini. The note acknowledged the efforts of Pius XII to protect the victims of Nazism; but it also requested "that a voice—a fatherly voice, the voice par excellence, that of Christ's Vicar—tell the world the truth, and bring the whole of this tragedy to light."[33]

De Gaulle's priority was to obtain the recall of Monsignor Valerio Valeri, the papal nuncio whom Pius XII intended to maintain in his post. André Latreille, an official in the Ministry of Education, was delegated to the Interior Ministry, headed by M. Tixier, for the purpose of carrying out this purge. On 26 July 1944, he received his instructions in an unsigned note which detailed the roles leading churchmen had played under Vichy. Their names had been entered on the lists, "A" and "A'." The aim was to make an example of a few individuals "at a very high level"; the possibility of summoning clergymen to appear before the special tribunals created to punish treason was evoked. Among the names on these lists was that of Cardinal Suhard, the archbishop of Paris. Suhard had received Marshal Pétain with all due solemnity at Notre Dame and had personally officiated at the funeral services for Philippe Henriot, the Vichy government minister assassinated on 27 June by Résistance fighters disguised as *miliciens* who had managed to gain entry to his apartments at the Ministry of Information. Cardinal Suchard was not allowed to participate in the *Magnificat* celebrated on 26 August 1944; Francis-Louis Closon and Segalat, both of them convinced Catholics and emissaries of the "provisional government," were charged with notifying him that he was not to set foot in the cathedral.* Among the clergymen affected by these measures were Monsignor Courbe, auxiliary bishop of Paris and secretary general of Action française; Monsignor Chappoulie, who represented the cardinals and archbishops at Vichy; and Archbishop Feltin de Bordeaux, who had not withdrawn authorization to publish newspapers favorable to the enemy from two priests in his diocese, Father Bergey, associated with *Soutanes de France*, and Canon Peuch, who published *La Liberté du Sud-Ouest* and *Voix française* in collaboration with Paul Lesourd. A second list, list B, contained the names of candidates for the cardinal's hat and bishop's miter: these were men who had greatly distinguished themselves in the struggle against the Vichy regime and had condemned the persecution of the Jews. At the head of the list were Monsignor Saliège of Toulouse (who, on 24 July 1942, declared, "the Jews are men, the Jews are women. One is not free to do anything one likes to them. . . . They are part of the human race. They are our brothers, like countless others. A Christian should not forget that"); Monsignor Théas de Montauban; Monsignor Bruno de Solages, the Rector of the Catholic faculties of Toulouse, who was then in prison; and Monsignor Chevrot, a priest who had taken over the parish of Saint François Xavier on behalf of the archbishopric of Paris. André Latreille, in his turn, sent a note to the Interior Minister in which he conceded that "if the bishops were under no obligation to engage in acts of resistance as such, one was nevertheless en-

---

*"Having frequently had occasion to see him and come to know his candor and his positions vis-à-vis the Germans—the Nazis—and having had ample opportunity to appreciate his courage, especially when the JOC [a Catholic organization for young workers] was attacked by the Gestapo, I was deeply pained by the affront he was thus made to bear. In my opinion, it was a profound mistake and a grave injustice," says Henri Bourdais, national vice-president of the JOC in Paris from 1941 to 1944 (Bourdais, *JOC*, p. 216).

titled to expect that they would remind people of Rome's condemnations of Nazism—particularly the memorable encyclical *Mit brennender Sorge* of March 1937—and repeat the warnings sounded by their fellow bishops in Belgium, Holland, Germany, or even certain voices in Rome."[34] However, Latreille expressed surprise that the only thing the Ministry saw fit to recall about Cardinal Gerlier of Lyons was his approval of Pétain's slogan, "Work, Family, Fatherland"—"these words are ours," the Cardinal had said—or his declaration, "France is Pétain, and Pétain, today, is France." The Ministry showed him no gratitude for his pastoral letter criticizing the treatment meted out to the Jews or for the courage he had shown in lodging protests with the *Wehrmacht* over the massacres of hostages or genuine resistance fighters. Again, Latreille found it regrettable that Monsignor Liénart, the cardinal bishop of Lille whose name figured on the list A', had not been "given due credit for his opposition to sending forced laborers to Germany with the *Service du travail obligatoire*." As for the protests of bishop Delay of Marseilles "against the treatment meted out to the Jews," they were simply not mentioned, even if it *was* true that Delay had celebrated a memorial mass for Philippe Henriot. Moreover, the deportation to Dachau of the "very pro-Vichy" bishop Piguet of Clermont was evoked in list A only by way of the euphemism "currently in prison." For Latreille, the behavior of a Girbaud in Nîmes or a Mesguen in Poitiers was more repugnant. About Monsignor Dutoit, archbishop of Arras, who had written a pastoral letter calling for voluntary collaboration, or Cardinal Baudrillart, Rector of the *Institut catholique* in Paris, who wrote in pro-Nazi papers like *Le Gerbe* and *Le Nouvelliste*, Latreille's text says nothing. "The more time went by, the less I was inclined to carry out a purge," Latreille confesses; yet he drew up a questionnaire that was sent to all the police chiefs in the Republic and used their responses to sketch a general picture of the situation on 24 February 1945. It showed, as he interpreted his findings, that "the clergy's attitude toward the German occupiers had been 'cold' and 'dignified,' a few individual lapses aside." Pétainism had made itself felt among the higher clergy more by way of "a kind of personal devotion than by calls to support the policies of the Vichy regime"; it was, however, true that the Church hierarchy had explicitly condemned the Resistance, contrary to the more circumspect attitude adopted by the lower clergy and the members of religious orders, especially after 1942.[35]

In the end, seven prelates were dismissed. A number of other clerics were promoted to the rank of cardinal: the archbishops of Toulouse, Rouen, and Rennes, Monsignors Saliège, Petit de Julleville, and Roques. In the meantime, Monsignor Roncalli had become the papal nuncio in Paris.

What Status for Jews in Post-War France?

Baptism, Again!

In London, Simone Weil was not assigned the dangerous mission she had hoped for—she would have like to be parachuted into France—but had to make do with a job as an editor in the civilian department of the Commission for activities concerning France. This department was directed by Francis-Louis Closon, known as "Vincent" in the Résistance. In a reminiscence,[36] Closon recalls how disconcerting his first meetings with Weil were; her talent for remaining an outsider made communicating with her very difficult. Closon soon resolved to leave her at liberty to write whatever she felt a need to—to "cough up whatever she had in her," as she herself puts it. Thus she was given the task of examining projects for the post-war reorganization of the country drawn up by the Résistance committees in the Unoccupied zone. On 2 December 1941, General de Gaulle had created four commissions "to seek solutions to the national and international problems that we will face after the war, whether economic, financial, social, legal, intellectual, or related to foreign policy matters."[37] Weil regretted having left Marseilles, now occupied by the Germans, who considered it the New Jerusalem on the Mediterranean. Convinced that "human intelligence, even in the case of the most intelligent people, is woefully inadequate to the problems of public life,"[38] she nevertheless set out her own ideas, notably within the framework of the Commission for State Reform, a body created by de Gaulle to draft a new Declaration of the Rights of Man. She proposed to replace the notion of law with that of justice and obligation. She was in search of something that would inspire the people of France. It seemed to her that restoring the dignity of labor by respiritualizing it, like rediscovering what patriotism really meant, were fundamental "needs of the soul"; she did not hesitate to say, as we have already noted, that "far from always preaching the exact opposite of its various battle-cries, we ought to adopt many of the ideas launched by the propaganda services of the National Revolution, but turn them into realities!"[39] The same went for the project of European unity: "The idea of Europe, of European unity, contributed a good deal towards the success of collaborationist propaganda in the early days. We cannot do too much to encourage, nourish such sentiments as these. It would be disastrous to create any opposition between them and patriotic sentiments."[40]

It was in the context of these activities that, in June 1942, Weil had occasion to comment on a project entitled "Basis for a Statute Regarding French Non-Christian Minorities of Foreign Origin." The project had been drawn up for the Civilian and Military Organization by Maxime Blocq-Mascart, an economist who was himself of Jewish descent. Blocq-Mascart held that a majority had the right to take measures directed against a minority, limiting, for example, the number of Jews in the administration or other high–ranking posts; he proposed to create a "Population Commissariat" whose policies would take their inspiration from the recent anthropobiological works of Dr. Martial, a racist scholar who had taught a course in anthropobiology at the Paris Faculty of Medicine in 1938–1939 and served as a member of the Supervisory Committee at Darquier de Pellepoix's Anthroposociological Institute.*

Weil seems to rally to certain of Martial's views:

> The central idea is correct: that it is not a matter of knowing whether the Jewish minority has this or that characteristic, but whether it exists. Correct also is the idea that this minority has as a common bond: the absence of the Christian heritage. However, it is dangerous to consider these accepted premises as stable and to make them correspond to a stable *modus vivendi*. The existence of such a minority does not represent a good thing; thus the objective must be to bring about its disappearance, and any *modus vivendi* must be a transition toward this objective. In this regard, official recognition of this minority's existence would be very bad because that would crystallize it.

How was this minority to be brought to disappear? Weil's suggestion was to encourage "mixed marriages and a Christian upbringing for future Jewish generations."[41]

While still in America, Weil had induced her brother to have his daughter Sylvie baptized and to arrange for his stepson Alain to make his first communion. "If a genuinely Christian inspiration—without the encroachment of dogma on intelligence—really impregnated the training, education, and upbringing of the youth in France, and even more the entire life of the country, neither the so-called Jewish religion nor the atheism typical of Jews emancipated from their religion would be strong enough to prevent contagion."[42]

Such positions are, to say the least, paradoxical for someone who had consistently protested against colonization and felt that assimilation should not be synonymous, for the assimilated people, with the loss of its roots and culture. What are we to make of the fact that, almost simultaneously, in another 1942 text, Weil deplored "the conquest by the French of the lands situated

---

*Dr. Martial was the author of *Vie et constance des races* (Paris, 1939) and *Français, qui es-tu?* (Paris, 1942). See Marrus and Paxton, *Vichy France and the Jews*, p. 190.

to the south of the Loire at the beginning of the thirteenth century," a conquest that stood, in her eyes, as an "atrocious" example of deracination? How can one accept her comparison between the French and Germans—"the French were as much foreigners and barbarians [to the people living south of the Loire] as the Germans are to us?" Above all, what is to be said of her statement to the effect that

> people who have their culture taken away from them either carry on without any at all, or else accept the odds and ends of the culture one condescends to give them. In any event, they don't stand out individually, so they appear to be assimilated. The real marvel is to assimilate populations so that they preserve their culture, though necessarily modified, as a living thing. It is a marvel which very seldom takes place.[43]

Yet Weil is well aware, and often repeats, that the destruction of the past is irreversible, that it is "perhaps the greatest of all crimes,"[44] that "loss of the past, whether it be collectively or individually, is the supreme human tragedy," and that it is precisely for this reason that peoples put up a resistance to being conquered![45] Indeed, does she herself not write, in her *Notebooks*, that the Jews, an "artificial people, a tribe when it entered Egypt that became a nation under slavery," failed to assimilate after four and a half centuries in Europe; that the Hebrews are inassimilable and, in the same measure, do not assimilate others; and that their cohesiveness has only been sustained by terrible violence?

Beginning in 1937, in *Le Mystère d'Israël* (originally published as *L'Impossible antisémitisme*),[46] Jacques Maritain, for his part, spoke out against the assimilation of the Jews, arguing that assimilation entailed the risk that they would abandon "the vocation of the house of Israel": "The mystical body of Israel is that of a special people. It has a temporal foundation and is at one level a community of flesh and blood; to spread throughout the world it has to be disjointed, broken up, and dispersed. The Diaspora—whose existence predates the Christian era—is the earthly, bloodied and battered pendant to the catholicity of the Church."[47] But it is this special vocation which makes the Jews "outsiders in a supernatural sense" whom the whole world execrates.[48] To be more precise, Maritain here speaks of "assimilation," a social and political phenomenon he carefully distinguishes from "settling down," which is a spiritual phenomenon: "an 'assimilated' Jew cannot be a Jew who has 'settled down.' " But, if "Yiddishism," which reflects, not a national language, but rather "the language of misery and dispersal, the slang of the Holy City,"[49] is not the solution to the Jewish question, neither is assimilation. Maritain observes that the Jews' desire to lose their identity, to melt, to be like the others, has always had fatal consequences for them and that God has always punished them for it, availing himself, at times, of the basest means:

> Never had there been Jews more assimilated than the German Jews. They were all the more attached to German culture for its having in part been their achievement. They had become totally German, which did not make them more discreet or humble. They were not only assimilated, but settled down, conciliatory and well reconciled with the Prince of this world. The Jews who become like others become worse than others. (When a Jew receives Christian grace, he is less than ever like others: he finds *his* Messiah.)[50]

In the 1920s, invoking St. Paul's Epistle to the Romans, Maritain cherished the hope that the Jews would convert. Was Zionism, then, the solution? Initially, Maritain did indeed pin his hopes on the Zionist movement, which Louis Massignon introduced him to as early as 1908. He went so far as to send a "Report on Zionism" to Pius XI in 1925, suggesting that the Church open negotiations with the Zionists: the Jews, converted to Catholicism, would simultaneously become members of the Catholic Church.[51] Pius XI did not accept this proposal. In any case, by 1937, Zionism seemed to Maritain to be quite as dangerous as assimilation; it was, at best, "a partial or provisional solution." He rejected the idea of "normalizing" the Jewish people; emphatically, the Jews must not become, at the spiritual level, "like others."

> Zionism . . . does not yet represent deliverance from exile; the return to Palestine is but the prelude to such deliverance. No more than individualist liberalism . . . can the Zionist state do away with the law of the desert and of the Galuth, which is not consubstantial with the Jewish people— this law *will* come to an end—but is essential to the mystical body and the vocation of Israel in the state of separation.[52]

But let us return to Simone Weil. One cannot but acknowledge, with Perrin, the obvious fact that "at the center of all her oppositions was her attitude to Israel, [which] was the key to all her resistance,"[53] and that her spontaneous sympathy for all oppressed peoples (did Dr. Bercher not declare that, if she had stayed in America, "she would surely have become a black"?)[54] operated to the exclusion of the Jewish people. It is also possible that Weil, who was, on a personal level, ever more deeply committed to Christian culture and the Christian faith and had her foot poised on the threshold of the Church—on the threshold and no further, but, still, on the threshold—regarded her own path as one every Jew had to follow. She often used the Greek expression *en hupomene*, "waiting." Commenting on her waiting attitude, she says, "it is true that I am near to [the Church], for I am at the door. But that does not mean that I am ready to enter. It is true that the slightest impulsion would be enough to make me enter; but there must be an impulsion, otherwise I may remain indefinitely on the threshold."[55]

Jew *and* German!

The idea of a mass conversion of the Jews was nothing new. One thinks of the debate between Mendelssohn and Lavater here: should the Jews melt into a broader collectivity in the name of universalism and reason? When Theodor Herzl, the founder of Zionism, started thinking about the problem, did he not envisage a conversion of all Jewish children "at the Church of Saint-Etienne, marching in solemn procession amid the pealing of the bells, in broad daylight, on a Sunday noon? Not shamefully, as has heretofore been the case with isolated individual conversions, but proudly!"[56] In the 1930s, which is to say, before leaving Germany, Arendt too examined the question of Jewish assimilation, which she links with that of the emancipation of the Jews in the modernity of the late eighteenth century; she discusses it in *Rahel Varnhagen: The Life of a Jewess*,[57] and also in "Aufklärung und Judenfrage" [The Enlightenment and the Jewish question].[58] The individual Jew who wished to assume a place in society had, she says, to deny the basic facts of his existence as if they were something shameful. Jews were only accepted if they gave up their "prejudices" and rejoined the Christians. "As the price of Jewish emancipation," Gershom Scholem writes, "the Germans demanded a resolute disavowal of Jewish nationality . . . indeed, like Wilhelm von Humboldt, [they] considered the disappearance of the Jews as an ethnic group a condition for taking up their cause."[59] This explains the considerable success of a proposal made by David Friedländer, one of the Elders of the Israelite Consistory, to the effect that the Jews should receive baptism *en masse*: one out of every ten Jews in Berlin subscribed to it. Rahel Varnhagen herself succumbed to the temptation in 1814. But Arendt never shared this feeling of ambivalence, which is precisely what rules out autobiographical interpretations of her book on Rahel: she did not have to make the long journey that, for Rahel, was the price of self-acceptance, the acceptance of a given. At the end of *The Origins of Totalitarianism*, Arendt writes: "modern man has come to resent everything given, even his own existence. . . . in his resentment of all laws merely given to him, he proclaims openly that everything is possible and believes secretly that everything is possible."[60] She invites us to make our peace with the given, to love the world and the human condition.

After the war, Arendt continued to militate in favor of creating

> the same national status for Jews throughout Europe, and, at the same time, the legal prosecution of anti-Semitism in every country, since only recognition of the rights of the people as a whole, not individual rights, can resolve the problem of the integration of the Jewish people into the future community of European peoples. This is the goal the Jewish underground movement is pursuing today, in solidarity with all the other underground movements in Europe.[61]

Arendt was afraid that the end of the war would do nothing to alter the situation of the refugees who had fought fascism and were now living outside the law, without civil rights. She cites, as an example, the fact that

> hardly had de Gaulle finished paying tribute to the Spanish maquis in a big public ceremony at Toulouse, and awarded medals to the most deserving of them for helping to liberate France, than the French army demanded that these same Spaniards, who had no consular protection and could only be considered stateless persons, either join the Foreign Legion or report to the mandatory labor batallions. The resistance movement in France, with its sense of honor and solidarity, is still strong enough to block execution of this decree. But hundreds of thousands of foreign Jews who had fought for the liberation of France under the blue and white flag were not allowed to march under that flag in the parade commemorating the November 11 Armistice.[62]

As further proof of Europe's inability to resolve the refugee problem, Arendt adduces the example of the Belgian government, which "had resumed stamping the identity papers of German-Jewish refugees still living on Belgian soil with the words 'nationality: German,' in spite of the fact that these Jews had been stripped of their civil rights."[63]

It should be clear enough by now that, whereas Simone Weil pleaded for the absorption of the minority by the majority, Hannah Arendt advocated recognition of the Jews' specificity. She even expressed a wish that the next German constitution "stipulat[e] . . . that any Jew, regardless of where he is born, can become a citizen of [the future German] republic, enjoying all rights of citizenship, solely on the basis of his Jewish nationality and without ceasing to be a Jew."[64] Jaspers unreservedly approved this proposal. Assimilation had never seemed to him to represent a real solution, involving as it did the risk that "something priceless would be lost if there were no more Jews, aware of themselves as Jews, in the world." He went so far as to wonder whether the solution was not "to desire Palestine but *not* go there, because the task is to live among *all* the peoples of the world, with them and against them as long as they are content to remain peoples and nothing more. This would be a new form of that influence 'from afar' which has perhaps always been characteristic of biblical religion."[65] One sees, given this position, why he requested Arendt's permission to use her suggestion (without naming her) that Germany pass "a law by which any Jew can apply for citizenship in Germany, and immediately be granted it while still remaining a Jew." Arendt was only too happy to comply: "Of course without naming the source. . . . It is meaningful only if it comes from a German in Germany."[66] In the same year, 1944, she observed that the thousand men who had already been granted temporary asylum by the U.S. government "were not refugees in the time-honored, sacred sense of the word," people to whom one would normally accord the "ancient right to asylum." What was at stake, in view of their numbers, was less the freedom and dignity of these persecuted souls considered as members of a people than their sheer physical survival.

These exiles did not inspire veneration, as they had in the past; rather, their misfortune awakened suspicion. Coming from "No-man's Land, for they could be neither deported nor expelled," these stateless persons stood outside the law; they were "enemy aliens" who, with "their naked humanity" and the pity they inspired, merely left the "eerie impression that they were something totally inhuman."[67]

1943

3 January: In the Old Port section of Marseilles, a bomb is set off in a bordello patronized by officers of the Wehrmacht. On 24 January, Hitler retaliates by issuing orders to raze the buildings in that section of Marseilles and haul 50,000 inhabitants of the city off to concentration camps. Twenty thousand people are affected by these measures of reprisal; they are arrested, sent to the camp at Gurs, then transferred to the camp at Drancy before being deported to death camps in Eastern Europe. These arrests do not, as in 1942, spark violent protests from the French Catholic bishops.

20 January: in the twenty-sixth issue of its bulletin *Défense de la France*, the Résistance organization of the same name, together with seven other movements, urges the two generals leading the Free French forces to "unite, as those fighting within France have united. . . . Let de Gaulle head the government, which he already represents in the eyes of France and foreign countries, and let Giraud assume command of military operations."[1]

25 January: Lucien Vidal-Naquet notes in his *Journal*: "We have just gone through several days and nights . . . during which the French police, obeying, alas, orders handed down in Berlin, have conducted massive search and arrest operations designed to furnish the Nazi Moloch with the quantity of human flesh he has determined in advance. Workers, women, and children have been indiscriminately arrested and thrown into sealed train cars, then hurriedly dispatched to Poland and Russia as forced laborers . . . I never understood as I do today all the tragedy that the simple world 'terror' can contain."[2]

The same day, Jacques Maritain delivers a lecture on "Le droit raciste et la vraie signification du racisme" [Racist laws and the real meaning of racism] at the *Ecole libre des hautes études*, a French university-in-exile: "Today, as we watch, all hell is unleashed on earth. And the devil, gentlemen, is calling the tune."[3]

Laval proposes that all Jews naturalized after 10 August 1927 be stripped of their French citizenship.

Première of *La Reine morte* [The dead queen] by Henry de Montherlant.

General Darlan is assassinated, General Giraud relieved of his command.

30 January: creation of the *Milice*.

2 February: the German 6th Army surrenders at Stalingrad.

5 February: a census of all men born between 1 January 1912 and 31 December 1921 is carried out with a view to creating a *Service du Travail Obligatoire*. The STO affects 600,000 young Frenchmen. Anti-Semitic persecution grows fiercer; the Freemasons come under attack; Communists are tracked down and arrested. General de Gaulle's popularity is on the rise and he is acquiring greater legitimacy.

Défense de la France reports the use of gas vans.

16 February: passage and promulgation of the law creating the STO.

April: the Warsaw ghetto uprising is crushed.

3 April: Léon Blum is transferred to Buchenwald. He will be held there for two years, in a private house, together with Georges Mandel. Mandel is released a few months before Blum, then turned over to the Germans and executed in Fontainebleau Forest by the French *Milice*.

15 April: creation of the National Council of the Résistance.

The most conservative members of *Défense de la France* are excluded from its ranks. The organization rallies to de Gaulle.

19 April: mass arrests of Jews in Nîmes, Avignon, Carpentras, Aix-en-Provence. The liquidation of the Warsaw ghetto begins. The ghetto rises up in revolt.

30 April: meeting between Laval and Hitler in Berchtesgaden.

27 May: first meeting of the National Council of the Résistance in Paris, presided over by Jean Moulin. One month later, Moulin is arrested and tortured.

Clandestine publication of Vercors's *Silence de la mer* [The sea's silence] by the *Editions de Minuit*.

The Résistance executes members of Jacques Doriot's *Parti populaire français*.

June: the formula of joint leadership by de Gaulle and Giraud carries the day in Algiers. The two men share leadership responsibilities in the French Committee of National Liberation.

From June on, the deportation convoys succeed one another without pause. The camp at Darcy is placed under the administrative control of

Hauptsturmführer Brünner. Twelve torture chambers are now in operation in the middle of Paris.

5 June: *Défense de la France* condemns Giraud and his machinations and recognizes de Gaulle as the leader of the Résistance. Accepting the idea that de Gaulle will head up the future provisional government, the Résistance bulletin demands that the Allies extend recognition to the French Committee of National Liberation.

Henri Frenay, however, facilitates the entry of Giraud's supporters into the Secret Army. Giraud's intention is to claim credit for the creation of the domestic Resistance movement.

Sartre publishes *The Flies*.

July: at Kursk, the Germans suffer their second major defeat at the hands of the Soviets.

20 July: the new issue of *Défense de la France* is given over to the atrocities perpetrated by the Nazis and the French police. The paper runs photographs of starving children and the bodies of Russian prisoners-of-war stacked up in mass graves.

Mussolini is overthrown. The Allies land in Sicily.

August: Simone de Beauvoir publishes *She Came to Stay*.

Première of Jean Giraudoux's *Sodome et Gomorrhe* and Paul Claudel's *The Satin Slipper*.

September: the Allies land on the Italian peninsula.

30 September: *Défense de la France* mentions the existence of Auschwitz in its thirty-seventh issue but says nothing about the gas chambers. "In the concentration camp at Oswiecim, in the Cracow diocese, 40,000 people are being subjected to unbelievable and, in the final analysis, lethal conditions. The mortality rate sometimes reaches 150 deaths per day. The dead are cremated to remove all traces of torture. Three crematoria at the gates of the camp are in daily operation. In all, more than 700,000 Jews have been murdered on Polish territory."[4]

October: Corsica is liberated.

13 November: Pétain tries to rid himself of Laval.

Disbelief

Pitchipoï*

"I did not understand what the extermination camps were," says Hélène Viannay. "I thought treatment of that kind was was only meted out to the

---

*At Drancy, *Pitchipoï* was the name the Jewish prisoners gave the deportation trains. They were unaware that these trains were bound for Auschwitz and Sobibor.

Russians. The same holds for the gas vans; I did not at all believe that they really existed. I thought it was a rumor that had been blown up."[5] The universalist ideology of the Résistance movement may explain why *Défense de la France* gave such little coverage to anti-Semitism. When Albert Cohen (Cohen had, as early as 20 June 1940, gone into exile in England, where he represented the Jewish Palestine Agency; he met with de Gaulle on the agency's behalf on 9 August)* demanded immediate action to save Jewish lives, Georges Boris replied that he objected to "anything that tended to recognize and perpetuate discrimination between Jewish and non-Jewish Frenchmen. Thus, if it becomes possible to find new ways to facilitate escapes, they should in principle be used to help anyone subject to Nazi persecution, not just Jews."[6] Raymond Aron agreed. "A simple argument leads me to regard [anti-Semitic laws] with relative equanimity. If the Germans win the war, the Jews will disappear from France and the rest of Europe. If they lose, the Statute on the Jews will not survive; it will vanish with the war itself."[7]

As early as 1942, Renée Blum informed her father-in-law, then imprisoned at Bourassol, of rumors to the effect that Jews had been burned alive in German camps. "Go on," was his reply, "you must be crazy!"[8] Only after the Americans had bombarded Buchenwald did Léon Blum and his third wife Janot, who had both been detained in a private house there since 3 April 1943, get a glimpse of the strange inmates of the camp and succeed in communicating with some of the French and Belgian deportees among them. From then on, the news that Blum had been interned spread like wildfire through the camp at Buchenwald.**

Yet, on 1 July 1942, the BBC had already broadcast, in French, news of the massacre of 700,000 Polish Jews. The newspaper *J'accuse*, in its issue of 2 October, reported that "the Boche torturers are burning and asphyxiating thousands of Jewish men, women, and children deported from France," while *Humanité* declared that the Nazis were performing "experiments with toxic gas on eleven thousand men, women, old people, and children who were part of the Jewish population deported from the two zones of France." On 17 December 1942, Anthony Eden, the British Foreign Minister, had denounced the mass executions of Jews in the Polish camps before the House of Commons. But skepticism in the face of the improbable prevailed. It took the ar-

* On plans for cooperation between the Zionists and de Gaulle, who hoped they would provide him with information about America and North Africa, see Rachel Galperin, "Activité sioniste: diplomatie et politique (1940–1944)," as well as the "Rapport confidentiel à l'exécutif de l'Agence juive," *Passages*, December 1995–January 1996.

**"We have learned Blum was here in 1944, in August. . . . He was recognized one day by some French and Belgian deportees who were making repairs in the SS villas, after the American bombing raids on the munitions factories of Buchenwald" (Jorge Semprun, *Literature or Life*, trans. Linda Coverdale [New York: Viking, 1997], p. 95).

rival in Palestine of a group of people from Poland before even the Jewish Agency could make up its mind, on 23 November 1942, to publish a report on Sobibor and Treblinka.[9]

What did we know at the time about repression in France and what we to-day call the Holocaust? Of the camps that had been established in our country, I can only recall hearing about Drancy and Pithiviers. We must also have heard about the camps in southwestern France, because the let-ter that the archbishop of Toulouse, Monsignor Saliège, wrote to con-demn what had taken place at Noé and Recebedou went from hand to hand in our house. But I do not remember ever hearing about the Camp at les Milles, near Aix-en-Provence. . . . The word Auschwitz? For us, it appeared for the first time in Louis Aragon's *Musée Grévin*:

Auschwitz, Auschwitz, o syllables soaked in blood,
Where people live and die an inch at a time.

Auschwitz was where the Communists deported in the 24 January 1943 convoy lost their lives.[10]

Lucien, Pierre Vidal-Naquet's father, speaks, in his *Journal* entry for 17 July 1943, of the "methodically organized 'annihilation of the Jews' through-out Europe." But did he realize the true import of his words? "Unlike my cousin Jacques Brunschwicg, for example, who had been promised by one of his playmates that he would end up as a bar of soap, I knew nothing and guessed nothing,"[11] Pierre Vidal-Naquet confesses.

Most Frenchmen were not even capable of recognizing General de Gaulle: the paper *Défense de la France* published photographs of him. Geneviève de Gaulle helped members of the organization of the same name get to know her uncle: "Rumor had it that de Gaulle was an illegitimate son of Pétain's, or that he was such a good friend of Pétain's that he had named his son Philippe and that the Maréchal was the boy's godfather . . . not even my comrades knew much."[12]

The three Résistance movements in southern France were more than will-ing to send their paramilitary groups to join a secret army whose leader was to be appointed by de Gaulle, but they had not yet acknowledged the Gen-eral's political authority. Moreover, the political parties had sensed that the Allies were going to win the war, and, discredited as they were by the 1940 defeat, were essaying a return to the scene in hopes of obtaining a share of political power after France had been liberated. De Gaulle faced the follow-ing alternative: he could either extend symbolic recognition to the political parties for the role they had played in the resistance movement, thus assur-

ing himself the legitimacy that the Americans persisted in denying him because of their preference for Giraud; or he could initiate a process leading to
the disappearance of the parties and put political leadership in the hands of
the authentic resistance movements. In *The Need for Roots*, Simone Weil, for
her part, advocates banishing political parties from political life altogether,
on the grounds that the interparty struggle under the Third Republic had
demonstrated the bankruptcy of democracy, but also because, as she put it,
"there is no such thing as a collective exercise of intelligence . . . the intelligence is defeated as soon as the expression of one's thoughts is preceded, explicitly or implicitly, by the little word 'we.' "[13]

Hannah Arendt heard about Auschwitz for the first time in 1943. She did
not credit these wild tales, any more than did her husband, who, she reminds
us, was a former military historian. Part of the reason for her incredulity was
that, "militarily, [Auschwitz] was unnecessary and uncalled for." Six months
later, however, Arendt and her husband had no choice but to face up to the
reality of the matter:

> That was the real shock. Before that we said: Well, one has enemies. That
> is entirely natural. Why shouldn't a people have enemies? But this was dif-
> ferent. It was really as if an abyss had opened. Because we had the idea that
> amends could somehow be made for everything else, as amends can be
> made for just about everything at some point in politics. But not for this.
> This ought not to have happened. And I don't mean just the number of vic-
> tims. I mean the method, the fabrication of corpses and so on—I don't
> need to go into that. This should not have happened. Something happened
> to which we cannot reconcile ourselves.[14]

The Free French Organization—A Fascist Party?

After de Gaulle had read Weil's "Réflexions sur la révolte" [Reflections on
the revolt], an essay in which she calls for the creation of a "Supreme Council of the Rebellion"—in this case, for once, the General read a work
of Weil's in its entirety—the decision was taken to create a National Council of the Résistance. The Council's first meeting was held on 27 May 1943.
Its president was Jean Moulin; he would soon be succeeded by Georges
Bidault.

Weil was still in London at the time, for Jean Cavaillès was opposed to
complying with her wish to parachute her into Occupied France. Although
she admired de Gaulle, whom she praised for having "saved the country's
honor at the moment when it fell into slavery," she dreaded the creation of a
Gaullist party, going so far as to wonder if, after the victory over fascism,

there would be any need to overturn the Vichy government. In her view, the constitution of a legitimate provisional government

> would imply [de Gaulle's] renouncing any subsequent political career. Concern about a subsequent career would create the risk of contaminating the complete purity which is indispensable for the exercise of political power in such terrible circumstances. In any case it is desirable that France, once she has regained her balance, should be led by a Frenchman who lived through her trial on her soil.[15]

In *The Need for Roots*, she writes, "there are some people, in America, for example, who ask themselves whether the French in London might not have leanings toward Fascism." In her view, that was not the right way to state the question: "the thing is to know whether the French in London possess the necessary means to prevent the people of France from sliding into Fascism, and at the same time stop them from falling into either Communism or anarchy."[16] In 1942, the Free French movement in London had seemed to her to deserve the halo due an organization of the loftiest inspiration; but, in 1943, in a discussion of the project of the "Revolutionary Group of French Republicans," a group that "would have been composed solely of people from the Résistance," she declares that "these people are completely, exclusively, and consciously Fascists. When they say that according to their intention their party would not be the only party, it is obvious that they are lying. . . . The elected leader who will be the head of the party will hold absolute power over the economic and cultural life of the country. They admit that they want to seize power by violence. . . . The cynicism with which all this is presented is scarcely believable."[17] After de Gaulle left for Algiers at the end of May, accompanied by André Philip, Maurice Schumann, and Francis-Louis Closon, Simone learned of the rivalry between him and Giraud. On 26 July, she sent Closon her letter of resignation: " 'I do not have, I cannot have, and I do not wish to have any direct or indirect, or even very indirect, connection with the French Résistance. . . . I disapprove of the continuation—confirmed by de Gaulle in an interview—of something called 'the movement of fighting France'; wherever I may be, whether here or in Africa, I don't consider myself a part of it."[18] This last letter, written less than a month before her death, remained in the possession of Maurice Schumann for many years. Francis-Louis Closon remarks that Weil "continued to hope that downtrodden Europe would rise up in a general revolt, and, relying solely on its own strength, would, when de Gaulle and Churchill issued the call, take command of the situation and drive out the invader: 'it is sheer torture to have the feeling that one has seen things that are true, but lacks the means to render them useful.' "[19]

However, as André Weil tells it, "already when [Simone Weil] went to London she had no great illusions about the so-called Free French movement. I had none at all because I had seen the beginnings of the movement in London in the summer of 1940."[20] Lucien Vidal-Naquet, for his part, noted in his *Journal* on 8 January 1943:

> When I hear, on English radio, a—veiled—account of the dissension between de Gaulle's and Giraud's partisans in North Africa, or when I learn that everyone who thinks he can use the fact that Laval has fired him to attest his civic spirit has rushed to Africa in the belief that, after one look at his attestation, people will forget the role he played when the armistice was signed and after the armistice was signed, then I understand the reasons for our defeat only too well.

And again on 11 July: "The disagrements between de Gaulle and Giraud saddened us deeply, while the Allies' inactivity had us looking to the future with more and more anxiety every day."[21] But Jacques Maritain sided with de Gaulle against Giraud, polemicizing on this issue with Saint-Exupéry, who was defended by Raymond Aron.[22]

What had aroused Weil's mistrust? It stemmed from accusations that she was a Pétainist:

> My sister . . . had discussions with the Gaullists in America and what she disliked most of all was their total intolerance towards anyone who was what they described as a "collaborator" in France: many of those so-called collaborators were perfectly honest and decent people who were doing their best under difficult circumstances. In fact, my sister mentions in a letter which has been published that the Gaullists were calling her a Pétainist, and conversely. She was of course condemned to be on bad terms with almost everybody—it was with her an old experience.[23]

In *The Need for Roots*, Weil calls punishment one of the needs of the soul: "the only way of showing respect for somebody who has placed himself outside the law is to reinstate him inside the law by subjecting him to the punishment ordained by the law."[24] The guilty man must, then, acknowledge that his punishment is just and consent freely to it. As to "responsibilities and punishments" for the crimes committed during the war and the occupation, Weil remarks that "the initial crime . . . from which almost all of the others have flowed automatically" was the June 1940 capitulation; she adds that this "collective crime of the entire nation" consisted in a lack of "heroism." Her conclusion is that "only those Frenchmen who were guilty of collusion with the enemy before the armistice" should be sent to prison.[25]

"French Professor Starves Herself to Death"

Baptized or Not?

On 15 April 1943, Simone Weil, who had come down with tuberculosis, was transferred to Middlesex Hospital, and on 30 July, at her request, to the sanitorium in Ashford, Kent. "What a lovely place to die!" she declared on her arrival there. To her friend Simone Deitz, she remarked, "if one day I fall into a coma and am entirely deprived of my will, then I should be baptized."[26] Father René de Naurois often came to see her. Refusing to take nourishment, she let herself waste away. When she died on 24 August, the headline in the *Tuesday Express* read, "French Professor Starves Herself to Death."[27] Did she, as Michel Narcy claims, allow herself to die "for political reasons . . . in the Ashford sanitorium . . . shunning a destiny different from that of her society and fellow citizens?"[28] "Her political ardor and her haste to join the ranks of the victims," Narcy also says, "are nothing more nor less than faith taken seriously."

Weil was buried in the Roman Catholic cemetery at Ashford on 30 August. The mourners were expecting a Catholic priest; either he was late or he took the wrong train. It hardly matters: Maurice Schumann said the prayers. It seems that people were unsure as to whether Simone had been baptized or not until Father de Naurois decided to dispel their doubts by confirming that she had not asked to receive baptism, and categorically denying that he had refused to baptize her because she would not accept the theory of the existence of limbo as an integral part of the faith.[29] In her *Profession of Faith*, published under the inappropriate title "Last Text," Weil writes: "I believe in God, the Trinity, the Incarnation, Redemption, the Eucharist, and the teachings of the Gospel."[30] Martin Buber, in a conversation with the Jewish thinker Samuel-Hugo Bergman, a friend of Kafka's and an enthusiastic admirer of Weil's, confessed to him that he "couldn't imagine a Jew really believing in the Trinity. In 'attributes,' perhaps—but in persons?"[31] However that might be, Weil explains that she does not affirm these beliefs "as one might affirm empirical facts or geometrical theorems," but rather that she adheres "through love . . . to the perfect, unseizable truth which these mysteries contain." Yet she refuses to recognize the Church's right "to set up, as being the truth, the commentaries with which she surrounds the mysteries of the faith, and much less still the right to use intimidation when, in imposing these commentaries, she exercises her power to deprive people of the sacraments." She is aware that she is fallible—indeed, as a consistent Cartesian, she doubts "even the things that appear . . . most manifestly certain" to her, adding that "this doubt bears equally on all my thoughts, those which are in agreement with the Church's teaching just as much as those which are in disagreement with it." And she resolves to "continue in this attitude" to her dying day, declaring that she is "sure that it is not sinful to talk like this."

At the same time, she acknowledges "an intense and ever-increasing desire for communion."[32] She admits, however, that if she were vouchsafed baptism, this would, given her attitude, represent a "break" with a "routine" that the Church has followed for at least seventeen centuries. "For this reason and for several others of a similar nature," she explains, "I have never up to now made a formal request to a priest for baptism."[33]

Henri Bergson's position was very different. He had asked for the Church's succor in dying. But the Church was slow to respond to his request, as it had been slow to respond to Simone's; by the time Canon Lelièvre had arrived at his bedside, the philosopher was dead. Lelièvre could only recite the prayer for the dead and bless the body. On 8 February 1937, Bergson had made out his last will and testament:

> My reflexions have led me closer and closer to Catholicism, in which I see the complete fulfillment of Judaism. I should have become a convert, had I not seen in preparation for years (in great part, alas, through the fault of a certain number of Jews entirely deprived of moral sense) the formidable wave of anti-Semitism which is to sweep over the world. I wanted to remain among those who tomorrow will be persecuted. But I hope that a Catholic priest will be good enough to come—if the Cardinal Archbishop of Paris authorizes it—to pray at my funeral. Should this authorization not be granted, it will be necessary to approach a rabbi, but without concealing from him, nor from anyone, my moral adherence to Catholicism, as well as my personal and first desire to have the prayers of a Catholic priest.[34]

In 1933, Bergson, whose Polish-born father came from a Hasidic family, had confessed to Sertillanges that "the Gospels are my true spiritual fatherland." It was left to his daughter, Jeanna, to take the final step.

The Kaddish for Hannah?

The same year, Hannah Arendt wrote "We Refugees," an essay in which, after painting a nightmarish portrait of "the first non-religious Jews persecuted . . . who answer[ed] with suicide," she describes her own situation as an exile in France:

> We were expelled from Germany because we were Jews. But having hardly crossed the French borderline, we were changed into "boches." We were even told that we had to accept this designation if we really were against Hitler's racial theories. During seven years we played the ridiculous role of trying to be Frenchmen—at least, prospective citizens; but at the beginning of the war we were interned as "boches" all the same. . . . After the Germans invaded the country, the French Government had only to change the name of the firm; having been jailed because we were Germans, we were not freed because we were Jews.

This article offered Arendt yet another opportunity to reflect on the condition of those pariahs who, after losing everything—their social, political, and legal status—refuse to maintain their Jewish identity, oblivious to the fact that they "represent the vanguard of their people—if they keep their identity. For the first time Jewish history is not separate but tied up with that of all other nations."[35]

That same month, in a review of Howard L. Brooks's *Prisoners of Hope*, Arendt once again drew attention to the anti-Semitic dimension of the Vichy government, which Brooks seems to have completely overlooked. While "the description of physical conditions in the concentration camps, the psychology of their inmates and the frequent ignorance of the French people of their very existence" are clearly pointed out, Arendt says, the fact "that these inmates are chiefly Jews is hardly mentioned, and that the whole institution is part of a political system is hardly understood." Brooks is thus betrayed into making "such remarks as that the commandant of one of these camps 'except for his anti-Semitism was quite amiable' or that bad camp conditions are due to 'military discipline and a blind addiction to regulations' "—this though the author was perfectly aware that most camp commandants "acted 'as though the camps were their personal property.' " In Arendt's opinion, there could be no doubt that the sums allocated to this "new and flourishing industry of the 'France Nouvelle' . . . go straight into the pockets of the commandants and their staff," since Pétain chose to "reward his former comrades" in the officer corps by this means.[36]

In February and March, *Aufbau* published a two-part article by Arendt on French political literature in exile.[37] We have already discussed the first installment, which is largely taken up with a defense of Georges Bernanos. In the second, Arendt expresses her gratitude to Yves Simon for recalling, in *The March to Liberation*, that the recent catastrophe was in part due to their generation's lack of interest in politics and public affairs; she also commends

Simon for denouncing the absurd conception of an "eternal Germany." She draws attention to several important observations made in this book: that the period of national wars is ending and that the French catastrophe provides the clearest possible proof that the nation, in the form it has taken heretofore, is disappearing. The ideas of the French Revolution, which, so the claim, had long been dead, seem to be rising from their ashes; there is no longer any escaping the basic political questions of our time. Arendt acclaims the finest passages in the book, in which Simon shows that the alternatives of the past—authority vs. freedom, a free-market or totally planned economy—are now deemed relevant only by "our enemies"; they result from the unimaginativeness of "thinkers" accustomed to identifying "the history of humanity with that of a small, privileged minority" and to confusing "liberalism's golden age with freedom's." On the other hand, Arendt objects strongly to Simone's resurrection of Sorel's notion of the elite.[38]

In April 1943, in an essay entitled "Why the Crémieux Decree Was Abrogated," Arendt tries to predict the consequences of the abrogation of the Crémieux Decree. She begins by casting a glance at the colonial policy of assimilation that France had maintained for two centuries, from the time of Jean-Baptiste Colbert on. In 1868, she recalls, the government of Napoleon III had decided to naturalize the Algerian Jews *en bloc*; Adolphe Crémieux, then the French Minister of Justice, applied the government's decree two years later. The reaction of the army and the colonial administration, convinced that this would cost them their privileges and prerogatives, was not late in coming: it did a great deal to fuel the increasingly virulent anti-Semitism rampant in the Algerian press from 1880 on. Indeed, Edouard Drumont even tried to drum up a French–style anti-Semitic campaign in Algeria. As the Dreyfus Affair unfolded, Algiers was shaken by violent pogroms (1898); Drumont succeeded in getting himself elected deputy to the French National Assembly thanks largely to the help of the mayor of Algiers, Max Régis, who had instigated the pogroms. This anti-Semitic propaganda continued to wreak havoc in Oran in 1925 and Constantine in 1934, gradually gaining ground among all the peoples of North Africa. In 1943, of its 7,234,084 inhabitants, 987,252 were Europeans; 853,209 of the Europeans were French citizens, and, of these, some 100,000 were Jews. General Giraud claimed to have abrogated the Crémieux Decree to eliminate the inequality between natives and Jews, who were in a privileged position. However, he glossed over the fact that the Muslims had for seventy years had the right to opt for French citizenship. His real motive was to bring the only segment of the Algerian population that had hitherto eluded his arbitrary rule under the control of his "dictatorship."[39]

In the same period, Arendt wrote "Die wahren Gründe für Theresienstadt" [The real reasons for Theresienstadt]. In this article, she brings out the connection between the persecutions of the Jews and the Nazi apparatus of domination, listing a number of measures which, in the name of "tolerance" or under cover of "protecting" the Jews, actually aimed to foment anti-Semitism among the people. The mass killings of Jews, she notes, took place only in sparsely populated regions.[40]

A fifth essay, "Portrait of a Period," is in fact a review of Stefan Zweig's *The World of Yesterday*. In this autobiography, Zweig, who "could not reconcile to the fact that his name had been pilloried by the Nazis like that of a 'criminal,' and that the famous Stefan Zweig had become the Jew Zweig," has apparently still not taken the measure of political developments and the rise of anti-Semitism; he continues to regard Lueger as "a kindly person whose 'official antisemitism never stopped him from being helpful and friendly to his former Jewish friends.' " The lesson is as clear as it was in the book Arendt wrote about Rahel Varnhagen. Faithful to the revolutionary Bernard Lazare, she argues that there is no escaping "the 'disgrace' of being a Jew" at the individual level, by cultivating the society of the famous; the only effective response is political commitment and "fight[ing] for the honor of the Jewish people as a whole."[41]

In "Can the Jewish–Arab Question Be Solved?" Arendt begins by once again deploring the fact that the Jews have played no role in the "wild game of power politics" ever since they abandoned the struggle to create a Jewish army, which, as we know, she very much wanted to see come into being from 1941 on. She then dismisses as equally untenable both the idea of a Jewish Commonwealth in Palestine, that is, an autonomous state "based on a prospective majority granting minority rights to the present majority," and Dr. Magnes' proposal to create a binational state which, she argues, would give the Jews permanent minority status in an Arab empire under the protectorate of a third party. The security of a Jewish national homeland could be adequately guaranteed only within the framework of a federation comparable to the United States, in which no state would enjoy supremacy over any other because all would govern together.[42]

Arendt died suddenly on 4 December 1975, after having waged many other battles. Two epigraphs to her last book, which she had barely begun— it was to be titled *Lectures on Kant's Political Philosophy*—* were found in her typewriter at her death. The first, taken from Cato the Elder, reads: *Victrix*

*This is thus a posthumous work made up of a postscript to *The Life of the Mind*, thirteen lectures on Kant's political philosophy delivered at the New School for Social Research in 1970 after a first version had been delivered at the University of Chicago in 1964, and, finally, notes on the imagination, taken from a New School seminar on Kant's *Critique of Judgement* which Arendt taught the same year she gave her lectures on Kant.

causa deis placuit, sed victa Catoni ["the winning cause pleased the gods, but the losing cause pleases Cato"]. The second comes from Goethe's *Faust*: "Könnt' ich Magie von meinem Pfad entfernen, / Stünd' ich Natur! vor dir ein Mann allein, / Dann wär's der Mühe wert, ein Mensch zu sein" [If I could banish Magic's fell creations / . . . Stood I, O Nature! Man alone in thee, / Then were it worth one's while a man to be!].

Arendt had arranged for the kaddish, a ritual she loved, to be recited by the graveside of her husband Heinrich Blücher, who was not Jewish. At her graveside, after much debate among her friends, a Psalm was read, first in Hebrew and then in English. The eulogy that her old friend Hans Jonas delivered on 8 December at the Riverside Memorial Chapel in New York ended with these words: "The world has become colder without you. You left us too early. We shall try to keep faith with you."[43]

Esther Beatified

Edith Stein, "a daughter of Israel blessed by the Cross," was beatified by John Paul II in Cologne on 4 May 1987, seven years after the formulation of a petition for her beatification. The decision was announced a few months earlier, on 26 January 1987, before the controversy surrounding the Carmel at Auschwitz had subsided. Thus Edith's name took its place on the roll of the blessed: St. Ursula, St. Gereon, Saints Madron, Boethius, Cunbert, Bruno, Herbert, Anno, Engelbert, Hermann, Joseph, Albert the Great. . . . In the homily that the Pope delivered in the stadium at Cologne-Mungersdorf, in the presence of Edith's twelve nephews and grand-nephews, former students, and hundreds of Carmelite friars and nuns, he quoted a letter of hers:

> I am confident that the Lord has taken my life for all [Jews]. I always have to think of Queen Esther, who was taken away from her people for the express purpose of standing before the King for her people. I am the very poor, weak, and small Esther, but the King who selected me is infinitely greater and more merciful.[44]

In his introductory address, Cardinal Hoeffner drew a parallel between Edith's destiny and Maximilien Kolbe's: "may Edith Stein's martyrdom at Auschwitz," he said, "help reconcile Germans and Jews." Her life seemed to him to illustrate a dictum of Husserl's: "deep down in Jews is radicalism and love faithful unto martyrdom."[45]

The Pope pointed out that, for Stein, neither the sacrament of baptism nor entry into the Cologne Carmel in 1933 signified "escape from the world or from responsibility." Rather, they were proof of "a resolute commitment to the heritage of Christ on the Cross." Father Xavier Tilliette, for his part, entitles the essay in which he pays homage to Stein's double heritage "Edith Stein, trait d'union entre Juifs et chrétiens" [Edith Stein, hyphen between Jews and Christians]."[46] "Her Jewish admirers," Tilliette says in this essay, "can rightfully consider her one of their own. The Christians who invoke her name wish to dissociate her memory neither from the Holocaust nor from the Passion of Christ." Underscoring the similarity with "Simone Weil, that other lover of the Cross, that other Jew, lay saint, and Christian without church or baptism," and emphasizing the parallels between these two destinies "patterned after the sufferings of the Crucified," Tilliette nevertheless expresses a preference for Edith, the "daughter of the Church, the baptized one." Not that, in his eyes, Weil has nothing to teach us or nothing that can move us. But, of the two, Stein alone "was chosen by the Lord as his instrument."[47] The woman whom Tilliette went on to call "the synagogue with the blindfold over her eyes," this figure of Jewish restlessness whom God denied the bloody death she longed for, would, if she had heard him, surely have cried out, *Anathema sit*!

Epilogue

"Righteous Women"?

Love for One's Neighbor

Even if Simone Weil claimed she had nothing to do with Jewish tradition and rejected the very idea of belonging to a people or collectivity, was her failure to perceive the "naked humanity" to which the war had reduced the Jews not proof that she lacked, if not pity, then, at least, the thoughtfulness Maritain calls for? This failure is all the more curious in that it is precisely this lack of qualities, this nudity, this anonymity which she takes to be, of all possible motives for compassion, the only pure one.* Did Weil succeed in being just—she who maintained that "from [her] earliest childhood [she] always had . . . the Christian idea of love for one's neighbour, to which [she] gave the name of justice, a name it bears in many passages of the Gospel"[1]; she who insisted that the righteous man was "the one who does not so much as know when or if he had clothed those who were naked"?[2] When she wrote these lines in 1942, was her ignorance of the "affliction" of the Jews so deep as to justify her failure to extend the Jews the benefits of the "miracle" which consists in the "look," the "attention" that the righteous bestow upon the afflicted?**

---

*"Christ has said who is the neighbour whom we are commanded to love. It is the naked, bleeding, and senseless body which we see lying in the road. What we are commanded to love first of all is affliction: the affliction of man, the affliction of God" (Simone Weil, "L'amour de Dieu et le malheur," in *Pensées sans ordre concernant l'armour de Dieu* [Paris: Gallimard, 1962], p. 121; "The Love of God and Affliction," in *On Science, Necessity, and the Love of God*, ed. and trans. Richard Rees [London: Oxford University Press, 1968], p. 192).

**"Those who are unhappy have no need for anything in this world but people capable of giving them attention . . . a very rare and difficult thing; it is almost a miracle; it *is* a miracle" (Weil, *Attente de Dieu*, p. 96; *Waiting on God*, p. 58).

"November 1942 was a turning point for us as it was for everybody else," writes Pierre Vidal-Naquet; "the Allied landing in North Africa was enthusiastically acclaimed, while the pact concluded with Darlan horrified everyone." On 11 November, the Germans—not "forces of occupation," but "operational troops"—invaded the Unoccupied Zone. On 17 December, Lucien Vidal-Naquet noted in his *Journal* that deportation "undoubtedly meant death."[3]

Was Simone Weil unaware of the existence of the camp at Drancy or the destination of the eastward-bound trains? The first deportations took place on 28 March 1942: Weil set sail for the United States in May and remained there until November, when she left for London. Did people in New York and London not know that Jews were being gassed to death? As early as 5 December 1941, the *New York Herald Tribune* stated that "the sum of it all indicates that the fate reserved for the Jews by the Nazis is worse than a status of serfdom—it is nothing less than systematic extermination."[4] Throughout spring and summer 1942, information about the mass killings was reaching Washington. By 1 July, one million Jews had been slaughtered in Eastern Europe. On 30 June and 2 July, the *New York Times* reprinted articles from the *London Daily Telegraph* of 25 June and 30 June which spoke of the "slaughter" of "more than 700,000 Polish Jews" through "the use of poison gas."[5] On 21 July, a large protest rally was organized in Madison Square Garden. News came pouring in during August and September. From his Swiss exile, Thomas Mann spoke of the total eradication of European Jewry and the gassing of thousands near Warsaw, on a radio program called, "Les Français parlent aux Français" that was broadcast by the BBC in London.[6] On 17 December, eleven Allied governments and de Gaulle's Comité de la France combattante issued a joint declaration on Hitler's intention to exterminate the European Jews. All the news from the occupied countries of Europe converged on London. Dr. Kac, who worked for the Free French Movement in London in the same building as Simone Weil, examined her on two occasions and spoke to her about the fate of the Jews:

In this period, particularly in London, we already knew about what the Germans called *Sonderbehandlung*—the special treatment reserved for Jews. We knew that the death agony of the Warsaw ghetto had already begun, following the first skirmishes with the Nazis in January 1943. We were already aware of the feverish activity reigning at East Railway Station in Warsaw, the *Umschlagplatz* where thousands of Jews destined for Treblinka were herded together every day. We had already heard that the naked bodies of Jews who had died of starvation were left lying on the sidewalks, covered with newspapers.[7]

It has to be recognized that, even if political circles in Washington and London learned of the "Final Solution" very early on, they did not believe what they heard, or else took no interest in it.

But Simone Weil did not concern herself with the ordeal of the Jews.* Did she not thus demonstrate a lack of that *Einfühlung* which Edith Stein had not only chosen as the subject of her dissertation but had also displayed when, shortly before her death at Auschwitz, she said to Father Hirschmann, "you don't know what it means to me to be a daughter of the chosen people—to belong to Christ, not only spiritually, but according to the flesh"⁸—or when she took her sister Rosa by the hand as they were being arrested, and, leaving her Carmel, said, "come; we're going for our people."⁹ Stein thus made Paul's words her own: *Hebraei sunt, et ego.* In Simone Weil, the mechanism of compassion is a complex one which requires that the soul be, in some sense, "divided in two"; mercy presupposes that the soul have an "impassible part," and, simultaneously, a "part . . . contaminated to the point of identification. This tension is passion, compassion."¹⁰ In the absence of such impassibility, of such a "point of eternity," one fails to perceive the misfortunate, or "is kept far away from them by difference of situation and lack of imagination, or else, if one really approaches them, pity is mixed with horror, disgust, fear, invincible repulsion."¹¹ Did "the impassible part" of Weil's soul take precedence over the capacity to be transported beyond the limits of the self? How are we to explain the fact that Weil paid such little attention to the Jewish people, her great sensitivity to all forms of human distress notwithstanding? (Simone de Beauvoir and Raymond Aron both recall how deeply upset she was upon learning that famine had broken out in China.)

Compassion being, for Weil, a veritable miracle,** an attribute that God alone may truly be said to possess, must we conclude that no human compassion is capable of assuming the burden of such affliction, of facing up to it?*** Yet do the compassionate not attest to the manifest presence of God here below? "When we are lacking in compassion we make a violent separation between a creature and God."¹² We cannot feel compassion, Weil also says, for what is close to us: "mercy implies an infinite distance."¹³ Did the Jewish cause seem too close to her, even if she denied being "one of them"?

---

*"The love of our neighbour in all its fullness simply means being able to say to him: 'What are you going through?' " (Weil, *Attente de Dieu*, p. 96; *Waiting on God*, p. 59).

**"Compassion for the afflicted is an impossibility. When it is really found, it is a more astounding miracle than walking on water, healing the sick, or even raising the dead" (Weil, "L'amour de Dieu et le malheur," p. 88; "On the Love of God and Affliction," p. 172).

***"To project one's being into an afflicted person. . . . Only Christ had done it. Only Christ and those men whose soul he possesses can do it." This is, Weil believes, the reason that Christ Himself received such little compassion while He was on earth: "it would have needed another Christ to have pity on Christ in affliction" (ibid., pp. 119–20 / pp. 191–92).

Was she afraid that she would not be sufficiently impersonal, like Rosa Luxemburg writing to Mathilde Wurm (and this in 1917): "What do you want with this particular suffering of the Jews? The poor victims on the rubber plantations in Putumayo, the Negroes in Africa with whose bodies the Europeans play a game of catch, are just as near to me."[14] Not sufficiently impersonal, and therefore not sufficiently universal? "Christianity will not be incarnated so long as there is not joined to it the Stoic's idea of filial piety for the city of the world, for the country of here below which is the universe."[15] It may be that Weil was unable to heed the voice of the prophet Isaiah: "peace, peace to him that is far off, and to him that is near." For Simone Weil, does "he that is near" exclude "him that is far off"? He that is truly near, our real neighbor, is God,[16] and God has the exclusive "monopoly on goodness." Does it follow that God Himself was lacking in compassion? Compassion and gratitude, which are as rare in this world as they are incomprehensible,[17] are, furthermore, too heavily compromised by considerations of "social prestige."[18] Must we conclude that, far from having been led to her grave by an excess of compassion, as certain writers suggest, Weil had a soul that was insufficiently possessed by Christ, in contrast to Stein, whose life and writings bear witness to the fact that "our love for human beings is proportionate to our love for God"? "For the Christian," Stein says, "there is no such thing as a 'stranger.' There is only the neighbor—the person who happens to be next to us, the person most in need of our help."[19]

Is it, however, essential to have faith in order to be just? "Hannah Arendt, not long before she died, told the following story on French radio. Once when she was a child . . . she said to the rabbi who was teaching her religion: 'You know, I have lost my faith.' And the rabbi responded: 'Who is asking you for it?' " Emmanuel Lévinas comments on this story, "What matters is not 'faith,' but 'doing'. . . . What do we believe with? With the whole body! With all our bones! (Psalm 35:10) What the rabbi meant was: 'Doing good is the act of belief itself.' "[20] We have already amply demonstrated that Hannah Arendt "did good" for the Jewish people, in a very concrete sense. But, in Arendt, one also finds reflections—free of all mysticism, to be sure, and intended rather as inquiries into the place of morality and the heart in politics—on the role of compassion and closely related concepts like pity, brotherhood, goodness, solidarity, and humanity, which she carefully distinguishes.

Pity: A Way of Practicing Nihilism?

Arendt's point of departure is provided by Rousseau, who postulates that man has, in addition to self-love, "an innate repugnance to see his fellow-man suffer," a repugnance of which "even beasts sometimes give perceptible signs."[21] Compassion, accordingly, does not require any participation of the will, inasmuch as we are spontaneously moved by affliction. At most, the judgment is brought into play as a means of discriminating between an "I" and a "Thou": "we suffer only as much as we believe [the other] to suffer."[22] To be sure, compassion also presupposes the appeal of the imagination: "no one becomes sensitive till his imagination is aroused and begins to carry him outside himself."[23] Indeed, "he who imagines nothing is aware only of himself; he is isolated in the midst of mankind." But who is the object of our compassion? The "repressed and persecuted," responds Arendt, that is, "the Jews, as far as the history of the nineteenth century is concerned." Compassion is, in a short, "the great privilege of pariah peoples"—in other words, of those known as the "*malheureux*" in the eighteenth century and the "*misérables*" in the nineteenth.[24] The ultimate objective of such compassion is the happiness of the many—a "novel idea in Europe"[25]—which will henceforth be claimed as a "right." But any notion of the "common good" implies the exercise of beneficence, the virtue par excellence discovered in 1672 by the Abbé de Saint Pierre and defined as follows by Voltaire: "What is virtue? Beneficence towards one's fellow-creatures."[26]

Rousseau "introduced compassion into political theory"—does Mallet du Pan not tell us that Marat read passages of the *Social Contract* to the assembled crowds?—but it was Robespierre who brought this "Virtue" onto the market-place.[27] For Rousseau, compassion consisted in an effort to ensure the happiness of the greatest number;[28] it therefore gave rise to a "*zèle compatissant*," an "imperious impulse which attracts us toward *les hommes faibles*," a "capacity to suffer with the 'immense class of the poor.' " But it also harbored certain dangers. Given the history of past revolutions, Arendt puts us on our guard against the pursuit of happiness, as distinct from the attempt to "establish justice for all."[29] Comparing the French and the American Revolutions, she remarks that, despite the issue of Black slavery, the social question played no role in the American Revolution; all indications were that the poor remained "invisible." This would explain why the men who led the American Revolution remained "men of action," whereas the French revolutionaries got entangled in the social question. Nietzsche had already stated that the equation good men = "men of pity" propounded by the philosophers was simply an "echo" of "the time of the French Revolution." He added that "every socialist system has placed itself as if involuntarily on the common ground of these teachings":[30] thus a sense of sympathy (*Mitempfindung*) and the social sense (*soziale Empfindung*) are closely associated in modern thought. Again, the French Revolution appeared to him to be the last great slave insurrection,[31] the last major political event to illustrate the ancient struggle of Judea against Rome.[32] It too brought the "good news" that "a gateway to happiness stands open for the poor and the lowly."[33] Politics, as Nietzsche saw it, was suffering from the disease of equality and the right of the greatest number to happiness.

In an attempt to work out a new conception of what it is to be humane, Arendt turned to Antiquity, "more experienced in political matters" than we are. Aristotle believed that compassion, like fear, prevents men from taking action. The Stoics, for their part, put compassion on a par with envy, " 'for the man who is pained by another's misfortune is also pained by another's prosperity' " (Cicero, *Tusculanae Disputationes* III, 21) . . . "Why pity rather than give assistance if one can? Or, are we unable to be open-handed without pity?"[34] Is "sharing joy" not "absolutely superior . . . to sharing suffering"—as Nietzsche also believed? Is it not the true condition for dialogue? Does compassion not lead, via perversion, to cruelty, so that one feels "pleasure where pain would naturally be felt"?[35] Compassion is of no value because it is a *passion*, one which consists in being "stricken with the suffering of someone else as though it were contagious."[36] Moreover, compassion, like goodness, is sympathy with a single suffering creature. Thus it is not susceptible of generalization: because it is a form of "cosuffering," it cannot be directed toward a group or class in its entirety. "Compassion, in this respect not unlike love, abolishes . . . distance"; "it remains, politically speaking, irrelevant and without consequence. In the words of Melville, it is incapable of establishing 'lasting institutions.' "[37] Such compassion is closely related to "fraternity" or "goodness": both are "mute," tending to find expression in "gestures and expressions of countenance," as is attested by the kiss bestowed by the Jesus who remains silent in the face of the Grand Inquisitor. The task of putting the affairs of the world in order falls to Captain Vere.

The same analysis may be found in Arendt's reflections on fraternity in "dark times." Fraternity "is not transmissible"; only pariah peoples can exercise this "virtue" among themselves. It "cannot be easily acquired by those who do not belong among the pariahs' that is, by those who have a different place in the world, one that prevents them from being "unburdened by care for the world," as the pariahs are; the pariahs' insouciance consists in sidestepping the conflicts that agitate mankind so as to take refuge in the "warmth" of human relationships, out of reach of all responsibility. Yet this warmth "exerts a great fascination upon all those who are so ashamed of the world as it is" and would also "like to take refuge in invisibility"[38] rather than assume responsibility for the world. The "element common to all men is not the world, but 'human nature.' " Involved here is a situation in which men "have moved so closely together that the interspace which we have called the world . . . has simply disappeared." Far from criticizing this "loss of the world," this "worldlessness," which is, after all, "a form of barbarism,"[39] Arendt acknowledges that it is "a great thing"; in her interview with Gaus, she even describes it as something very beautiful,* to the extent that it can generate a "kindliness and sheer goodness of which human beings are otherwise scarcely capable."[40] From a political point of view, however, she points out that such fraternity—which has, she adds, "never yet survived the hour of liberation by so much as a minute"—is "absolutely irrelevant."[41]

If goodness and fraternity have no place in politics, the reason is not that they condemn us to inaction,** but rather that, paradoxically, "when goodness appears openly, it is no longer goodness, though it may still be useful as organized charity or an act of solidarity." Goodness and fraternity are "truly not of this world" and must avoid public exposure, lest they lose their "specific character of goodness, of being done for nothing but goodness' sake":[42] " 'let not thy left hand know what thy right hand doeth.' " Just as Socrates did not wish to be called wise, so Jesus "thought and taught that no man can be good";*** "the talmudic story of the thirty-six righteous men, for the sake of whom God saves the world" also tells us that these men are "known to nobody, least of all to themselves." Doomed to be forgotten, to disappear without a trace, good works are not human but superhuman; it is for this reason that "goodness . . . as a consistent way of life, is not only impossible within the confines of the public realm, it is even destructive of it."[43] Arendt has learned the lesson taught by "the poets" Melville and Dostoyevsky: that "absolute goodness is hardly any less dangerous than absolute evil, that it does not consist in selflessness . . . and that it is beyond virtue."[44] John XXIII, to whom Arendt pays tribute in "A Christian on St. Peter's Chair," saw, precisely, that pure goodness cannot be exercised within the framework of religious and political institutions. Thus goodness, while it is an admirable quality in personal relations, is incapable of penetrating the political sphere and resolving its problems. Pity fares no better at Arendt's hands: unlike compassion, it is not a passion, but a *feeling*. It can therefore be generalized to take in an entire people, or a mass, because it is not bound

---

*"But it was something very beautiful, this standing outside of all social connections" (Hannah Arendt, "Was bleibt? Es bleibt die Muttersprache," in *Gespräche mit Hannah Arendt*, ed. Adelbert Reif [Munich: Piper, 1976], p. 28; " 'What Remains? The Language Remains': A Conversation with Günter Gaus," in *Essays in Understanding, 1930–1954*, ed. Jerome Kohn [New York: Harcourt Brace, 1994], p. 17).

***"Jesus knew what *action* is better than anybody else" (Hannah Arendt, " 'Remarks' to the American Society of Christian Ethics [1973], MSS Box 70 011838, cited in Margaret Canovan, *Hannah Arendt: A Reinterpretation of Her Political Thought* [London: Cambridge University Press, 1992], p. 147).

****"Why callest thou me good? None is good, save one, that is, God" (Luke, 18:19; see also Matthew 6).

up with the singularity of a unique individual. As opposed to compassion, which is mute, pity is eloquent, and, "because it is not stricken in the flesh," it too can keep its distance and "enter the marketplace."[45] But the disadvantage of pity is that it does not outlive the action it inspires: born with affliction, it dies when affliction does. Moreover, pity is dangerous. "*Par pitié, par amour, pour l'humanité, soyez inhumains!*": for Arendt, these words, taken at random from a petition of the Paris Commune, indicate that as soon as Robespierre had elevated pity to a position of power, it "engendered cruelty and contempt for the law."[46] The heart and feelings, one sees, clearly have no place in politics; they are "a place of darkness," and "emphasis on the heart as the source of political virtue" is misplaced. To be sure, "the heart begins to beat properly only when it has been broken or is being torn in conflict, but this is a truth which cannot prevail outside the life of the soul and within the realm of human affairs."[47] From the moment goodness enters the public realm, it leads inexorably to the appearance of crimes and criminality, for, "in politics, more than anywhere else, we have no possibility of distinguishing between being and appearance." Nobody, perhaps, perceived the danger inherent in doing good more sharply than Machiavelli, who boldly counterposed to Socrates' "be the way you would like to appear to others" his own "appear the way you would like to be," and taught men " 'how not to be good.' "[48]

Toward a Politics of Friendship?

What Sort of Justice, What Sort of Humanity?

Arendt's concern, then, is to devise a new conception of humaneness, one capable of serving as a guide to political action in dark times. But, since the passion of compassion and the sentiment of pity must be excluded from the public realm, since the heart is emphatically out of place in politics, and since humaneness cannot consist in an *imitatio Christi*, what is to be done to keep the world humane? What is the right response to evil and totalitarianism? Arendt was in search of a *principle*; she was faithful, in this respect, to Montesquieu, who, in *The Spirit of the Laws*, had brought to light the driving force behind monarchy (whose motivating principle is glory) and tyranny (motivated by fear). Could solidarity—even if, to the extent that it is rooted in reason, it can seem cold and abstract because it involves ideas rather than love—furnish the principle capable of guiding and inspiring action? Did Arendt regard solidarity as the political counterpart to pity? Initially, she apparently did, for, as we have seen, in 1942 she put all her hope in the upsurge of solidarity the French people showed when, despite its own suffering, it stood up against the Vichy regime's plans to carry out massive deportations of Jews. Solidarity protects us from the "sea of emotion"; but this virtue has its vice, namely, that because solidarity can be extended by generalization to humanity as a whole, thus attaining the level of the universal, it is completely independent of oppression, weakness, or poverty: it includes even the rich and the powerful in its embrace.

Arendt would seem to contrast humaneness and solidarity. This is what is suggested by her very beautiful preface to *Die verborgene Tradition*,[49] in which she admonishes those who were fortunate enough to survive the deluge of Auschwitz against the temptation of yielding "to despair or scorn for humankind." She suggests, rather, that they imitate "Noah in his ark," urging them to express their gratitude to the Noahs who "float around out there on the world's seas" trying to join their arks in a single convoy. It was in Jaspers that Arendt found her "model of how human beings can speak with each other, despite the prevailing conditions of the deluge." Jaspers was delighted by her preface, especially the comparison with Noah, who could be represented, depending on the kind of political regime under consideration, by "individualists," "aristocrats," "reactionaries," or even "unsocial elements." The Ark was, for Jaspers, "the outlook that *will* carry the future."[50] Incidentally, Jaspers himself, who had delivered a lecture entitled "Vom europäischen Geist" (On the European spirit) at the *Rencontres internationales* held in Geneva in September 1946, had been very favorably impressed by a number of former French Resistance fighters he met on this occasion. Answering the letter in which he expressed his admiration for them, Arendt wrote: "What you had to say about the French of the Résistance made me very happy. Yes, I know, there are still some genuine human beings."[51] She considered Albert Camus to be one of them. He was, in her eyes, a man of integrity blessed with great political insight; she saw in him a new type of human being, one who was simply European "without any 'European nationalism,' " and who felt "at home everywhere" in the world. Flight from reality was no solution either, however successful certain attempts to escape—Heine's, Rahel's, Chaplin's, Kafka's—had been on the personal or artistic level, since power comes into existence only where men act in concert. Our question is thus twofold: "how much reality must be retained even in a world become inhuman if humanity is not to be reduced to an empty phrase or a phantom"?[52]

The principle which is independent of the human warmth that, fusing pariahs and the persecuted, isolates them from the rest of the world, the principle capable of inspiring the type of joint action that confers power on the world even as it humanizes it, this love of a special kind bears the name *philia*, or friendship.* "A German and a Jew, and friends. But wherever such a friendship succeeded at that time . . . a bit of humanness in a world become inhuman had been achieved."[53] Hannah Arendt found an example of this Greek *philanthropia*—this inclination to share the world with other men, this Roman *humanitas* which yet remains political, this humanity which, for us moderns, is "a mere effect of education"—in the injunction "we must, must be friends!" found in *Nathan the Wise*, the classic drama of friendship in Arendt's eyes, the work of that "completely political person," Lessing. The model for friendship is thus political, and friendship between citizens—the condition for general well-being—depends on discourse, dialogue, care for the world that we have in common. For the world does indeed "remain 'in-human' in a very literal sense unless it is constantly talked about by human beings." It "is not humane just because it is made by human beings, and it does not become humane just because the human voice sounds in it, but only when it has become the object of discourse."[54] Justice here requires the quest for truth and consensus to allow a plurality of voices to be heard. Should this plurality be reduced to singularity, "the world . . . would vanish altogether."[55]

Simone Weil had, at the age of fifteen, invented an imaginary "unknown friend" for herself; yet she too warned against the trap of solidarity, which was almost as dangerous as love in her eyes, and accordingly rejected it in the name of friendship.** In her view as in Arendt's, the unifying force of love rules out friendship,*** that "miracle" which consists in keeping one's dis-tance from the person one loves.**** Friendship respects the autonomy of the other, respects his difference, his otherness; it does not seek to devour him and does not confuse the I and the Thou. As if she were echoing Arendt, Weil praises this respect for distance, this "kind of 'friendship' without inti-macy and without closeness . . . a regard for the person from the distance which the space of the world puts between us."[56] This distance, restraint, or reserve, which both our philosophers argued was constitutive of friendship, may perhaps be linked in its turn to the concept of "shame" (*Scham*) which

*I indeed love 'only' my friends' (Hannah Arendt and Gershom Scholem, "Eichmann in Jerusalem: An Exchange of Letters between Gershom Scholem and Hannah Arendt," in Han-nah Arendt, *The Jew as Pariah: Jewish Identity and Politics in the Modern Age*, ed. Ron H. Feldman [New York: Grove Press, 1978], p. 246).
**"Nothing is more contrary to friendship than solidarity, be it a question of solidarity based on comradeship, personal sympathy, or membership in a common social group, or the same po-litical conviction, the same nation, the same religious confession" (Weil, *Intuitions préchrétiennes*, p. 140; *Intimations of Christianity*, p. 177).
***"There is not friendship where distance is not kept and respected" (Weil, *Attente de Dieu*, p. 205; *Waiting on God*, p. 136).
****"The miracle of friendship consists in being able "to view from a certain distance, and without coming any nearer, the very being who is necessary to him as food. It requires the strength of soul that Eve did not have" (Weil, *Attente de Dieu*, p. 204; *Waiting on God*, p. 135).

Nietzsche contrasted with the obscenity of pity (*Mitleid*). He had found a
model for such "shame" in the Greek *aidos*, a word Simone Weil found it
"impossible to translate," noting that "it is no credit to us that neither in
French nor, to my knowledge, in any other modern language, have we a
word to express this shade of meaning."[57] Nietzsche, for his part, attempted
a translation: "*Aidos* is emotion and fear at the thought of offending the gods
and men and breaking the eternally immutable laws; it is the instinct of veneration (*Ehrfurcht*) become a habit with men of nobility, a kind of disgust at
the idea of offending what is venerable. The Greek aversion for excess
(*hubris*), for any being which exceeds its own limits, is something *extremely
aristocratic* that harks back to the earliest forms of nobility. An offense against
aidos is a terrible thing to behold for anyone who is familiar with what *aidos*
is."[58] There can be no question of glossing this dense aphorism of Nietzsche's
here. Let us simply and provisionally remark that, for Simone Weil, *aidos*
"refers to the particular sort of respect which we owe to an unfortunate being when he implores us," and that she finds an illustration of it in Aeschylus' *The Suppliants*.[59] An entry in her *Notebooks* reads: "Respect. *Aidos*."[60]
Friendship is a quest for justice, balance, or harmony between contraries.
Weil returns repeatedly in her work to the Pythagoreans' definition of it:
"friendship is an equality made of harmony." But harmony is unity between
contraries, the contraries being "myself and the other." She cites Socrates in
the *Gorgias*: "It is communion which unites the heavens and the earth, the
gods and men, in friendship, order (*kosmiotèta*), restraint, justice."[61] That is
why "the most beautiful friendship," for Weil, is "that between companions
in combat," "far from hot baths"—witness the final verses of the *Iliad*, in
which Achilles weeps, " 'dreaming of his much-loved companion.' "[62]

In Weil, however, contrary to Arendt, for whom *philia politike* is friendship
between equals—for, in the *polis*, no-one is governed and no-one governs—
the harmony of contraries is incompatible with the notion of equality: there
can be harmony only between "things which are [not] of the same species, of
the same root, and of the same station." The most valuable friendship is
therefore that which binds two beings together less by way of their mutual
affinities than their differences. Justice and equality are distinct. That is why
Weil singles out for criticism Aquinas's commentary on a passage in Aristotle's *Ethics* (8, 7) cited by Jacques Maritain:

> Friendship . . . cannot exist between beings too far removed from one an-
> other. Friendship presupposes that they are close to one another and have
> attained to equality with one another. It is the part of friendship to make
> an equal use of the equality already existing between men. And it is the part

of justice to bring to equality those who are unequal: once this equality has been attained, the task of justice is accomplished. And in that way equality is at the term of justice and is at the beginning and origin of friendship.[63]

Thus, while friendship with a god is impossible in Aristotle, for Weil, the true friend, "the perfect friend,"[64] is God; our worldly friendships are merely the "image of that original and perfect friendship which belongs to the Trinity."[65] Aristotle is accordingly "the blighted tree that bears only rotten fruit." In Weil, this third element which binds men together in a friendship that is the most difficult friendship of all—for how is it possible to bind together already homogeneous fragments "of the same species, of the same root, and of the same station," which consequently have no empty space or distance between them?—is God, who slips in between them. " 'Is it true,' " Nietzsche has a little girl ask her mother, " 'that God is present everywhere? . . . I think that's indecent!' "[66]

Creation and De-creation

But how does Weil arrive at this "union of love" between the two beings who are as unlike as can be, the Creator and His creature? Michel Narcy has proposed an extremely illuminating interpretation which turns on the key concept of "de-creation."[67] For Weil, who appears, on this point, close to the Gnostics, and even to the sixteenth-century Kabbalistic doctrine developed by Isaac Luria (Luria rejects the theory of creation by emanation), the true religions are those in which God is conceived as surrendering his omnipotence out of love for us, so that man may exist.[68] If God were omnipresent, Luria remarks, the world could not have been created, for how can the Other be brought into being starting out from the Same? So that the world might exist, then, God had to withdraw into Himself, leaving an empty space (*tehiru*). Creation is contradiction, self-limitation, abdication: God asked us if we wished to be created and we answered that we did. Hence the creation by no means involves, for God, an extension of His being, the production of something beyond Himself; rather, by withdrawing, God enables a part of being to be "other than God."[69] Since divine omnipotence consists in a voluntary abdication, a sacrifice,[70] man, out of love for God, can only "repeat in the opposite sense the abdication of God";[71] that is, he can only consent to renounce his existence and be a mere "creature," or, in other words, to be "nothing."[72] Man's love for God, the model friendship, even implies the renunciation of all other friendships, "that of one friend for another, of a woman for her lover, of a child for its father, of a child for its mother. That is why we have the Virgin. Even the renunciation by parents of their child; that is why we have the Holy Family."[73]*

Man's response to the divine creation should consist of a "destruction" of existence within himself and consent to "non-existence," in an analogous "abdication" of his power over the world.** It is in this way that man perfects creation,[74] participating in the work of the Divinity: to Him who has given me the gift of being, I can give something in return only by ceasing to be.[75] This extinction of desire in us, our willingness to be reduced to the point we occupy in space and time, is known as "detachment."*** It is, moreover, only a variant of suicide; yet we know that Weil rejected suicide.**** In Weil, as we have seen, friendship requires that we reach the level of universality, renouncing our membership in groups of any kind and abandoning the personal pronoun "we." But it also requires "renunciation of the power to think of everything in the first person." This renunciation alone "grants to a man the knowledge that other men are his fellows."[76] However, as a result of her desire to do away with the "I" and the "We," Weil once again distances herself from Judaism, which not only "welcomes and affirms . . . the 'I' of love . . . and binds the 'I' more closely to the 'Thou,' "[77] but also posits "the 'We' that may say in truth: 'Our Father.' "[78] It would thus seem that Weil fails

---

*Raymond Bénichou was the first to point out the convergence between Weil's hypothesis of de-creation and Kabbalistic doctrine in his 1953 lecture, "Simone Weil, prophétesse égarée" (in Raymond Bénichou, *Ecrits juifs* [Alger, 1957], pp. 39–65). Miklos Vetö likewise sees in the Weilian conception of de-creation—the rejection of existence in the form in which it has been given to me—an echo of the notion of *tsimtsum* (see Vetö, *La Métaphysique religieuse de Simone Weil* [Paris: Vrin, 1971], pp. 20ff.). This is plainly what Dominique Bourel also wishes to suggest: in an account of the reception of Weil's work in Jerusalem, and, especially, of Samuel-Hugo Bergman's enthusiastic reaction to her thought, Bourel urges us to "confront Simone Weil's thinking with the great Kabbalistic texts" (see Bourel, "Simone Weil et Samuel-Hugo Bergman," in *Le Grand Passage* [Paris: Albin Michel, 1994], pp. 71–74). Rabbi Richard Freund has tried to show that there is a relation between "the Jewish mystic tradition and Simone Weil"; even if Weil knew nothing of Judaism, he argues, her conception of an "absent" or "hidden" God, drawn from the works of Christian and Gnostic mystics, is also to be found in most Jewish mystical writings. This becomes particularly clear when Weil writes that "the world, to the extent that it is entirely devoid of God, is God Himself" (Freund, *Cahiers Simone Weil* 10, no. 3 [September 1987]). However, Weil herself evokes Chinese traditions and certain Christian texts in support of her idea that divine creation consists in the withdrawal of God (Weil, *Intuitions préchrétiennes*, p. 30; *Intimations of Christianity*, p. 96).

**"Just as the divine Word, equal to God, emptied itself out in order to become a slave, so we should become equal to the Divine word in emptiness and slavery" (Weil, *Intuitions préchrétiennes*, pp. 168–223, 170, 264. See also Simone Weil, *La Pesanteur et la grâce* [Paris: Plon, 1988], pp. 20–21; *Gravity and Grace*, trans. Arthur Wills [Lincoln: University of Nebraska Press: 1997], pp. 55–56).

***"Every attachment is of the same nature as sexuality. In that Freud is right (but only in that)" (Weil, *La Connaissance surnaturelle*, p. 252; *First and Last Notebooks*, p. 287).

****"Two ways of killing ourselves: suicide or detachment" (Weil, *Pesanteur*, p. 23/*Gravity and Grace*, p. 60).

to grasp the ethic of action that Hasidism preaches: the Hasidic teaching would "bridge the gulf between love of God and love of man,"[79] since the commandment to love our neighbor reduces the distance between God and man to the extent that it makes God and the world coincide. But even if Weil had been acquainted with Kabbalistic doctrine and had not rejected it on the grounds that it had been contaminated by Judaism, she would certainly not have accepted the corollary, developed, in particular, by sixteenth-century Hasidism: by assigning a personal identity to the divine sparks scattered abroad when the vases were shattered, it implies that man should become a subject, find the sparks of each thing again, and, through his activity, restore order to the world.[80]

In Weil, God's movement of withdrawal is itself "love"; His renunciation, which makes it possible to create someone other than Himself in the finitude of temporality, constitutes the divine "caress."[81] This divine abdication of omnipotence must find its pendant in a corresponding act of consent in us, an obedience to necessity, a renunciation of the search for a final purpose in the universe. To "the most piercing words of the Gospel—'my God, my God, why hast thou forsaken me?'[82]—the only possible response is the incomprehensible perfection of love . . . the love which passeth all understanding."[83] Christ Himself emitted this cry, wrenched from him by his suffering. To this cry, "there is no reply. . . . this whole universe is empty of finality."[84] There is no consolation to be had from the world. Since reality, for human beings, is no more nor less than "contact with necessity,"[85] the true reply, the only reply, the only thing we can give back to Him Who has nothing more to give us, because he has already given us too much, is consent to necessity and the possibility of affliction.* That is why the experience of affliction "makes the passage to the other side of that door possible, makes the true face of harmony visible . . . rends the veils which separate us from the beauty of the world and the beauty of God." This is what is revealed by the end of the book of Job,[86] one of the few books of the Old Testament to find grace in Weil's eyes—even if, at several points in her work, she raises questions about its authorship.**

As God's only response to the "why?" of those who are crucified is silence, and as necessity is indifferent to moral values,*** man, who is free to consent to necessity or not, may be tempted to rebel, to reject God and accuse Him

---

*"Consent [to necessity] constitutes participation in the Cross of Christ" (Weil, *Intuitions préchrétiennes*, p. 149; *Intimations of Christianity*, p. 184).

**"Job must be a discovered text of some other religion. . . . But what religion? Phoenician? Canaanite?" (Weil, *La Connaissance surnaturelle*, p. 245; *First and Last Notebooks*, p. 280).

***"Righteous men and criminals receive an equal share of the benefits of the sun and of the rain" (Weil, *Intuitions préchrétiennes*, p. 150; *Intimations of Christianity*, p. 184).

of wrongdoing.* However, in the absence of our Friend par excellence, we can only testify to our love for Him through obedience, queen of the virtues, which, for Weil, goes hand in hand with poverty and chastity. Since God created a world in which good and evil co-exist[87] and cannot make this world better by destroying evil, which "can do no harm to what is good,"[88] it follows that He chooses to let evil exist. We must do the same, that is, "accept the existence of all that exists, including the evil, excepting only that portion of evil which we have the possibility and the obligation of preventing."[89] For, while we must certainly refuse to allow ourselves to do evil and must be penitent when we have, the defining feature of evil is simply that it partakes less of the reality of things.** Because evil has its origins in the superabundance of divine goodness, "the universe" can only be "beautiful, even including evil, which, as a part of the order of the world, has a terrible sort of beauty."[90] The fact that evil exists does not, then, prevent us from "lov[ing] God through the evil which one hates."[91] On the contrary: only to the soul that has not ceased to love God will it one day be given "to hear the silence itself as something infinitely more full of significance than any response, like God Himself speaking. It knows then that God's absence down here is the same thing as the secret presence on earth of the God who is in heaven."[92]

Amor Fati et Amor Mundi

The other name for this detachment is *amor fati*. An "Albanian story" provides Weil with an illustration of it: "whatever loathsome drink the witch gives her she must drink it and say it is delicious."[93] *Amor fati*, Weil's "unconditional yes" even to evil, is "the Christian virtue excellent above all others,"[94] an idea that Alain had already expressed: "There exist duties of acceptance, or, if you like, of obedience. To accept oneself as one is is the homage we pay to the dead . . . [and] to history . . . whoever breaks this bond destroys his tools."[95] But, for Alain, acceptance is "only half of religion"; the other half is "revolt, demanding one's rights, a call to struggle against what is and for what should be."[96] Weil, as we hope to have shown, was a rebel of this kind. She rebelled not only against her own situation, but also against society as it was, and she aspired to a better future.

Christianity and Stoicism are twin modes of thought. That explains why Weil, citing Marcus Aurelius and Diogenes Laertius, claimed to be a Stoic

---

*"One can only excuse men for evil by accusing God of it. If one accuses God one forgives, because God is the Good" (Weil, *La connaissance surnaturelle*, p. 39; *First and Last Notebooks*, p. 94).

**"Evil when we are in its power is not felt as evil but as a necessity, or even a duty" (Weil, *Pesanteur*, p. 85; *Gravity and Grace*, p. 121).

while rejecting the impassivity of Roman Stoicism: for her, "true Stoicism [was] the Stoicism of the Greeks, from which Saint John, or perhaps Christ, borrowed the terms of 'Logos' and 'pneuma.' "[97] In this, too, the disciple was faithful to her master Alain, who regarded the Stoics as peerless models of piety for whom it was *this* world that represented reason.* "Everything, without any exception," writes Weil, "joys and sorrows alike, ought to be welcomed with the same inward attitude of love and thankfulness."[98] For Alain, such veneration for what is by no means amounts to resignation and does not imply renunciation of the right to act: "as soon as you see a way forward," says Marcus Aurelius, "make haste to pursue it."

Weil appealed to the thought of Rosa Luxemburg in defense of her own brand of Stoicism. In a review of Luxemburg's *Letters from Prison*,[99] she lingers over Rosa's endless hymn to the beauty of the world, which her prison cells often separated her from, and praises her "virile attitude towards misfortune, which is what is ordinarily meant by the term Stoicism."[100] In a letter to Sonja Liebknecht, Luxemburg wrote:

> In your card, you ask: "Why do these things happen?" Dear child, life is like that, and always has been. Sorrow, and parting, and unsatisfied yearnings, are just a part of life. We have to take everything as it comes, and to find beauty in everything. That's what I manage to do. Not from any profound wisdom, but simply because it is my nature. I feel instinctively that this is the only right way of taking life, and that is why I am truly happy in all possible circumstances. I would not spare anything out of my life, or have it different from what it has been and is. If only I could bring you to my way of looking at things. . . . ![101]

For Luxemburg, as she repeatedly confirms in her letters to Liebknecht, it is futile to be indignant or curse one's existence: one should not passively submit to events, but accept them as "conditions of existence," however terrible, and endure "all the turns of fortune with a fair amount of equanimity."[102] Like Weil, Luxemburg is determined to accept necessity: " 'what for?' is not, in fact, a concept for the whole of life and its forms."[103] Ultimately, for Rosa Luxemburg, humanity resides in this acquiescence to everything life brings one's way: "Being genuinely human means happily throwing one's life on 'fate's great scale', if necessary, but, at the same time, enjoying every bright day and every beautiful cloud. . . . The world is very beautiful even with all its horrors."[104] Equally Stoic is an emotion which Luxemburg evinces

---

*"However violent, unjust, or ruthless it may appear, that is what one must venerate" (Alain, *Propos sur la religion* [Paris: Presses universitaires de France, 1938], p. 160).

in many passages and which Weil also testifies to: the feeling "of being at home in the universe, whatever event it may produce."[105]

But why does Weil so insistently call attention to Luxemburg's fierce love of life, despite her own attitude of detachment from the world and consent to death, the only way of obeying God that she could see (along with work)? How are we to reconcile Weil's texts on the beauty and love of the world with her feeling of being in exile, her occasional condemnations of the world, her longing for rootedness and, simultaneously, her desire to tear up all roots? We must, doubtless, discover a passage between Rosa Luxemburg's pagan Stoicism and the Christian Stoicism Weil claimed as her own: "This world is uninhabitable . . . we must flee to the next . . . but the door is shut."[106]* From the concept of world, we need to make a transition to the concept of universe: in the unprecedented age that is ours, writes Weil, universality, which had been "implicit," must become "explicit." If she remained forever poised on the threshold of the Catholic church, the reasons, as we have seen, were that she thought the Church was catholic—universal—in name only, hated the Church's "patriotism," and believed that "the children of God should not have any other country here below but the universe itself," so that Catholics should not be "bound by so much as a thread to any created thing, unless it be to creation in its totality."[107] The only thing that Weil contests in Luxemburg is her faith in the spontaneity of the Revolution. Indeed, as early as 1933, she drew the conclusion that the magic word "revolution" had lost all force. "We are living," she wrote, "through a period bereft of a future . . . for a long time now the working class has shown no sign of that spontaneity on which Rosa Luxemburg counted."[108]

Hannah Arendt had the good fortune to outlive Simone Weil. She had the opportunity to witness the Hungarian uprising of 1956, which she enthusiastically hailed. From her mother, who fervently admired Rosa Luxemburg even though she belonged to a circle opposed to the Spartacus movement, Arendt inherited her fervent admiration for the Polish revolutionary, painting a beautiful portrait of her in *Men in Dark Times*. When she told her daughter about the insurrection, news of which had just arrived from Berlin, Martha Arendt added this exhortation: "you must pay attention, this is a historical moment!"[109] Heinrich Blücher was also a passionate reader of Luxemburg. In her review of J. P. Nettl's biography of Luxemburg, Arendt, like Weil, underscored not only Rosa's confession about her own temperament— that she was "capable of 'setting a prairie on fire' "—but also her "manliness . . . unparalleled in the history of German socialism."[110] However, far

---

*Or again: "This world is the closed door. It is a barrier. And, at the same time, it is the way through" (Weil, *Pesanteur*, p. 164; *Gravity and Grace*, p. 200).

from relating Luxemburg's sense of being "at home in the world" to Stoicism, she linked it to her Jewishness: this "home" could be reduced to a single point, and, as she was a Jew before all else, did not coincide with any "fatherland."[111] She saw in this an illusion typical of "Jewish intellectuals," who, in contrast to assimilated Jews, liked to "think that they had no 'fatherland,' for their fatherland actually was Europe."[112] Here we find praise similar to that she lavished on the new type of European incarnated, in her eyes, by Camus. But Arendt's fatherland (unlike Weil, Arendt had a deep desire for roots, and delightedly immersed herself in the American Constitution when she was naturalized in 1951, a procedure she took very seriously) was not the universe, or the next world of the Christians; it was this world, even if all nationalistic feelings have become obsolete with the decline of the nation-state. Consent to necessity—the opposite of which is not "contingence or accident, but freedom"—is likewise not something Arendt could approve. We are all aware, she says in *The Life of the Mind*, that "everything that appears to human eyes, everything that occurs to the human mind, everything that happens to mortals for better or for worse is 'contingent,' including their own existence." She then quotes these lines by her friend W. H. Alden:

> Unpredictably, decades ago, You arrived
> among that unending cascade of creatures spewed
> from Nature's maw. A random event, says Science.
> Random my bottom! A true miracle, say I,
> for who is not certain that he was meant to be?[113]

Arendt unweariedly sought to understand the why and the how of dark times, and she enlisted this understanding, not in the service of Weil's absolute *amor fati*, of faith in God and the world to come, but rather in that of a reconciliation with reality, of the *love for a world* to which men are born strangers.* The need for reconciliation derives from the fact that an Auschwitz was possible in this world. But, even if understanding is "an unending activity," only understanding allows us to "be at home in the world." That is why Arendt analyzed the "terrible originality" of totalitarianism, which consists less in the advent of a new idea than in the reversal of all our moral categories, in obedience to a commandment the Decalog did not foresee: "Thou shalt kill!"[114] In 1945, she was already asking, in the *Origins of Totalitarianism*: What had happened? Why had it happened? How was it possible? The book appeared in 1951. A few years later, Arendt told Karl Jaspers

*"Every single person needs to be reconciled to a world into which he was born a stranger and in which, to the extent of his distinct uniqueness, he always remains a stranger" (Arendt, "Understanding and Politics," p. 308).

of her intention to write a book on political theory that would confirm her reconciliation with the world: "I've begun so late, really only in recent years, to truly love the world that I shall be able to do that now. Out of gratitude, I want to call my book on political theories 'Amor Mundi.' "[115] The book in fact appeared as *The Human Condition* in 1958; a German version, entitled *Vita Activa oder vom tätigen Leben* [Vita activa, or, the active life], was published in Stuttgart in 1960. As Paul Ricœur suggests in his preface to the French translation, *La Condition de l'homme moderne*, the book is a work of "resistance and reconstruction."

Because the crisis of our age is political, the response to it must also be political, contrary to what is suggested by Christianity, which displaces concern for the world and the duties bound up with it onto a concern for the soul and its salvation. Tertullian provides a good example: "nothing," he says, "is more alien to us than public affairs." This political response on the part of men, which, according to Arendt, testifies to their love and concern for the world, their desire to assume responsibility for it, is underwritten by action. But what do we mean by the world? It does not only consist in the divine creation of the heavens and the earth, nor is it identical with what precedes our birth, with the "limited space for the movement of men and the general condition of organic life."[116] In other words, it is not merely what man finds (*invenire*) when he is born. The world is also "related to the human artifact, the fabrication of human hands, as well as the affairs which go on among those who inhabit the man-made world together."[117] What comes about in consequence of our exercising our wills transforms the world *qua* "fabrica Dei" into a natural fatherland for man.[118] The world common to all of us "transcends our lifespan into past and future alike . . . it is what we have in common not only with those who live with us, but also with those who were here before us and with those who will come after us."[119] To be sure, if it is to withstand this succession of generations, the common world must appear in public; that is, men must have the courage to bear voluntary witness to it, to act on the public stage by producing the unexpected and infinitely improbable. To act, as the Greek word *archein* and the Latin *agere* indicate, "means to take an initiative, to set something into motion." And it is precisely because they are themselves "*initium*, newcomers and beginners by virtue of birth," that men act.[120] Arendt once again evokes Augustine, the teacher of her youth: "[initium] ergo ut esset, creatus est homo ante quem nullus fuit" (that there be a beginning, man was created before whom there was nobody). It is because each newborn child is unique that one can say no one existed before it was born: as such, he or she embodies our hope for wholly unprecedented words and deeds. By way of a corrective to the irreversibility of actions, human beings are endowed with the capacity to forgive, which is the act of undoing what has been done; at the same time, confronted with the "unpredictability" and "incalculability" of the future, they are endowed with the eminently human, audacious capacity to promise. Moreover, both pardon and promise "depend on plurality, on the presence and acting of others, for no one can forgive himself and no one can feel bound by a promise made only to himself."[121]

However, if the world that is already there before I am born is to become a fatherland for me, if I am to feel at home in it, if it is to be divested of its strangeness, then activity in the sense of *fabricare* is not enough. To make the world a world, one must also love it, appreciate its diversity, desire to share it with others. That is what an Eichmann refused to do. Arendt would have liked to hear his judges address him in these terms:

> And just as you supported and carried out a policy of not wanting to share the earth with the Jewish people and the people of a number of other nations—as though you and your superiors had any right to determine who should and should not inhabit the world—we find that no one, that is, no member of the human race, can be expected to want to share the earth with you. This is the reason, and the only reason, you must hang.[122]

In contrast, Arendt celebrates the courage of Walter Gurian, who was fully conscious of his own status as pariah. Even while remaining a stranger to the world, he succeeded in accomplishing our common task: "he . . . established his home in this world . . . through friendship."[123] Those who make the world are, then, those who love it, *dilectores mundi*. Loving the world implies being responsible for it, implies feeling responsible even for acts that we ourselves have not committed: while guilt can only be individual, responsibility is vicarious, on condition, of course, that we belong to a group or collectivity. The feeling of responsibility "is the price we pay for the fact that we live our lives not by ourselves but among our fellow men, and that the faculty of action, which, after all, is the political faculty par excellence, can be actualized only in one of the many and manifold forms of human community."[124] Ultimately, the *amor mundi* that Arendt evokes presupposes that we revitalize two dimensions of existence "which Greek antiquity ignored altogether, discounting the keeping of faith as a very uncommon and not too important virtue and counting hope among the evils of illusion in Pandora's box. It is this faith in and hope for the world that found perhaps its most glorious and most succinct expression in the few words with which the Gospels announced their 'glad tidings': 'A child has been born unto us.' "[125] The faith that Hannah Arendt holds out is not faith in God, but in the "Creation," a faith in the intrinsic value of every human being and in love conceived as the appropriate response to the arrival of each newcomer, capable of renewing the world we have in common. This miraculous, thaumaturgical capacity of action is itself rooted in the hope associated with new birth. Whenever Arendt chanced to encounter, in society, a student in whose conversation she glimpsed hope for a new beginning of the eternal *humanum*, she would whisper, Hans Jonas reports, one of her favorite lines from Goethe's *Faust*: "For the soil again engenders them as it ever has before."[126] If such a newcomer is in no sense a "divine savior," birth itself *is* divine, for "the world's potential salvation lies in the very fact that the human species regenerates itself constantly and forever."[127]

Notes

Prologue

1. Bertolt Brecht, "To Those Born Later," in *Poems, 1913–1956*, ed. John Willett and Ralph Manheim, trans. Edith Anderson et al. (New York: Methuen, 1976), pp. 318, 320.
2. "Writing history is a matter of giving dates their physiognomy." Walter Benjamin, "Zentralpark," in *Gesammelte Schriften*, ed. Rolf Tiedemann and Hermann Schweppenhäuser (Frankfurt: Suhrkamp, 1974), vol. 1, book 2, p. 661.

Part I. The Formative Years
Three Childhoods

1. Edith Stein, *Werke*, vol. 7: *Aus dem Leben einer jüdischen Familie. Das Leben Edith Steins: Kindheit und Jugend* (Freiburg: Herder, 1985); *Collected Works*, vol. 1: *Life in a Jewish Family: Her Unfinished Autobiographical Account*, trans. Josephine Koeppel (Washington: Institute of Carmelite Studies, 1986).
2. Ibid., p. 42 / p. 72.
3. Wladimir Rabi, "Entretiens sur S. Weil, la Résistance et la question juive," *Les nouveaux cahiers*, no. 63 (Winter 1980–1981), p. 64.
4. Hannah Arendt, "Was bleibt? Es bleibt die Muttersprache," in *Gespräche mit Hannah Arendt*, ed. Adelbert Reif (Munich: Piper, 1976), p. 16; " 'What Remains? The Language Remains': A Conversation with Günter Gaus," trans. Joan Stambaugh, in Hannah Arendt, *Essays in Understanding 1930–1954*, ed. Jerome Kohn (New York, Harcourt Brace, 1994), p. 7.
5. Uwe Johnson, "Il me faut remercier," *Cahiers du Grif* (Paris: Tierce / Deux Temps, 1986), p. 7.
6. Stein, *Aus dem Leben*, p. 47; *Life in a Jewish Family*, p. 73.
7. Erna Biberstein-Stein, *Aufzeichnungen* (New York, 1949).
8. Stein, *Aus dem Leben*, p. 47; *Life in a Jewish Family*, p. 73.
9. *Le grand passage* (Paris: Albin Michel, 1994), p. 9.
10. "André Weil, a Scientist, Discusses His Sister with Malcolm Muggeridge," in Simone Weil, *Gateway to God*, ed. David Raper et al. (Glasgow: Collins, Fontana Books, 1974), p. 157.
11. Hannah Arendt, letter of 23 March 1947, in *Hannah Arendt–Karl Jaspers: Briefwechsel, 1926–1969*, ed. Lotte Köhler and Hans Sauer (Munich: Piper, 1985), p. 116; *Correspondence*

Hannah Arendt–Karl Jaspers, 1926–1969, trans. Robert and Rita Kimber (New York: Harcourt Brace Jovanovich, 1992), p. 80.
  12. Arendt, "Was bleibt?" pp. 16–17; "What Remains?" p. 7.

Schooling and Teachers

  1. Stein, *Aus dem Leben,* p. 51; *Life in a Jewish Family,* p. 77.
  2. Arendt, "Was bleibt?" p. 19; "What Remains?" p. 9.
  3. Simone Weil, *Attente de Dieu* (Paris: Fayard, 1966), p. 38; *Waiting on God,* trans. Emma Craufurd (London: Routledge and Kegan Paul, 1951), p. 17.
  4. Simone Pétrement, *La vie de Simone Weil,* 2 vols. (Paris: Fayard, 1983), 1:102.
  5. Simone Pétrement, *Simone Weil: A Life,* trans. Raymond Rosentha (New York: Pantheon, 1976), p. 74.
  6. Stein, *Aus dem Leben,* p. 190; *Life in a Jewish Family,* p. 222.
  7. Hedwig Conrad-Martius, in Edith Stein, *Briefe an Hedwig Conrad Martius* (Munich: Kösel, 1961), p. 65, cited in Wilhelmine Boehm, *Edith Stein à la lumière de la ressuscité,* trans. Elisabeth de Solms (Paris: Médiaspaul, 1985), p. 37.
  8. Stein, *Aus dem Leben,* p. 191; *Life in a Jewish Family,* p. 222.
  9. Philibert Secretan, introduction to Edith Stein, *Phénoménologie et philosophie chrétienne* (Paris: Cerf, 1987), p. viii.
  10. Fritz Brentano, ed., "Briefe Franz Brentanos an Hugo Bergman," *Philosophical and Phenomenological Research* 7 (1946–1947): 104; cited in John M. Oesterreicher, *Walls Are Crumbling: Seven Jewish Philosophers Discover Christ* (London: Hollis and Carter, 1953), p. 44.
  11. Stein, *Aus dem Leben,* p. 219; *Life in a Jewish Family,* p. 250.
  12. Ibid., p. 230 / p. 260.
  13. Ibid., p. 283 / p. 316.
  14. Jacques Maritain, cited in Louis Bouyer, *Women Mystics: Hadewijch of Antwerp, Teresa of Avila, Thérèse of Lisieux, Elizabeth of the Trinity, Edith Stein,* trans. Anne Englund Nash (San Francisco: Ignatius, 1993), p. 173.
  15. Stein, *Aus dem Leben,* p. 239; *Life in a Jewish Family,* p. 269.
  16. Ibid., p. 371 / p. 411 [translation modified].
  17. Ibid., p. 371 / p. 410.
  18. Ibid., p. 371 / p. 411.
  19. Alain, "Journal" (unpublished), cited in Pétrement, *Simone Weil,* p. 26.
  20. [TN: *Diplôme d'études supérieures,* the approximate equivalent of a C. phil. degree.]
  21. Pétrement, *La vie de Simone Weil,* 1: 157.
  22. [TN: The highest competitive teacher's examination in France.]
  23. Pétrement, *Simone Weil,* p. 73.
  24. Arendt, "Was bleibt?" p. 18; "What Remains?" p. 9.
  25. Hans Jonas, "Hannah Arendt: Words Spoken at Her Funeral Service," *Partisan Review* 42 (1976): 12.
  26. Hannah Arendt, "Martin Heidegger at 80," trans. Albert Hofstadter, *New York Review of Books* 17, no. 6 (21 October 1971), pp. 50–54.
  27. Ibid., p. 50.
  28. Ibid., p. 51.
  29. Ibid., pp. 50–51.
  30. Ibid., pp. 50–52.
  31. Ibid., pp. 50–51.
  32. Ibid., pp. 53n., 54.
  33. Ibid., p. 53.
  34. Ibid., pp. 54n., 53n.
  35. Ibid., p. 54.

36. Hannah Arendt, "Was ist Existenz-Philosophie?" in *Sechs Essays*, Schriften der Wandlung 3 (Heidelberg: Lambert Schneider, 1948), pp. 48–80; "What Is Existential Philosophy?" trans. Robert and Rita Kimber, in Arendt, *Essays in Understanding*, pp. 163–187.

37. Hannah Arendt, "Heidegger the Fox" [extract from Arendt's *Denktagebuch* for 1953], trans. Robert and Rita Kimber, in Arendt, *Essays in Understanding*, p. 361.

38. Arendt, letters of 29 September 1949 and 4 March 1951, in *Briefwechsel Arendt–Jaspers*, pp. 178, 204; *Correspondence*, pp. 142, 167–168.

39. Arendt, letter of 19 February 1966, ibid., p. 663 / p. 628.

40. Ettinger, *Hannah Arendt / Martin Heidegger* (New Haven: Yale University Press, 1995). French translation by Nicolas Guilhot (Paris: Le Seuil, 1995).

41. Hannah Arendt, *The Human Condition* (Chicago: University of Chicago Press, 1958), p. 237.

42. Ibid.

43. Ibid., p. 239.

44. Ibid., pp. 237–242.

45. Ibid., p. 242.

46. Hannah Arendt, "Zueignung an Karl Jaspers," in *Sechs Essays*, pp. 5–10; Hannah Arendt, "Karl Jaspers: A Laudatio," trans. Clara Winston and Robert Winston, in Hannah Arendt, *Men in Dark Times* (New York: Harcourt Brace and World, 1968), pp. 71–80. Hannah Arendt, "Karl Jaspers: Citizen of the World," in *Men in Dark Times*, pp. 81–94.

47. Arendt, *Human Condition*, p. 243.

48. Arendt, letter of 1 November 1961, in *Briefwechsel Arendt–Jaspers*, p. 494; *Correspondence*, p. 457.

49. Elisabeth Young-Bruehl, *Hannah Arendt: For Love of the World* (New Haven: Yale University Press, 1982), p. 405.

50. Hannah Arendt, *The Life of the Mind*, 2 vols. (New York: Harcourt Brace Jovanovich, 1978), vol. 1: *Thinking*, pp. 77–78.

"Amicus Plato"

1. Edith Stein, preface to Thomas Aquinas, *Untersuchungen über die Wahrheit* (*Quaestiones disputatae de veritate*), in Stein, *Werke*, vol. 3 (Freiburg: Herder, 1952), p. 7, and Stein, *Werke*, vol. 2: *Endliches und ewiges Sein: Versuch eines Aufstieges zum Sinn des Seins* (Freiburg: Herder, 1950), p. 12.

2. Edith Stein, "Husserls Phänomenologie und die Philosophie des heiligen Thomas von Aquino: Versuch einer Gegenüberstellung," *Jahrbuch für Philosophie und phänomenologische Forschung*, suppl. vol. (1929): *Festschrift, Edmund Husserl zum 70. Geburtstag gewidmet*, p. 324.

3. Edith Stein, "Die weltanschauliche Bedeutung der Phänomenologie," in *Werke*, vol. 6: *Welt und Person: Beitrag zum christlichen Wahrheitsstreben* (Freiburg: Herder, 1962), p. 14.

4. Ibid., pp. 15–16.

5. Ibid., p. 13.

6. Ibid., p. 17.

7. Edith Stein, Remarks (in German), in *La phénoménologie: Journée d'étude de la société thomiste* (Kain, Belgium, and Juvisy, France: Cerf, [1932]), pp. 109–111.

8. Edith Stein, "Husserls transzendentale Philosophie," in *Werke*, 6:35. [Review of *Cartesian Meditations*. Husserl's book was initially published in French translation.]

9. Stein, "Husserls Phänomenologie," pp. 315–316.

10. Ibid., p. 316.

11. Ibid., p. 321.

12. Ibid.

13. Stein, "Weltanschauliche Bedeutung der Phänomenologie," p. 17.

14. Hans Jonas, "Philosophie: Rétrospective et prospective à la fin du siècle," trans. Jean Greisch, *Le messager européen* 7 (1993): 334.

15. Hannah Arendt, "Concern with Politics in Recent European Political Thought," in Arendt, *Essays in Understanding,* pp. 428–447.

16. Etienne Gilson, *Les métamorphoses de la Cité de Dieu* (Louvain, 1952), p. 51.

17. Arendt, "Concern with Politics," p. 436.

18. Hannah Arendt, *Was ist Politik?: Fragmente aus dem Nachlaß,* ed. Ursula Ludz (Munich: Piper, 1993), p. 106.

19. Hannah Arendt, "French Existentialism," in Arendt, *Essays in Understanding,* pp. 188–193.

20. Simone Weil, letter of 1942 to Jean Wahl, *Deucalion 4: Etre et pensée, Cahiers de Philosophie* 36 (October 1952): 253–257; *Seventy Letters,* ed. and trans. Richard Rees (London: Cambridge University Press, 1965), p. 161.

21. Simone Weil, *Cahiers,* 3 vols., vol. 2 (Paris: Plon, 1953), p. 96; *The Notebooks of Simone Weil, 1940–1942,* 2 vols., trans. Arthur Wills (London: Routledge and Kegan Paul, 1956), 1: 203.

22. Arendt, "Concern with Politics," p. 443.

23. Jonas, "Philosophie," p. 335.

24. Arendt, "Existenz-Philosphie," p. 66; "Existential Philosophy," p. 176.

25. Hans Jonas, *Wissenschaft als persönliches Erlebnis* (Göttingen: Vandenhoeck und Ruprecht, 1987), pp. 19–20.

26. Stein, "Weltanschauliche Bedeutung der Phänomenologie," p. 16.

27. Edith Stein, "Martin Heideggers Existentialphilosophie," in *Werke,* 6: 99. [The English translation here is meant to reflect Stein's misunderstanding of Heidegger.]

28. Ibid., p. 112.

29. Ibid., p. 126.

30. Stein, *Endliches und ewiges Sein,* pp. 29–30.

31. Simone Weil, "Some Reflections on the Idea of Value" (unpublished manuscript), cited in Pétrement, *La vie de Simone Weil,* 2: 321; Pétrement, *Simone Weil,* p. 406.

32. Simone Weil, *Leçons de philosophie,* ed. Anne Reynaud-Guérithault (Paris: Plon, 1989); *Lectures on Philosophy,* trans. Hugh Price (Cambridge: Cambridge University Press, 1978).

33. Pétrement, *Simone Weil,* p. 231.

34. Ibid., p. 105.

35. Raymond Aron, *Mémoires* (Paris: Julliard, 1983), p. 41.

36. Alain, *Correspondance avec Elie et Florence Halévy* (Paris: Gallimard, 1957), p. 251.

37. Pétrement, *Simone Weil,* p. 436.

38. Pétrement, *La vie de Simone Weil,* 2:181.

39. Alain, *Propos sur la religion* (Paris: Presses universitaires de France, 1938), p. 25.

40. Ibid., p. 199.

Three Ways of Being a Woman

1. Arendt, "Was bleibt?" p. 11; "What Remains?" p. 3.

2. Hans Jonas, "Acting, Knowing, Thinking: Gleanings from Hannah Arendt's Philosophical Work," *Social Research* 1 (1977): 25.

3. Young-Bruehl, *Hannah Arendt,* p. 272.

4. Arendt, "Was bleibt?" p. 9; "What Remains?" p. 2.

5. Young-Bruehl, *Hannah Arendt,* p. 272.

6. Hannah Arendt, "Rosa Luxemburg, 1871–1919," in *Men in Dark Times,* pp. 33–56.

7. Jonas, "Acting, Knowing, Thinking," p. 25.

8. Karl Jaspers, letter of 13 October 1959, in *Briefwechsel Arendt-Jaspers,* p. 789, n. 1; letter of 3 October 1959, *Correspondence,* p. 754, n. 2.

9. Hannah Arendt, *Rahel Varnhagen: Lebensgeschichte einer deutschen Jüdin aus der Romantik* (Munich: Piper, 1959); *Rahel Varnhagen: The Life of a Jewess,* ed. Liliane Weissberg, trans. Richard Winston and Clara Winston (Baltimore: Johns Hopkins University Press, 1997).

10. Romaeus Leuven, *Heil im Unheil. Das Leben Edith Steins: Reife und Vollendung*, trans. Sister Bernalda (Freiburg: Herder, 1983), in Stein, *Werke* 10:22–23, cited in Florent Gaboriau, *Edith Stein philosophe* (Paris: FAC, 1989), p. 42. Edith Stein, *Die Frau: Ihre Aufgabe nach Natur und Gnade* (Munich, 1949); Edith, Stein, *Collected Works*, vol. 2: *Essays on Women*, trans. Freda Mary Oben, 2d ed. (Washington: Institute of Carmelite Studies, 1996).

11. Stein, *Werke*, vol. 5: *Die Frau; Collected Works*, vol. 2: *Essays on Women*.

12. Edith Stein, "Probleme der Frauenbildung," *Werke*, vol. 5: *Die Frau*, p. 120; Edith Stein, "Problems of Woman's Education," in *Collected Works*, 2:173.

13. Ibid., p. 133n./p. 279n.

14. Edith Stein, "Das Ethos der Frauenberufe," *Werke*, 5:5; "The Ethos of Women's Professions," in *Collected Works*, 2:47.

15. Georges Bataille, *The Blue of Noon*, trans. Harry Mathews (New York: Urizen, 1978).

16. Pétrement, *Simone Weil*, pp. 26–28.

17. Ibid., p. 28.

18. Simone Weil, letter to a pupil, cited in Pétrement, *La vie de Simone Weil*, 2:36–37; Pétrement, *Simone Weil*, p. 236.

19. Simone Weil, letter to Jérôme Carcopino, cited in Pétrement, *La vie de Simone Weil*, 2:289–291; Pétrement, *Simone Weil*, pp. 390–392.

20. "Simone Weil, anarchiste et chrétienne," *L'âge nouveau*, no. 61 (May 1951): p. 20; cited in Pétrement, *Simone Weil*, p. 421.

21. Paul Giniewski, *Simone Weil ou la haine de soi* (Paris: Berg International, 1978).

22. Simone Weil, cited in Pétrement, *La vie de Simone Weil*, 2, p. 291n.; Pétrement, *Simone Weil*, p. 554n.

Amor Fati and the Fate of the Jews

1. Renata Posselt [Teresia Renata de Spiritu Sancto], *Edith Stein*, trans. Cecily Hastings and Donald Nicholl (London: Sheed and Ward, 1952), p. 59.

2. Ibid.

3. Edith Stein, *Etre fini et être éternel*, trans. Etienne de Sainte-Marie (Paris: Nauwelaerts, 1957), extracted in Edith Stein, *Dans la puissance de la Croix*, ed. Waltraud Herbsmith, trans. Thomas Soriano (Montrouge, France: Nouvelle Cité, 1982), p. 62.

4. Léon Poliakov, *L'impossible choix? Les crises d'identité juive* (Paris: Austral, 1994).

5. Weil, *Attente de Dieu*, p. 25; *Waiting on God*, p. 9.

6. Weil, *Cahiers*, 2:243; *Notebooks, 1940–1942*, 1:299.

7. Simone Weil, *Lettre à un religieux* (Paris: Gallimard, 1951), pp. 17, 49, 83; *Letter to a Priest*, trans. A. F. Wills (London: Routledge and Kegan Paul, 1953), pp. 15, 43, 74. See also Weil, *Attente de Dieu*, p. 246; *Waiting on God*, p. 169.

8. Joseph-Marie Perrin and Gustave Thibon, *Simone Weil as We Knew Her*, trans. Emma Craufurd (London: Routledge and Kegan Paul, 1953), p. 76.

9. Ibid.

10. Weil, *Attente de Dieu*, p. 176; *Waiting on God*, p. 117.

11. Simone Pétrement, "Un échange de lettres entre G. Aubourg et S. Pétrement," *Cahiers Simone Weil* 11, no. 1 (March 1988): 11.

12. Weil, *Lettre à un religieux*, p. 14; *Letter to a Priest*, p. 11.

13. Weil, *Attente de Dieu*, p. 24; *Waiting on God*, p. 9.

14. Simone Weil, *L'enracinement* (Paris: Gallimard, 1949), p. 61; *The Need for Roots: Prelude to a Declaration of Duties toward Mankind*, trans. Arthur Wills (London: Routledge and Kegan Paul, 1952), p. 41.

15. Ibid., p. 180 / pp. 134–135.

16. Alain, *Propos sur la religion*, p. 137.

17. Weil, *Enracinement*, p. 209; *The Need for Roots*, p. 157.

18. Weil, *Enracinement*, p. 133; *The Need for Roots*, p. 97.

19. Weil, *Cahiers*, 2: 242; *Notebooks, 1940–1942*, 1: 298.

20. Ibid., p. 244 / p. 300.

21. Weil, *Attente de Dieu*, p. 41; *Waiting on God*, p. 16.

22. Pétrement, *Simone Weil*, p. 205.

23. Simone Weil, letter of January 1935 to Albertine Thévenon, cited in Pétrement, *La vie de Simone Weil*, 2:29; *Seventy Letters*, p. 15.

24. Simone Weil, "Journal d'usine," *Œuvres complètes*, vol. 2: *Ecrits historiques et politiques*, book 2: *L'expérience ouvrière et l'adieu à la révolution, juillet 1934–juin 1937* (Paris: Gallimard, 1991), p. 253; "Factory Journal," in *Formative Writings, 1929–1941*, ed. and trans. Dorothy Tuck McFarland and Wilhelmina Van Ness (Amherst: University of Massachusetts Press, 1987), p. 225.

25. Weil, *Attente de Dieu*, p. 42; *Waiting on God*, pp. 19–20.

26. Weil, *Enracinement*, p. 380; *The Need for Roots*, pp. 286, 288.

27. Weil, *Attente de Dieu*, p. 43; *Waiting on God*, p. 20.

28. Ibid.

29. Charles Péguy, "Portrait de Bernard Lazare," in *Notre jeunesse*, in Charles Pégvy, *Œuvres complètes: Œuvres en prose, 1909–1914* (Paris: Gallimard, Pléiade), pp. 551–562; "A Portrait of Bernard Lazare," in Bernard Lazare, *Job's Dungheap: Essays on Jewish Nationalism and Social Revolution*, ed. Hannah Arendt, trans. Harry Lorin Binnse (New York: Schocken, 1948), pp. 15–40.

30. Bernard Lazare, *Le fumier de Job* (Paris: Circé, 1990), p. 8.

31. Ibid., p. 20.

32. Bernard Lazare, *Antisemitism, Its History and Causes*, trans. anon. (London: Britons Publishing, 1967).

33. Bernard Lazare, "Contre l'antisémitisme," in Bernard Lazare, *Juifs et antisémites* (Paris: Allia, 1992), p. 114.

34. Lazare, *Le fumier de Job*, p. 8.

35. Lazare, *Juifs et antisémites*, p. 175.

36. Weil, *Cahiers*, 3:246–247; *Notebooks, 1940–1942*, 2: 575–576.

37. Weil, *Attente de Dieu*, p. 47 / *Waiting on God*, p. 23.

38. Ibid., p. 45 / p. 21.

39. Ibid., p. 76 / p. 42.

40. Ibid., p. 54 / p. 27.

41. Ibid.

42. Edith Stein, letter of 12 February 1928 to Callista Kopp, in *Werke*, vol. 8: *Selbstbildnis in Briefen*, Part 1: 1916–1934 (Freiburg: Herder, 1976), p. 54, excerpted in Stein, *Dans la puissance*, ed. Herbstrith p. 47; Stein, *Collected Works*, 5: 54.

43. Weil, *Attente de Dieu*, p. 61; *Waiting on God*, p. 32.

44. Simone Weil, "Israël et les Gentils," in *Pensées sans ordre concernant l'amour de Dieu* (Paris: Gallimard, 1962), p. 53.

45. Joseph-Marie Perrin, *Mon dialogue avec Simone Weil* (Paris: Nouvelle Cité, Rencontres, 1984), p. 92; Angelo Roncalli [John XXIII], "Opening Address to the Second Vatican Council," in *The Documents of Vatican II*, ed. Walter J. Abbott (London: Geoffrey Chapman, 1966), p. 716, cited in Peter Hebblethwaite, *Pope John XXIII: Shepherd of the Modern World* (Garden City, N.Y.: Doubleday, 1985), p. 433 (translation modified by Hebblethwaite).

46. Simone Weil, letter to Hélène Honnorat, cited in Pétrement, *La vie de Simone Weil*, 2: 417; partially cited in Pétrement, *Simone Weil*, p. 468.

47. Perrin and Thibon, *Simone Weil as We Knew Her*, p. 119.

48. Weil, *Lettre à un religieux*, p. 14; *Letter to a Priest*, p. 12.

49. Alain, *Propos sur la religion*, p. 199.

50. Weil, *Attente de Dieu*, p. 80; *Waiting on God*, p. 44.

51. Ibid., p. 81 / p. 45.

52. Ibid., p. 25 / p. 52.

53. Ibid., p. 26 / p. 9.
54. Karl Jaspers, letter of 15 February 1951, in *Briefwechsel Arendt–Jaspers*, p. 201; *Correspondence*, p. 165.
55. Arendt, letter of 4 March 1951, ibid., p. 202 / pp. 165–166.
56. Stein, *Aus dem Leben*, p. 3; *Life in a Jewish Family*, p. 24.
57. Hannah Arendt, "Herzl and Lazare," in Hannah Arendt, *The Jew as Pariah: Jewish Identity and Politics in the Modern Age*, ed. Ron H. Feldman (New York: Grove Press, 1978), pp. 125–130.
58. Arendt, letter of 29 January 1946, in *Briefwechsel Arendt–Jaspers*, p. 65; *Correspondence*, p. 29.
59. Arendt, *Rahel Varnhagen, Lebensgeschichte*, p. 15; *Rahel Varnhagen, Life*, p. 85.

Part II. Commitment to the Things of This World
1933

1. Raymond Aron, *Mémoires* (Paris: Julliard, 1983), p. 63.
2. George Steiner, "Das lange Leben der Metaphorik: Ein Versuch über die Shoah," *Akzente* 3 (1987): 194–212.
3. Renata Posselt [Teresia Renata de Spiritu Sancto], *Edith Stein*, trans. Cecily Hastings and Donald Nicholl (London: Sheed and Ward, 1952), p. 117.
4. Ibid., pp. 118–119.
5. Ibid., p. 119.
6. Georges Passelecq and Bernard Suchecky, *The Hidden Encyclical of Pius XI: The Vatican's Lost Opportunity to Oppose Nazi Racial Policies* (New York: Harcourt Brace, 1987).
7. Posselt, *Edith Stein*, p. 120.
8. Edith Stein, letter of 19 July 1936 to Petra Brüning, in Edith Stein, *Werke*, vol. 9: *Selbstbildnis in Briefen*, Part 2: 1934–1942 (Freiburg: Herder, 1976), pp. 60–61; *Collected Works*, vol. 5: *Self-Portrait in Letters, 1916–1942*, trans. Josephine Koeppel (Washington: Institute of Carmelite Studies, 1993), p. 230.
9. Posselt, *Edith Stein*, p. 120.
10. Stein, letter of 14 April 1939 to Walter Warnach, in *Werke*, 9:135; *Collected Works*, 5:307.
11. Stein, letter of 3 September 1936 to Petra Brüning, ibid., pp. 64–65 / p. 237.
12. Alois Huning, *Edith Stein und Peter Wust: Von der Philosophie zum Glaubenszeugnis* (Münster, Westphalia, Germany: Regensberg, 1969), p. 34.
13. Edith Stein, "Beiträge zur philosophischen Begründung der Psychologie und der Geisteswissenschaften. Erste Abhandlung: Psychische Kausalität," *Jahrbuch für Philosophie und phänomenologische Forschung* 5 (1992): 76.
14. Posselt, *Edith Stein*, p. 164.
15. Hannah Arendt, "Was bleibt? Es bleibt die Muttersprache," in *Gespräche mit Hannah Arendt*, ed. Adelbert Reif (Munich: Piper, 1976), p. 21; " 'What Remains? The Language Remains': A Conversation with Günter Gaus," trans. Joan Stambaugh, in Hannah Arendt, *Essays in Understanding, 1930–1954*, ed. Jerome Kohn (New York: Harcourt Brace, 1994), p. 11.
16. Simone Weil, "Conditions d'une révolution allemande: 'Et Maintentant?' de Léon Trotsky," *Œuvres complètes*, 2: *Ecrits historiques et politiques*, book 1: *L'engagement syndical, 1927–juillet 1934*, ed. Géraldi Leroy (Paris: Gallimard, 1988), pp. 108–115.
17. Ibid., p. 115.
18. Simone Weil, "La situation en Allemagne," in *Œuvres complètes*, 2, book 1, pp. 141–142; "The Situation in Germany," in *Formative Writings, 1929–1941*, ed. and trans. Dorothy Tuck McFarland and Wilhelmina Van Ness (Amherst: University of Massachusetts Press, 1987), p. 97.
19. Simone Weil, "Premières impressions d'Allemagne," in *Œuvres complètes* 2.1.116; cited in Simone Pétrement, *Simone Weil: A Life*, trans. Raymond Rosenthal (New York: Pantheon, 1976), pp. 130–131.

20. Weil, "Premières impressions d'Allemagne," p. 117; cited in Pétrement, *Simone Weil*, p. 132.

21. Simone Weil, "Impressions d'Allemagne (août et septembre): L'Allemagne en attente," in *Œuvres complètes*, 2.1.127.

22. Simone Weil, "Sur la situation en Allemagne: Quelques remarques sur la réponse de la MOR" (*L'Ecole emancipée*, 7 May 1933), in *Œuvres complètes*, 2.1.207–212.

23. Ibid., p. 211.

24. Ibid., p. 212; partially cited in Pétrement, *Simone Weil*, p. 156.

25. Simone Weil, "Réflexions sur la guerre," in *Œuvres complètes*, 2.1.298; "Reflections on War," in *Formative Writings*, p. 247.

26. See Jean-François Sirinelli, *Deux intellectuels dans le siècle: Sartre et Aron* (Paris: Fayard, 1995).

27. Jean-Paul Sartre, foreword to Paul Nizan, *Aden, Arabie*, trans. Joan Pinkham (New York: Columbia University Press, 1987), p. 22.

28. Arendt, "Was bleibt?" p. 13; "What Remains?" p. 5.

29. Simone Weil, *Attente de Dieu* (Paris: Fayard, 1966), p. 24; *Waiting on God*, trans. Emma Craufurd (London: Routledge and Kegan Paul, 1951), p. 8.

30. Cited in Michel Winock, Esprit: *Des intellectuels dans la cité, 1930–1950* (Paris: Seuil, 1996), p. 92.

1935

1. Marc Augé and Aurélien Moline, *Paris, Années 1930: Roger-Viollet* (Paris: Hazan, 1996).

2. Ibid., p. 649.

3. [TN: *Diplome d'études supérieures*, the approximate equivalent of a C. phil. degree.]

4. Simone Weil, *Réflexions sur les causes de la liberté et de l'oppression*, in *Œuvres complètes*, 2.2.31; *Oppression and Liberty*, trans. Arthur Wills and John Petric (London: Routledge and Kegan Paul, 1958), p. 39.

5. Hannah Arendt, letter of 7 April 1956, in *Hannah Arendt–Karl Jaspers: Briefwechsel, 1926–1969*, ed. Lotte Köhler and Hans Sauer (Munich: Piper, 1985), p. 320; *Correspondence Hannah Arendt–Karl Jaspers, 1926–1969*, trans. Robert and Rita Kimber (New York: Harcourt Brace Jovanovich, 1992), p. 283.

6. "In the following chapter, Karl Marx will be criticized." Hannah Arendt, *The Human Condition* (Chicago: University of Chicago Press, 1958), p. 79.

7. John Locke, *The Second Treatise of Government*, in *Two Treatises of Government*, ed. Peter Laslett (London: Cambridge University Press, 1963), p. 329.

8. Weil, *Réflexions sur les causes*, p. 92; *Oppression and Liberty*, pp. 106–107.

9. Arendt, *Human Condition*, pp. 85–86.

10. Ibid. p. 108.

11. Weil, *Réflexions sur les causes*, p. 71; *Oppression and Liberty*, p. 83.

12. Ibid., p. 35/p. 44.

13. Simone Weil, "Y a-t-il une doctrine marxiste?" in *Réflexions sur les causes de la liberté et de l'oppression* (Paris: Gallimard, 1955); p. 229; "Is There a Marxist Doctrine?" in *Oppression and Liberty*, p. 174.

14. Ibid., p. 37/p. 45.

15. Ibid., p. 37/p. 46.

16. Ibid., p. 34/p. 43.

17. Homer, *Iliad*, 6. 458.

18. Arendt, *Human Condition*, p. 131n.

19. Ibid., p. 131.

20. Weil, *Réflexions sur les causes*, *Œuvres complètes*, p. 59; *Oppression and Liberty*, p. 70.

21. Arendt, *Human Condition*, p. 122.

22. Weil, *Réflexions sur les causes*, p. 43; *Oppression and Liberty*, p. 53.

23. Arendt, *Human Condition*, p. 126n.

24. Ibid., p. 133.

25. Ibid., p. 132.

26. Simone Weil, "Expérience de la vie d'usine: Lettre ouverte à Jules Romains," in *Œuvres complètes*, 2.2.301; "Factory Work," trans. Felix Giovanelli, *Politics* 3, no. 11 (December 1946), reprinted in *The Simone Weil Reader*, ed. George A. Panichas (London: Moyer Bell, 1977), p. 66.

27. Simone Weil, review of Louis de Broglie et al., *L'avenir de la science*, in *Sur la science* (Paris: Gallimard, 1966), pp. 179–180; "Scientism: A Review," in *On Science, Necessity, and the Love of God*, ed. and trans. Richard Rees (London: Oxford University Press, 1968), pp. 26–27.

28. Simone Weil, "Le groupement de 'l'Ordre nouveau,' " in *Œuvres complètes*, 2.2.325, 327.

29. Arendt, letter of 26 March 1955, in *Briefwechsel Arendt–Jaspers*, pp. 294–295; *Correspondence*, pp. 257–258.

30. Hannah Arendt, *The Life of the Mind*, 2 vols. (New York: Harcourt Brace Jovanovich, 1978), vol. 1: *Thinking*, p. 78.

31. Weil, *Réflexions sur les causes*, p. 30; *Oppression and Liberty*, p. 38.

32. Arendt, *Human Condition*, p. 134.

33. Weil, *Réflexions sur les causes*, p. 30; *Oppression and Liberty*, p. 38.

34. Arendt, *Human Condition*, p. 134.

35. Weil, *Réflexions sur les causes*, pp. 89–90; *Oppression and Liberty*, p. 104.

36. Alain, letter of 14 January 1934, cited in Pétrement, *Simone Weil*, p. 231.

37. Simone Weil, "Journal d'usine," in *Œuvres complètes*, 2.2.269.

38. Ibid., p. 262/p. 193.

39. Simone Weil, *L'enracinement* (Paris: Gallimard, 1949), p. 63; Simone Weil, *The Need for Roots: Prelude to a Declaration of Duties toward Mankind*, trans. Arthur Wills (London: Routledge and Kegan Paul, 1952), p. 43.

40. Alain, *Politique* (Paris: Presses universitaires de France, 1962), p. 1.

41. Simone Weil, *Enracinement*, p. 91; *The Need for Roots*, p. 64.

42. Simone Weil, "Antigone" (16 May 1936), *Œuvres complètes*, 2.2.333–338; "Antigone," in *Intimations of Christianity among the Ancient Greeks*, ed. and trans. Elisabeth Chase Geissbuhler (London: Routledge and Kegan Paul, 1957), pp. 18–23.

43. Simone Weil, "Science et perception chez Descartes," *Œuvres complètes*, vol. 1: *Premiers écrits philosophiques* (Paris: Gallimard, 1988), p. 217; "Science and Perception in Descartes," in *Formative Writings*, p. 85.

44. Weil, *Réflexions sur les causes*, p. 91; *Oppression and Liberty*, p. 106.

45. Arendt, *Human Condition*, p. 123.

46. Ibid. p. 134.

47. Ibid. p. 46.

48. Ibid. pp. 119–121.

49. Ibid. p. 118.

50. Ibid. p. 135.

51. Weil, *Réflexions sur les causes*, p. 90; *Oppression and Liberty*, p. 104.

52. Ibid., p. 71/p. 83.

53. Ibid., p. 106/p. 122.

54. Simone Weil, "Sur l'idée de Ganuchaud et Canguilhem," *Œuvres complètes*, 2.1.49 (summer 1928).

55. Martin Heidegger, *What Is Called Thinking?* trans. D. Wieck and J. Glenn Gray (New York: Harper and Row 1968), p. 159.

56. Arendt, Letter of 18 September 1946, in *Briefwechsel Arendt–Jaspers*, p. 95; *Correspondence*, p. 58.

57. Arendt, "Was bleibt?" p. 27; "What Remains?" p. 17.

58. Ibid., p. 17/p. 7.

59. Hannah Arendt and Gershom Scholem, "An Exchange," in *The Jew as Pariah: Jewish Identity and Politics in the Modern Age*, ed. Ron H. Feldman (New York: Grove Press, 1978), p. 246.
60. Ibid.
61. Arendt, "Was bleibt?" p. 31; "What Remains?" p. 20.
62. Arendt and Scholem, "An Exchange," p. 246.
63. Hannah Arendt, "To Save the Jewish Homeland," in Arendt and Scholem, *Jew as Pariah*, p. 186.
64. Mary McCarthy, letter of 17 October 1969, in *Between Friends: The Correspondence of Hannah Arendt and Mary McCarthy, 1949–1975*, ed. Carol Brightman (New York: Harcourt Brace, 1995), p. 246.
65. Arendt, letter of 17 October 1969, in *Between Friends*, pp. 248–249.
66. Ibid., p. 249.
67. Hannah Arendt, "Die jüdische Armee: Der Beginn einer jüdischen Politik?" *Aufbau*, 14 November 1941, reprinted. in Arendt, *Die Krise des Zionismus: Essays und Kommentare*, 2 vols., vol. 2, ed. Eike Geisel and Klaus Bittermann, Critica Diabolis 23 (Berlin: Tiamat, 1989), p. 168.
68. Guillaume de Tarde, *Les nouveaux cahiers*, no. 38 (1 Feb. 1939), p. 20.

1936

1. Ilan Greilsamer, *Blum* (Paris: Flammarion, 1996), p. 347.
2. Michael R. Marrus and Robert O. Paxton, *Vichy France and the Jews* (New York: Basic Books, 1981), p. 39.
3. Paul Claudel, letter to H. Daniel-Rops, in *Les Juifs*, ed. H Daniel-Rops (Paris: Plon, Présences, 1937), p. vii, cited in Bernard Doering, "Maritain's Idea of the Chosen People," in *Jacques Maritain and the Jews*, ed. Robert Royal (Mishawaka, Ind.: American Jacques Maritain Association, 1994), p. 33.
4. Greilsamer, *Blum*, p. 391.
5. Philibert Secretan, preface to Edith Stein, *La prière de l'Eglise* (Geneva: Ad Solem, 1995), p. 5.
6. Edith Stein, "Das Gebet der Kirche," in *Wege der Stille* (Frankfurt: Kaffke, 1978), p. 26; Edith Stein, "The Prayer of the Church," *Collected Works*, vol. 4: *The Hidden Life*, ed. Lucy Gelber and Michael Linssen, trans. Waltraut Stein (Washington: Institute of Carmelite Studies, 1992), pp. 7, 148 n.1.
7. Alain, *Politique*, LXX, p. 221.
8. Ibid., XCVIII, p. 296.
9. Ibid., LXXIII, p. 228.
10. Ibid., LXXXV, p. 262.
11. Winock, *Esprit*, pp. 125, 132, 160.
12. Weil, letter to Urbain and Albertine Thévenon, Autumn 1934, cited in Simone Pétrement, *La vie de Simone Weil*, 2 vols. (Paris: Fayard, 1983), 2:9; Pétrement, *Simone Weil*, pp. 217–218.
13. Simone Weil, "Notre Front populaire: Journal d'un militant," p. 69, cited in Géraldi Leroy, "Simone Weil et le Front populaire," *Cahiers Simone Weil* 2, no. 1 (March 1979).
14. Claude Jamet, *Journal* [extract], *Cahiers Simone Weil* 5, no. 1 (March 1982).
15. Simone Weil, "A propos de *La condition humaine*," in *Œuvres complètes*, 2.1.318–319; partially cited in Pétrement, *Simone Weil*, pp. 209–210.
16. Simone Weil, review of Rosa Luxemburg, *Letters from Prison*, in *Œuvres complètes*, 2.1. 300–301; cited in Pétreinent, *Simone Weil*, p. 184 (translation modified).
17. Simone Weil, letter to Georges Bernanos, in *Ecrits historiques et politiques* (Paris: Gallimard, 1960), p. 221; Simone Weil, *Selected Essays, 1931–1943*, ed. and trans. Richard Rees (London: Oxford University Press, 1962), pp. 172–175.

18. Clara Zetkin, cited in Maurice Baumont, *La faillite de la paix, 1918–1939* (Paris: Presses universitaires de France, Peuples et civilisations, 1961), p. 719.

19. Simone Weil, "Que se passe-t-il en Espagne?" in *Œuvres complètes,* 2.2.403; "Untitled Fragment on Spain," in *Formative Writings,* p. 255.

20. Simone Weil, "Journal d'Espagne," in *Œuvres complètes,* 2.2. p. 375.

21. Simone Weil, "Réflexions pour déplaire," in *Œuvres complètes,* 2.2. 388; "Reflections That No One Is Going to Like," in *Formative Writings,* pp. 256–257.

22. Simone Weil, "Faut-il graisser les godillots?" in *Œuvres complètes,* 2.2. 386; "Do We Have to Grease Our Combat Boots?" in *Formative Writings,* pp. 257–258.

23. Simone Weil, "Non-intervention généralisée" (unpublished draft, 1936–1937), in *Œuvres complètes,* vol. 2, book 3: *Vers la guerre, 1937–1940,* ed. Simone Fraisse (Paris: Gallimard, 1989), p. 44; "Broadening the Policy of Nonintervention," in *Formative Writings,* pp. 261–262.

24. Simone Weil, "Les rapports franco-allemands" (unpublished draft), *Œuvres complètes,* 2.3.48.

25. Simone Weil, fragment of a letter to Emmanuel Mounier, in "Un épisode de la guerre d'Espagne vu par Simone Weil," *Cahiers Simone Weil* 6, no. 4 (December 1983), pp. 293–296.

26. Jamet, entry for 28 December 1938, "Journal," *Cahiers Simone Weil* 5, no. 1 (March 1982), p. 4.

27. Simone Weil, "Ne recommençons pas la guerre de Troie" (April 1937), *Œuvres complètes,* 2.3. p. 55; "The Power of Words," in *Selected Essays,* p. 159.

28. Hannah Arendt, "On the Nature of Totalitarianism: An Essay in Understanding," in Arendt, *Essays in Understanding,* p. 347.

29. Hannah Arendt, "The Seeds of a Fascist International," in Arendt, *Essays in Understanding,* p. 140.

30. "Hannah Arendt," obituary, *New York Times,* 5 Dec. 1975, cited in Elisabeth Young-Bruehl, *Hannah Arendt: For Love of the World* (New Haven: Yale University Press, 1982), p. 140.

31. Arendt, "Nature of Totalitarianism," p. 349.

32. Arendt, "Fascist International," p. 147.

33. Arendt, "Nature of Totalitarianism," pp. 355–356.

34. "Ne recommençons pas la guerre de Troie," p. 55; "Power of Words," p. 160.

35. Ibid., p. 55/p. 161.

36. Simone Weil, "Le danger de guerre et les conquêtes ouvrières" (*Syndicats,* no. 28, 22 April 1937), in *Œuvres completes,* 2, 1. 72–73.

37. Alain, *Propos sur la religion* (Paris: PUF, 1938), p. 137.

1938

1. Louis-Ferdinand Céline, *Bagatelles pour un massacre* (Paris: Denoël, 1938).

2. Marrus and Paxton, *Vichy France and the Jews,* p. 40.

3. Louis-Ferdinand Céline, *L'école des cadavres* (Paris: Denoël, 1938), p. 264, cited in ibid., p. 42.

4. Hilda Graef, "Edith Stein et les dons du saint Esprit," *La vie spirituelle,* December 1975, pp. 504–515, cited in Jean-François Thomas, *Simone Weil et Edith Stein: Malheur et souffrance* (Paris: Culture et Vérité, 1988), p. 166.

5. Posselt, *Edith Stein,* p. 129.

6. Edith Stein, *Wie ich in den Kölner Karmel kam,* ed. Maria Amat Neyer (Würzburg: Echter, 1994).

7. Rosa Luxemburg, letter of 26 January 1917 to Luise Kautsky.

8. Jacques Maritain, "Les Juifs parmi les nations," in *Le mystère d'Israël* (Paris: Desclée de Brouwer, 1990), p. 75; Jacques Maritain, *A Christian Looks at the Jewish Question* (New York: Longmans, Green, 1939), p. 16.

9. Jacques Maritain, *La nouvelle revue française*, no. 297 (1 June 1938).

10. Henriette Psichari-Renan, *Les convertis de la Belle Epoque* (Paris: Editions rationalistes, 1971).

11. André Gide, *Cahiers André Gide* (Petite Dame) 4 (1918–1929) (Paris: Gallimard, 1973), p. 35. Cited in Greilsamer, *Blum*, p. 45.

12. Léon Bloy, *Le salut par les Juifs* (Paris: Henri Aniéré, 1906), cited in Jacques Maritain, *Antisemitism* (London: Geoffrey Bles, Centenary Press, 1939), p. 22. [*Antisemitism* is an expanded version of "Les Juifs parmi les nations."]

13. Jacques Maritain, *L'impossible antisémitisme*, with a foreword by Pierre Vidal-Naquet, "Jacques Maritain et les Juifs" (Paris: Desclée de Brouwer, 1994), p. 163.

14. Bloy, *Le salut par les Juifs*, pp. 13–15, partially translated in John Hellmann, "The Jews in the 'New Middle Ages,' " in *Jacques Maritain and the Jews*, p. 14.

15. Simone Weil, "Pour une négociation immédiate," in *Œuvres complètes* 2.3. 78–79.

16. Simone Weil, "Réflexions sur la conférence de Bourché," in *Œuvres complétes*, 2.3. p. 90; "Reflections on Bouché's Lecture," in *Formative Writings*, p. 270.

17. Simone Weil, "L'Europe en guerre pour la Tchécoslovaquie?", in *Œuvres complétes*, 2.3. 81–86; "A European War over Czechoslovakia?" in *Formative Writings*, pp. 264–268.

18. Ibid., pp. 82–83 / pp. 265–266.

19. Simone Weil, letter to Gaston Bergery, in *Ecrits historiques et politiques*, p. 286; cited in Pétrement, *Simone Weil*, p. 326.

20. Pétrement, *Simone Weil*, p. 326.

21. Weil, *Attente de Dieu*, p. 44; *Waiting on God*, p. 21. See also Weil, letter of 12 May 1942 to Joë Bousquet, in Simone Weil, *Pensées sans ordre concernant l'amour de Dieu* (Paris: Gallimard, 1962), p. 45; Simone Weil, *Seventy Letters*, ed. and trans. Richard Rees (London: Cambridge University Press, 1965), p. 142.

22. Weil, letter of 12 May 1942 to Joë Bousquet, in *Pensées sans ordre*, p. 81; *Seventy Letters*, p. 140.

23. Winock, *Esprit*, p. 180.

24. Georges Bernanos, *Nous autres français* (Paris: Gallimard, 1939), pp. 739–740, cited in Winock, *Esprit*, p. 185.

25. Maritain, "Les Juifs parmi les nations," in *Mystère d'Isreal*, pp. 116–117, and *A Christian Looks at the Jewish Question*, p. 41

26. Raïssa Maritain, *We Have Been Friends Together: Memoirs*, trans. Julie Kernan (New York: Longmans, Green, Golden Measure Books, 1942).

27. Maritain, *Mystère d'Israël*, p. 184; see further p. 224. See also Léon Bloy, *Le Vieux de la montagne* (Paris: Mercure de France, 1963).

28. J. Maritain, *Mystère d'Israël*, p. 217, cited in Michael Novak, "Maritain and the Jews," in Royal, *Jacques Maritain and the Jews*, p. 123.

29. Maritain, *Mystère d'Israël*, p. 217.

30. "Jews and Catholics," *Je suis partout*, no. 384 (1 April 1938), in Maritain, *L'impossible antisémitisme*, pp. 169–170.

31. Ibid., pp. 193–194.

32. Ibid., pp. 211, 214.

33. Arendt, letter of 17 August 1946, in *Briefwechsel Arendt–Jaspers*, p. 92; *Correspondence*, p. 56.

34. Hannah Arendt, "From the Dreyfus Affair to France Today," *Jewish Social Studies* 4 (1942): 195–240, included, with modifications, in Hannah Arendt, *The Origins of Totalitarianism*, 3d ed. (New York: Harcourt, Brace, Harvest Books, 1973), pp. 89–120.

35. Arendt, *Origins of Totalitarianism*, p. 118. See also Arendt, review of Bruno Weil, *Historia del Crimen Judicial mas Escandaloso del Siglo XIX*, *Jewish Social Studies* 5 (1943): 205.

36. Hannah Arendt, "Christianity and Revolution," *The Nation* 161, no. 12 (22 September 1945), reprinted in Arendt, *Essays in Understanding*, pp. 151–155. Raïssa Maritain's book was

later published in French as *Les grandes amitiés.* Arendt also reviewed, in *Aufbau,* a book originally published in English by Jacques Maritain: *Ransoming the Time,* trans. Harry Lorin Binsse
(New York: Scribner's, 1941).

37. Jacques Maritain, *L'antimoderne,* in Jacques Maritain, *Œuvres complètes,* 2: 928ff.

38. This information is taken from Pierre Vidal-Naquet, *Réflexions sur le génocide, la mémoire
et le présent,* vol. 3 (Paris: La Découverte, 1995), pp. 40ff.

39. Jacques Maritain, "A propos de la question juive," in Maritain, *Œuvres complètes,* 2:1198;
cited in Doering, "Maritain's Idea of the Chosen People," in Royal, *Jacques Maritain and the
Jews,* p. 27.

40. Maritain, "A propos de la question juive," in Maritain, *Œuvres complètes,* vol. 2:1197.

41. Georges Bernanos, *A Diary of My Times,* trans. Pamela Morris (London: Boriswood,
1938), p. 75.

42. Hannah Arendt, "Franz Kafka: A Revaluation," in Arendt, *Essays in Understanding,* p. 72.

43. Hannah Arendt, "Französische politische Literatur im Exil," *Aufbau,* 28 February 1943,
pp. 7, 8, and 26 March 1943, p. 8.

44. Georges Bernanos, *Nous autres français,* ed. Jacques Chabot, in Georges Bernanos, *Essais
et écrits de combat,* vol. 1 (Paris: Gallimard, Pléiade, 1971), p. 618.

45. Ibid., p. 648.

46. Ibid., p. 735.

47. Arendt, "Französische politische Literatur im Exil," p. 8.

48. Jan H. Nota, "Edith Stein und der Entwurf für eine Enzyklika gegen Rassismus und Antisemitismus," *Freiburger Rundbrief* 26, no. 97–100 (1975): 35–41.

49. Memorandum sent to Father Joseph A. Murphy on 3 July 1938, cited in Passelecq and
Suchecky, *Hidden Encyclical,* pp. 36–37.

50. Passelecq and Suchecky, *Hidden Encyclical,* pp. 253–254.

51. Ibid., p. 98.

52. Jean Tonneau, *Le Pape, la guerre et la paix: Pie XII a-t-il parlé?* (Paris: Cerf, 1942).

53. Posselt, *Edith Stein,* p. 184.

1939

1. *Le Voltigeur,* no. 11 (1 March 1939), cited in Winock, *Esprit,* p. 200.

2. Claudel, letter to H. Daniel-Rops, p. xx.

3. Jean Giraudoux, *Pleins pouvoirs* (Paris: Gallimard, 1939), p. 59, cited in Marrus and Paxton, *Vichy France and the Jews,* p. 53.

4. Giraudoux, *Pleins pouvoirs,* pp. 63, 65, 76, cited in Marrus and Paxton, *Vichy France and
the Jews,* p. 5.

5. Pierre Drieu La Rochelle, *Gilles* (Paris: Gallimard, 1939), p. 562, cited in Marrus and
Paxton, *Vichy France and the Jews,* p. 46.

6. Erna Biberstein-Stein, *Aufzeichnungen* (New York, 1949), p. xix.

7. Waltraud Herbstrith, *Edith Stein: A Biography,* trans. Bernard Bonowitz (San Francisco:
Ignatius, 1992), pp. 168–169.

8. Simone Weil, "Note sur la suppression générale des partis politiques," in *Ecrits de Londres et dernières lettres* (Paris: Gallimard, 1980), pp. 135, 148.

9. Arendt, *Human Condition,* p. 7.

10. Hannah Arendt, *Was ist Politik?: Fragmente aus dem Nachlaß,* ed. Ursula Ludz (Munich:
Piper, 1993), pp. 21–122.

11. Ibid., pp. 106–107.

12. Arendt, *Human Condition,* p. 244.

13. Simone Weil, "Quelques réflexions sur les origines de l'hitlerisme," in *Œuvres complètes,*
2.3.172; "The Great Beast," in *Selected Essays,* p. 93.

14. Arendt, *Was ist Politik?* p. 117.

15. Weil, "Quelques réflexions sur les origines de l'hitlerisme," p. 176; "The Great Beast," p. 96.

16. Weil, *Enracinement*, p. 222; *The Need for Roots*, p. 167.

17. Simone Weil, draft of a letter, in *Ecrits historiques et politiques*, p. 103.

18. Ibid., p. 104.

19. Ibid., p. 105.

20. Weil, "Quelques réflexions sur les origines de l'hitlerisme," p. 187; "The Great Beast," p. 107.

21. Weil, *Enracinement*, p. 198; *The Need for Roots*, p. 148.

22. Ibid., p. 208 / p. 156.

23. Weil, "Quelques réflexions sur les origines de l'hitlerisme," p. 181; "The Great Beast," p. 102.

24. Ibid.

25. Weil, *Enracinement*, pp. 181–183, 215; *The Need for Roots*, pp. 134–136, 161–162.

26. Weil, "Quelques réflexions sur les origines de l'hitlerisme," p. 210; "The Great Beast," p. 131.

27. Arendt, "Keinen Kaddisch wird man singen," *Aufbau*, 19 June 1942, p. 19.

28. Arendt, *Was ist Politik?* p. 115.

29. Ibid., p. 116.

30. Ibid., p. 117.

31. Ibid., p. 121.

32. Simone Weil, *Cahiers*, 3 vols., vol. 1 (Paris: Plon, 1951), p. 57; *The Notebooks of Simone Weils 1940–1942*, 2 vols., trans. Arthur Wills (London: Routledge and Kegan Paul, 1956), 1:32.

33. Arendt, *Was ist Politik?*, p. 72.

34. Ibid., p. 80.

35. Ibid., p. 88.

36. Ibid., p. 89.

37. Ibid., pp. 105–106.

38. Simone Weil, "L'*Iliade*, ou la poème de la force," in *La source grecque* (Paris: Gallimard, 1953), p. 11; Simone Weil, "The *Iliad*, Poem of Might," in Simone Weil, *Intimations of Christianity among the Ancient Greeks*, ed. and trans. Elisabeth Chase Geissbuhler (London: Routledge and Kegan Paul, 1957), p. 24. See also Simone Weil, *La pesanteur et la grâce* (Paris: Plon, 1988), p. 67; Simone Weil, *Gravity and Grace*, trans. Arthur Wills (Lincoln: University of Nebraska Press, 1997).

39. Simone Weil, "En quoi consiste l'inspiration occitanienne?", in *Ecrits historiques et politiques*, p. 83; "The Romanesque Renaissance," in *Selected Essays*, p. 53.

40. Simone Weil, *Lettre à un religieux* (Paris: Gallimard, 1951), p. 47; *Letter to a Priest*, trans. A. F. Wills (London: Routledge and Kegan Paul, 1953), p. 41.

41. Weil, *Attente de Dieu*, p. 243; *Waiting on God*, p. 167.

42. Ibid., p. 245 / p. 168.

43. Weil, "*Iliade*, poème de la force," p. 11; "*Iliad*, Poem of Might," p. 24.

44. Ibid., p. 12 / p. 25.

45. Simone Weil, Draft of the conclusion to "L'*Iliade*, ou le poème de la force," in *Œuvres complétes*, 2.3.298.

46. Arendt, *Was ist Politik?* p. 92.

47. Ernst Jünger, *The Storm of Steel*, trans. Basil Creighton (London: Chatto and Windus, 1929).

48. Carl von Clausewitz, *On War*, ed. Anatol Rapoport, trans. J. J. Graham (London: Penguin, 1982), p. 119.

49. Arendt, *Was ist Politik?* Fragment 3d, p. 133.

50. Ibid.

51. Ibid., p. 29.

52. Simone Weil, "Réflexions en vue d'un bilan" (draft, spring–summer 1939), in *Œuvres complétes*, 2.3, 99–116; "Cold War Policy in 1939," in *Selected Essays*, pp. 177–194.

53. Weil, "Quelques réflexions sur les origines de l'hitlerisme," p. 198; "The Great Beast," p. 119.

54. Simone Weil, "Réflexions sur la barbarie," *Œuvres complètes*, 2.3. 224; "The Great Beast," p. 144.

55. Weil, "Quelques réflexions sur les origines de l'hitlerisme," p. 209; "The Great Beast," p. 130.

56. Weil, *Enracinement*, p. 186; *The Need for Roots*, p. 138.

57. Ibid., p. 345 / p. 262.

58. Simone Weil, Letter to Jean Giraudoux, in *Œuvres complètes*, 2.3 27; *Seventy Letters*, p. 110.

59. Arendt, *Origins of Totalitarianism*, p. 157.

60. Arendt, letter of 17 August 1946, in *Briefwechsel Arendt–Jaspers*, p. 92; *Correspondence*, p. 55.

61. Arendt, "From the Dreyfus Affair to France Today." This essay first appeared in *Jewish Social Studies*, whose editor-in-chief was the historian Salo Baron.

62. Arendt, *Origins of Totalitarianism*, p. 90.

63. Bernard-Henri Lévy, *L'idéologie française* (Paris: Grasset, 1981), p. 107.

64. Ibid., p. 109.

65. Georges Bernanos, *La grande peur des bien-pensants: Edouard Drumont*, ed. Joseph Jurt, in *Essais et écrits de combat*, vol. 1:336.

66. Ibid., pp. 149, 296, 328, 329.

67. Ibid., p. 329.

68. Simone Weil, *Cahiers*, 3:133; *Notebooks, 1940–1942*, 2:500.

69. Hannah Arendt, "A Reply to Eric Voegelin," in Arendt, *Essays in Understanding*, p. 406.

70. Arendt, *Origins of Totalitarianism*, pp. 465–466.

71. Eric Voegelin, *Die politischen Religionen* (Stockholm: Bermann-Fischer, 1939), p. 8.

72. Ibid., pp. 57–58.

73. Raymond Aron, "L'avenir des religions séculières" (1944), in *Histoire et politique* (Paris: Julliard, 1975), p. 370.

74. Weil, *Enracinement*, p. 119; *The Need for Roots*, p. 87.

75. Weil, *Cahiers*, 3.136; *Notebooks, 1940–1942*, 2:502.

76. Hannah Arendt, "Understanding and Politics (The Difficulties of Understanding)," in *Essays in Understanding*, p. 309.

77. Arendt, "Understanding and Politics," pp. 309–312.

78. Hannah Arendt, "Des Teufels Redekunst," *Aufbau*, 8 May 1942, p. 20, and "The Image of Hell" (1946), in Arendt, *Essays in Understanding*, p. 198.

79. Arendt, "Religion and the Intellectuals," in Arendt, *Essays in Understanding*, p. 228.

80. Ibid., p. 230.

81. Waldemar Gurian, *Bolshevism: An Introduction to Soviet Communism* (Notre Dame, Ind.: University of Notre Dame Press, 1952).

82. Arendt, "Religion and Politics," p. 384.

83. Arendt, "Reply to Eric Voegelin," pp. 401–408.

84. Ibid., p. 407.

85. Hannah Arendt, "Concern with Politics in Recent European Political Thought," in Arendt, *Essays in Understanding*, p. 436.

86. Weil, *Enracinement*, p. 302; *The Need for Roots*, p. 229.

87. Ibid., pp. 323–329 / pp. 244–250.

88. Arendt, "The Image of Hell," pp. 201–202.

89. Arendt, letter of 17 December 1946, in *Briefwechsel Arendt—Jaspers*, p. 106; *Correspondence*, p. 69.

90. Weil, *Enracinement*, p. 287 / *The Need for Roots*, p. 217.

91. Ibid., p. 285 / p. 216.
92. Ibid., p. 186 / p. 139.
93. Ibid. p. 350 / p. 265.
94. Ibid. p. 286 / p. 217.
95. Ibid., p. 292 / p. 221.
96. Ibid., p. 292 / p. 222.
97. Ibid., p. 328 / p. 249.
98. Ivo R. Malan, "Simone Weil et la responsabilité des écrivains," *Cahiers Simone Weil* 2, no. 3 (September 1979): 161; Weil, "The Responsibility of Writers," in Weil, *On Science*, p. 166.
99. Simone Weil, letter to *Cahiers du Sud*, *Cahiers du Sud*, no. 310 (1951), p. 428, cited in *Cahiers Simone Weil* 10, no. 4 (December 1987): 356. See also *Enracinement*, pp. 38, 106; *The Need for Roots*, pp. 24–25, 76.
100. Hannah Arendt, *Eight Exercises in Political Thought: Between Past and Future* (New York: Viking, 1968), p. 226.
101. Plato, *The Phaedrus*, trans. R. Hackforth, in *Collected Dialogues*, ed. Edith Hamilton and Huntington Cairns (Princeton: Princeton University Press, 1961), Bollingen Series 71, 245a, p. 492.
102. Arendt, letter of 30 September 1973, in *Between Friends*, pp. 343–344.
103. Arendt, *Human Condition*, pp. 55–56.
104. Hans Jonas, "Immortality and the Modern Temper," *Harvard Theological Review* 55 (1962): 3.

Part III. Exile
1940

1. Cited in Renée Bédarida, *Les armes de l'esprit*: Témoignage chrétien, *1941–1944* (Paris: Editions ouvrières, 1977), p. 13.
2. Raïssa Maritain, *We Have Been Friends Together: Memoirs*, trans. Julie Kernan (New York: Longmans, Green, Golden Measure Books, 1942), p. vii.
3. Arthur Koestler, *Scum of the Earth* (New York: Macmillan, 1948), p. 24.
4. Ibid., p. 249.
5. Georges Bernanos, *Correspondance inédite*, ed. Albert Béguin and Jean Murray (Paris: Plon, 1971), vol. 2: 1934–1948, p. 334.
6. Georges Bernanos, *Le chemin de la croix des âmes*, p. 29, cited in Michel Winock, *Esprit: Des intellectuels dans la cité, 1930–1950* (Paris: Seuil, 1996), p. 217.
7. Koestler, *Scum of the Earth*, p. 25.
8. Ibid.
9. Ibid., pp. 254–256 (translation modified).
10. Ibid., p. 26.
11. Henri Bourdais, *La JOC sous l'Occupation allemande: Témoignages et souvenirs de Henri Bourdais* (Paris: Editions de l'Atelier / Editions ouvrières, 1995).
12. Emmanuel Mounier, *Entretiens*, X, p. 44, cited in Winock, *Esprit*, p. 216.
13. *Lettres de Claire Girard, Roger Lescaret* (Paris, 1954–1993), p. 28, cited in Pierre Vidal-Naquet, *Réflexions sur le génocide, les Juifs, la mémoire et le présent*, vol. 3 (Paris: La Découverte, 1995), p. 19.
14. Bédarida, *Armes de l'esprit*, p. 58.
15. Ibid., pp. 16, 20.
16. Mounier, *Entretiens*, XII, 18 May 1941, cited in Winock, *Esprit*, p. 217.
17. Pierre Bitoun, *Les hommes d'Uriage* (Paris: La Découverte, 1988).
18. "Archives judiciaires, dossiers de la section spéciale de la cour d'appel d'Aix-en-Provence, Archives départementales des Bouches-du-Rhône, série 8 W, dossier 22. Document no. 1: pièce 119 de la procédure," *Cahiers Simone Weil* 17, no. 4 (December 1994), p. 217.

19. Hannah Arendt, "Keinen Kaddisch wird man singen," *Aufbau*, 19 June 1942, p. 19.
20. Hannah Arendt, "Die wahren Gründe für Theresienstadt," *Aufbau*, 3 Sept. 1943, p. 21.
21. Ibid.
22. Hannah Arendt, "We Refugees," *Menorah Journal* 31 (1943), reprinted in Hannah Arendt, *The Jew as Pariah: Jewish Identity and Politics in the Modern Age*, ed. Ron H. Feldman (New York: Grove Press, 1978), p. 59.
23. Lotte Eisner, *Exilés en France* (Paris: Maspero), cited in a note to Arthur Koestler, *La lie de la terre*, in *Œuvres autobiographiques* (Paris: Laffont, 1994), p. 1132.
24. Koestler, *Scum of the Earth*, p. 23.
25. Elisabeth Young-Bruehl, *Hannah Arendt: For Love of the World* (New Haven: Yale University Press, 1982), p. 15.
26. Carol Brightman, Introduction to *Between Friends: The Correspondence of Hannah Arendt and Mary McCarthy, 1949–1975* (New York: Harcourt Brace, 1995).
27. Simone Weil, *Œuvres complètes*, vol. 6: *Cahiers*, book 1: *1933–septembre 1941*, ed. Aylette Degrâces et al. (Paris: Gallimard, 1994), p. 154.
28. Koestler, *Scum of the Earth*, p. 279.
29. Simone Weil, *La connaissance surnaturelle* (Paris: Gallimard, 1950), p. 173; Simone Weil, *First and Last Notebooks*, trans. Richard Rees (New York: Oxford, 1970), p. 215.
30. Simone Weil, *Attente de Dieu* (Paris: Fayard, 1966), p. 177; Simone Weil, *Waiting on God*, trans. Emma Craufurd (London: Routledge and Kegan Paul, 1951), p. 117.
31. Ibid., p. 39 / p. 16.
32. Simone Weil, *Lettre à un religieux* (Paris: Gallimard, 1951), p. 19; *Letter to a Priest*, trans. A. F. Wills (London: Routledge and Kegan Paul, 1953), p. 16.
33. Simone Weil, "Israël et les Gentils," in *Pensées sans ordre concernant l'amour de Dieu* (Paris: Gallimard, 1962), p. 52.
34. Ibid., p. 51.
35. Weil, *Lettre à un religieux*, p. 35; *Letter to a Priest*, p. 30.
36. Weil, "Israël et les Gentils," p. 52.
37. Weil, *Attente de Dieu*, p. 240; *Waiting on God*, p. 165.
38. Weil, *Lettre à un religieux*, p. 23; *Letter to a Priest*, p. 19.
39. Ibid., p. 49/p. 13.
40. Weil, "Israël et les Gentils," p. 54.
41. Simone Weil, *L'enracinement* (Paris: Gallimard, 1949), p. 311; Simone Weil, *The Need for Roots: Prelude to a Declaration of Duties toward Mankind*, trans. Arthur Wills (London: Routledge and Kegan Paul, 1952), p. 235.
42. Ibid., p. 305/p. 232.
43. Weil, *Connaissance surnaturelle*, p. 173; *First and Last Notebooks*, p. 215.
44. Emmanuel Lévinas, "Simone Weil against the Bible," *Difficult Freedom: Essays on Judaism*, trans. Séan Hand (London: Athlone, 1990), p. 137.
45. Martin Buber, *On Judaism*, ed. Nahum N. Glatzer (New York: Schocken, 1967), p. 20.
46. Simone Pétrement, *La vie de Simone Weil* (Paris: Fayard, 1983), 2:291; Simone Pétrement, *Simone Weil: A Life*, trans: Raymond Rosenthal (New York: Pantheon), p. 554.
47. Lévinas, "Simone Weil against the Bible," p. 133.
48. Salomon Malka, *Monsieur Chouchani. L'énigme d'un maître du XXe siècle: Entretiens avec Elie Wiesel* (Paris: Lattès, 1994).
49. Joseph-Marie Perrin, *Mon dialogue avec Simone Weil* (Nouvelle Cité: Rencontres, 1984), p. 99.
50. Ibid., p. 137.
51. Joseph-Marie Perrin and Gustave Thibon, *Simone Weil as We Knew Her*, trans. Emma Craufurd (London: Routledge and Kegan Paul, 1953), p. 60.
52. Simone Weil, *Intuitions préchrétiennes* (Paris: Fayard, 1985), p. 168; Simone Weil, *Intimations of Christianity among the Ancient Greeks*, trans. Elisabeth Chase Geissbuhler (London: Routledge and Kegan Paul, 1957), p. 199.

53. Lévinas, "Simone Weil against the Bible," p. 139.

54. Ibid., p. 134.

55. Simone Pétrement, *Le dualisme dans l'histoire de la philosophie des religions: Introduction à l'étude du dualisme platonicien, du gnosticisme et du manichéisme* (Paris: Gallimard, 1946), and Simone Pétrement, *A Separate God: The Christian Origins of Gnosticism*, trans. Carol Harrison (San Francisco: Harper, 1990).

56. Simone Weil, extracts from a letter to André Weil, in *Sur la science* (Paris: Gallimard, 1966), p. 242; cited in Pétrement, *Simone Weil*, p. 370.

57. Pétrement, *Simone Weil*, p. 37.

58. Ibid., p. 34.

59. Pétrement, *Separate God*, p. 74.

60. Ibid., p. 14.

61. Perrin, *Mon dialogue avec Simone Weil*, p. 101.

62. Weil, *Connaissance surnaturelle*, p. 299; *First and Last Notebooks*, p. 329.

63. Ibid., p. 90/p. 140.

64. Simone Weil, *Cahiers*, 3 vols., vol. 1 (Paris: Plon, 1951), p. 51; *The Notebooks of Simone Weil, 1940–1942*, 2 vols., trans. Arthur Wills (London: Routledge and Kegan Paul), 1:28. See also ibid., p. 206/p. 170.

65. Henri de Lubac et al., *Israël et la foi chrétienne* (Freiburg: Editions de la Librairie de l'Université [Luf], 1942), pp. 9–39.

66. Ibid., pp. 280–281.

67. Arendt, *The Human Condition* (Chicago: University of Chicago Press, 1958), p. 10.

68. Ibid., p. 20.

69. Ibid., pp. 243–44.

70. Hannah Arendt and Gershom Scholem, "An Exchange," in Hannah Arendt, *The Jew as Pariah: Jewish Identity and Politics in the Modern Age*, ed. Ron H. Feldman (New York: Grove Press, 1978), p. 247.

71. Hannah Arendt, "Ein christliches Wort zur Judenfrage," *Aufbau*, 5 June 1942, p. 19.

72. Hans Jonas, "Der Gottesbegriff nach Auschwitz: Eine jüdische Stimme," in Hans Jonas and Fritz Stern, *Reflexionen finsterer Zeit*, ed. Otfried Hofius (Tübingen: Mohr, 1984), pp. 65–66.

73. Weil, *Enracinement*, p. 152; *The Need for Roots*, pp. 112–11

74. Hannah Arendt, "Understanding and Politics (The Difficulties of Understanding)," in Hannah Arendt, *Essays in Understanding, 1930–1954*, ed. Jerome Kohn (New York: Harcourt Brace, 1994). p. 31

75. Ibid.

76. Ibid.

77. Ibid.

78. Ibid.

79. Ibid.

80. Hannah Arendt, "On the Nature of Totalitarianism," in Arendt, *Essays in Understanding*, p. 348.

81. Hannah Arendt, *The Origins of Totalitarianism*, 3d ed. (New York: Harcourt, Brace, Harvest Books, 1973), p. 459.

82. Ibid.

83. Simone Weil, "Quelques réflexions sur les origines de l'hitlerisme," in *Œuvres complètes*, vol. 2: *Ecrits historiques et politiques*, book 3: *Vers la guerre, 1937–1940*, ed. Simone Fraisse (Paris: Gallimard, 1989), p. 209; Simone Weil, "The Great Beast," in *Selected Essays, 1931–1943*, ed. and trans. Richard Rees (London: Oxford University Press, 1962), p. 130.

84. Simone Weil, *Cahiers*, 3 vols., vol. 2 (Paris: Plon, 1953), p. 9; *Notebooks, 1940–1942*, 1:147.

85. Simone Weil, *Cahiers*, 3 vols., vol. 3 (Paris: Plon, 1951), p. 31; *Notebooks, 1940–1942*, 2:432.

86. Arendt, *Origins of Totalitarianism*, p. 445.

87. Hannah Arendt, *Was ist Politik?: Fragmente aus dem Nachlaß*, ed. Ursula Ludz (Munich: Piper, 1993), p. 127.

88. Raymond Aron, "L'essence du totalitarisme selon Hannah Arendt," in *Histoire et politique* (Paris: Julliard, 1975), p. 424.

89. Hannah Arendt, "Waldemar Gurian, 1903–1954," in *Men in Dark Times* (New York: Harcourt Brace and World, 1968), pp. 253–262.

90. Waldemar Gurian, *The Future of Bolshevism*, trans. E. I. Watkin (London: Sheed and Ward, 1936).

91. Elie Halévy, *The Era of Tyrannies: Essays on Socialism and War*, trans. R. K. Webb (London: Penguin, 1967).

92. We are here following François Furet, *Le passé d'une illusion: Essai sur l'idée communiste au XXe siècle* (Paris: R. Laffont/Calmann-Lévy, 1995).

93. Aron, "L'essence du totalitarisme selon Hannah Arendt," p. 425.

94. Furet, *Le passé d'une illusion*, pp. 496, 500.

95. Rudolf Augstein et al., *Historikerstreit: Die Dokumentation der Kontroverse um die Einzigartigkeit der nationalsozialistischen Judenvernichtung* (Munich: Piper, 1987).

1941

1. Cited in Henri Michel, *The Second World War*, trans. Douglas Parmée (London: Deutsch, 1975), p. 206.

2. Cited in Bédarida, *Armes de l'esprit*, p. 30.

3. Pierre Drieu la Rochelle, *La nouvelle revue française*, August 1941, cited in Michael R. Marrus and Robert O. Paxton, *Vichy France and the Jews* (New York: Basic Books, 1981), p. 58.

4. Olivier Wieviorka, *Une certaine idée de la Résistance* (Paris: Seuil, 1995), p. 25.

5. *Défense de la France*, no. 1, 15 August 1941.

6. Marrus and Paxton, *Vichy France and the Jews*, p. 197.

7. Paul Claudel, Letter to H. Daniel-Rops, in *Les Juifs*, ed. H. Daniel-Rops (Paris: Plon, Présences, 1937), pp. 325–326.

8. Bourdais, *JOC*, p. 128.

9. Edith Stein, letter to Ambrosia Antonia Engelmann, presumably written in December 1941, in Edith Stein, *Werke*, vol. 9: *Selbstbildnis in Briefen*, Part 2: 1934–1942 (Freiburg: Herder, 1976), p. 167; *Collected Works*, vol. 5: *Self-Portrait in Letters, 1916–1942*, trans. Josephine Koeppel (Washington: Institute of Carmelite Studies, 1993), p. 341.

10. Pétrement, *Simone Weil*, p. 412.

11. Perrin, *Mon dialogue avec Simone Weil*, p. 65.

12. Ibid., p. 66.

13. Perrin and Thibon, *Simone Weil as We Knew Her*, p. 122.

14. Perrin, *Mon dialogue avec Simone Weil*, p. 102.

15. See Pétrement, *Simone Weil*, p. 395. For an English translation of Simone Weil's letter, see letter to Déodat Roché of 23 January 1941, in *Seventy Letters*, ed. and trans. Richard Rees (London: Oxford University Press, 1965), pp. 129–131.

16. A. Fraixe, "Simone Weil et les *Cahiers du Sud*," *Cahiers Simone Weil* 12, no. 2 (June 1988): 177.

17. *Cahiers Simone Weil* 2, no. 4 (December 1979): 181.

18. "Lettres de Simone Weil à Gustave Thibon et de Gustave Thibon à Simone Weil," *Cahiers Simone Weil* 4, no. 2 (June 1981): 79.

19. Ibid., p. 78.

20. Perrin, *Mon dialogue avec Simone Weil*, p. 108.

21. Hannah Arendt, *Crises of the Republic: Lying in Politics, Civil Disobedience, On Violence, Thoughts on Politics and Revolution* (New York: Harcourt Brace Jovanovich, 1972), pp. 93, 99.

22. Marie-Louise Blum, "Entretien sur Simone Weil, la Résistance et la question juive," *Cahiers Simone Weil* 4, no. 2 (June 1981): 79–80.

23. Perrin and Thibon, *Simone Weil as We Knew Her*, p. 125.

24. Perrin, *Mon dialogue avec Simone Weil*, p. 73.

25. Raïssa Maritain, *Au creux du rocher* (Paris: Alsatia, 1954).

26. Simone Weil, letter of 18 October 1941 to Xavier Vallat, cited in Pétrement, *La vie de Simone Weil*, 2:377–379; Pétrement, *Simone Weil*, p. 444.

27. Simone Weil, letter to André Weil, cited in Pétrement, *La vie de Simone Weil*, 2:305; Pétrement, *Simone Weil*, p. 396.

28. Simone Weil, "Deux lettres à Huguette Baur," *Cahiers Simone Weil* 17, no. 1 (March 1994): 109 n.4.

29. Hannah Arendt, letter of 18 November 1945, in *Hannah Arendt–Karl Jaspers: Briefwechsel, 1926–1969*, ed. Lotte Köhler and Hans Sauer (Munich: Piper, 1985), p. 59; *Correspondence Hannah Arendt–Karl Jaspers, 1926–1969*, trans. Robert and Rita Kimber (New York: Harcourt Brace Jovanovich, 1992), p. 23.

30. Hannah Arendt, "Der Dank vom Hause Juda? Offener Brief an Jules Romains," *Aufbau*, 24 October 1941, p. 7.

31. Hannah Arendt, "Die jüdische Armee—Der Beginn einer jüdischen Politik?" *Aufbau*, 14 January 1941, reprinted. in Hannah Arendt, *Die Krise des Zionismus: Essays und Kommentare*, 2 vols., vol. 2, ed. Eike Geisel and Klaus Bitterman, Critica Diabolis 23 (Berlin: Tiamat, 1989), pp. 167–170.

32. Ibid., p. 168.

33. Ibid., pp. 168–169.

34. Hannah Arendt, "Mit dem Rücken an der Wand," *Aufbau*, 3 July 1942, reprinted in Arendt, *Die Krise des Zionismus*, 2:185.

35. Hannah Arendt, "Papier und Wirklichkeit," *Aufbau*, 10 April 1942, reprinted in Arendt, *Die Krise des Zionismus*, 2:178.

36. Hannah Arendt, "Die 'sogenannte Jüdische Armee,' " *Aufbau*, 22 May 1942, reprinted in Arendt, *Die Krise des Zionismus*. 2:180.

37. Hannah Arendt, "Des Teufels Redekunst," *Aufbau*, 8 May 1942, p. 20.

38. Arendt, "Mit dem Rücken an der Wand," p. 185.

39. Arendt, "Die 'sogenannte Jüdische Armee,' " p. 180.

40. Hannah Arendt, "Eine Lehre in sechs Schüßen," *Aufbau*, 11 August 1944, p. 15.

41. Hannah Arendt, "Die Tage der Wandlung," *Aufbau*, 28 July 1944, p. 16.

42. Arendt, "Die 'sogenannte Jüdische Armee,' " p. 183.

43. Arendt, "Keinen Kaddisch," p. 19.

44. Arendt, "Des Teufels Redekunst," p. 20.

1942

1. Arendt, "Keinen Kaddisch," p. 19.

2. Marrus and Paxton, *Vichy France and the Jews*, p. 95.

3. Bédarida, *Armes de l'esprit*, p. 52.

4. Walter Laqueur, *The Terrible Secret: Suppression of the Truth about Hitler's "Final Solution"* (Boston: Little, Brown, 1980), p. 13.

5. *Cahiers Jacques Maritain* 16–17:4.

6. Ibid., p. 88, cited in Vidal-Naquet, *Réflexions sur le génocide*, 3:58.

7. Arendt, "Keinen Kaddisch," p. 19.

8. Marrus and Paxton, *Vichy France and the Jews*, p. 233.

9. Jacques Maritain, *Messages* (New York: Maison française, 1945), in Jacques Maritain, *Mystère d'Israël* (Paris: Desclée de Brouwer, 1994), pp. 159–160.

10. Jacques Maritain, "Atonement for All," *Commonweal* 36 (1942): 509, cited in Vidal-Naquet, *Réflexions sur le génocide*, 3:58.

11. Wieviorka, *Une certaine idée de la Résistance*, p. 208.

12. Ibid., "Témoignage d'un Français juif," *Le journal de Maître Lucien Vidal-Naquet* (September 1942–February 1944): 115, 119, 124, 125.

13. Vidal-Naquet, *Réflexions sur le génocide*, 3:164.

14. Ibid., p. 262.

15. Pétrement, *Simone Weil*, p. 468.

16. Simone Weil, letter to Jean Wahl, cited in Pétrement, *La vie de Simone Weil*, 2:446; Pétrement, *Simone Weil*, pp. 487–488.

17. Vidal-Naquet, *Réflexions sur le génocide*, 3:59.

18. "Un échange de lettres entre Simone Weil et Jacques Maritain," *Cahiers Simone Weil* 3, no. 2 (June 1980).

19. Matthew 10:23.

20. Etty Hillesum, *Letters from Westerbork*, trans. Arnold J. Pomerans (New York: Pantheon, 1986).

21. Edith Stein, "Die Seelenburg," in Stein, *Werke*, vol. 6: *Welt und Person: Beitrag zum christlichen Wahrheitsstreben* (Freiburg: Herder, 1962), p. 67.

22. Edith Stein Archive, cited in Waltraud Herbstrith, *Edith Stein: A Biography*, trans. Bernard Bonowitz, 5th ed. (San Francisco: Ignatius, 1992), pp. 198–199.

23. Renata Posselt [Teresia Renata de Spirit, Sancto], *Edith Stein*, trans. Cecily Hastings and Donald Nicholl (London: Sheed and Ward, 1952).

24. "Keinen Kaddisch," p. 19.

25. Hannah Arendt, "*The Deputy*: Guilt by Silence?" in *Amor Mundi: Explorations in the Faith and Thought of Hannah Arendt*, ed. James Bernaver (Boston: Nijhoff, 1987), p. 56.

26. Ibid., p. 53.

27. Ibid., p. 53–56.

28. Ibid., p. 57–58.

29. Hannah Arendt, "Angelo Giuseppe Roncalli: A Christian On St. Peter's Chair from 1958 to 1963," in *Men in Dark Times*, p. 62.

30. McCarthy and Arendt, letters of 16 December and 21 December 1968, in *Between Friends*, pp. 225, 232.

31. Arendt, "Angelo Giuseppe Roncalli," p. 62.

32. Hannah Arendt, "Was geht in Frankreich vor?" *Aufbau*, 25 September 1942, p. 18.

33. Cited in Vidal-Naquet, *Réflexions sur le génocide*, 3: 60.

34. André Latreille, *De Gaulle, la Libération et l'Eglise catholique* (Paris: Cerf, 1978), p. 38.

35. Ibid., p. 56.

36. Francis-Louis Closon, "Témoignage sur Simone Weil," *Cahiers Simone Weil* 5, no. 3 (September 1982).

37. Jacques Cabaud, *Simone Weil à New York et à Londres: Les quinze derniers mois, 1942–1943* (Paris: Plon, 1967), p. 42.

38. Simone Weil, "Remarques sur le nouveau projet de Constitution," in *Simone Weil, Ecrits de Londres et dernières lettres* (Paris: Gallimard, 1980), p. 90.

39. Weil, *Enracinement*, p. 211; *The Need for Roots*, p. 158.

40. Ibid., p. 211 / pp. 158–159.

41. Simone Weil, "Bases d'un statut des minorités françaises non chrétiennes et d'origine étrangère," cited in Pétrement, *La vie de Simone Weil*, 2: 477; Pétrement, *Simone Weil*, p. 509.

42. Ibid.

43. Weil, *Enracinement*, pp. 139–141; *The Need for Roots*, pp. 101–104.

44. Ibid., p. 52 / p. 49.

45. Ibid., p. 154 / p. 114.

46. Jacques Maritain, *L'impossible antisémitisme*, in Jacques Maritain, *Les Juifs*, ed. H. Daniel-

Rops (Paris: Plon 1937); reprinted in Jacques Maritain, *Questions de conscience* (Paris: Desclée de Brouwer, 1938).

47. Maritain, *Mystère d'Israël*, p. 39.

48. Maritain, *Mystère d'Israël*, p. 52; Jacques Maritain, *A Christian Looks at the Jewish Question* (New York: Longmans, Green, 1939), p. 29.

49. Maritain, *Mystère d'Israël*, p. 28; Jacques Maritain, "The Mystery of Israel," trans. Harry Lorin Binnse, in *The Social and Political Philosophy of Jacques Maritain: Selected Readings*, ed. Joseph W. Evans and Leo R. Ward (London: Geoffrey Bles, 1956), pp. 225, 234.

50. Ibid., p. 53 / p. 234.

51. Vidal-Naquet, *Réflexions sur le génocide*, 3: 45.

52. Maritain, *Mystère d'Israël*, p. 58; "Mystery of Israel," p. 239.

53. Perrin and Thibon, *Simone Weil as We Knew Her*, p. 59.

54. Pétrement, *Simone Weil*, p. 478.

55. Perrin and Thibon, *Simone Weil as We Knew Her*, p. 46.

56. A. Boyer, *Theodor Herzl* (Paris: Albin Michel, 1991).

57. Hannah Arendt, *Rahel Varnhagen: Lebensgeschichte einer deutschen Jüdin aus der Romantik* (Munich: Piper, 1959); Hannah Arendt, *Rahel Varnhagen: The Life of a Jewess*, ed. Liliane Weissberg, trans. Richard Winston and Clara Winston (Baltimore: Johns Hopkins University Press, 1997).

58. Hannah Arendt, "Aufklärung und Judenfrage," *Zeitschrift für die Geschichte der Juden in Deutschland* 4 (1932): 65–77, reprinted in Hannah Arendt, *Die verborgene Tradition: Acht Essays* (Frankfurt: Suhrkamp, 1976), pp. 108–126.

59. Gershom Scholem, "Jews and Germans," trans. Werner J. Dannhauser, in *On Jews and Judaism in Crisis: Selected Essays*, 2 vols., ed. Werner J. Dannhauser (New York: Schocken, 1976), 1: 75.

60. Hannah Arendt, *Origins of Totalitarianism*, 1st ed. (New York: Harcourt, Brace, 1951), p. 438.

61. Hannah Arendt, "Für Ehre und Ruhm des jüdischen Volkes," *Aufbau*, 21 April 1944, pp. 1, 2.

62. Hannah Arendt, "Die Entrechteten und Entwürdigten," *Aufbau*, 15 December 1944, p. 13.

63. Ibid., p. 16.

64. Arendt, letter of 17 August 1946, in *Briefwechsel Arendt–Jaspers*, p. 89; *Correspondence*, p. 53.

65. Karl Jaspers, letter of 20 July 1947, ibid., pp. 131–132 / p. 95.

66. Arendt, letter of 3 May 1947, ibid., p. 122 / p. 85.

67. Hannah Arendt, "Gäste aus dem Niemandsland," *Aufbau*, 30 June 1944, p. 15.

1943

1. Wieviorka, *Une certaine idée de la Résistance*, p. 201.

2. Vidal-Naquet, *Réflexions sur le génocide*, 3: 155–156.

3. Maritain, *Mystère d'Israël*, p. 166.

4. Wieviorka, *Une certaine idée de la Résistance*, p. 89.

5. Ibid.

6. Emmanuel d'Astier, French Interior Ministry Archives, F1A 3735, 1 March 1944, cited in ibid., p. 91.

7. Raymond Aron, *Mémoires* (Paris: Julliard, 1983), p. 175.

8. Ilan Greilsamer, *Blum* (Paris: Flammarion, 1996), p. 478.

9. Marrus and Paxton, *Vichy France and the Jews*, p. 348.

10. Vidal-Nacquet, *Réflexions sur le génocide*, 3: 128.

11. Ibid., p. 129.

12. Wieviorka, *Une certaine idée de la Résistance*, p. 206.

13. Weil, *Enracinement*, p. 41; *The Need for Roots*, p. 26.

14. Hannah Arendt, "Was bleibt? Es bleibt die Muttersprache," in *Gespräche mit Hannah Arendt*, ed. Adelbert Reif (Munich: Piper, 1976), p. 24; Hannah Arendt, " 'What Remains? The Language Remains': A Conversation with Günter Gaus," in Arendt, *Essays in Understanding*, pp. 13–14.

15. Simone Weil, "La légitimité du gouvernement provisoire," in Weil, *Ecrits de Londres*, pp. 70–71; Simone Weil, "The Legitimacy of the Provisional Government," trans. Peter Winch, *Philosophical Investigations* 53 (1987): 96.

16. Weil, *Enracinement*, p. 232; *The Need for Roots*, p. 174.

17. Cited in Pétrement, *La vie de Simone Weil*, 2: 477–478; Pétrement, *Simone Weil*, p. 510.

18. Simone Weil, letter of 26 July 1943 to Francis-Louis Closon, cited in Pétrement, *La vie de Simone Weil*, 2: 508; Pétrement, *Simone Weil*, p. 531.

19. Francis-Louis Closon, "Témoignage," *Cahiers Simone Weil* 5, no. 3 (September 1982).

20. "André Weil, a Scientist, Discusses His Sister with Malcolm Muggeridge," in Simone Weil, *Gateway to God*, ed. David Raper et al. (Glasgow: Collins, Fontana Books, 1974), p. 157.

21. Vidal-Naquet, *Réflexions sur le génocide*, 3: 135, 144.

22. Ibid., p. 58.

23. "André Weil Discusses His Sister," p. 157.

24. Weil, *Enracinement*, p. 33; *The Need for Roots*, pp. 20–21.

25. Cited in Pétrement, *La vie de Simone Weil*, 2: 476; Pétrement, *Simone Weil*, p. 508.

26. Cabaud, *Simone Weil*, p. 71.

27. Ibid., p. 517.

28. Michel Narcy, *Simone Weil: Malheur et beauté du monde* (Paris: Centurion, 1967), p. 91.

29. Maurice Schumann, "Mes entretiens avec Simone Weil à Londres en 1943," *Cahiers Simone Weil* 13, no. 1 (March 1990): 49–50.

30. Simone Weil, "Dernier texte," in *Pensées sans ordre*, p. 149; Simone Weil, "Last Text," trans. David Raper, in *Gateway to God*, p. 72.

31. Martin Buber, cited in D. Bourel, "S. Weil et Samuel-Hugo Bergman," in *Le grand passage* (Paris: Albin Michel, 1994), p. 72.

32. Weil, "Dernier texte," p. 151; "Last Text," pp. 72–73.

33. Ibid., p. 152 / p. 74.

34. Philippe Delattre, "Les dernières années de Henri Bergson," *Revue philosophique*, no. 38 (March–August 1941); cited in John M. Oesterreicher, *Walls Are Crumbling: Seven Jewish Philosophers Discover Christ* (London: Hollis and Carter, 1953), opposite plate 15.

35. Arendt, "We Refugees," pp. 55–66.

36. Hannah Arendt, review of *Prisoners of Hope*, by Howard L. Brooks, *Jewish Social Studies* 5 (1943): 79–80.

37. Hannah Arendt, "Französische politische Literatur im Exil," *Aufbau*, 26 February 1943, pp. 7–8, and 26 March 1943, p. 8.

38. Yves Simon, *La marche à la délivrance* (New York: Maison française, 1942).

39. Hannah Arendt, "Why the Crémieux Decree Was Abrogated," *Contemporary Jewish Record* 6 (1943): 115–123.

40. Hannah Arendt, "Die wahren Gründe für Theresienstadt," *Aufbau*, 3 September 1943, p. 21.

41. Hannah Arendt, "Portrait of a Period," *Menorah Journal* 31 (1943): 307–314, reprinted in Arendt, *Jew as Pariah*, pp. 112–124.

42. Hannah Arendt, "Can the Jewish-Arab Question Be Solved?" *Aufbau*, 17 December 1943, p. 1.

43. Hans Jonas, "Hannah Arendt: Words Spoken at Her Funeral Service," *Partisan Review* 42 (1976): 13.

44. Karol Wojtyla [John Paul II], "Homily for the Beatification of Edith Stein," ed. and trans. John Sullivan, *Carmelite Studies* 4 (1987): 306.

45. Cited in Elisabeth de Miribel, *Edith Stein, 1891–1942* (Paris: Seuil, 1954).
46. Xavier Tilliette, *Actualité religieuse dans le monde*, 15 April 1987, pp. 36–37.
47. Xavier Tilliette, "Le souvenir d'Edith Stein," *Etudes*, April 1956, pp. 3–14.

Epilogue

1. Simone Weil, *Attente de Dieu* (Paris: Fayard, 1966), p. 40; Simone Weil, *Waiting on God*, trans. Emma Craufurd (London: Routledge and Kegan Paul, 1951), p. 18.
2. Simone Weil, "Israël et les Gentils," in *Pensées sans ordre concernant l'amour de Dieu* (Paris: Gallimard, 1962), p. 52.
3. Pierre Vidal-Naquet, *Mémoires*, vol. 1: *La brisure et l'attente, 1930–1955* (Paris: Seuil, Découverte, 1995), p. 122.
4. Walter Laqueur, *The Terrible Secret: Suppression of the Truth about Hitler's "Final Solution"* (Boston: Little, Brown, 1980), p. 93.
5. Ibid., pp. 73–74.
6. Ibid., p. 44.
7. Paul Giniewsky, *Simone Weil ou la haine de soi* (Paris: Berg, 1978), p. 332.
8. Waltraud Herbstrith, *Edith Stein: A Biography*, trans. Bernard Bonowitz (San Francisco: Ignatius, 1985), p. 63.
9. Ibid., cited in Wilhelmine Boehm, *Im Schatten von Golgotha: Edith Stein* (Meitingen-Freising, Germany: Kyrios, 1980).
10. Simone Weil, *La connaissance surnaturelle* (Paris: Gallimard, 1950), p. 39; Simone Weil, *First and Last Notebooks*, trans. Richard Rees (London: Oxford University Press, 1970), pp. 94–97.
11. Ibid., p. 42 / p. 97.
12. Ibid., p. 49 / p. 103.
13. Ibid., p. 38 / p. 93.
14. Rosa Luxemburg, Letter of 16 February 1917 to Mathilde Wurm, in *The Letters of Rosa Luxemburg*, ed. Stephen Eric Bronner, ed., 2d ed. (Atlantic Highlands, N.J.: Humanities Press, 1993), p. 179.
15. Weil, *Connaissance surnaturelle*, p. 39.
16. Weil *Attente de Dieu*, p. 213; *Waiting on God*, p. 142.
17. Ibid.
18. Simone Weil, *Intuitions préchrétiennes* (Paris: Fayard, 1985), p. 75; Simone Weil, *Intimations of Christianity among the Ancient Greeks*, ed. and trans. Elisabeth Chase Geissbuhler (London: Routledge and Kegan Paul, 1957), p. 135.
19. Edith Stein, *Wege zur inneren Stille* (Aschaffenburg, 1987), pp. 61–62, cited in Herbstrith, *Edith Stein*, pp. 86–87.
20. Emmanuel Lévinas, *In the Time of the Nations*, trans. Michael B. Smith (Bloomington: Indiana University Press, 1994), p. 164.
21. Jean-Jacques Rousseau, *On the Origins of Inequality among Men*, in Jean-Jacques Rousseau, *The First and Second Discourses*, ed. Roger D. Masters, trans. Roger D. Masters and Judith R. Masters (New York: St. Martin's, 1964), p. 130.
22. Jean-Jacques Rousseau, "Essay on the Origin of Language," trans. John H. Moran, in Jean-Jacques Rousseau and Johann Gottfried Herder, *Two Essays on the Origin of Language* (Chicago: University of Chicago Press, 1986), p. 32.
23. Jean-Jacques Rousseau, *Emile, or Education*, trans. Barbara Foley (London: Dent, Everyman's Library, 1925), p. 184.
24. Hannah Arendt, *Von der Menschlichkeit in finsteren Zeiten: Gedanken zu Lessing* (Hamburg, 1960); Hannah Arendt, "On Humanity in Dark Times: Thoughts about Lessing," trans. Clara Winston and Richard Winston, in *Men in Dark Times* (New York: Harcourt Brace and World, 1968), pp. 13–14.

25. Saint-Just to the Convention, 26 February 1794.

26. Voltaire, *Philosophical Dictionary*, ed. and trans. H. I. Woolf (New York: Knopf, 1924); http://history.hanover.edu/texts/voltaire/volvirt.htm. Translation modified.

27. Hannah Arendt, *On Revolution* (Harmondsworth, Great Britain: Penguin, 1979), p. 81.

28. Ibid., p. 75.

29. Arendt, "On Humanity in Dark Times," p. 14.

30. Friedrich Nietzsche, *Daybreak: Thoughts on the Prejudices of Morality*, trans. R. J. Hollingdale (London: Cambridge University Press, 1982), pp. 82–83.

31. Friedrich Nietzsche, *Beyond Good and Evil: Prelude to a Philosophy of the Future*, trans. Helen Zimmern (London: Allen and Unwin, 1967), §46, p. 66.

32. Friedrich Nietzsche, *The Genealogy of Morals: A Polemic.*

33. Friedrich Nietzsche, *The Will to Power*, trans. Walter Kaufmann and R. J. Hollingdale (New York: Random House, 1967), p. 123.

34. Arendt, "Humanity in Dark Times," pp. 14–15.

35. Ibid., 15.

36. Arendt, *On Revolution*, p. 85.

37. Ibid., p. 86.

38. Arendt, pp. 14–16.

39. Ibid., pp. 13–17.

40. Ibid., p. 13.

41. Ibid., pp. 16–17.

42. Hannah Arendt, *The Human Condition* (Chicago: University of Chicago Press, 1958), pp. 74–75.

43. Ibid., pp. 75–77.

44. Arendt, *On Revolution*, p. 82.

45. Ibid., p. 89.

46. Ibid., p. 96.

47. Ibid., p. 97.

48. Arendt, *Human Condition*, p. 77.

49. Hannah Arendt, "Zueignung an Karl Jaspers," in *Die verborgene Tradition: Acht Essays* (Frankfurt: Suhrkamp, 1976), pp. 7–11; Hannah Arendt, "Dedication to Karl Jaspers," trans. Robert and Rita Kimber, in Arendt, *Essays in Understanding*, pp. 212–216. [There exists no English translation of *Die verborgene Tradition* as a whole.]

50. Karl Jaspers, letter of 19 March 1947, in *Hannah Arendt–Karl Jaspers: Briefwechsel, 1926–1969*, ed. Lotte Köhler and Hans Sauer (Munich: Piper, 1985), p. 112; *Correspondence Hannah Arendt–Karl Jaspers, 1926–1969*, trans. Robert and Rita Kimber (New York: Harcourt Brace Jovanovich, 1992), p. 66.

51. Arendt, letter of 11 November 1946, ibid., p. 101 / p. 64.

52. Arendt, "On Humanity in Dark Times," p. 22.

53. Ibid., p. 23.

54. Ibid., p. 24.

55. Ibid., p. 31.

56. Arendt, *Human Condition*, p. 243.

57. Weil, *Intuitions préchrétiennes*, p. 107; *Intimations of Christianity*, pp. 71–72.

58. Friedrich Nietzsche, *La Volonte de Puissance*, vol. 2, trans. Bianquis (Paris: Gallimard, 1942), no. 436 [book 14, pt. 1, §238].

59. Weil, *Intuitions préchrétiennes*, p. 107; *Intimations of Christianity*, pp. 71–72.

60. Simone Weil, *Cahiers*, 3 vols., vol. 1 (Paris: Plon, 1951), p. 12; *The Notebooks of Simone Weil, 1940–1942*, 2 vols., trans. Arthur Wills (London: Routledge and Kegan Paul, 1956), 1: 3.

61. Weil, *Intuitions préchrétiennes*, p. 98; *Intimations of Christianity*, p. 155.

62. Simone Weil, "*L'Iliade*, ou le poème de la force," in Simone Weil, *La source grecque* (Paris: Gallimard, 1953), p. 35; Simone Weil, "The *Iliad*, Poem of Might," in *Intimations of Christianity*, p. 47.

63. Weil, *Connaissance surnaturelle*, p. 327; *First and Last Notebooks*, p. 355.

64. Weil, *Attente de Dieu*, p. 214; *Waiting on God*, p. 142.

65. Ibid., p. 207 / p. 137.

66. Friedrich Nietzsche, preface to the second edition of *The Gay Science*, trans. Walter Kaufmann (New York: Vintage, 1974), §4, p. 38.

67. Michel Narcy, "La parole pacifiée d'Emile Novis," *Sud* (1990): 130ff.

68. Weil, *Attente de Dieu*, p. 132; *Waiting on God*, p. 88.

69. Ibid., p. 161 / p. 107.

70. Weil, *Connaissance surnaturelle*, pp. 168, 264; *First and Last Notebooks*, pp. 212, 300.

71. Ibid., p. 170 / p. 213.

72. Ibid., p. 175 / p. 217.

73. Simone Weil, *Cahiers*, 3 vols., vol. 3 (Paris: Plon, 1956), p. 10; *Notebooks, 1940–1942*, 2:419 (translation modified).

74. Weil, *Connaissance surnaturelle*, pp. 170, 264; *First and Last Notebooks*, pp. 212, 300.

75. Simone Weil, *Cahiers*, 3 vols., vol. 2 (Paris: Plon, 1956), p. 358; *Notebooks, 1940–1942*, vol. 2: 379.

76. Weil, *Intuitions préchrétiennes*, p. 138; *Intimations of Christianity*, p. 175.

77. Martin Buber, *On Judaism*, ed. Nahum N. Glatzer (New York: Schocken, 1967), p. 210.

78. Ibid., p. 211.

79. Ibid.

80. We are here following M. A. Ouaknin, *Tsimtsoum: Introduction à la méditation hébraïque* (Paris: Albin Michel, 1992).

81. Ibid., p. 92.

82. Weil, *Intuitions préchrétiennes*, p. 85; *Intimations of Christianity*, p. 143.

83. Ibid., p. 131 / p. 169.

84. Ibid., p. 168 / pp. 198–199.

85. Ibid., p. 142 / p. 178.

86. Ibid., p. 164 / p. 196.

87. Simone Weil, *La pesanteur et la grâce* (Paris: Plon, 1988), p. 94; *Gravity and Grace*, trans. Arthur Wills (Lincoln: University of Nebraska Press, 1997), p. 130.

88. Weil, *Connaissance surnaturelle*, p. 271; *First and Last Notebooks*, p. 304.

89. Ibid., p. 268 / pp. 84–85.

90. Weil, *Connaissance surnaturelle*, p. 271; *First and Last Notebooks*, p. 329.

91. Ibid., p. 57 / p. 110.

92. Weil, *Intuitions préchrétiennes*, p. 168; *Intimations of Christianity*, p. 199.

93. Weil, *Connaissance surnaturelle*, p. 271; *First and Last Notebooks*, p. 271.

94. Weil, *Intuitions préchrétiennes*, p. 58; *Intimations of Christianity*, p. 120.

95. Alain, *Propos sur la religion* (Paris: Presses universitaires de France, 1938), p. 4.

96. Ibid.

97. Weil, *Attente de Dieu*, pp. 150, 64; *Waiting on God*, p. 127. See also Weil, *L'enracinement* (Paris: Gallimard, 1949), pp. 244–245; *The Need for Roots: Prelude to a Declaration of Duties toward Mankind*, trans. Arthur Wills (London: Routledge and Kegan Paul, 1952), pp. 276–277.

98. Weil, *Enracinement*, p. 364; *The Need for Roots*, p. 276.

99. Rosa Luxemburg, *Briefe aus dem Gefängnis* (Berlin: Dietz, 1953).

100. Simone Weil, review of Rosa Luxemburg, *Letters from Prison*, in *Œuvres complètes*, vol. 2: *Ecrits historiques et politiques*, book 1: *L'engagement syndical, 1927–juillet 1934*, ed. Géraldi Leroy (Paris: Gallimard, 1988), p. 300; cited in Simone Pétrement, *Simone Weil: A Life*, trans. Raymond Rosenthal (New York: Pantheon, 1976), p. 184.

101. Rosa Luxemburg, letter of 19 April 1917 to Sonja Liebknecht.

102. Luxemburg, letter of 2 August 1917 to Sonja Liebknecht.

103. Luxemburg, letter of 23 May 1917 to Sonja Liebknecht, in *The Letters of Rosa Luxemburg*, ed Stephen Eric Bronner, p. 209.

104. Luxemburg, letter of 28 December 1916 to Mathilde Wurm, in ibid., p. 173 (translation modified).

105. Weil, review of Luxemburg, *Letters from Prison*, p. 306; cited in Pétrement, *Simone Weil*, p. 184.

106. Weil, *Cahiers*, 3:83; *Notebooks, 1940–1942*.

107. Weil, *Attente de Dieu*, p. 80; *Waiting on God*, p. 44.

108. Simone Weil, "Réflexions sur les causes de la liberté et de l'oppression," in *Œuvres complètes*, vol. 2, book 2: *L'expérience ouvrière et l'adieu à la révolution, juillet 1934–juin 1937*, ed. Géraldi Leroy and Anne Roche (Paris: Gallimard, 1991), p. 30; Simone Weil, *Oppression and Liberty*, trans. Arthur Wills and John Petric (London: Routledge and Kegan Paul, 1958), pp. 38–39.

109. Elisabeth Young-Bruehl, *Hannah Arendt: For Love of the World* (New Haven: Yale University Press, 1982), p. 28.

110. Hannah Arendt, "Rosa Luxemburg, 1871–1919," in Arendt, *Men in Dark Times*, p. 44.

111. Ibid., p. 37.

112. Ibid., p. 42.

113. Hannah Arendt, *The Life of the Mind*, 2 vols. (New York: Harcourt Brace Jovanovich, 1978), vol. 1: *Thinking*, p. 60.

114. Hannah Arendt, "Understanding and Politics (The Difficulties of Understanding)," in Arendt, *Essays in Understanding*, pp. 308–310.

115. Arendt, Letter of 6 August 1955, in *Briefwechsel Arendt–Jaspers*, p. 301; *Correspondence*, p. 264.

116. Arendt, *Human Condition*, p. 52.

117. Ibid.

118. Hannah Arendt, *Der Liebesbegriff bei Augustin* (Berlin: J. Springer, 1929), Hannah Arendt, *Love and Saint Augustine*, ed. Joanna V. Scott and trans. Judith C. Stark, (Chicago: University of Chicago Press, 1996).

119. Arendt, *Human Condition*, p. 55.

120. Ibid., p. 177.

121. Ibid., p. 237.

122. Hannah Arendt, *Eichmann in Jerusalem: A Report on the Banality of Evil* (New York: Viking, 1963), pp. 255–256.

123. Hannah Arendt, "Waldemar Gurian, 1903–1954," in Arendt, *Men in Dark Times*, p. 262.

124. Hannah Arendt, "Collective Responsibility," in James W. Bernauer, ed., *Amor Mundi: Explorations in the Faith and Thought of Hannah Arendt* (Boston: Nijhoff, 1987), p. 50.

125. Arendt, *Human Condition*, p. 247.

126. Johann Wolfgang von Goethe, *Faust*, part 2, act 3, trans. W. Arndt, cited in Hans Jonas, "Acting, Knowing, Thinking: Gleanings from Hannah Arendt's Philosophical Work," *Social Research* 1 (1977): 31.

127. Arendt, *On Revolution*, p. 211.

Bibliography

Works by Hannah Arendt

(Works originally published in German are here listed in both English and, where appropriate, German language editions.)

Books

Crises of the Republic: Lying in Politics, Civil Disobedience, On Violence, Thoughts on Politics and Revolution. New York: Harcourt Brace Jovanovich, 1972.

Eichmann in Jerusalem: A Report on the Banality of Evil. New York: Viking, 1963.

Eight Exercises in Political Thought: Between Past and Future. New York: Viking, 1968.

Essays in Understanding, 1930–1954. Ed. Jerome Kohn. New York: Harcourt Brace, 1994.

The Human Condition. Chicago: University of Chicago Press, 1958.

The Jew as Pariah: Jewish Identity and Politics in the Modern Age. Ed. Ron H. Feldman. New York: Grove, 1978.

Der Liebesbegriff bei Augustin. Berlin: J. Springer, 1929.

The Life of the Mind. 2 vols. New York: Harcourt Brace Jovanovich, 1978.

Love and Saint Augustine. Ed. and Trans. Joanna V. Scott and Judith C. Stark. Chicago: University of Chicago Press, 1996.

Men in Dark Times. New York: Harcourt Brace and World, 1968.

On Revolution. Harmondsworth, Great Britain: Penguin, 1979.

The Origins of Totalitarianism. 1st ed. New York: Harcourt, Brace, 1951.

The Origins of Totalitarianism. 3d ed. New York: Harcourt, Brace, Harvest Books, 1973.

Rahel Varnhagen: Lebensgeschichte einer deutschen Jüdin aus der Romantik. Munich: Piper, 1959.

Rahel Varnhagen: The Life of a Jewess. Ed. Liliane Weissberg. Trans. Richard and Clara Winston. Baltimore: Johns Hopkins University Press, 1997.
Sechs Essays. Schriften der Wandlung 3. Heidelberg: Lambert Schneider, 1948.
Die verborgene Tradition: Acht Essays. Frankfurt: Suhrkamp, 1976.
Was ist Politik?: Fragmente aus dem Nachlaß. Ed. Ursula Ludz. Munich: Piper, 1993.

Correspondence

Between Friends: The Correspondence of Hannah Arendt and Mary McCarthy, 1949–1975. Ed. Carol Brightman. New York: Harcourt Brace, 1995.
Correspondence Hannah Arendt–Karl Jaspers, 1926–1969. Trans. Robert and Rita Kimber. New York: Harcourt Brace Jovanovich, 1992.
Hannah Arendt–Karl Jaspers: Briefwechsel, 1926–1969. Ed. Lotte Köhler and Hans Sauer. Munich: Piper, 1985.
Hannah Arendt–Martin Heidegger: Briefe, 1925–1975. Ed. Ursula Ludz. Frankfurt: Vittorio Klostermann, 1998.

Articles and Essays

"Aufklärung und Judenfrage." *Zeitschrift für die Geschichte der Juden in Deutschland* 4 (1932): 65–77.
"Can the Jewish-Arab Question Be Solved?" *Aufbau*, 17 December 1943, p. 1 and 31, December 1943, p. 1.
"Ein christliches Wort zur Judenfrage." *Aufbau*, 5 June 1942, p. 19.
"Collective Responsibility." In *Amor Mundi: Explorations in the Faith and Thought of Hannah Arendt*. Ed. James W. Bernauer. Boston: Nijhoff, 1987, pp. 43–50.
"Der Dank vom Hause Juda? Offener Brief an Jules Romains." *Aufbau*, 24 October 1941, p. 7.
"*The Deputy*: Guilt by Silence?" In *Amor Mundi: Explorations in the Faith and Thought of Hannah Arendt*. Ed. James W. Bernauer. Boston: Nijhoff, 1987, pp. 51–58.
"Die Entrechteten und Entwürdigten." *Aufbau*, 15 December 1944, pp. 13, 16.
"Französische politische Literatur im Exil." *Aufbau*, 26 February 1943, pp. 7–8, and 26 March 1943, p. 8.
"From the Dreyfus Affair to France Today." *Jewish Social Studies* 4 (1942): 195–240.
"Für Ehre und Ruhm des jüdischen Volkes." *Aufbau*, 21 April 1944, pp. 1, 2.
"Gäste aus dem Niemandsland." *Aufbau*, 30 June 1944, p. 15.
"Die jüdische Armee—Der Beginn einer jüdischen Politik?" *Aufbau*, 14 January 1941. Reprinted in *Die Krise des Zionismus: Essays und Kommentare*, 2 vols., vol. 2, ed. Eike Geisel and Klaus Bitterman, pp. 167–170. Critica Diabolis 23. Berlin: Tiamat, 1989.
"Keinen Kaddisch wird man singen." *Aufbau*, 19 June 1942, p. 19.
"Eine Lehre in sechs Schüßen." *Aufbau*, 11 August 1944, p. 15.
"Martin Heidegger at 80." Trans. Albert Hofstadter. *New York Review of Books* 17, no. 6 (21 October 1971), pp. 50–54.
"Mit dem Rücken an der Wand." *Aufbau*, 3 July 1942. Reprinted in *Die Krise des Zion-*

ismus: Essays und Kommentare. 2 vols., vol. 2, ed. Eike Geisel and Klaus Bitterman, pp. 184–86. Critica Diabolis 23. Berlin: Tiamat, 1989.

"Papier und Wirklichkeit." *Aufbau,* 10 April 1942, pp. 15, 16.

"Portrait of a Period." *Menorah Journal* 31 (1943): 307–314.

Review of Bruno Weil, *Historia del Crimen Judicial mas Escandaloso del Siglo XIX. Jewish Social Studies* 5 (1943): 205.

Review of Howard L. Brooks, *Prisoners of Hope. Jewish Social Studies* 5 (1943): 79–80.

"Die 'sogenannte Jüdische Armee.' " *Aufbau,* 22 May 1942. Reprinted in *Die Krise des Zionismus: Essays und Kommentare.* 2 vols., vol. 2, ed. Eike Geisel and Klaus Bitterman, pp. 179–183. Critica Diabolis 23. Berlin: Tiamat, 1989.

"Die Tage der Wandlung." *Aufbau,* 28 July 1944, p. 16.

"Des Teufels Redekunst." *Aufbau,* 8 May 1942, p. 20.

"Die wahren Gründe für Theresienstadt." *Aufbau,* 3 September 1943, p. 21.

"Was bleibt? Es bleibt die Muttersprache." In *Gespräche mit Hannah Arendt.* Ed. Adelbert Reif. Munich: Piper, 1976, pp. 9–34.

"Was geht in Frankreich vor?" *Aufbau,* 25 September 1942, p. 18.

"We Refugees." *Menorah Journal* 31 (1943): 69–77.

"Why the Crémieux Decree Was Abrogated." *Contemporary Jewish Record* 6 (1943): 115–23.

Works by Edith Stein [Teresia Benedicta a Cruce]

(Works originally published in German are here listed in both German and, where available, English language editions.)

Collected Works

Werke. Ed. Lucy Gelber and Romaeus Leuven. Freiburg: Herder, 1950–.

Vol. 1 (1983): *Kreuzeswissenschaft: Studie über Johannes a Cruce,* 2d ed.

Vol. 2 (1950): *Endliches und ewiges Sein: Versuch eines Aufstieges zum Sinn des Seins.*

Vol. 3 (1952): Thomas Aquinas, *Untersuchungen über die Wahrheit (Quaestiones disputatae de veritate).* Ed. and trans. Edith Stein.

Vol. 5 (1959): *Die Frau: Ihre Aufgabe nach Natur und Gnade.*

Vol. 6 (1962): *Welt und Person: Beitrag zum christlichen Wahrheitsstreben.*

Vol. 7 (1985): *Aus dem Leben einer jüdischen Familie. Das Leben Edith Steins: Kindheit und Jugend.*

Vol. 8 (1976): *Selbstbildnis in Briefen,* Part 1: 1916–1934.

Vol. 9 (1976): *Selbstbildnis in Briefen,* Part 2: 1934–1942.

[Vol. 10 {Biography} (1983): Romaeus Leuven, *Heil im Unheil. Das Leben Edith Steins: Reife und Vollendung.* Trans. Sister Bernalda.]

Vol. 11 (1987): *Verborgenes Leben: Hagiographische Essays, Meditationen, geistliche Texte.*

Collected Works. Washington: Institute of Carmelite Studies, 1986–.

Vol. 1 (1986): *Life in a Jewish Family: Her Unfinished Autobiographical Account.* Trans. Josephine Koeppel.

Vol. 2 (1996): *Essays on Women*. 2d ed. Trans. Freda Mary Oben.
Vol. 5 (1993): *Self-Portrait in Letters, 1916–1942*. Trans. Josephine Koeppel.

Other Books

Dans la puissance de la croix. Walter Herbstrith, Ed. and trans. T. Soriano. Nouvelle cité, Spiritualité, 1982 [short selections from Stein's writings].
Die Frau: Ihre Aufgabe nach Natur und Gnade. Munich, 1949.
The Science of the Cross: A Study of St. John of the Cross. Trans. Hilda Graef. London: Burns and Oates, 1960.
Wege zur inneren Stille. Aschaffenburg, 1987.
Wie ich in den Kölner Karmel kam. Ed. Maria Amat Neyer. Würzburg: Echter, 1994.
Writings of Edith Stein. Ed. and trans. Hilda Graef. Westminster, Md.: Newman, 1956.

Essays and Remarks

"Beiträge zur philosophischen Begründung der Psychologie und der Geisteswissenschaften. Erste Abhandlung: Psychische Kausalität." *Jahrbuch für Philosophie und phänomenologische Forschung* 5 (1922): 1–116.
"Husserls Phänomenologie und die Philosophie des heiligen Thomas von Aquino: Versuch einer Gegenüberstellung." *Jahrbuch für Philosophie und phänomenologische Forschung*, suppl. vol. (1929): *Festschrift, Edmund Husserl zum 70. Geburtstag gewidmet*, pp. 315–38.
Remarks (in German), in *La phénoménologie: Journée d'étude de la société thomiste*. Kain, Belgium and Juvisy, France: Cerf [1932], pp. 108–112.

Works by Simone Weil

Collected Works

Œuvres complètes. Published under the direction of André A. Devaux and Florence de Lussy. Paris: Gallimard, 1988–.
Vol. 1: *Premiers écrits philosophiques* (1988).
Vol. 2, book 1, ed. Géraldi Leroy (1988): *Ecrits historiques et politiques: L'engagement syndical, 1927–juillet 1934*.
Vol. 2, book 2, ed. Géraldi Leroy and Anne Roche (1991): *Ecrits historiques et politiques: L'expérience ouvrière et l'adieu à la révolution, juillet 1934–juin 1937*.
Vol. 2, book 3, ed. Simone Fraisse (1989): *Vers la guerre, 1937–1940*.
Vol. 6, book 1, ed. Aylette Degrâces et al. (1994): *Cahiers, 1933–septembre 1941*.

Other Books

Attente de Dieu. Paris: Fayard, 1966.
Cahiers. Vol. 1. Paris: Plon, 1951.
Cahiers. Vol. 2. Paris: Plon, 1953.
Cahiers. Vol. 3. Paris: Plon, 1956.

La connaissance surnaturelle. Paris: Gallimard, 1950.

Ecrits de Londres et dernières lettres. Paris: Gallimard, 1980.

Ecrits historiques et politiques. Paris: Gallimard, 1953.

L'enracinement. Paris: Gallimard, 1949.

First and Last Notebooks. Trans. Richard Rees. New York: Oxford University Press, 1970.

Formative Writings, 1929–1941. Ed. and Trans. Dorothy Tuck McFarland and Wilhelmina Van Ness. Amherst: University of Massachusetts Press, 1987.

Gateway to God. Ed. and trans. David Raper. Glasgow: Collins, Fontana Books, 1974.

Gravity and Grace. Trans. Arthur Wills. Lincoln: University of Nebraska Press, 1997.

Intimations of Christianity Among the Ancient Greeks. Ed. and trans. Elisabeth Chase Geissbuhler. London: Routledge and Kegan Paul, 1957.

Intuitions préchrétiennes. Paris: Fayard, 1985.

Leçons de philosophie. Ed. Anne Reynaud-Guérithalut. Paris: Plon, 1989.

Lectures on Philosophy. Trans. Hugh Price. London: Cambridge University Press, 1978.

Letter to a Priest. Trans. A. F. Wills. London: Routledge and Kegan Paul, 1953.

Lettre à un religieux. Paris: Gallimard, 1951.

The Need for Roots: Prelude to a Declaration of Duties toward Mankind. Trans. Arthur Wills. London: Routledge and Kegan Paul, 1952.

The Notebooks of Simone Weil, 1940–1942. Trans. Arthur Wills. 2 vols. London: Routledge and Kegan Paul, 1956.

On Science, Necessity, and the Love of God. Ed. and trans. Richard Rees. London: Oxford University Press, 1968.

Oppression and Liberty. Trans. Arthur Wills and John Petric. London: Routledge and Kegan Paul, 1958.

Pensées sans ordre concernant l'amour de Dieu. Paris: Gallimard, 1962.

La pesanteur et la grâce. Paris: Plon, 1988.

Selected Essays, 1931–1943. Ed. and trans. Richard Rees. London: Oxford University Press, 1962.

Seventy Letters. Ed. and trans. Richard Rees. London: Oxford University Press, 1965.

The Simone Weil Reader. Ed. George A. Panichas. London: Moyer Bell, 1977.

La source grecque. Paris: Gallimard, 1953.

Sur la science. Paris: Gallimard, 1966.

Waiting on God. Trans. Emma Craufurd. London: Routledge and Kegan Paul, 1951.

Essays and Correspondence

"Deux lettres à Huguette Baur." *Cahiers Simone Weil* 17, no. 1 (March 1994).

"Un échange de lettres entre Simone Weil et Jacques Maritain." *Cahiers Simone Weil* 3, no. 2 (June 1980).

"Factory Work." Trans. Felix Giovanelli. *Politics* 3, no. 11 (December 1946).

Fragment of a letter to Emmanuel Mounier. In "Un épisode de la guerre d'Espagne vu par Simone Weil." *Cahiers Simone Weil* 6, no. 4 (December 1983).

"The Legitimacy of the Provisional Government." Trans. Peter Winch. *Philosophical Investigations* 53 (1987): 87–98.

Letter of 1942 to Jean Wahl. *Deucalion* 4: *Etre et pensée, Cahiers de Philosophie* 36 (October 1952), pp. 253–57.

Letter to *Cahiers du Sud*. In *Cahiers Simone Weil* 10, no. 4 (December 1987).

"Lettres de Simone Weil à Gustave Thibon et de Gustave Thibon à Simone Weil." *Cahiers Simone Weil* 4, no. 2 (June 1981).

"Notre Front populaire: Journal d'un militant." In Géraldi Leroy, "Simone Weil et le Front populaire." *Cahiers Simone Weil* 2, no. 1 (March 1979).

General Works

Alain (Emile Chartier), *Les arts et les dieux*. Paris: Gallimard, Pléiade, 1958.

———. *Correspondance avec Elie et Florence Halévy*. Paris: Gallimard, 1957.

———. *Politique*. Paris: Presses universitaires de France, 1962.

———. *Propos sur la religion*. Paris: Presses universitaires de France, 1938.

———. *Propos d'économique*. Paris: Gallimard, Pléiade, 1958.

Ancelet-Hustache, J. *Convertis du XXᵉ siècle*. Paris: Casterman/Foyer Notre-Dame, 1958.

"Archives judiciaires, dossiers de la section spéciale de la cour d'appel d'Aix-en-Provence, Archives départementales des Bouches-du-Rhône, série 8 W, dossier 22. Document no. 1: pièce 119 de la procédure." *Cahiers Simone Weil* 17, no. 4 (Dec. 1994).

Aron, Raymond. *Histoire et politique*. Paris: Julliard, 1975.

———. *Mémoires*. Paris: Julliard, 1983.

Aron, Robert. *Histoire de Vichy, 1940–1944*. Paris: Fayard, 1954.

Auden, W. H. *Collected Poems*. New York, 1976.

Augé, Marc, and Aurélien Moline. *Paris, Années 1930: Roger-Viollet*. Paris: Hazan, 1996.

Augstein, Rudolf, et al. *Historikerstreit: Die Dokumentation der Kontroverse um die Einzigartigkeit der nationalsozialistischen Judenvernichtung*. Munich: Piper, 1987.

Bataille, Georges. *The Blue of Noon*. Trans. Harry Mathews. New York: Urizen, 1978.

———. *Œuvres complètes*, vol. 3. Paris: Gallimard, 1971.

Baumont, Maurice. *La faillite de la paix, 1918–1939*. Paris: Presses universitaires de France, Peuples et civilisations, 1961.

Bédarida, Renée. *Les armes de l'esprit: Témoignage chrétien, 1941–1944*. Editions ouvrières, 1977.

Bénichou, R. *Ecrits juifs*. Alger, 1957.

Benjamin, Walter. "Zentralpark." In *Gesammelte Schriften*, vol. 1. Ed. Rolf Tiedemann and Hermann Schweppenhäuser. Frankfurt: Suhrkamp, 1974.

Bernanos, Georges. *Correspondance inédite, 1934–1948*. Ed. Albert Béguin and Jean Murray. Paris: Plon, 1971.

———. *A Diary of My Times*. Trans. Pamela Morris. London: Boriswood, 1938.

———. *Essais et écrits de combat*, vol. 1. Paris: Gallimard, Pléiade, 1971.

Biberstein-Stein, Erna. *Aufzeichnungen*. New York, 1949.

Bitoun, Pierre. *Les hommes d'Uriage*. Paris: La Découverte, 1988.

Bloy, Léon. *Le salut par les Juifs*. Paris: Henri Aniéré, 1906.

————. *Le vieux de la montagne*. Mercure de France, 1963.

Blum, Léon. *Souvenirs sur l'Affaire*. Paris: Gallimard, 1935 and 1981.

Blum, Marie-Louise. "Entretien sur Simone Weil, la Résistance et la question juive." *Cahiers Simone Weil* 4, no. 2 (June 1981).

Blum, Marie-Louise, and Jacques Madaule. "Témoignages sur Simone Weil." *Cahiers Simone Weil* 2, no. 4 (December 1979).

Boehm, Wilhelmine. *Edith Stein à la lumière du ressuscité*. Trans. Elisabeth de Solms, OSB. Paris: Médiaspaul, 1985.

Bourdais, Henri. *La JOC sous l'Occupation allemande: Témoignages et souvenirs de Henri Bourdais*. Paris: Editions de l'Atelier /Editions ouvrières, 1995.

Bourel, D. "Simone Weil et Samuel-Hugo Bergman." In *Le grand passage*. Paris: Albin Michel, 1994.

Bouyer, Louis. *Women Mystics: Hadewijch of Antwerp, Teresa of Avila, Thérèse of Lisieux, Elizabeth of the Trinity, Edith Stein*. Trans. Anne Englund Nash. San Francisco: Ignatius, 1993.

Boyer, A. *Theodor Herzl*. Paris: Albin Michel, 1955.

Brecht, Bertolt. *Poems, 1913–1956*. Ed. John Willett and Ralph Manheim. Trans. Edith Anderson et al. New York: Methuen, 1976.

Brentano, Fritz, ed. "Briefe Franz Brentanos an Hugo Bergman." *Philosophical and Phenomenological Research* 7 (1946–1947).

Brightman, Carol. Introduction to *Between Friends: The Correspondence of Hannah Arendt and Mary McCarthy, 1949–1975*. New York: Harcourt Brace, 1995.

Buber, Martin. *On Judaism*. Ed. Nahum N. Glatzer. New York: Schocken, 1967.

Cabaud, Jacques. *Simone Weil à New York et à Londres: Les quinze derniers mois, 1942–1943*. Paris: Plon, 1967.

Cahiers Paul Claudel 7: La figure d'Israël. Paris: Gallimard, 1968.

Canovan, Margaret. *Hannah Arendt: A Reinterpretation of Her Political Thought*. London: Cambridge University Press, 1992.

Céline, Louis-Ferdinand. *Bagatelles pour un massacre*. Paris: Denoël, 1938.

————. *L'école des cadavres*. Paris: Denoël, 1938.

Claudel, Paul. Letter. In *Les Juifs*. Paris: Plon, Présences, 1937.

Clausewitz, Carl von. *On War*. Ed. Anatol Rapoport. Trans. J. J. Graham. London: Penguin, 1982.

Closon, Francis-Louis. "Témoignage sur Simone Weil." *Cahiers Simone Weil* 5, no. 3 (septembre 1982).

Courtois, R. "*Edith Stein, fille d'Israël*." In *Convertis du XXe siècle*. Ed. J. Ancelet-Hustache. Paris: Casterman/Foyer Notre-Dame, 1958.

Daniel-Rops, H., ed. *Les Juifs*. Paris: Plon, 1937.

Défense de la France, no. 1 (15 August 1941).

Delattre, Philippe. "Les dernières années de Henri Bergson." *Revue philosophique*, no. 38 (March–August 1941).

Derrida, Jacques. *Politics of Friendship*. Trans. George Collins. London: Verso, 1997.

Devaux, A. "Première introduction à l'œuvre d'Edith Stein." *Cahiers universitaires catholiques*, June–July 1956.

Drieu La Rochelle, Pierre. *Gilles*. Paris: Gallimard, 1939.

Eisner, Lotte. *Exilés en France*. Paris: Maspero.

Ettinger, Elzbieta. *Hannah Arendt, Martin Heidegger*. New Haven: Yale University Press, 1995.

Fraixe, A. "Simone Weil et les *Cahiers du Sud*." *Cahiers Simone Weil* 12, no. 2 (June 1988).

Freund, Richard. *Cahiers Simone Weil* 10, no. 3 (September 1987).

Furet, François. *Le passé d'une illusion: Essai sur l'idée communiste au XXe siècle*. Paris: R. Laffont/Calmann-Lévy, 1995.

Gaboriau, Florent. *Edith Stein philosophe*. Paris: FAC, 1989.

Gide, André. *Cahiers André Gide*. Paris: Gallimard, 1973.

Gilson, Etienne. *Les métamorphoses de la Cité de Dieu*. Louvain, 1952.

Giniewski, Paul. *Simone Weil ou la haine de soi*. Paris: Berg International, 1978.

Giraudoux, Jean. *Pleins pouvoirs*. Paris: Gallimard, 1939.

Graef, Hilda. *Le philosophe et la croix: Edith Stein*. Paris: Cerf, 1955.

Graetz, H. *La construction de l'historie juive*, followed by *Gnosticisme et Judaïsme*. Ed. and trans. M. Ruben Hayoun. Paris: Cerf, 1992.

Greilsamer, Ilan. *Blum*. Paris: Flammarion, 1996.

Gurian, Waldemar. *Bolshevism: An Introduction to Soviet Communism*. Notre Dame, Ind.: University of Notre Dame Press, 1952.

———. *The Future of Bolshevism*. Trans. E. I. Watkin. London: Sheed and Ward, 1936.

Halévy, Elie. *The Era of Tyrannies: Essays on Socialism and War*. Trans. R. K. Webb. London: Penguin, 1967.

Hebblethwaite, Peter. *Pope John XXIII: Shepherd of the Modern World*. Garden City, N.Y.: Doubleday, 1985.

Heidegger, Martin. *What Is Called Thinking?* Trans. D. Wieck and J. Glenn Gray. New York: Harper and Row, 1968.

Herbstrith, Waltraud. *Edith Stein: A Biography*. Trans. Bernard Bonowitz. San Francisco: Ignatius, 1985.

Hillesum, Etty. *Letters from Westerbork*. Trans. Arnold J. Pomerans. New York: Pantheon, 1986.

Huning, Alois. *Edith Stein und Peter Wust: Von der Philosophie zum Glaubenszeugnis*. Münster, Westphalia, Germany: Regensberg, 1969.

Jamet, Claude. *Journal* [extract]. *Cahiers Simone Weil* 5, no. 1 (March 1982).

Johnson, Uwe. "Il me faut remercier." *Cahiers du Grif*. Paris: Tierce/Deux Temps, 1986.

Jonas, Hans. "Acting, Knowing, Thinking: Gleanings from Hannah Arendt's Philosophical Work." *Social Research* 1 (1977): 25–43.

———. *Entre le néant et l'éternité*. Ed. and trans. Sylvie Courtine-Denamy. Paris: Belin, 1996.

———. "Der Gottesbegriff nach Auschwitz: Eine jüdische Stimme." In Jonas and Fritz Stern, *Reflexionen finsterer Zeit*. Ed. Otfried Hofius. Tübingen: Mohr, 1984, pp. 63–84.

———. "Hannah Arendt: Words Spoken at Her Funeral Service." *Partisan Review* 42 (1976): 12–13.

———. "Immortality and the Modern Temper." *Harvard Theological Review* 55 (1962): 1–20.

———. "Philosophie: Rétrospective et prospective à la fin du siècle." Trans. Jean Greisch. *Le messager européen* 7 (1993): 331–48.

———. *La religion gnostique.* Trans. L. Evrard. Paris: Flammarion, 1978.

———. *Wissenschaft als persönliches Erlebnis.* Göttingen: Vandenhoeck und Ruprecht, 1987.

Jünger, Ernst. *The Storm of Steel.* Trans. Basil Creighton. London: Chatto and Windus, 1929.

Koestler, Arthur. *Dialogue with Death.* New York: Macmillan, 1942.

———. *Scum of the Earth.* New York: Macmillan, 1948.

Laqueur, Walter. *The Terrible Secret: Suppression of the Truth about Hitler's "Final Solution."* Boston: Little, Brown, 1980.

Latreille, André. *De Gaulle, la Libération et l'Eglise catholique.* Paris: Cerf, 1978.

Lazare, Bernard. *Antisemitism, Its History and Causes.* Trans. anon. London: Britons Publishing, 1967.

———. "Contre l'antisémitisme." In *Juifs et antisémites.* Paris: Allia, 1992.

———. *Le fumier de Job.* Paris: Circé, 1990.

———. *Job's Dungheap: Essays on Jewish Nationalism and Social Revolution.* Ed. Hannah Arendt. Trans. Harry Lorin Binnse. New York: Schocken, 1948.

———. *Juifs et antisémites.* Paris: Allia, 1992.

Le grand passage. Paris: Albin Michel, 1994.

Lévinas, Emmanuel. *Difficult Freedom: Essays on Judaism.* Trans. Sean Hand. Baltimore: Johns Hopkins University Press, 1990.

———. *In the Time of the Nations.* Trans. Michael B. Smith. Bloomington: Indiana University Press, 1994.

Lévy, Bernard-Henri. *L'idéologie française.* Paris: Grasset, 1981.

Locke, John. *The Second Treatise of Government.* In *Two Treatises of Government.* Ed. Peter Laslett. London: Cambridge University Press, 1963.

Lubac, Henri de, et al. *Israël et la foi chrétienne.* Fribourg: Editions de la Librairie de l'Université, 1942.

Lucan. *Pharsalia: Dramatic Episodes of the Civil War.* Trans. Robert Graves. London: Cassell, 1961.

Luxemburg, Rosa. *Briefe aus dem Gefängnis.* Berlin: Dietz, 1953.

———. *The Letters of Rosa Luxemburg.* 2d ed. Ed. Stephen Eric Bronner. Atlantic Highlands, New Jersey: Humanities Press, 1993.

———. *Letters to Karl and Luise Kautsky from 1896 to 1918.* New York: Gordon Press, 1975.

———. *Prison Letters to Sophie Liebknecht.* Trans. Eden and Cedar Paul. Leeds: Independent Labor Party, 1972.

L'Yvronnet, L. F. "Chronologie." In *Le grand passage.* Paris: Albin Michel, 1994.

Malan, Ivo R. "Simone Weil et la responsabilité des écrivains." *Cahiers Simone Weil.* Vol. 2, no. 3 (September 1979).

Malka, Salomon. *Monsieur Chouchani. L'énigme d'un maître du XXe siècle: Entretiens avec Elie Wiesel.* Paris: Lattès, 1994.

Maritain, Jacques. *L'antimoderne.* In *Œuvres complètes,* vol. 2.

———. *Antisemitism.* London: Geoffrey Bles, Centenary Press, 1939.

———. "Atonement for All." *Commonweal* 36 (1942).

———. *A Christian Looks at the Jewish Question*. New York: Longmans, Green, and Co., 1939.

———. *L'impossible antisémitisme*. Reprint in *Les Juifs*. Ed. H. Daniel-Rops. Paris: Plon, 1937 and in Maritain, *Questions de conscience*. Paris: Desclée de Brouzer, 1938.

———. Letter. *Cahiers Jacques Maritain* 16–17: 4.

———. *Messages*. New York: Maison française, 1945.

———. *Le mystère d'Israël*. Paris: Desclée de Brouwer, 1990.

———. "The Mystery of Israel." Trans. Harry Lorin Binnse. In *The Social and Political Philosophy of Jacques Maritain: Selected Readings*. Ed. Joseph. W. Evans and Leo R. Ward. (London: Geoffrey Bles, 1956).

———. *La nouvelle revue française*, no. 297 (1 June 1938).

———. *Questions de conscience*. Paris: Desclée de Brouwer, 1938.

———. *Ransoming the Time*. Trans. Harry Lorin Binnse. New York: Scribner's, 1941.

———. *The Social and Political Philosophy of Jacques Maritain: Selected Readings*. Ed. Joseph W. Evans and Leo R. Ward. London: Geoffrey Bles, 1956.

Maritain, Raïssa. *Au creux du rocher*. Paris: Alsatia, 1954.

———. *We Have Been Friends Together: Memoirs*. Trans. Julie Kernan. New York: Longman's, Green, Golden Measure Books, 1942.

Marrus, Michael R., and Robert O. Paxton. *Vichy France and the Jews*. New York: Basic Books, 1981.

Michel, Henri. *La deuxième guerre mondiale: Les succès de l'Axe, 1939–1943*. Paris: Presses universitaires de France, 1968/1977.

———. *The Second World War*. Trans. Douglas Parmee. London: Deutsch, 1975.

Miribel, Elisabeth de. *Edith Stein. 1891–1942*. Paris: Seuil, 1954.

Narcy, Michel. "La parole pacifiée d'Emile Novis." *Sud* (1990).

———. *Simone Weil: Malheur et beauté du monde*. Paris: Centurion, 1967.

Neher, A. *L'Exil de la parole*. Paris: Seuil, 1970.

Nevin, T. R. *Simone Weil: Portrait of a Self-Exiled Jew*. Chapel Hill: University of North Carolina Press, 1991.

Nietzsche, Friedrich. *Beyond Good and Evil: Prelude to a Philosophy of the Future*. Trans. Helen Zimmern. London: Allen and Unwin, 1967.

———. *Daybreak: Thoughts on the Prejudices of Morality*. Trans. R. J. Hollingdale. London: Cambridge University Press, 1982.

———. *The Gay Science*. Trans. Walter Kaufmann. New York: Vintage, 1974.

———. *The Genealogy of Morals: A Polemic*. Trans. Walter Kaufmann. New York: Vintage, Random House, 1969.

———. *La volonte de puissance*. Trans. Bianquis. Paris: Gallimard, 1942.

———. *The Will to Power*. Trans. Walter Kaufmann and R. J. Hollingdale. New York: Random House, 1967.

Nizan, Paul. *Aden, Arabie*. Trans. Joan Pinkham. New York: Columbia University Press, 1987.

Nolte, Ernst. *Les mouvements fascistes: L'Europe de 1919 à 1945*. Ed. Alain Renaut. Trans. R. Laureillard. Paris: Calmann-Lévy, 1991.

Nota, Jan H. "Edith Stein und der Entwurf für eine Enzyklika gegen Rassismus und Antisemitismus." *Freiburger Rundbrief* 26, no. 97–100 (1975): 35–41.

Oesterreicher, John M. *Walls Are Crumbling: Seven Jewish Philosophers Discover Christ.* London: Hollis and Carter, 1953.

Ouaknin, M. A. *Tsimtsoum: Introduction à la méditation hébraïque.* Paris: Albin Michel, 1992.

Passelecq, Georges, and Bernard Suchecky. *The Hidden Encyclical of Pius XI: The Vatican's Lost Opportunity to Oppose Nazi Racial Policies.* New York: Harcourt Brace, 1987.

Péguy, Charles. *Œuvres complètes: Œuvres en prose, 1909–1914.* Paris: Gallimard, Pléiade.

Perrin, Joseph-Marie. *Mon dialogue avec Simone Weil.* Paris: Nouvelle Cité, Rencontres, 1984.

Perrin, Joseph-Marie, and Gustave Thibon. *Simone Weil as We Knew Her.* Trans. Emma Craufurd. London: Routledge and Kegan Paul, 1953.

Petit, J. Bernanos. *Bloy, Claudel, Péguy: Quatre écrivains catholiques face à Israël.* Paris: Calmann-Lévy, 1972.

Pétrement, Simone. *Le dualisme dans l'histoire de la philosophie des religions: Introduction à l'étude du dualisme platonicien, du gnosticisme et du manichéisme.* Paris: Gallimard, 1946.

———. "Un échange de lettres entre G. Aubourg et S. Pétrement." *Cahiers Simone Weil* 11, no. 1 (March 1988).

———. *A Separate God: The Christian Origins of Gnosticism.* Trans. Carol Harrison. San Francisco: Harper, 1990.

———. *Simone Weil: A Life.* Trans. Raymond Rosenthal. New York: Pantheon, 1976.

———. *La vie de Simone Weil,* 2 vols. Paris: Fayard, 1983.

Plato, *The Phaedrus.* Trans. R. Hackforth. In *The Collected Dialogues of Plato.* Ed. Edith Hamilton and Huntington Cairns, pp. 475–525. Princeton: Bollingen Series 71, Princeton University Press, 1961.

Poliakov, Léon. *L'impossible choix? Les crises d'identité juive.* Paris: Austral, 1994.

Posselt, Renata. [Teresia Renata de Spiritu Sancto]. *Edith Stein.* Trans. Cecily Hastings and Donald Nicholl. London: Sheed and Ward, 1952.

Psichari-Renan, Henriette. *Les convertis de la Belle Epoque.* Paris: Editions rationalistes, 1971.

Rabi, Wladimir. "Entretien sur S. Weil, la résistance et la question juive." *Les nouveaux cahiers,* no. 63 (Winter 1980–1981).

———. *Simone Weil: Philosophe, historienne et mystique.* Paris: Aubier, 1978.

Reinach, A. *Gesammelte Schriften.* Halle: Max Niemayer, 1921.

Rousseau, Jean-Jacques. *Emile, or Education.* Trans. Barbara Foley. London: Dent, Everyman's Library, 1925.

———. "Essay on the Origin of Language." Trans. John H. Moran. In Rousseau and Johann Gottfried Herder, *Two Essays on the Origin of Language.* Chicago: University of Chicago Press, 1986.

———. *On the Origins of Inequality Among Men.* In *The First and Second Discourses.* Ed. Roger D. Masters. Trans. Masters and Judith R. Masters. New York: St. Martin's, 1964.

Royal, Robert, ed. *Jacques Maritain and the Jews.* Mishawaka, Inc.: American Jacques Maritain Association, 1994.

Saint-Sernin, B. *L'action politique selon Simone Weil*. Paris: Cerf, 1988.

Sartre, Jean-Paul. *Carnets de la drôle de guerre*. Paris: Gallimard, 1991.

———. Foreword to Paul Nizan, *Aden, Arabie*. Trans. Joan Pinkham. New York: Columbia University Press, 1987.

Scholem, Gershom. *On Jews and Judaism in Crisis: Selected Essays*. Ed. Werner J. Dannhauser. 2 vols. New York: Schocken, 1976.

Schumann, Maurice. "Mes entretiens avec Simone Weil à Londres." *Cahiers Simone Weil* 13, no. 1 (March 1990).

Secretan, Philibert. Introduction to Edith Stein, *Phénoménologie et philosophie chrétienne*. Paris: Cerf, 1987.

———. Preface to Edith Stein, *La prière de l'Eglise*. Geneva: Ad Solem, 1995.

Semprun, Jorge. *L'écriture ou la vie*. Paris: Gallimard, 1994.

Simon, Yves. *La marche à la délivrance*. New York: Maison française, 1942.

Sirinelli, Jean-François. *Deux intellectuels dans le siècle: Sartre et Aron*. Paris: Fayard, 1995.

Steiner, George. "Das lange Leben der Metaphorik: Ein Versuch über die Shoah." *Akzente* 3 (1987): 194–212.

Tarde, Guillaume de. *Les nouveaux cahiers*, no. 38 (1 Feb. 1939).

Thomas, Jean-François. *Simone Weil et Edith Stein: Malheur et souffrance*. Paris: Culture et Vérité, 1988.

Tillich, Paul. *Ecrits contre les nazis, 1932–1935*. Paris: Cerf, 1994.

Tilliette, Xavier. *Actualité religieuse dans le monde*, 15 April 1987.

———. "Le souvenir d'Edith Stein." *Etudes*, April 1956.

Tonneau, Jean. *Le Pape, la guerre et la paix: Pie XII a-t-il parlé?* Paris: Cerf, 1942.

Vetö, Miklos, *La Metaphysique religieuse de Simone Weil*. Paris: Vrin, 1971.

Vidal-Naquet, Pierre. "Jacques Maritain et les Juifs." In Maritain, *L'impossible antisémitisme*. Paris: Desclée de Brouwer, 1994.

———. *Mémoires*, vol. 1: *La brisure et l'attente, 1930–1955*. Paris: Seuil, Découverte, 1995.

———. *Réflexions sur le génocide, la mémoire et le présent*, vol. 3. Paris: La Découverte, 1995.

Voegelin, Eric. *Die politischen Religionen*. Stockholm: Bermann-Fischer, 1939.

Voltaire, *Philosophical Dictionary*. Ed. and trans. H. I. Woolf. New York: Knopf, 1924; http:\\history.hanover.edu/texts/voltaire/volvirt.htm.

Weil, André, and Muggeridge, Malcolm. "André Weil, a Scientist, Discusses His Sister with Malcolm Muggeridge." In Weil, *Gateway to God*, ed. David Raper et al., pp. 103–47. Glasgow: Collins, Fontana Books, 1974.

Wieviorka, Olivier. *Une certaine idée de la Résistance*. Paris: Seuil, 1995.

Winock, Michel. *Esprit: Des intellectuels dans la cité, 1930–1950*. Paris: Seuil, 1996.

Wojtyla, Karol [Pope John Paul II]. "Homily for the Beatification of Edith Stein." Ed. and trans. John Sullivan. Carmelite Studies 4 (1987): 298–306.

Young-Bruehl, Elisabeth. *Hannah Arendt: For Love of the World*. New Haven: Yale University Press, 1982.

Zweig, Stefan, *Le monde d'hier*. Paris: Belfond, 1948, rpt. 1982.

Index